Maker Innovations Series

Jump start your path to discovery with the Apress Maker Innovations series! From the basics of electricity and components through to the most advanced options in robotics and Machine Learning, you'll forge a path to building ingenious hardware and controlling it with cutting-edge software. All while gaining new skills and experience with common toolsets you can take to new projects or even into a whole new career.

The Apress Maker Innovations series offers projects-based learning, while keeping theory and best processes front and center. So you get hands-on experience while also learning the terms of the trade and how entrepreneurs, inventors, and engineers think through creating and executing hardware projects. You can learn to design circuits, program AI, create IoT systems for your home or even city, and so much more!

Whether you're a beginning hobbyist or a seasoned entrepreneur working out of your basement or garage, you'll scale up your skillset to become a hardware design and engineering pro. And often using low-cost and open-source software such as the Raspberry Pi, Arduino, PIC microcontroller, and Robot Operating System (ROS). Programmers and software engineers have great opportunities to learn, too, as many projects and control environments are based in popular languages and operating systems, such as Python and Linux.

If you want to build a robot, set up a smart home, tackle assembling a weather-ready meteorology system, or create a brand-new circuit using breadboards and circuit design software, this series has all that and more! Written by creative and seasoned Makers, every book in the series tackles both tested and leading-edge approaches and technologies for bringing your visions and projects to life.

More information about this series at https://link.springer.com/bookseries/17311.

Building Digital Twin Metaverse Cities

Revolutionizing Cities with Emerging Technologies

Xiangming Samuel Li

Apress®

Building Digital Twin Metaverse Cities: Revolutionizing Cities with Emerging Technologies

Xiangming Samuel Li
Northeastern University
Boston, MA, USA

ISBN-13 (pbk): 979-8-8688-0810-4   ISBN-13 (electronic): 979-8-8688-0811-1
https://doi.org/10.1007/979-8-8688-0811-1

Copyright © 2024 by Xiangming Samuel Li

This work is subject to copyright. All rights are reserved by the Publisher, whether the whole or part of the material is concerned, specifically the rights of translation, reprinting, reuse of illustrations, recitation, broadcasting, reproduction on microfilms or in any other physical way, and transmission or information storage and retrieval, electronic adaptation, computer software, or by similar or dissimilar methodology now known or hereafter developed.

Trademarked names, logos, and images may appear in this book. Rather than use a trademark symbol with every occurrence of a trademarked name, logo, or image we use the names, logos, and images only in an editorial fashion and to the benefit of the trademark owner, with no intention of infringement of the trademark.

The use in this publication of trade names, trademarks, service marks, and similar terms, even if they are not identified as such, is not to be taken as an expression of opinion as to whether or not they are subject to proprietary rights.

While the advice and information in this book are believed to be true and accurate at the date of publication, neither the authors nor the editors nor the publisher can accept any legal responsibility for any errors or omissions that may be made. The publisher makes no warranty, express or implied, with respect to the material contained herein.

    Managing Director, Apress Media LLC: Welmoed Spahr
    Acquisitions Editor: Miriam Haidara
    Development Editor: James Markham
    Coordinating Editor: Jessica Vakili

Cover designed by eStudioCalamar

Distributed to the book trade worldwide by Apress Media, LLC, 1 New York Plaza, New York, NY 10004, U.S.A. Phone 1-800-SPRINGER, fax (201) 348-4505, e-mail orders-ny@springer-sbm.com, or visit www.springeronline.com. Apress Media, LLC is a California LLC and the sole member (owner) is Springer Science + Business Media Finance Inc (SSBM Finance Inc). SSBM Finance Inc is a **Delaware** corporation.

For information on translations, please e-mail booktranslations@springernature.com; for reprint, paperback, or audio rights, please e-mail bookpermissions@springernature.com.

Apress titles may be purchased in bulk for academic, corporate, or promotional use. eBook versions and licenses are also available for most titles. For more information, reference our Print and eBook Bulk Sales web page at http://www.apress.com/bulk-sales.

Any source code or other supplementary material referenced by the author in this book is available to readers on GitHub (https://github.com/Apress). For more detailed information, please visit https://www.apress.com/gp/services/source-code.

If disposing of this product, please recycle the paper

Table of Contents

About the Author xi

About the Technical Reviewer xiii

Acknowledgments xv

Introduction: Building the Cities of Tomorrow xvii

Part I: Getting Started: A Problem Statement 1

Chapter 1: Rapid Global Urbanization 3
   Summary 6

Chapter 2: Problem Statement and Solution Overview 7
   A Problem Statement 7
   Our Solution Overview 9
   Summary 10

Chapter 3: Book Proposition and Unique Selling Points 11
   Research Gap 11
   Summary 13

Part II: First Thing First: A New Smart City Design 15

Chapter 4: What Are Novel Theoretical Frameworks over There 17
   Metaverse 18
   Digital Twin 20
   City 22

TABLE OF CONTENTS

Smart Cities 22

Smart City Indicator 23

Preliminary Digital Twins for Building Information Model (BIM) 25

Summary 25

Chapter 5: An Architectural Design of Digital Twin Metaverse Cities 27

Physical City 28

Digital City 30

Summary 32

Chapter 6: A Digital Twinning Process for Metaverse Cities 35

CRISP-DM Process 36

Data Visualization 38

Data Analytics 40

    Data Analytics Techniques 42

Data-Driven Digital Twinning Process 45

A Preliminary Digital Twin Metaverse City Example: Virtual Singapore (VP) 47

Summary 49

Part III: The Building Blocks: What Are Emerging Technologies 51

Chapter 7: Rising Emerging Information Technologies: Core 53

5G Mobile Networks 53

Internet of Things (IoT) 57

Big Data Analytics 62

Artificial Intelligence (AI) 65

Cloud Computing 70

Blockchain 73

TABLE OF CONTENTS

Digital Platform 76
Summary.. 82

Chapter 8: Rising Emerging Information Technologies: Enablers........ 83

Robotic Automation 83
Augmented Reality (AR) and Virtual Reality (VR) 88
3D Printing 92
Autonomous Driving (AD) 96
Drone and UAV 100
Cybersecurity 103

Part IV: Showing Me Real Examples: Smart City Showcases 109

Chapter 9: Showcases of Emerging ITs for Digital Twin Metaverse Cities: *Core*... 111

Smart Transportation 111
Smart Green Energy 113
Smart Home 116
Smart Housing 120
Smart Streetlight 123
Smart Environment 125

Chapter 10: Showcases of Emerging ITs for Digital Twin Metaverse Cities: *Services* 129

Smart Healthcare 130
Smart Senior Caring 137
Smart Education 141
Smart Retailing 147
Smart Recycling 155
Smart Disaster Response 162
Smart Vertical Farming 166

vii

TABLE OF CONTENTS

Part V: Showing Me How: The Development Tools and Prototypes 171

Chapter 11: Harnessing Digital Twin Development Tools to Build Digital Twin Cities 173

    1. AWS IoT TwinMaker 174

    2. Microsoft Azure Digital Twins 177

    3. Siemens MindSphere 180

    4. PTC ThingWorx 182

    5. IBM Maximo Asset Monitor 185

    6. Dassault Systèmes 3DEXPERIENCE 188

    7. GE Digital Predix 191

    8. Ansys Twin Builder 194

    9. Bosch IoT Suite 197

    10. SAP Digital Twin 200

    11. Oracle Digital Twin 202

    12. Autodesk Tandem 205

Chapter 12: Crafting Metaverse Cities: Unveiling the Cutting-Edge Development Tools 211

    1. Unity 212

    2. Unreal Engine (UE) 215

    3. Nvidia's Omniverse 218

    4. Amazon Sumerian 221

    5. Roblox Studio 224

    6. CryEngine 227

    7. Blender 230

    8. Autodesk Maya 233

    9. SketchUp 236

10. ZBrush 239

11. Tilt Brush 242

12. ChatGPT for Metaverse 245

13. Gemini for Metaverse 248

14. SpatialOS 251

15. Decentraland SDK 254

16. Meta Spark 257

Chapter 13: Digital Twin Metaverse Prototypes: *Smart Living* 263

Sustainable Smart Homes 264

Virtual Healthcare Clinic 273

Eco-Friendly Urban Transportation Hub 281

Smart Education Centers 290

Public Safety and Emergency Response Simulation 296

Urban Farming and Green Spaces 304

Chapter 14: Digital Twin Metaverse Prototypes: *Smart Working* 313

Virtual Coworking Spaces 314

Augmented Reality Training Modules 321

Smart Office Management System 327

Professional Development and Networking Hub 333

AI-Powered Virtual Assistants 339

Virtual Reality Design and Prototyping Studio 344

Chapter 15: Digital Twin Metaverse Prototypes: *Smart Entertainment and Cities* 351

1. Virtual Concert and Event Arena 352

2. Interactive Public Art Installations 360

3. Metaverse Theme Park 367

TABLE OF CONTENTS

    4. Digital Twin Museums and Galleries 373

    5. Smart Sports Complex 380

    6. City-Wide Game and Scavenger Hunt 386

    7. Metaverse Music Festival Experience 393

    8. A Metaverse City Prototype Using Unreal Engine (UE) 400

Part VI: What Is Next: Just Do It What Is Next: Just Do It 411

Chapter 16: Managing Successful Smart City Projects 413

Chapter 17: Navigating Change: Smart City Transformation and Cutover Strategies 419

Chapter 18: Leadership for the Future: New Skills for Smart City Development and Management 425

    1. Humility in AI-Driven Smart City Leadership 427

    2. Adaptability in Smart City Leadership 428

    3. Engagement for Smart City Cohesion 428

    4. Visionary Leadership in the AI Era 428

Conclusion and Calling for Immediate Actions 435

Appendix A: Building Digital Twin–Based Modern Management Information Systems (MMIS) 439

Bibliography 463

Index 483

About the Author

Xiangming Samuel Li has 23 years of intensive management and leadership experience in global ICT multinationals, including Nortel, Nokia, Motorola, BTI, Linaro, and Anhub in the United States, Canada, and Asia, and he is credited with successful technology management for the world's first touchscreen Linux smartphone, Motorola A760; the first global Nokia mobile Internet application, MIA; and the pioneering Android mobile platform, SavaJe OS. Dr. Li also has over ten years of high education teaching experience. He is currently actively engaged in academic research and teaching roles at Northeastern University Boston Campus, Anna Maria College, University Canada West, the University of Waterloo, the University of Toronto, Hangzhou Dianzi University, and the Zhejiang University of Technology. Samuel holds an MBA degree from the University of Toronto in the Global Executive MBA program, a master's degree in System Design Engineering, and a bachelor' degree in Computer Science. He is currently pursuing a PhD in Management Science from the University of Waterloo, focusing on advanced study in the Internet platform sharing economy, big data/AI/machine learning, and online trust and reputation systems. Dr. Li has published various papers and books in subjects of IT management, digital transformation, data analytics, machine learning, AI, etc.

About the Technical Reviewer

Massimo Nardone has more than 25 years of experience in security, web and mobile development, cloud, and IT architecture. His true IT passions are security and Android. He has been programming and teaching others how to program with Android, Perl, PHP, Java, VB, Python, C/C++, and MySQL for more than 20 years. He holds a master of science degree in computing science from the University of Salerno, Italy. He has worked as a CISO, CSO, security executive, IoT executive, project manager, software engineer, research engineer, chief security architect, PCI/SCADA auditor, and senior lead IT security/cloud/SCADA architect for many years. His technical skills include security, Android, cloud, Java, MySQL, Drupal, COBOL, Perl, web and mobile development, MongoDB, D3, Joomla, Couchbase, C/C++, WebGL, Python, Pro Rails, Django CMS, Jekyll, Scratch, and more. He was a visiting lecturer and supervisor for exercises at the Networking Laboratory of the Helsinki University of Technology (Aalto University). He also holds four international patents (in the PKI, SIP, SAML, and proxy areas). He is currently working for Cognizant as head of cybersecurity and CISO to help clients in areas of information and cybersecurity, including strategy, planning, processes, policies, procedures, governance, awareness, and so forth. In June 2017, he became a permanent member of the ISACA Finland Board. Massimo has reviewed more than 45 IT books for different publishing companies and is the coauthor of *Pro Spring Security: Securing Spring Framework 5 and Boot 2-based Java Applications* (Apress, 2019), *Beginning EJB in Java EE 8* (Apress, 2018), *Pro JPA 2 in Java EE 8* (Apress, 2018), and *Pro Android Games* (Apress, 2015).

Acknowledgments

To my dear Li family: Anna, Dave, and Wendy, for your unwavering support.

Heartfelt appreciation to editors Miriam Haidara, Nirmal Selvaraj, and James Markham for your excellent support and to technical reviewer Massimo Nardone for your expertise.

Deepest thanks to Professors Keith Hipel and Bon Koo at the University of Waterloo for your invaluable research guidance. Special thanks to Professor Mike Barlow, co-author of *Smart Cities, Smart Future: Showcasing Tomorrow*, who always advises me on how to position this book for a large audience and great global impact.

Sincere gratitude to my colleagues and friends at University Canada West, Northeastern University, and Hangzhou Dianzi University for their encouragement, including Dr. Turi Abeba Nigussie, Dr. Hu Weihua, and Dr. Barry Bo.

Introduction: Building the Cities of Tomorrow

Amid the Industry 4.0, this book sets forth a vision for integrating advanced digital technologies into urban infrastructure, presenting a compelling value proposition to address urban challenges. We introduce the transformative concept of metaverse digital twins, bridging the digital-physical divide with advanced ICTs like IoT, 5G, and AI. Amid the global economic shifts accelerated by the Covid-19 pandemic, this presents an opportunity for governments to fast-track the creation of digital twin metaverse cities. This book, grounded in the author's extensive academic research and industry experience, aims to guide the development of these cities, offering a unique architectural framework and smart city solutions to foster urban digital transformation.

In an era where cities swell beyond their seams, the challenges of urbanization—housing shortages, gridlocked streets, overburdened healthcare systems, scarce employment opportunities, and the ever-looming specter of pollution. More than just statistics, this trend reflects real-world stories of people seeking better lives in urban jungles. You can image the bustling streets of New York, the architectural marvels of Barcelona, the vibrant markets of Mumbai, and the illuminated skylines of Shanghai as a testament to the human aspiration but also a hotspot for urbanization challenges.

These compelling challenges cry out for innovative solutions. Traditional urban development strategies have made strides, yet they often fall short in integrating advanced technologies and practical implementation tools. This book proposes a transformative vision: the creation of digital twin metaverse cities. Harnessing the power of emerging technologies, it offers a comprehensive approach to not only envision but to materialize the cities of tomorrow.

In this book, you are expected to explore the following insights and learn new skills in building digital twin metaverse cities, revolutionizing urban spaces through emerging technologies:

- From Challenges to Solutions: We begin by dissecting the complex problem statements that modern cities face—crowded housing, relentless traffic, stretched healthcare systems. Here we ask: How can we turn these challenges into opportunities? This book explores not just answers but actional solutions to build the digital twin metaverse cities using the marvels of emerging technologies.

- Architectural Innovation: At the heart of this vision lies the novel architecture of digital twin metaverse cities. This architectural marvel is not just a blueprint but a dynamic, living representation of the urban landscape, continually evolving with its real-world counterpart. This architectural ingenuity is a blend of your imagination with reality, where virtual intelligent models mirror our physical cities. This design innovation also serves the future of smart city planning and management.

- Emerging Technologies—the Building Blocks: The book delves into the world of emerging technologies such as 5G, IoT, AI, robotics, AR/VR, 3D printing, blockchain, digital platform, cybersecurity, etc. (total 13). These are not just isolated technologies but the integral building blocks of our smart digital twin

INTRODUCTION: BUILDING THE CITIES OF TOMORROW

metaverse cities. And each plays a unique role in creating a seamless, interconnected urban ecosystem, transforming how we live, work, and interact for better lives in the smart cities.

- Practical Applications and Prototypes: Beyond theoretical frameworks, the book will journey through inspiring case studies and cutting-edge engineering prototypes, showing how these emerging technologies are being used to build smarter and more efficient cities. For example, you can see how smart traffic lights dynamically adjust to fluctuating traffic patterns, intelligent energy systems self-optimize for efficiency, robotic caregivers provide continuous support to our senior family members, metaverse education systems deliver real-time effective learning outcomes to students, and innovative vertical farms harness environmental condition to cultivate foods even at night. These a dozen real-world examples serve as a testament to the viability and transformative potential of digital twin smart cities.

- Learning New Skills of Building Digital Twin Smart Cities: In this pivotal section of our book, we embark on an exploration of 28 state-of-the-art development tools essential for crafting digital twin smart cities. We delve into the functionalities of leading tools like Microsoft Azure Digital Twins, Amazon AWS IoT TwinMaker, Ansys, SAP Digital Twin, Oracle Digital Twin, and the Bosch IoT Suite, examining their distinct capabilities and contributions to smart city development. Special focus is dedicated to innovative tools such as GE Digital Twin, IBM Digital Twin Exchange, Siemens

INTRODUCTION: BUILDING THE CITIES OF TOMORROW

MindSphere, and Meta Platforms for Facebook Metaverse, highlighting their impact on creating and managing digital spaces. Moreover, we scrutinize the metaverse modeling capabilities of the Unity and Unreal 3D Engine, coupled with the AI-driven insights provided by OpenAI ChatGPT and Google Gemini's large language models (LLMs). This segment not only showcases practical examples of smart city applications but also aims to equip you with the practical know-how to leverage these sophisticated tools, transforming theoretical understanding into actionable skills for the future of urban development.

Expanding upon this foundation, we will employ the avant-garde engineering tools to conceptualize and develop 20 digital twin metaverse city prototypes across domains of smart living, working, entertaining, and cities. These prototypes range from sustainable smart homes and virtual healthcare clinics to smart education centers, virtual coworking spaces, smart office management systems, AI-powered virtual assistants, virtual concert and event arenas, metaverse theme parks, and smart sports complexes and culminate in a comprehensive metaverse city prototype.

You are invited to join us in a step-by-step journey to initiate the construction of each prototype. This hands-on approach not only kick-starts your journey but also guides you to continue the development independently, thereby mastering the essential skills for smart city construction through a pragmatic "learning by doing" methodology.

- Navigating the Management Maze: In the intricate journey of building digital twin smart cities, this book goes beyond the technological blueprints to unravel the "management maze." It's not just about mastering technology but also about mastering the art and science of management. Here, we dive deep into the essentials of project management, emphasizing how to effectively plan, execute, and monitor complex urban development projects. Change management is another key focus, equipping readers with strategies to handle the dynamic nature of such transformative projects, ensuring adaptability and resilience. Leadership skills are also a cornerstone, as the book provides insights into inspiring and guiding diverse teams toward a shared vision. Additionally, we explore modern management information systems (MMIS), showcasing their crucial role in decision-making and efficiency enhancement. This comprehensive guide is designed to mold readers into not just city builders but visionary leaders in the realm of digital urban transformation.

- Embark on a Journey to Build More Smart Cities: Each page of this book extends an invitation to explore, learn, and actively contribute to shaping the future of our cities. Whether you're a seasoned professional, an urban planner, a passionate city builder, a technology enthusiast, a smart city scholar, or simply curious about the potential of our future cities, this book welcomes you with open arms and holding valuable insights for you. As you turn the pages, you'll embark on an exciting journey beyond theoretical frameworks, acquiring new skills of developing digital twin metaverse cities, honing your acumen of managing successful smart city projects, and exploring the uncharted territories of urban digital transformation in action. More than just a compendium of ideas, this book is a powerful call to action for visionaries, innovators, creators, and builders, an invitation to roll up your sleeves and be part of building the smart cities of tomorrow.

INTRODUCTION: BUILDING THE CITIES OF TOMORROW

Unique Selling Points

In comparison to similar titles like Barlow and Levy [3] and Gassmann [4], this book offers a unique architectural plan for metaverse digital twin cities, coupled with a data-centric development process. It thoroughly examines the advanced ICTs that form the backbone of these cities and provides pragmatic strategies for their digital evolution. The book offers practical insights into leveraging new technologies and engineering tools to craft groundbreaking digital twin metaverse cities, with the goal of driving significant advances in urban digitalization. This book offers an exciting glimpse into the latest digital twin metaverse development tools (total 28) and engineering prototypes (total 20), inspiring readers to envision and create the future of urban living. Additionally, it tackles key management challenges and introduces an MIS architecture that integrates metaverse digital twin ideas, making it an invaluable resource to a wide array of readers interested in smart cities and digital innovation.

In this book, you'll embark on a journey through the creation of digital twin metaverse cities, from architectural design to practical applications. Covering the building blocks of these cities with emerging ICTs, the book provides a comprehensive look at modernizing enterprise systems using these technologies. It culminates in a call to action for building metaverse cities, supported by agile project management and new leadership skills.

Chapters at a Glance

Each chapter of this book is a steppingstone in the journey to build digital twin metaverse cities:

Chapters 1–3: Introduce a hard-to-ignore argument for building digital twin metaverse cities

Chapter 4: Examines theoretical frameworks, such as the metaverse and digital twin for smart cities

Chapter 5: Proposes an architectural design for digital twin metaverse cities.

Chapter 6: Details a data-driven digital twinning process for smart cities

Chapter 7: Focuses on core emerging technologies for building the digital twin metaverse cities (total 7)

Chapter 8: Explores enabling technologies that support the development of these cities (total 6)

Chapter 9: Showcases applications of ICTs in core smart city services (total 6)

Chapter 10: Demonstrates how digital twin metaverse contributes to various city services (total 7)

Chapter 11: Reviews 12 digital twin development tools

Chapter 12: Examines 16 tools for creating immersive metaverse environments

Chapters 13–15: Present 20 prototypes in smart living, working, and entertaining

Chapter 16: Discusses project management strategies for smart city projects

Chapter 17: Focuses on change management during smart city transitions

Chapter 18: Explores new leadership skills required for managing smart cities

Appendix A: Introduces a modern MIS architecture based on the digital twin metaverse concept

PART I

Getting Started: A Problem Statement

Why choose city life over a quaint village? As more people flock to urban areas, what pressing issues emerge? This book delves into these questions, exploring how emerging technologies can address urban challenges with innovative solutions. It's not just about the problems but who cares and why it matters. Here, we introduce a compelling proposition for building digital twin metaverse cities, a concept that promises to revolutionize our urban future. So, let's embark on this journey together, uncovering the potential of these technological marvels.

CHAPTER 1

Rapid Global Urbanization

The phenomenon of urban migration is fundamentally reshaping our world. An increasing number of people are drawn to cities in pursuit of better employment opportunities and an enhanced quality of life. Currently, over half of the global population resides in urban areas, a figure that is projected to rise to approximately 70% by 2050.[1] Projections from the United Nations, as illustrated in Figure 1-1, highlight a significant global population growth from 7.6 billion in 2018 to an estimated 9.8 billion by 2050. This represents an approximate 30% increase, indicating a substantial expansion in the global populace within just a few decades. Such growth emphasizes the escalating demands and challenges for our planet, and its urban centers are poised to confront in the impending years.

---

[1] https://www.un.org/development/desa/en/news/population/2018-revision-of-world-urbanization-prospects.html

CHAPTER 1   RAPID GLOBAL URBANIZATION

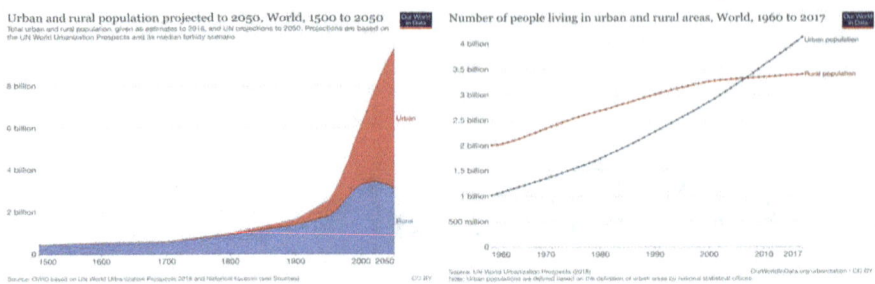

Figure 1-1. *World's population growth—urban vs. rural (source: UN World Urbanization Prospects, 2018)*[2]

This urban shift is not just a trend; it's a significant pivot in human history. The year 2007 marked a historic moment when, for the first time, more people lived in cities than in rural areas. Estimates suggest a dramatic shift in global living patterns, with urban populations expected to be more than double those in rural areas. According to the figures, this translates to approximately 6.7 billion people residing in cities, compared to 3.1 billion in rural locations. This trend underscores a significant tilt toward urban living on a global scale.

For example, Vancouver in Canada, renowned as one of the most livable cities globally, exemplifies the dramatic urban expansion. Over the past 64 years, its population has skyrocketed by 432%, growing from a modest 556,369 residents in 1950 to a bustling 2,406,529 in 2014. This growth trajectory is not slowing; projections indicate a further 23% increase by 2035, bringing the population to nearly 3 million [1]. Such rapid growth in Vancouver mirrors broader urbanization trends and highlights the evolving dynamics of city living, where urban spaces transform to accommodate an ever-increasing population.

---

[2] https://ourworldindata.org/urbanization?source=content_type%3Areact%7Cfirst_level_url%3Aarticle%7Csection%3Amain_content%7Cbutton%3Abody_link

CHAPTER 1   RAPID GLOBAL URBANIZATION

According to Statista's 2021 predictions,[3] the urban landscape is rapidly evolving, with an expected surge in the number of megacities. By 2030, it's anticipated that the globe will host 49 cities each with populations exceeding 10 million, a significant increase from the 33 recorded in 2018. This growth underscores a global trend toward urbanization, particularly in developing countries. A staggering 8.8% of the world's population, or around 752 million people, will reside in these megacities.

Notably, most of these burgeoning urban giants will be located in developing nations, such as India, China, Brazil, Mexico, Egypt, and Bangladesh. Figure 1-2 shows the megacities of the world with at least 10 million habitants in 2018 and 2030, respectively. This shift represents a crucial transformation in the demographic and cultural fabric of these nations and poses both challenges and opportunities for urban development.

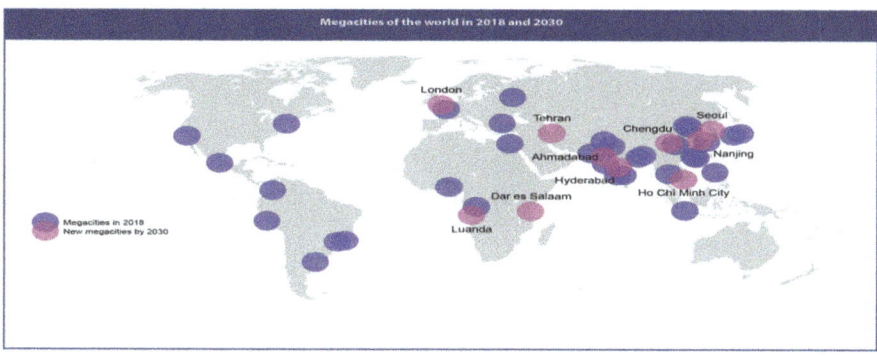

Figure 1-2. *The world's megacities with 10+ million inhabits in 2018 and 2030 (source: the UN report[4])*

---

[3] https://www.statista.com/
[4] https://www.un.org/en/events/citiesday/assets/pdf/the_worlds_cities_in_2018_data_booklet.pdf

CHAPTER 1   RAPID GLOBAL URBANIZATION

Summary

The rapid urbanization of our world presents a complex tapestry of challenges and opportunities, reshaping the future of our cities and the essence of urban living. Understanding and navigating these changes is critical as we strive to create urban environments that are not only populous but also sustainable and flourishing. This chapter sets the stage for our exploration of these issues. In Chapter 2, we will delve deeper into the specific challenges posed by this urbanization and begin to outline our proposed solutions to address them effectively.

CHAPTER 2

Problem Statement and Solution Overview

In this chapter, let's dive into a critical issue that's at the heart of our urban landscapes. We'll start by framing a problem statement that really captures the essence of the challenges we're facing in our rapidly urbanizing world. Then, we'll pivot to exploring some exciting solutions. Information and Communication Technologies (ICTs) are at the forefront of this exploration, offering innovative ways to tackle the most pressing challenges that come with city living.

A Problem Statement

The exponential growth of urban populations has led to numerous pressing challenges in cities, including environmental pollution, traffic congestion, pandemics, homelessness, poverty, and crime. This growth also strains resources such as energy, water, transportation, healthcare, education, food, and housing. Despite a decrease in the proportion of urban inhabitants living in slums in developing countries, the absolute number continues to rise, exacerbating issues like inadequate housing and limited access to essential services. Cities are major energy consumers, responsible for a significant portion of greenhouse gas emissions. Moreover, urban areas have been the epicenters of Covid-19 infections, with a high concentration of cases and deaths, illustrating the vulnerability of densely populated areas to global health crises. This situation highlights the urgent need for immediate action from governments and businesses to address the complexities of rapid urbanization.

According to the UN, although the proportion of urban inhabitants living in slums, i.e., informal settlements in the developing countries, decreased from 47% in 1990 to 37% in 2005, the absolute number is still rising due to rapid urbanization. These slums lack sufficient housing, water, drainage, and sanitation and have limited or no access to education, healthcare, and urban living, caused by massive migration from rural areas to cities. According to Statista (2021), about two-thirds of energy is consumed by the cities, accounted for 70% of all greenhouse gas emissions. Cities also have been considered the epicenters of Covid-19 infections, as 90% of cases were reported in urban areas.

The World Health Organization (WHO)[1] reports that total infections (confirmed cases) of Covid-19 by March 17, 2024, are about 775 million and total deaths are estimated 7 million. And the leading infective countries are the United States, China, India, France, Germany, Brazil, and South Korea, spreading to all over the world, regardless of the most advanced countries like the United States, France, and Germany with the highest urbanization (see Figure 2-1).

---

[1] https://COVID-1919.who.int/

CHAPTER 2   PROBLEM STATEMENT AND SOLUTION OVERVIEW

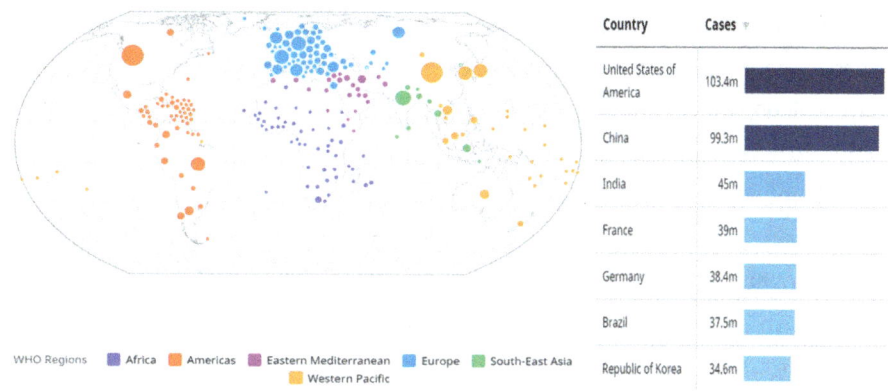

Figure 2-1. *Accumulative number of Covid-19 cases reported to WHO and top infective countries (source: 2024-4-2 WHO[5])*

In a nutshell, the rapid increase in urban populations has led to critical issues in cities globally, including environmental degradation, resource scarcity, and increased vulnerability to health crises. This situation urgently calls for action to create sustainable, safe, and livable urban environments for the burgeoning urban population. Without immediate intervention from governments and businesses, the safety and quality of life in urban areas worldwide are at serious risk.

Our Solution Overview

Thankfully, the swift advancement of Information and Communication Technologies (ICTs) offers promising solutions to the growing urban issues. This includes the development of smart cities [2][3][4], which integrate technologies like 5G networking, the Internet of Things (IoT), artificial intelligence (AI), robotics, cloud computing, augmented/virtual reality (AR/VR), 3D printing, blockchain, and digital platforms [5][6]. These innovative solutions can significantly improve urban living, work environments, and leisure spaces. For instance, Amsterdam has pioneered smart city projects, utilizing car-sharing apps to cut CO_2 emissions and smart lighting systems to enhance safety and reduce energy use [7]. Another example is Songdo, South Korea, a newly built smart city designed to optimize quality of life, using ICT to automate services and improve public transportation and waste management [8].

In brief, we will harness ICT to tackle urban challenges, with a focus on pioneering smart city designs. This includes the creation of the digital twin metaverse cities and the digital twinning processes. Our journey will incorporate advanced technologies such as 5G, IoT, AI, robotics, AR/VR, and cloud computing, all aimed at enhancing urban living in key areas such as transportation, healthcare, and energy efficiency. We will evaluate and recommend state-of-the-art engineering tools for smart city development, demonstrating how our solutions can transform urban areas into more efficient, sustainable, and habitable environments. We will guide you through building various digital twin metaverse city prototypes using these tools, encompassing aspects of smart living, working, and entertaining in urban settings, which will refine your city-building expertise. Lastly, we will tackle crucial management issues essential for the proliferation of digital twin metaverse cities.

Summary

This chapter addresses the critical challenges of rapid urbanization, such as environmental degradation, resource scarcity, and vulnerability to health crises like COVID-19. It emphasizes the need for urgent action from governments and businesses to create sustainable urban environments. Information and Communication Technologies (ICTs) are presented as key solutions through smart city initiatives, leveraging technologies like 5G, IoT, AI, and digital twin metaverse cities. These technologies aim to improve urban living, transportation, and energy efficiency, transforming cities into more sustainable and livable spaces for the future.

CHAPTER 3

Book Proposition and Unique Selling Points

In this chapter, we discuss overcoming the limitations of current smart city projects, particularly their isolated approach, by introducing the concept of metaverse digital twins. It explores using technologies like IoT, 5G, AR/VR, AI, and robotics to merge physical and virtual realms. The book leverages the author's academic and industrial expertise to provide a systematic approach to utilizing metaverse digital twins in urban development. It offers a unique perspective by proposing a novel architectural design for these cities, utilizing advanced ICTs, and equipping valuable skills for future urbanization projects. This chapter outlines the book's unique contribution to smart city development and the creation of cutting-edge metaverse cities.

Research Gap

Current smart city pilot projects often function in isolation, using a "silo" approach where one or two technologies target specific urban problems [7]. For example, IoT sensors and Wi-Fi networks are deployed for intelligent streetlighting, while mobile apps and 4G networks support services like

CHAPTER 3   BOOK PROPOSITION AND UNIQUE SELLING POINTS

Uber Eats and Instacart. However, these initiatives lack integrated and comprehensive data sharing, echoing the outdated siloed management information systems (MIS) in businesses (Figure 3-1). This leads to fragmented applications, much like in traditional MIS where functions such as human resources, manufacturing, sales, and finance operated independently, often supported by separate software from vendors like SAP, Oracle, or Microsoft. These isolated applications result in inefficient management due to the lack of centralized data sharing [9][10].

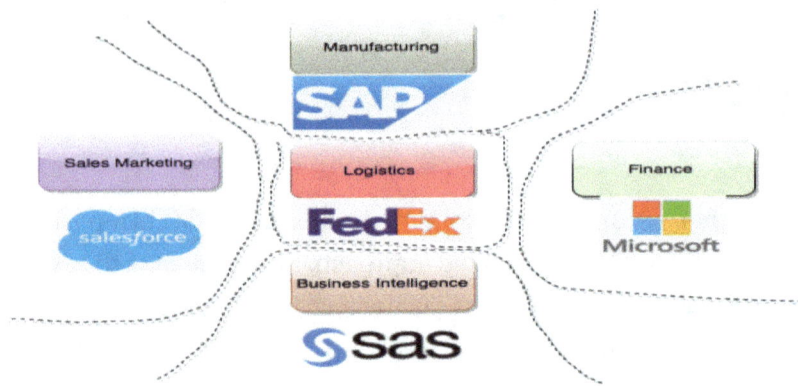

Figure 3-1. *Traditional data "silo" management information system (MIS) applications (source: author's development)*

Similarly, the "silo" smart city pilot projects lack the true essence of being "smart." They fail to fully utilize emerging ICTs, thus not realizing the full potential of smart cities for the growing urban populations. For instance, Amsterdam's city initiatives like citySDK and Beacon network, Barcelona's digital city efforts in public transportation and infrastructure, and Atlanta's SmartATL projects, though ambitious, were implemented independently by various vendors [7]. This lack of integration led to suboptimal outcomes and inefficient use of resources and did not meet the goals of smart cities, as evidenced by challenges highlighted in the IHS Markit 2018 survey like slow government response and growing citizen dissatisfaction (see Figure 3-2).

CHAPTER 3   BOOK PROPOSITION AND UNIQUE SELLING POINTS

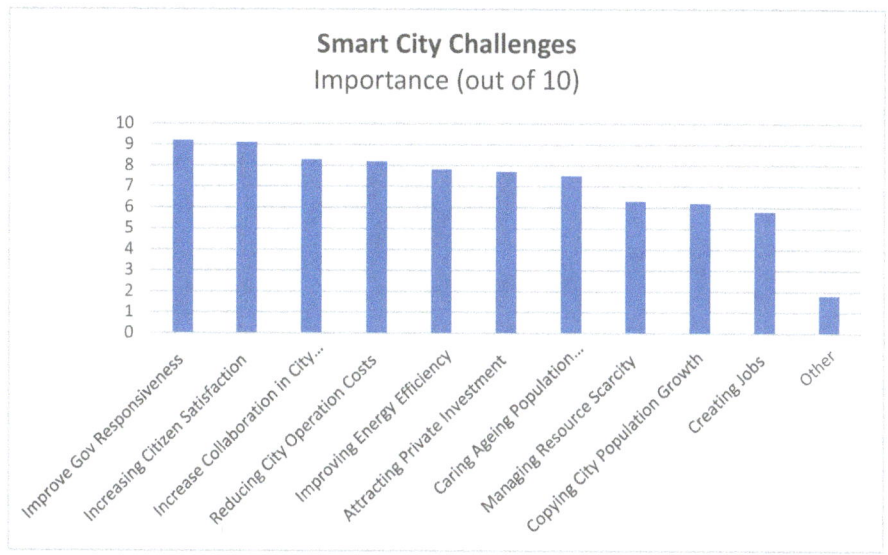

Figure 3-2. Major challenges for smart city projects (source: author's development based on IHS[1])

Summary

This chapter dived into a critical issue with current smart city projects: their siloed approach with outdated technologies and methodologies. We introduced the concept of "metaverse digital twins," a revolutionary approach that merges the physical and virtual worlds using advanced technologies like 5G, IoT, AR/VR, and AI. Leveraging the author's expertise, the book offers a structured approach for utilizing these digital twins. We'll explore a novel architectural design for these cities, equipping you with the practical skills needed for future projects. This comprehensive approach tackles the limitations of existing efforts, paving the way for the creation of truly integrated and innovative smart cities.

---

[1] https://www.usmayors.org/wp-content/uploads/2018/06/2018-Smart-Cities-Report.pdf

PART II

First Thing First: A New Smart City Design

We professionals always start with a "cool" engineering design or blueprint as a first step to building any successful project. Part 2 encompasses Chapters 4–6. Chapter 4 initiates with a thorough literature review, exploring relevant concepts such as metaverse, digital twin, smart cities, and smart city indicators. Following this, I will introduce an innovative architectural design for metaverse digital twin cities, covering elements like physical city, city functions, data collection, cloud-based data platform, service delivery platform, and city governance. Additionally, Chapter 5 delves into the specifics of this architectural design, providing a detailed overview of how the digital twin metaverse cities are structured. In Chapter 6, the focus shifts to proposing a novel data-driven digital twinning process tailored for smart cities.

PART II

First Thing First: A New Smart City Design

We professionals always start with a "cool" engineering design or blueprint as a first step to building any successful project. Part 2 encompasses Chapters 4–6. Chapter 4 initiates with a thorough literature review, exploring relevant concepts such as metaverse, digital twin, smart cities, and smart city indicators. Following this, I will introduce an innovative architectural design for metaverse digital twin cities, covering elements like physical city, city functions, data collection, cloud-based data platform, service delivery platform, and city governance. Additionally, Chapter 5 delves into the specifics of this architectural design, providing a detailed overview of how the digital twin metaverse cities are structured. In Chapter 6, the focus shifts to proposing a novel data-driven digital twinning process tailored for smart cities.

CHAPTER 4

What Are Novel Theoretical Frameworks over There

In this chapter, I will delve into the theoretical frameworks underpinning the concepts of metaverse, digital twin, city, smart cities, and smart city indicators. The metaverse is explored as a virtual 3D environment where users interact through avatars, mirroring the physical world for purposes like online gaming, virtual travel, ecommerce, and entertainment. The digital twin concept, introduced by Grieves, is defined as an integrated simulation of a physical system, constantly updated based on real-time data and historical footprints. The chapter will also provide insights into the evolving definition of cities and the increasing acceleration of urbanization, leading to the emergence of megacities with complex problems. Smart cities, leveraging emerging technologies like IoT, 5G, AI, robotics, and metaverse/digital twins, aim to address urbanization challenges. Additionally, smart city indicators are presented, offering a set of measures to evaluate the effectiveness of smart city functions, covering aspects such as environment, living standard, education, mobility, economy, and governance. The proposed theoretical framework sets the stage for the subsequent architectural design and digital twinning process discussions.

Metaverse

Metaverse is a combined word of "meta" and "universe." "Meta" means beyond/after/behind such metaphysics or meta-economy according to the ancient Greeks. "Universe" includes all existing matter and space considered as a whole or the cosmos according to Oxford English dictionary. The word "metaverse" was created by American writer Neal Stephenson in 1992 in his speculative science fiction named *Snow Crash* [11]. Here, metaverse is a massive virtual environment, in parallel to the physical worlds, where users interact with each other through digital avatars. According to the encyclopedia, "Metaverse is the post-reality universe, a perpetual and persistent multiuser environment merging physical reality with digital virtuality [12]."

Thus, I attempt to define the metaverse, abbreviated from "meta" (transcending) and "universe," as a specifically crafted virtual 3D realm where participants engage as interactive avatars. This virtual universe mirrors the physical world, offering diverse experiences like online gaming, virtual travel, social interactions, ecommerce, and entertainment. It harnesses emerging technologies such as 3D graphics, AR/VR/MR, IoT, blockchain, AI, robotics, and modern user interfaces to create rich and immersive experiences that blur the lines between reality and the virtual worlds.

Wang and colleagues [13] have conceptualized a continuum for digital twins within the metaverse, emphasizing the seamless integration of both virtual and physical realms. They outline three distinct stages in the evolution of the metaverse as illustrated in Figure 4-1. The first stage involves digital twins, which are detailed digital replicas of physical entities, capturing various attributes such as movement and appearance based on real data [14]. The second stage, digital natives, concentrates on the generation of native digital content within these virtual realms, often embodied by avatars. This content can either be linked to their physical analogs as digital twins or exist solely in the digital domain, contributing to diverse ecosystems, including economics and cultures. The third and final stage, physical-virtual reality, represents the culmination of the metaverse's development, where the digital and physical worlds coalesce, fostering a dynamic and self-sustaining virtual environment that operates in tandem with the physical world, allowing for a wide array of activities across multiple virtual platforms.

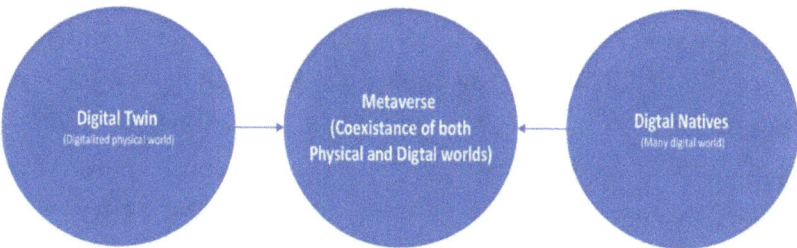

Figure 4-1. *Metaverse as digital twins and digital native continuum (author's development based on [13])*

Significantly, we find ourselves at an early stage in the development of the metaverse. At this juncture, the concept of digital twins serves as a foundational element, marking the initial phase where our physical environment begins its transition into the digital realm. These digital twins are essentially virtual duplicates of our physical world, providing a diverse range of virtual representations. Simultaneously, avatars, representing humans, are actively generating new content within these virtual spaces. Eventually, this process leads to the integration of physical and digital realms, culminating in a metaverse that is a blend of both realities, akin to a form of "Sur-reality" as described by Wang et al. [13].

CHAPTER 4   WHAT ARE NOVEL THEORETICAL FRAMEWORKS OVER THERE

Digital Twin

The concept of the digital twin was first introduced by Grieves in 2003 within the realm of product life cycle management, encompassing three main elements: the physical product, its digital counterpart, and the connecting data links [14]. This idea has evolved significantly with advancements in technologies like data collection, telecommunications, and data analytics. NASA expanded upon this concept, defining the digital twin as a comprehensive, multi-scale simulation that mirrors the real-life counterpart using up-to-date sensor data and historical information [15]. This definition highlights the dynamic nature of digital twins, continuously updated to reflect real-world changes. Since then, the digital twin has become a popular research topic.[1] More recently, Apte and Spano [16][2] described the digital twin as a dynamic model facilitating cost-effective and low-risk innovative experimentation. The rebranding of Facebook to "Meta Platforms" underscores the growing significance of digital twins, marrying the concept with the metaverse vision, where the physical and digital worlds interconnect, enabling social connections through digital avatars.[3]

Expanding on Grieves' initial concept from 2003, a digital twin encompasses three dimensions: the physical product, its digital representation, and the data linkage between the two [14]. An illustrative example, as shown in Figure 4-2, is a digital twin of a motor. Here, the digital motor mirrors its physical counterpart, connected through continuous data and information exchange—a process known as digital twinning.

---

[1] https://www.nature.com/articles/d41586-019-02849-1
[2] https://sloanreview.mit.edu/article/the-digital-twin-opportunity/
[3] https://about.facebook.com/meta/

CHAPTER 4   WHAT ARE NOVEL THEORETICAL FRAMEWORKS OVER THERE

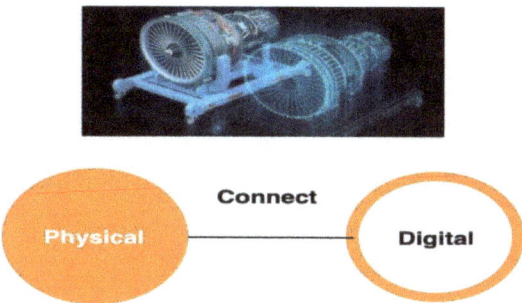

Figure 4-2. *Digital twins in three dimensions (author's development based on source [14])*

Tao et al. [17] have further improved the three-dimension model to a five-dimension digital twin model shown in Figure 4-3, including physical entity (PE), virtual entity (VE), data (DD), services (SS), and their connections (CN). Where DD is the data conveyed between PE and VE, SS are the services for both PE and VE, and CN is the connection of different parts like sensors, actuators, and devices. Further, DD creates new services (SS) such as command, automation, optimization, maintenance, and self-management, which is mission critical to a digital twin.

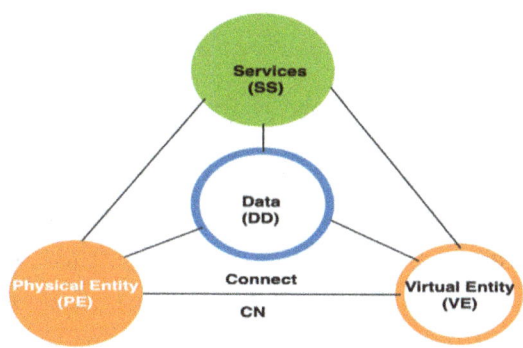

Figure 4-3. *Digital twins in five dimensions (author's development based on source [17])*

CHAPTER 4   WHAT ARE NOVEL THEORETICAL FRAMEWORKS OVER THERE

City

The concept of a "city" as defined by dictionaries like Oxford and Merriam-Webster typically refers to a large, significant urban area, distinguished from towns and villages by its size, population, and importance. This traditional view encapsulates cities as hubs of high population density, iconic architecture, diverse services, and governance. Historically, cities emerged as centers of the human civilization, driven by developments in agriculture, trade, and social organization. Today, as per the International Telecommunication Union (ITU), modern cities fulfill key roles in areas such as living, mobility, economy, and governance. Rapid urbanization, particularly in countries like China and India, has led to the rise of megacities, bringing complex challenges like traffic congestion, pollutions, and the strain on resources.

Smart Cities

To address the complex issues faced by growing cities, the academic and business sectors are focusing on sustainable living solutions through emerging ICTs like IoT, 5G, AI, and robotics, leading to the development of smart cities. Peters [18] defines "smart city" as a region utilizing these technologies to enhance resource use, efficiency, and living quality. For instance, Lal and Houghtalin [7] showcase Amsterdam, Barcelona, and Atlanta as examples of smart cities, each targeting specific urban issues like environmental concerns and infrastructure improvements. These cities represent a trend toward intelligent and sustainable urban areas [19] where advanced technologies are employed to optimize urban functions, reduce pollutions, and improve quality of life. This transformation is embodied in the concept of smart or digital twin metaverse cities, where cutting-edge ICTs are applied to solve urban challenges and enhance living standards.

Thus, I define smart cities, or digital twin metaverse cities, as modern urban areas transformed by emerging ICTs like IoT, 5G, AI, robotics, and metaverse/digital twins. These technologies are strategically applied to address critical urbanization challenges across living, transportation, environment, society, economy, and governance. The aim is to significantly enhance urban living standards and overall the human well-being. A prime example is Singapore, which, despite its lack of natural resources, is transitioning from an industrial base to a high-tech, intelligent island. This shift is part of the Singaporean government's extensive initiative to not just spur economic growth but also to substantially improve the quality of life for its residents [20].[4]

Smart City Indicator

Smart cities might mean different things to different people, depending on the level of smart city development. Therefore, scholars and developers have proposed standardized measures to gauge a city's progress toward becoming "smart." One such framework involves six smart city indicators, as depicted in Figure 4-4. These indicators are widely recognized and used for assessing various functions within a smart city, offering a uniform approach to evaluate their effectiveness and advancement [21] [22].

---

[4] https://youtu.be/xi6r3hZe5Tg

CHAPTER 4   WHAT ARE NOVEL THEORETICAL FRAMEWORKS OVER THERE

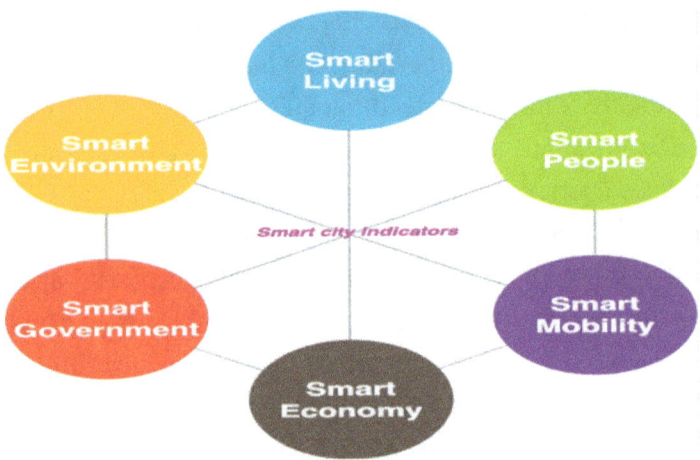

Figure 4-4. *The six smart city indicators (author's development based on source [21])*

Examining more closely in a smart city, the "smart environment" indicator evaluates how ICTs are used to enhance the natural environment and city livability, covering aspects like pollution control and energy efficiency. "Smart living" assesses life quality through factors like smart housing and healthcare access. "Smart people" focuses on education and job opportunities, fostering talent development and community engagement. "Smart mobility" measures transport system efficiency, including eco-friendly options and traffic management. "Smart economy" looks at business innovation and economic activities, supporting diverse economic participants. Finally, "smart government" evaluates effective governance and citizen interaction, leveraging ICTs for citizen services and public engagement.

Preliminary Digital Twins for Building Information Model (BIM)

The digital twin concept might have been initially used for a Building Information Modeling (BIM) in urban settings [23], offering substantial improvements to construction project management. This approach facilitates real-time updates from physical structures to their BIM counterparts, enhancing structural integrity evaluations, energy efficiency, and minimizing errors. BIM utilizes traditional communication technologies like camera, CCTV, and various sensors for data collection, leading to precise building designs and maintenance schedules. However, its usage predominantly targets individual buildings, not extending to broader city-wide solutions, and the technology in BIM remains relatively limited and passive. Furthermore, addressing data privacy concerns within building management is essential.

Summary

This chapter unpacked the key terms for smart city development: metaverse (virtual worlds), digital twin (real-world replicas), city (urban centers), smart city (tech-driven solutions), and smart city indicators (progress measurement). We'll explore how these concepts, along with advanced digital twins and emerging technologies, pave the way for the book's proposed framework for building innovative, data-driven smart cities of the future.

CHAPTER 5

An Architectural Design of Digital Twin Metaverse Cities

In this chapter, I will utilize metaverse digital twin concepts, emerging ICTs, smart city frameworks, and city functional indicators to develop an innovative architectural design for digital twin metaverse cities. This design integrates two key elements, the physical city and digital city, connected through a data-driven digital twinning process. The physical city covers tangible aspects and urban functions, utilizing IoTs for data collection. The digital city, on the other hand, comprises a data platform, service delivery modules, and governance structures. This chapter, drawing on my extensive ICT industry experience[1] and a thorough literature review, aims to present a groundbreaking approach to smart city architecture, incorporating the metaverse continuum, the five-dimensional digital twin model, smart city indicators, and various ICTs discussed in Chapters 5–8.

---

[1] https://www.linkedin.com/in/samuel-li-027a842/

CHAPTER 5   AN ARCHITECTURAL DESIGN OF DIGITAL TWIN METAVERSE CITIES

I propose a distinctive architectural design for digital twin metaverse cities, as depicted in Figure 5-1. The design features two primary components: the physical city and digital city. This visual representation succinctly captures the essence of a smart city's architecture, where the physical and digital realms converge through a digital twin framework. The "physical city" layer, depicted at the bottom, includes tangible assets and infrastructure vital to urban life, alongside essential city functions like governance and environment. Above it, "data collection" denotes the role of IoT devices in gathering critical information. The "digital city" layer represents the data, service delivery platform, and management aspect, all crucial for a city's digital transformation. This clear, layered approach illustrates the interconnectivity and flow from the physical foundation to the digital superstructure of a smart city. Furthermore, these components are interconnected through data and information, underpinned by a data-driven digital twinning process, a concept explored in Chapter 6. The following upcoming sections will delve deeper into the specifics of each component, providing a comprehensive understanding of this innovative design.

Physical City

The *physical city* component of smart cities encompasses concrete elements and vital data collection mechanisms. It consists of

- Physical city layer, which includes all tangible entities such as buildings, houses, hospitals, schools, churches, businesses, and infrastructure components like transportation, telecommunication, energy, water systems, parks, and recreational facilities. It also covers all forms of life from residents to wildlife and flora.

- City function layer, which represents six fundamental aspects of urban life: environment, living conditions, people, mobility, economic activities, and governance. These are measured by six smart city indicators that assess a city's level of "smartness."

- Data collection layer, which is a network of countless IoT sensors, actuators, mobile devices, and various communication technologies such as Wi-Fi and 5G. These instruments collect a wide range of real-time data, setting a stage for in-depth discussion in subsequent chapters.

This structure forms the groundwork for data integration within the digital twin metaverse city framework.

CHAPTER 5   AN ARCHITECTURAL DESIGN OF DIGITAL TWIN METAVERSE CITIES

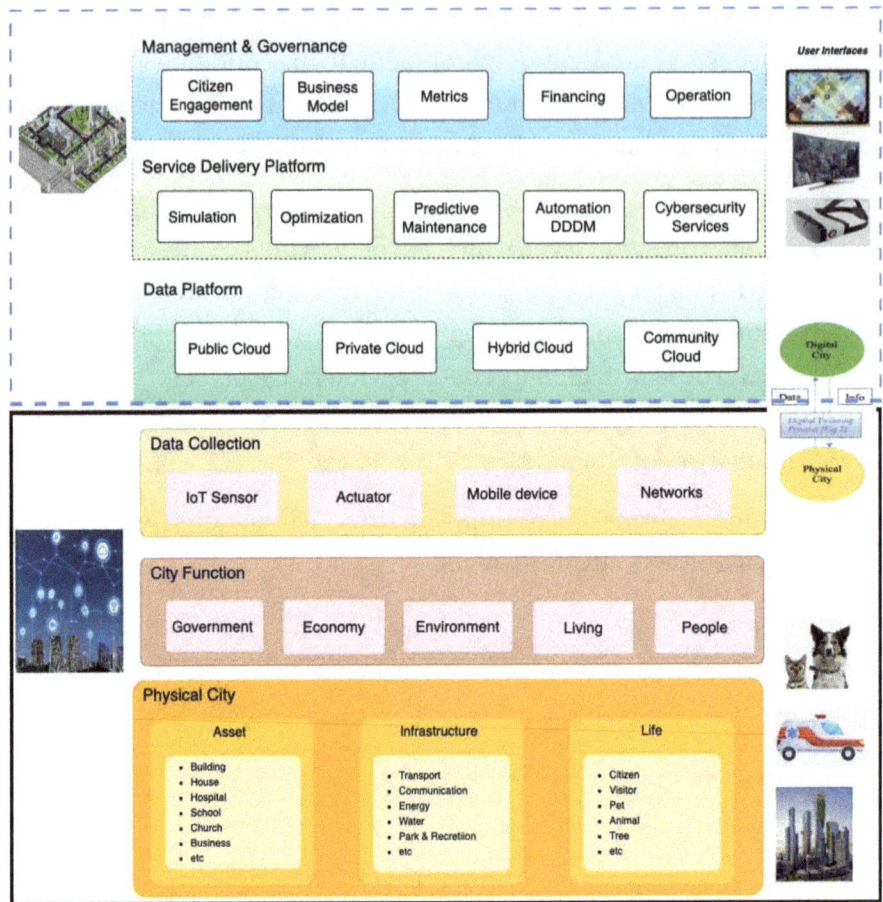

Figure 5-1. *An architectural design of metaverse digital twin cities (source: author's development)*

Digital City

Digital city, the virtual counterpart of the smart city, consists of layers that manage, process, and govern the data collected from the physical city. It includes

- Data platform, which centralizes data storage in different types of clouds based on the data privacy needs. For example, public data such as traffic updates and census information might be stored in a public cloud, while sensitive personal data might be stored in a private cloud.

- Service delivery platform, which is a sophisticated layer where data is analyzed to provide rich on-demand intelligent services. This includes processes like data visualization and AI-driven analytics that lead to actionable intelligent services for the physical city, such as energy optimization in buildings, educational services for kids, senior companionship at home, and predictive maintenance for the physical cities.

- City management and governance, which operates at a higher level to facilitate citizen engagement, public-private partnerships, innovative business models, project financing, smart city indicators' evaluation, and the oversight of operational efficiency and safety.

This digital infrastructure is pivotal for the data-driven management of smart cities, utilizing modern cloud services and intelligent analytics to improve urban life. The seamless integration of the physical and digital cities is enabled by a digital twinning process to be discussed in Chapter 6, which encompasses both "push" and "pull" operations. This means that any changes in the physical environment, such as updates to assets, prompt corresponding updates in the digital blockchain systems. Conversely, digital algorithms can proactively deactivate equipment to prevent unfortunate accidents. User interfaces, including avatars and holograms within the digital cities, aid in visualizing and overseeing smart city key performance indicators and critical assets. Tools such as Ansys,

Roblox, Unity, Unreal Engine, Meta Spark, Blender, Amazon AWS IoT, GE Predix, and Microsoft Azure Digital Twin, which will be explored in subsequent chapters, are crucial for constructing these interconnected digital twin metaverse cities.

It is essential to acknowledge that, within a smart city, purely digital assets may exist solely in the metaverse, as detailed in the metaverse continuum. These assets can range from projected structures like buildings and highways to conceptual features such as mountains, lakes, oceans, islands, theme parks, and sports complex, offering citizens metaverse living and entertaining experiences for a multitude of activities. Furthermore, Chapter 6 delineates a strategy for smart city development that is predicated on data-driven digital twinning, fostering a dynamic and interactive urban fabric.

Summary

We have traversed the development of metaverse and digital twin concepts, evolving from a foundational three-dimensional framework to a more intricate five-dimensional model. This advanced model encapsulates the quintessential elements of physical and digital realms, their interconnections, and the pivotal layers of data and services. Furthermore, we have revisited the transition from rural to urban settings and the ensuing challenges to maintaining and enhancing quality of life.

The innovative architectural design proposed herein, rooted in metaverse digital twin principles, presents a visionary blueprint for the smart cities of tomorrow. It melds the tangible aspects of city life with digital breakthroughs, with the goal of augmenting the urban experience through cutting-edge ICT solutions. These solutions are gauged against a suite of smart city functional indicators, guaranteeing a comprehensive approach to urban development.

CHAPTER 5 AN ARCHITECTURAL DESIGN OF DIGITAL TWIN METAVERSE CITIES

The insights amassed in this chapter lay the groundwork for the ensuing chapters, which will delve into the data-driven processes required to synchronize the physical and digital dimensions of smart cities. We will also examine the role of core and enabling ICTs in this transformational journey, providing tangible examples and case studies. This architectural blueprint, therefore, aspires to inspire and direct researchers, practitioners, and policymakers on their path to achieving the vision of smart and digitally integrated cities.

CHAPTER 6

A Digital Twinning Process for Metaverse Cities

In this chapter, I will focus on the data-driven digital twinning process (DDTP) for metaverse cities, an extension of the architectural framework from Chapter 5. The process, energized by the Data Analytics Flywheel (DAFW), includes a series of steps: understanding the problem, collecting and preparing data, visualizing it, modeling, evaluating models, and deploying the best solution. This cycle ensures the continuous alignment and updating of both the physical and digital aspects of a city. The chapter will wrap up with Virtual Singapore as a case study, underscoring the importance of systematic execution and research in the development of smart metaverse cities.

The structure from Chapter 5 involves six layers, dividing tangible city elements and their digital reflections. This chapter will introduce a DDTP that serves as a conduit, fostering a symbiotic relationship between these realms. Starting with a literature survey, it will progress to depict the DDTP as the engine driving intelligent services crucial for the actualization of truly smart cities.

CRISP-DM Process

The CRISP-DM Process [24], standing for Cross-Industry Standard Process for Data Mining, is a widely adopted methodology for data mining and analytics across various industries. It involves six principal phases shown in Figure 6-1:

- Business Understanding: This initial phase focuses on understanding the project objectives and requirements from a business perspective, then converting this knowledge into a data mining problem definition and a preliminary plan to achieve the objectives.

- Data Understanding: The data understanding phase starts with an initial data collection and proceeds with activities to get familiar with the data, to identify data quality problems, or to discover initial insights into the data.

- Data Preparation: The data preparation phase covers all activities needed to construct the final dataset from the initial raw data. Data preparation tasks are likely to be performed multiple times and not in any prescribed order. Tasks include table, record, and attribute selection, as well as transformation and cleaning of data for modeling tools.

- Modeling: In this phase, various modeling techniques are selected and applied, and their parameters are calibrated to optimal values. Typically, there are several techniques for the same data mining problem type. Some techniques have specific requirements on the form of data. Therefore, stepping back to the data preparation phase is often necessary.

- Evaluation: At this stage in the project, you have experimented with various models that appears to have high quality, from a data analysis perspective. Before proceeding to final deployment of the "best" models, it is important to more thoroughly evaluate the models and review the steps executed to construct the models, to be certain it properly achieves the business objectives. A key objective is to determine if there is some important business issue that has not been sufficiently considered. At the end of this phase, a consensus decision on the use of the data mining results should be reached.

- Deployment: Creation of the model is generally not the end of the project. Even if the purpose of the model is to increase knowledge of the data, the knowledge gained will need to be organized and presented in a way that is useful to the business. Depending on the requirements, the deployment phase can be as simple as generating a report or as complex as implementing a repeatable data mining process across the business. In many cases, it will be the customer, not the data analyst, who will carry out the deployment steps. However, even if the analyst will not carry out the deployment effort, it is important for the customer to understand up front what actions will need to be carried out in order to actually make use of the created models.

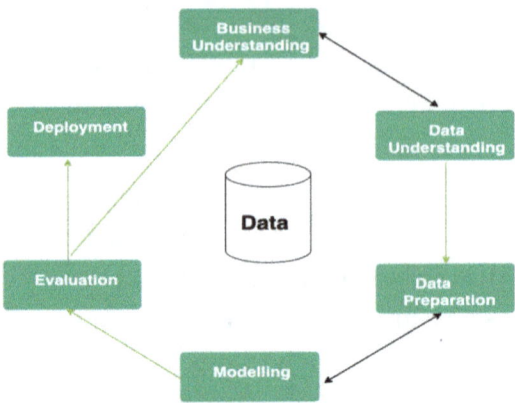

Figure 6-1. *The **CR**oss-Industry Standard **P**rocess for **D**ata **M**ining (CRISP-DM, author's development based on source [24])*

Each phase plays a crucial role in extracting meaningful insights from data, which in turn contributes to an informed decision-making process.

Data Visualization

"A picture is worth a thousand words." Data visualization is an indispensable component of data analytics, serving as a precursor to complex modeling. Tools such as Tableau, PowerBI, Python, R, and even simple Excel are employed to visually reveal data trends and correlations. Tableau, a leader in the BI sphere, simplifies the visualization process with its user-friendly interfaces, offering a wide array of graphical representations like bar, pie, map, distribution, and line charts. It aids in real-time decision-making by enabling the creation of BI dashboards that present critical organizational key performance indicators (KPIs), such as revenue, profit, costs, products, customer, and employee.

The foundation of effective data visualization lies in the Gestalt principles of visual perception [25]. These principles, grounded in psychology, dictate how we group and interpret visual arrays, suggesting that our perceptions are often organized by the overall form rather than isolated components. They include

- Closure: We perceive incomplete elements as complete figures, filling in gaps to form a coherent image.

- Continuity: Our perception favors seamless, uninterrupted continuities in lines and patterns.

- Figure/Ground: This principle assists in distinguishing between the main element and the background in a visual scene.

- Proximity: Elements placed in proximity are seen as related, forming a collective perception.

- Similarity: Similar elements are naturally categorized together, whether by shape, color, or size.

- Enclosure: Items enclosed within a boundary are perceived as a collective unit.

- Common Fate: Elements moving in the same direction are regarded as part of a single group.

These principles are crucial to data visualization, as they inform the organization and presentation of data for optimal understanding and interpretive efficiency. Tableau's interfaces, reminiscent of Excel, facilitate straightforward data connection and visualization through intuitive drag-and-drop actions. Users can choose from over 20 different visual types to best convey their data insights.

An effective use of Tableau for data visualization is the construction of BI dashboards. These dashboards synthesize entity metrics, or KPIs, onto a single display, aiding management in real-time decision-making and enhancing productivity for digital entrepreneurs in urban retail environments.

Figure 6-2 illustrates a Tableau BI dashboard, which visualizes a city retail store's KPIs like revenue, profit, product, and regional performance, offering real-time support for management decisions through graphs such as bar, map, and color.

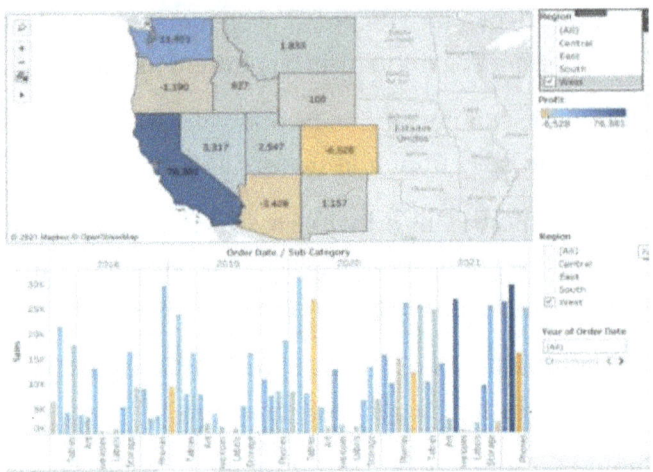

Figure 6-2. *An example of Tableau interactive dashboard displaying KPIs: sales, profit, product details (source: author's development using Tableau)*

Data Analytics

Data analytics is a process or methodology of extracting information or knowledge from raw data using various data analytics techniques, aimed to improve decision outcomes [26]. The rapid development in the data analytics field is attributed to explosive growth of big data, advancing computing power, and innovative computing algorithms or called models. According to Gartner (2017),[1] data analytics can be categorized to descriptive, diagnostics, predictive, and prescriptive analytics shown in Figure 6-3, which are all based on data, leading to final informative decision-making and problem-solving with different degree of decision automation [27].

---

[1] https://www.gartner.com/en/information-technology/glossary/descriptive-analytics

To elucidate further, the four categories of data analytics, as defined by Gartner, are

- Descriptive Analytics: Often the initial phase of data analysis, descriptive analytics summarizes historical data to establish trends and patterns, serving as a foundation for further analysis.

- Diagnostic Analytics: This approach delves into data to ascertain reasons behind past outcomes, leveraging sophisticated analytical techniques like correlation and pattern recognition to uncover the "why."

- Predictive Analytics: Leveraging algorithms and machine learning models, predictive analytics forecasts future events by analyzing historical data, providing a probabilistic assessment of what might occur next.

- Prescriptive Analytics: At the forefront of analytics, prescriptive analytics employs advanced algorithms to recommend actions or acting directly and determine optimal solutions, significantly informing automation and decision-making in various domains.

Each of these analytics types adds a layer of sophistication and insight, providing a deeper understanding of data which can lead to more informed and automated decision-making. The diagram in Figure 6-3 from Gartner illustrates these concepts and their contributions to the decision-making process.

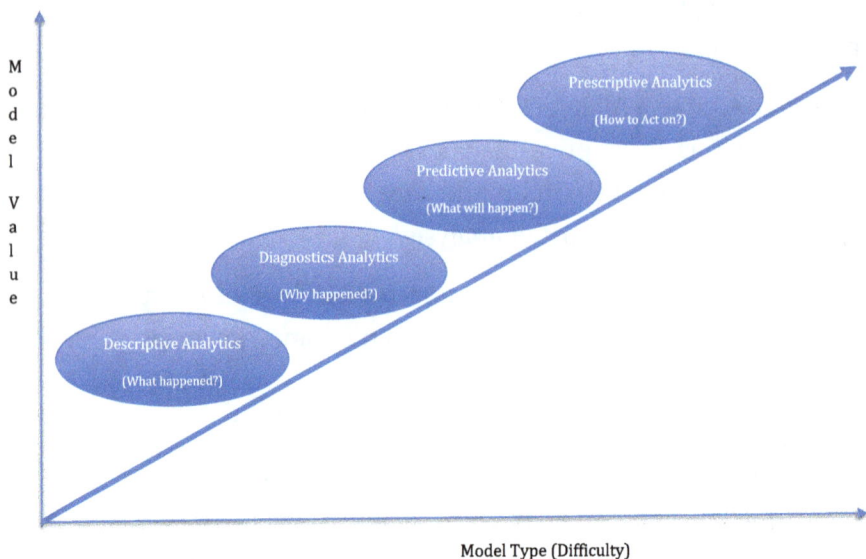

Figure 6-3. *Data analytics and decision automation (author's development based on source: Gartner, March 2012)*

Data Analytics Techniques

Data analytics techniques, encompassing machine learning models, fall into three broad categories: unsupervised learning (USPL), supervised learning (SPL), and deep learning (DL) [26].

- Clustering groups items based on similarity, with no prior labels available, hence the term unsupervised learning (USPL). K-Means is a popular algorithm in this category, where "K" determines the number of optima clusters, and "Means" refers to the average distance to the centroid within clusters.

- Classification, a form of supervised learning (SPL), uses labeled data to predict outcomes. For instance, it can determine whether a new customer will make a purchase as a conversion rate. Algorithms like Naive Bayes (NB), decision tree (DT), linear regression (linear), logistic regression (LR), and support vector machine (SVM) are widely used in SPL for predicting categorized outcomes.

- Artificial neural networks (ANN), or deep learning (DL), mimic the human brain's neural networks. ANNs consist of multiple layers that process unstructured datasets. Convolutional neural networks (CNNs) are excellent for image processing, while recurrent neural networks (RNNs), including long short-term memory (LSTM) networks, are adept at processing sequential data, making them suitable for applications like natural language processing and chatbots. The recent widespread adoption of ChatGPT is an example of generative AI, which is based on deep learning large language models (LLMs).

Figure 6-4 illustrates these data analytics processes and techniques, which are integral to the innovative data-driven digital twinning process for smart metaverse cities discussed in the subsequent sections.

CHAPTER 6   A DIGITAL TWINNING PROCESS FOR METAVERSE CITIES

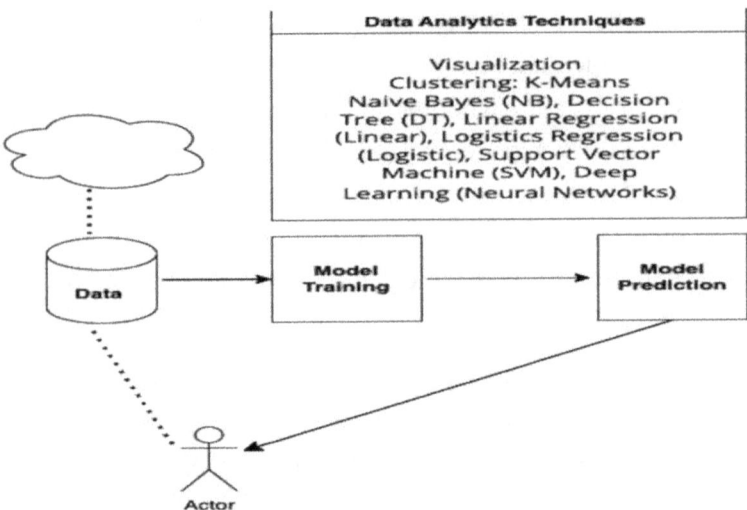

Figure 6-4. *Data analytics process and techniques (author's development)*

In concluding the above literature review, we've traversed the foundational processes and methodologies essential for the operationalization of digital twinning in metaverse cities. This journey has included a deep dive into the CRISP-DM process, the elucidation of data visualization's pivotal role, and the classification of data analytics into descriptive, diagnostic, predictive, and prescriptive categories, as per Gartner's framework. The discussion of data analytics techniques has brought to light the functionalities and applications of clustering, classification, and deep learning algorithms, setting the stage for their integration into our digital twinning process. As we move forward, the forthcoming chapter seeks to propose a formalized digital twinning process, drawing upon the insights gathered here to foster intelligent, data-driven urban ecosystems that enhance the quality of life and operational efficiency within our burgeoning smart cities.

Data-Driven Digital Twinning Process

The data-driven digital twinning process (DDTP) for metaverse cities is a crucial living mechanism that breathes life into the architectural designs of smart cities, as illustrated in Chapter 5. This process, detailed in Figure 6-5, fueled by the latest advancements in ICTs, including the Internet of Things (IoT), augmented and virtual reality (AR/VR), big data, artificial intelligence (AI), robotics, and other data analytics techniques discussed in Chapters 7 and 8, is the key to generating various intelligent services to activate "smart" digital twin metaverse cities proposed in Chapter 5.

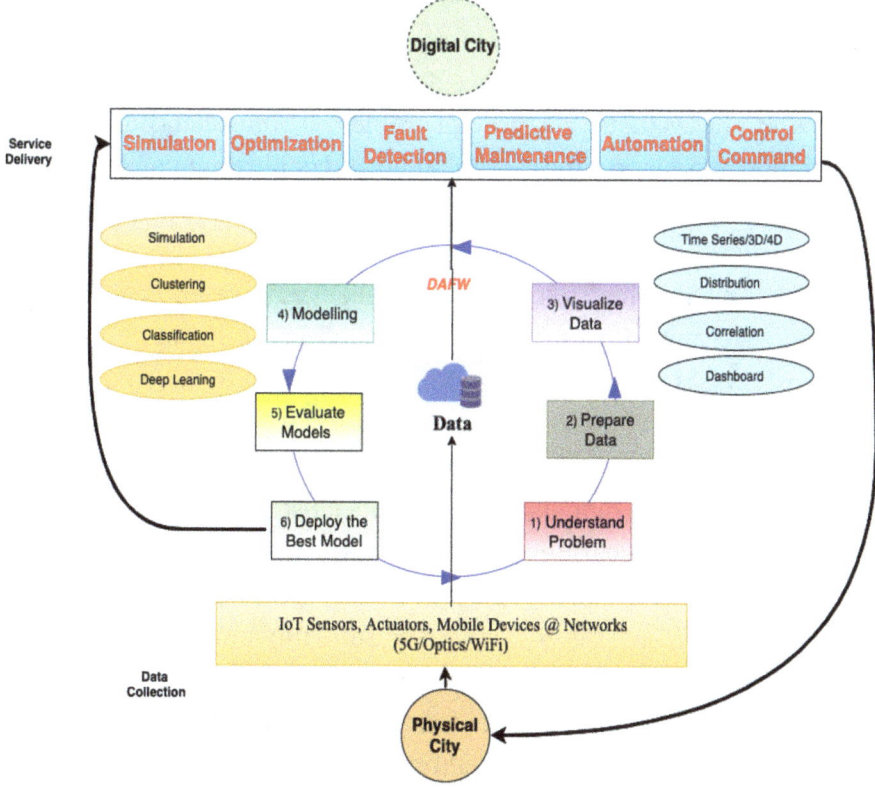

Figure 6-5. Digital twinning process–based decision-making for smart metaverse cities (source: author's development)

CHAPTER 6   A DIGITAL TWINNING PROCESS FOR METAVERSE CITIES

At the core of the DDTP is the collection of data from the physical city assets, such as buildings, hospitals, schools, businesses, vertical farms, streets, highways, energy facilities, sewage systems, people, animals, and trees. These elements make up the physical layer of a smart city and are organized into six main functions: environment, mobility, people, living, economy, and government. This data is then stored in cloud systems—public, private, hybrid, or community—based on the data's sensitivity and the regulation governance. For instance, public data from city administrations and services should be openly shared, while private business and personal data need to be protected according to privacy laws.

The heart of the DDTP is the Data Analytics Flywheel (DAFW), a dynamic force that maintains city livability by renewing itself in rhythm with the city's pulse. Inspired by the CRISP-DM process, the DAFW includes six phases that cycle through problem scoping, data collection, visualization, modeling, model evaluation, and deployment of the best models. These phases culminate in the generation of specific smart city intelligent services.

As this cycle unfolds, specific urban challenges are pinpointed, and raw data is amassed, processed, and visualized through intuitive interfaces, such as displays, TVs, and 3D/4D headsets. Refined data is then analyzed using machine learning techniques—unsupervised learning (USPL), supervised learning (SPL), or deep learning (DL)—and incorporated into models for simulation, clustering, classification, forecasting, and deep learning. These models—encompassing simulation, optimization, fault detection, predictive maintenance, automation, and control command—are rigorously assessed and implemented to provide intelligent services that meet the city's various requirements.

Intelligent services that emerge from this process include autonomous public transportation, robotic firefighting, telemedicine, educational services, senior care chatbots, and round-the-clock cybersecurity for urban safety.

The process is dynamic and iterative, enabling continuous refinement and synchronization between the physical and digital manifestations of the city. The digital city remains agile and responsive, evolving with the physical city to optimize smart city operations. The DAFW is the engine of this transformation, turning raw data into actionable insights that drive various city facets, all under the watchful eye of smart city indicators and city governance frameworks.

In sum, the data-driven digital twinning process, driven by the DAFW, is the innovative force behind the continuous evolution and synchronization of digital twin metaverse cities. It cultivates a responsive and adaptive digital city that learns and develops in tandem with its physical counterpart, thus delivering superior operations and intelligent services for an enriched urban experience. Subsequent sections will present preliminary examples to illustrate such a data-driven digital twinning process that powers our smart cities.

A Preliminary Digital Twin Metaverse City Example: Virtual Singapore (VP)

Virtual Singapore stands as a testament to Singapore's vision of a "smart nation," representing an ambitious leap toward the future of urbanization and digital economies.[2] This project is a concerted effort by the government, academic institutions, citizens, and private entities to construct a digital twin—a dynamic, 3D city model and data platform that encapsulates the essence of Singapore.

---

[2] https://www.nrf.gov.sg/programmes/virtual-singapore

At the heart of Virtual Singapore are several functionalities designed to propel smart city innovation:

- Virtual Experimentation Lab: Serving as a sandbox for urban design and infrastructure planning, this facilitates experiments like mobile network planning, spatial visualizations, and 3D urban simulations.

- Intelligent Service Testbed: This platform assesses and validates smart city services, such as crowd management and emergency evacuation procedures.

- Analytical Decision-Making Hub: This integrated setup supports urban planning by analyzing traffic flows, pedestrian dynamics, and public safety measures.

- Research and Development Resource: With city data at their fingertips, researchers and technologists can forge new frontiers in smart city tech, including advanced three-dimensional tools.

The Singapore government's report highlights how Virtual Singapore benefits public agencies, the research community, citizens, and private enterprises. It acts as a crucible for service innovation, business analytics, and collaborative problem-solving.

Yet, Virtual Singapore remains an initial prototype, not fully realizing the six components of a digital twin metaverse city as conceptualized in our digital twin metaverse city framework, shown in Figure 5-1. It lacks a comprehensive adoption of the DAFW-centric process, proposed in Figure 6-5, which is crucial for generating real-time intelligent services like automated control, predictive maintenance, and fault detection.

There lies a significant opportunity for Virtual Singapore to systematically evolve into a full-fledged digital twin metaverse city, integrating sophisticated intelligent service generation to enhance the "smartness" of Singapore.

Summary

The data-driven digital twinning process (DDTP) proposed in this chapter is nothing short of a paradigm shift for smart city development. At its core, the DDTP is energized by the Data Analytics Flywheel (DAFW), a dynamic, iterative engine that turns raw city data into actionable intelligence, powering the continuous evolution of both the physical and the digital realms of an urban environment.

The first step in this groundbreaking process is the meticulous collection of data, which is gathered from myriad IoT devices embedded throughout the city's infrastructure. This data is then securely stored, with public data made openly available to foster community engagement and innovation, while private data is protected in accordance with privacy laws and regulations.

The heartbeats of this process are the cycles of the DAFW, which mirror the rhythms of an urban life. These cycles begin with problem identification, where specific city challenges are pinpointed and defined. From there, the process transitions into data preparation, where the collected data is cleansed and organized, followed by data visualization to tease out initial patterns and insights.

Sophisticated modeling techniques are then applied to the prepared data, employing cutting-edge algorithms across simulation, clustering, classification, and deep learning. This step is collaborative, drawing on the expertise of a diverse team of professionals, such as data scientists, engineers, and domain-specific experts.

The next phase involves the careful evaluation of the models, using a variety of performance metrics to select the optimal solution for deployment. The chosen model is then integrated into the service delivery platform of the digital twin city, where it commands real-time intelligent services, driving innovation and efficiency.

CHAPTER 6   A DIGITAL TWINNING PROCESS FOR METAVERSE CITIES

The DDTP is a living, breathing process. It's not static; it's perpetually in motion, constantly refining itself through feedback loops that enhance city operations and services. As data flows back from the services in operation, the DAFW is triggered anew, propelling the cycle forward and ensuring the city's digital twin remains in lockstep with its physical counterpart.

This process is as vital to a city as the human heart is to the body, circulating the "blood" of data to sustain and improve the city's livability. It's an innovative model designed to create adaptable, responsive, and intelligent urban environments that not only react to current needs but also proactively prepare for future challenges.

In closing, the DDTP, fueled by the DAFW, represents an architectural and operational leap forward for digital twin cities. It encapsulates a vision where the metaverse and physical reality coalesce, yielding smart cities that are more than just habitable—they are sentient, adaptive, and, above all, intrinsically linked to the well-being and progression of human society. This is not just a proposal; it's a blueprint for the future, inviting further research and development to bring this vision to life in cities around the world.

Worth noting is the evolving landscape of data analytics modeling techniques, particularly deep learning AI, which is poised to further enhance the Data Analytics Flywheel (DAFW) amid rapid advancements in AI and machine learning techniques. Upcoming chapters will delve into a variety of emerging ICTs that act as both core components and enablers as building blocks to construct digital twin metaverse cities, proposed in Chapters 5 and 6. These discussions will unfold in Chapters 7 and 8, providing a comprehensive exploration of the technological forefront shaping the future of digital twin metaverse cities.

PART III

The Building Blocks: What Are Emerging Technologies

Parts 1 and 2 of this book articulate a transformative blueprint for the future of urban living. In Chapter 5, I unveiled a pioneering architectural design for digital twin metaverse cities, a groundbreaking vision that intricately weaves the fabric of the physical and digital realms to architect an intelligent urban landscape. The meticulously crafted design delineates the synergy between infrastructure, governance, and technological orchestration. In Chapter 6, we advanced this narrative by detailing a sophisticated digital twinning process, the lifeblood of our envisioned metropolises. And we introduced a Data Analytics Flywheel (DAFW) as the central cog in the perpetual machine of urban innovation. It is a manifesto for real-time, bidirectional synchronization of the tangible and virtual, ensuring that the city's pulse is constantly tuned to the rhythm of data and digital evolution. In Part 3, we will dive into the essential components that construct digital twin metaverse cities: the core and enabling emerging technologies. Core technologies are the backbone of this new urban landscape, featuring advancements such as 5G networks, IoTs, big data analytics, AI, cloud computing, blockchain, and digital platforms. Concurrently, enabling technologies act as catalysts for innovation

PART III   THE BUILDING BLOCKS: WHAT ARE EMERGING TECHNOLOGIES

and integration, bringing robotic automation, AR/VR, 3D printing, autonomous vehicles, drones and UAVs, and cybersecurity into the fold. These technologies are not just tools but also transformative forces that will be meticulously examined for their roles in revolutionizing cities with digital twin capabilities.

CHAPTER 7

Rising Emerging Information Technologies: Core

As we embark on Part 3, we are delving into the technological underpinnings that make such advancements possible. This chapter will explore the core and enabling technologies that are the building blocks of digital twin metaverse cities, including the likes of 5G networks and IoTs, as well as innovations in AI, cloud computing, and cybersecurity, among others. These technologies not only empower the infrastructure but also drive the functionality that will transform urban environments into intelligent and interconnected ecosystems.

5G Mobile Networks

Mobile networks have revolutionized the way we connect, enabling seamless communications across the globe and unlocking the potential value of both people and things. From the analog voice calls of 1G in the 1980s to the broadband digital services of 3G, each generation has brought a major technological leap approximately every decade. The evolution, as depicted in Figure 7-1, culminates with 4G introducing LTE and WiMax, supporting high-speed Internet services and preparing the ground for the Internet of Things (IoT) revolution, leading to an estimate of 9 billion connected mobile devices by 2019—more than the global population—with expectations of reaching 24 billion by the end of 2020 [28].

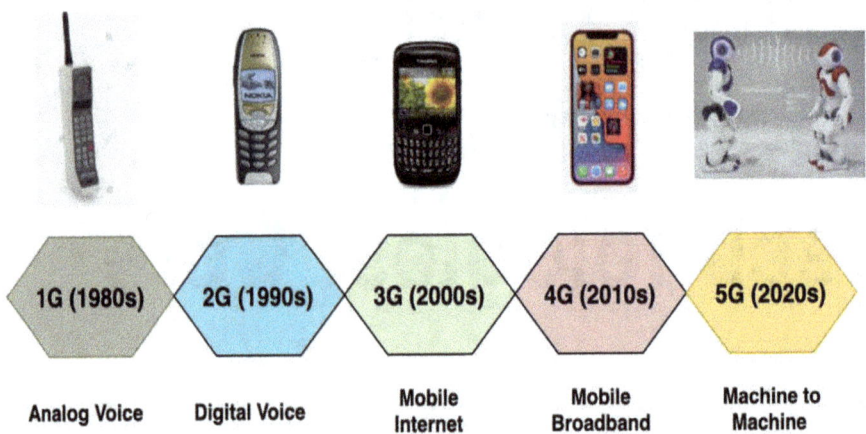

Figure 7-1. Mobile technology evolution from 1G to 5G (source: author's development)

In the era of 5G, introduced in 2018 by tech giants like Ericsson, Nokia, and Huawei, we experience up to 100 times faster speeds than 4G's, with significantly lower latency rates. This breakthrough heralds the advent of next-generation applications such as machine-to-machine (M2M) communication, IoT, AI, autonomous driving, telesurgery, remote education, and more [29].

Mobile networks comprise a core network, which is the backbone of mobile communications, and a radio access network, or base station, which connects users wirelessly to the Internet [30]. Core technologies of 5G include millimeter waves, small cell networks, Massive MIMO, beamforming, network slicing, and full duplex, each contributing to a robust and secure communication infrastructure, as illustrated in Figure 7-2.

CHAPTER 7   RISING EMERGING INFORMATION TECHNOLOGIES: CORE

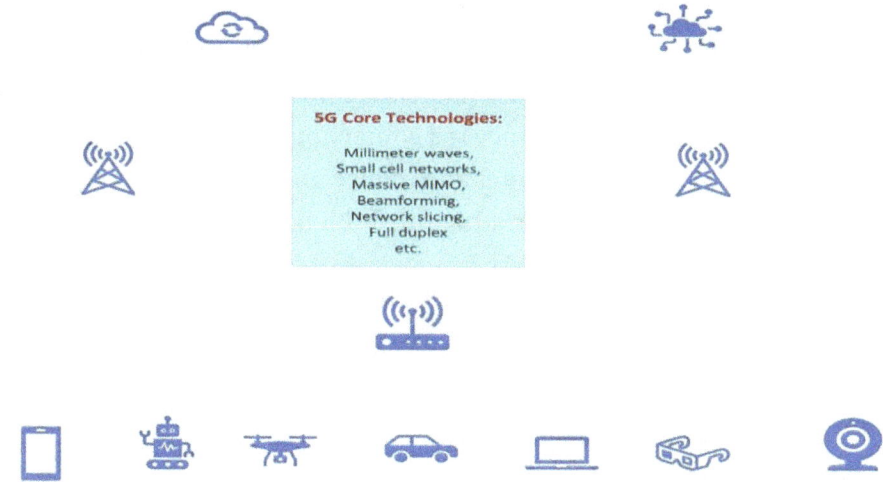

Figure 7-2. *General architecture of 5G mobile networks (source: author's development based on [29])*

5G technology represents a significant leap forward in mobile network architecture, distinguished by its adoption of *millimeter waves*, which have traditionally been used in radar and satellite communications. These high-frequency bands, specifically those above 24 GHz, offer the potential for large bandwidths, enabling broadband-level speeds and capacity that were previously unattainable in mobile communications. Millimeter waves, however, present a challenge in that they can be more susceptible to signal attenuation, particularly over long distances and through various obstructions. To address this, small cell networks become crucial, as they can be deployed in dense configurations to boost signal fidelity and ensure consistent service delivery in urban environments and high-traffic areas, as detailed in source.

Advancements in antenna technology also play a pivotal role in enhancing the 5G network. *Massive MIMO (Multiple Input Multiple Output)* significantly augments network capacity by employing a higher number of antennas at both the transmitter and receiver to facilitate more simultaneous data transmissions. This technique allows for a more efficient use of the spectrum, effectively multiplying the capacity of a wireless connection without requiring additional spectrum bandwidth, hence revolutionizing how signal channels are managed and optimized. This elevation in network efficiency is a cornerstone of the 5G architecture, affording users increased data rates and reduced latency for a myriad of applications, from streaming ultra-high-definition video to enabling the tactile Internet, as explored in [31].

Another revolutionary aspect of 5G technology is *beamforming*, which directs the transmission power to targeted users to improve signal strength and reduce interference. This dynamic adaptation of the antenna patterns ensures a focused and efficient transmission, enhancing user experience by delivering a stronger and more reliable connection. Moreover, the concept of network slicing further reinforces the customizable nature of 5G networks. Network slicing permits the creation of multiple virtual networks on a single physical infrastructure. These virtual end-to-end networks can be optimized for specific service requirements, whether they cater to high-speed data services, low-latency applications, or massive IoT deployments, therefore providing tailored connectivity solutions as diverse as the applications they serve, as outlined in [32].

Each of these core technologies—millimeter waves, small cell networks, Massive MIMO, beamforming, and network slicing—collectively build the robust framework that enables 5G to support a new era of digital communication. They represent a harmonized suite of advancements that address the increasing demands for high-speed, high-capacity, and low-latency wireless services.

The promise of 5G extends to facilitating M2M communications for automation across IoT devices, driving innovations like telesurgery, where surgeons perform operations remotely, supported by 5G's high-speed and reliable data transmission [33].

For smart cities, as conceptualized in Figure 5-1 of Chapter 5, 5G is foundational. It supports the massive and simultaneous connections necessary for urban areas, enhancing public resources, quality of life, and energy efficiency [34]. Yet, the deployment of 5G also presents challenges, including significant energy demands, the need for heightened computing power, and addressing data privacy and security concerns within a rigid global regulatory environment [35].

In essence, 5G lays the groundwork for the infrastructure and digital ecosystem of digital twin metaverse cities, offering robust telecommunication advancements essential for modern urban life. As 5G-fueled services like autonomous vehicles and smart home assistance become more prevalent, tackling the challenges of energy consumption, computational demands, privacy, security, and international regulation will be paramount for researchers and urban developers.

Internet of Things (IoT)

In the vanguard of Industry 4.0, the Internet of Things (IoT) is pivotal, transforming how we interact with the world around us. With an estimated growth to 75 billion devices by 2025 shown in Figure 7-3, IoTs represent a key pillar in the fourth industrial revolution, spanning from mechanization to the current cyber-physical systems. These interconnected devices offer a digital pulse of our world, akin to sensory cells, capturing data that feeds into the greater ecosystem of big data and AI, propelling advancements in various sectors.

CHAPTER 7   RISING EMERGING INFORMATION TECHNOLOGIES: CORE

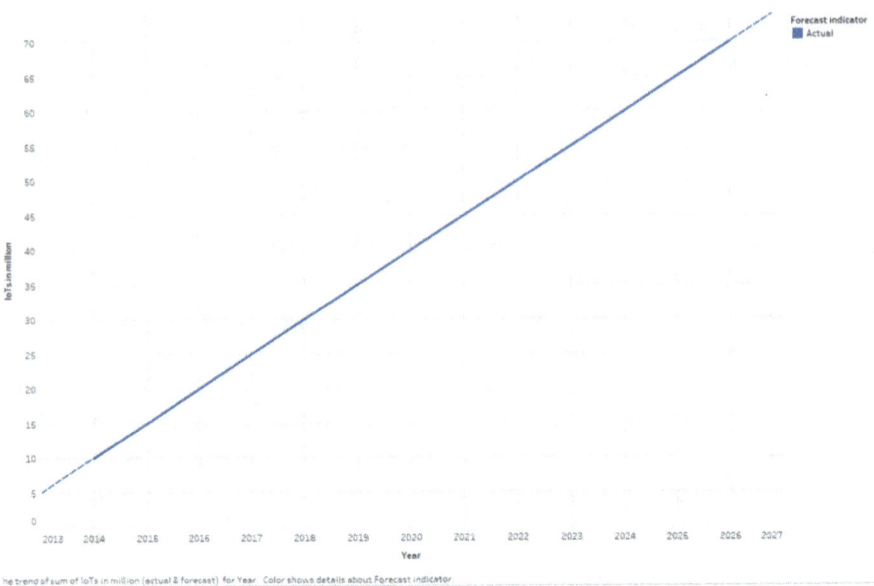

Figure 7-3. *An exponential growth of IoT devices from 2015 to 2025 (source: author's development using Tableau based on Statista, Germany, 2021[1])*

The maturation of 5G networking technology is a driving force in this data revolution, supporting IoTs with their promise of unprecedented speed, lower latency, and enhanced capacity. The integration of IoTs within the urban fabric is essential for the evolution of the digital twin metaverse cities [36], laying out a network of sensors and intelligent devices in every nook and cranny of urban life.

Defined as a mesh of connected entities, IoTs span an array of sensors, actuators, and mobile devices that collaborate to streamline and automate city functions. This network is the lifeblood of smart cities, with data flowing through IoTs to inform analytics and decision-making processes that enhance optimization and automation [37].

---

[1] https://www.statista.com/statistics/471264/iot-number-of-connected-devices-worldwide/

CHAPTER 7   RISING EMERGING INFORMATION TECHNOLOGIES: CORE

The Internet of Things (IoT) encompasses a diverse range of sensors that detect various environmental elements like temperature, sound, touch, smell, and pressure. Alongside these sensors, there are different types of actuators such as linear, rotary, and stepper, as well as a variety of mobile devices, including smartphones, drones, and self-driving vehicles. This broad array of IoT components is illustrated in Figure 7-4. In the context of a smart city, these sensors, actuators, and devices are embedded within various elements of the urban fabric, enabling M2M communication. Data collected from these sources feeds into data analytics models, which play a crucial role in analyzing, monitoring, and automating various aspects of city life, driving optimization and enhancing the functionality of the physical city.

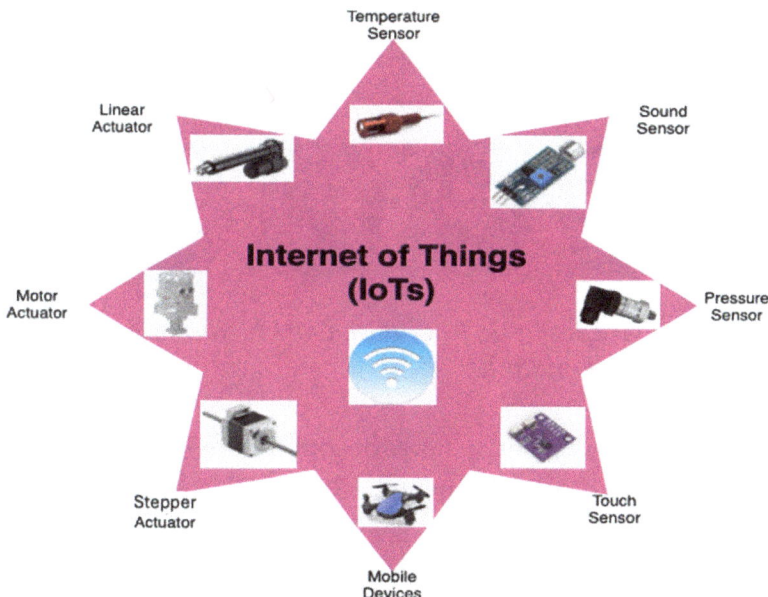

Figure 7-4. *Internet of Things (IoTs)—various sensor, actuator, and device (source: author's development)*

CHAPTER 7 RISING EMERGING INFORMATION TECHNOLOGIES: CORE

A simple scheme of how IoT works can be illustrated in Figure 7-5. IoT sensors can be categorized based on their collected analog signals, such as temperature, proximity, pressure, humility, vibration, chemical, and solar radiation, for example, temperature sensor, GPS locator, moisture measure, motion detector, etc. These IoT sensors capture analogical data from the environment, then convert to digital data through the usage of converter and microcontroller. After this, the data is sent to IoT networks by the gateway devices, then stored in the cloud, where the data is processed and analyzed. Further, the information is directed back to IoT devices, where actions like automation and optimization can be performed.

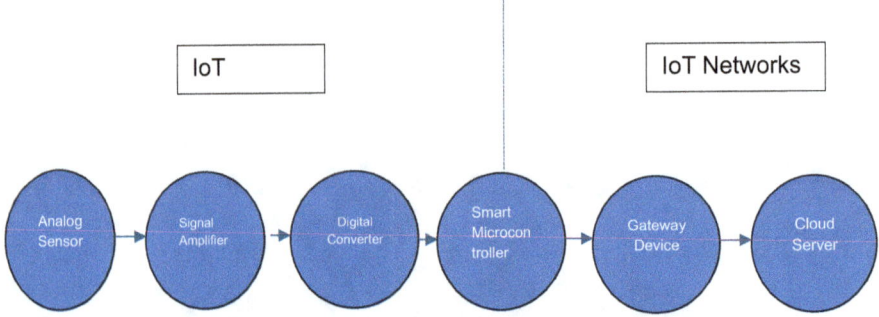

Figure 7-5. How does an IoT network work? (source: author's development based on [38])

The IoT offers an expansive range of applications, greatly benefiting smart cities with its diverse capabilities. Gartner's 2018 report highlights that there are more connected IoT devices globally than people, with over 25 billion devices already in production (refer to Figure 7-3). A significant portion of these devices are consumer-oriented products like smart TVs and speakers, while in the corporate realm, smart electric meters and commercial security cameras are prevalent.

IoT's utility extends far beyond leisure and personal communication. It plays a pivotal role in enhancing societal functions across various sectors such as education, healthcare, agriculture, and urban safety. In healthcare, IoT technology has revolutionized medical treatments and diagnostics. Common medical devices, when connected to the Internet, can gather valuable data, providing deeper insights into symptoms and enabling remote care. This has been particularly transformative for conditions like diabetes, which affects a significant portion of global adult population and requires continuous monitoring. Continuous glucose monitors (CGMs) are a prime example, allowing patients, families, and healthcare providers to track blood glucose levels in real time, making timely interventions possible.

In education, IoTs open up possibilities for more personalized learning experiences. Technologies like neuroscience transmitters can monitor students' performances, helping educators tailor teaching strategies to individual needs. This concept of a "smart school" not only connects teachers, students, and parents but also ensures real-time updates on student learning progress.

The advancement of 5G mobile networks is set to dramatically increase the capabilities of IoTs. With its high-speed data transfer, reliability, robust security, and massive connection capacity, 5G will enable millions, even billions, of IoT devices to communicate seamlessly. This will facilitate a wide range of data-intensive applications from mobile phones, home sensors, vehicles, and beyond.

However, the implementation of IoT in smart cities is not without challenges. The cost per device can influence the scale of IoT deployment and the density of data collection. The quality and reliability of IoT devices, along with maintenance requirements, are crucial factors that impact large-scale installations. Security is another critical aspect, both in terms of the physical security of the devices and the privacy of the data they collect. Addressing these challenges is essential for the successful development and application of IoTs in various industries within smart cities.

To encapsulate, IoTs are primed to be the nerve centers of metaverse smart cities, facilitating data collection and analysis that inform actions to optimize performance and enhance life quality. The synergy of 5G and IoTs will be instrumental in this transformative journey, though addressing cost, quality, and security challenges will be imperative for their successful integration into the smart city paradigm.

Big Data Analytics

Big data represents the immense volume of data amassed for decision-makers, characterized by the 5V model: volume, variety, velocity, veracity, and value, as depicted in Figure 7-6. Volume refers to the significant quantities of data from diverse sources. Variety encompasses different data types like texts, emails, videos, games, and financial transactions. Velocity signifies the rapid rate of data acquisition and analysis. Veracity indicates the reliability and relevance of data, acknowledging that not all data is useful or accurate. Finally, value underscores the primary goal of transforming this vast data into actionable insights for data-driven decision-making or automation in the physical world.

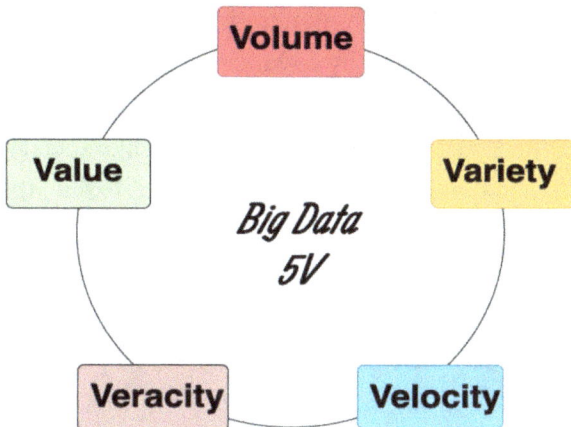

Figure 7-6. *Big data 5V model (source: author's development based on [39])*

Big data can be analyzed according to the type of information gathered. Three types of big data include structured, unstructured, and semi-structured. Structured data is the easiest to analyze, because it is already organized and the information could fit into rows and columns. Examples of structured data are age, billing, contact information, expenses, and your ID numbers. But, this structured data only accounts for only 20% of total data,[2] which is decreasing because of an exponential growth of other data types. Comparatively, unstructured data is one coming from all different social media applications such as video, photo, gesture, tweet, mail, link, share, game, metaverse, etc. And unstructured data is hard to process and analyze, but it has a lot of value. Finally, semi-structured data is a mix of both structured and unstructured data.

The evolution of big data has unfolded in three major phases.[3] Phase I involved the development of management information systems (MIS) for business intelligence. Phase II, spanning from 2000 to 2010, saw the rise of

---

[2] https://www.altexsoft.com/blog/structured-unstructured-data/
[3] https://www.bigdataframework.org/short-history-of-big-data/

the Internet and web applications generating diverse unstructured data. The current Phase III is marked by advancements in mobile technology, from 4G to 5G, enabling the collection of vast, varied data, including location-based and person-centered information like social media. With rapid growth of digital twin metaverse, I would argue that we are in Phase IV of big data with massive immersive data sources like 3D/4D environments.

Big data analytics employs sophisticated tools to process and analyze data, unearthing valuable insights like trend, pattern, and correlation. These analytics extend to various applications, from digital marketing to supply chain logistics, with data often stored in cloud-based databases like MongoDB and Cassandra. Analytical tools like Tableau and Power BI, along with programming languages such as Python, R, and Java, play crucial roles in this process. Figure 7-7 illustrates popular applications of big data analytics from the business analytics aspect.

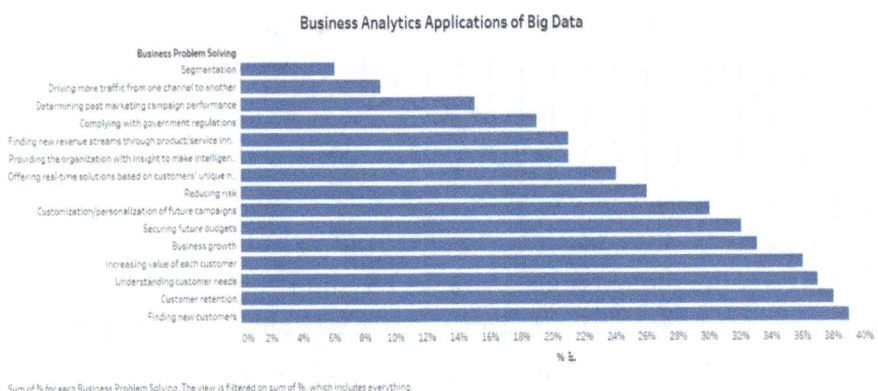

Figure 7-7. *Big data analytics—turning big data into insights (source: author's development using Tableau based on data[4])*

---

[4] https://www.edq.com/globalassets/white-papers/the-impact-of-bad-contact-data-quality.pdf

For example, in logistics and manufacturing, big data optimizes routing and maintenance, reducing costs and enhancing precision. In digital marketing, it backs decision-making with comprehensive Internet data, allowing for personalized marketing strategies and efficient targeting.

The challenges of big data analytics include growing demands for computational resources, a shortage of skilled professionals, and cybersecurity risks. The reliance on advanced computing systems, like GPU, grid, and quantum computing, underscores the need for more trained professionals in big data analytics.

In a nutshell, 5V big data is akin to the new oil in the modern economy and urban living. Collected in real time through IoT devices connected via 5G networks, stored in cloud databases, and analyzed using data visualization and machine learning, big data insights enhance life in physical cities. From improved asset utilization to full automation and enhanced quality of life, big data analytics is pivotal in shaping smart metaverse cities.

Artificial Intelligence (AI)

The explosion of 5V big data has catalyzed critical advancements in artificial intelligence (AI). As a distinct branch of computer science, AI is dedicated to creating machines that emulate human intelligence, performing tasks that typically require human cognition [40]. AI, generally encompassing machine learning and deep learning, has recently grown exponentially with advancements in computing power and software innovation. Notably, the AI market is projected to soar, reaching an estimated $500 billion by 2024, with a significant percentage of companies worldwide incorporating AI in some capacity. By the year 2025, 95% of customer interactions will be powered by AI.[5]

---

[5] https://aibusiness.com/document.asp?doc_id=760184

CHAPTER 7   RISING EMERGING INFORMATION TECHNOLOGIES: CORE

AI's evolution or even called AI revolution is evident in its key areas: machine learning, deep learning, and natural language processing (NLP), illustrated in Figure 7-8. Machine learning (ML) algorithms sift through extensive datasets to discern patterns and inform decisions. Deep learning (DL), a subset of ML, is inspired by the neural networks of the human brain, comprising multiple interconnected layers that analyze data for tasks like classification and prediction. This field has burgeoned, giving rise to virtual assistants, language translation services, autonomous vehicles, facial recognition systems, and generative AI, such as ChatGPT and Gemini, as large language models (LLMs). These technologies are increasingly integrating into every aspect of our lives.

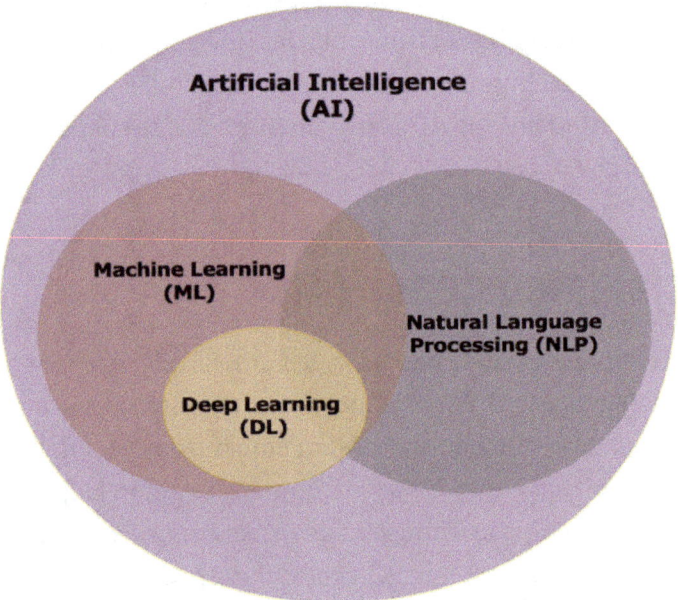

Figure 7-8. AI—machine learning, deep learning, and NLP (source: author's development)

NLP, a facet of AI, allows machines to understand and interact using human language, enabling communication with AI robots in languages like English, Spanish, or Chinese. ChatGPT, an advanced large language model (LLM), exemplifies this capability, and we'll delve further into its intricacies in Chapters 13 and 14 of this book with prototyping an online digital assistant using ChatGPT APIs.

AI's applications are as varied as they are transformative, touching upon ecommerce, robotics, healthcare, and beyond. GE's Predix AI, for an example, uses sensor data to anticipate equipment failure, facilitating timely preventive maintenance. Google's Waymo and Tesla utilize AI for autonomous driving, processing environmental data to navigate safely. In healthcare, AI's precision in early cancer detection exemplifies its potential for life-saving diagnostics, where AI can detect cancer at an early stage as precision medicine, based on data analytics on various stained tumor slides or radiology images and historic dataset [41].

Figure 7-9 illustrates the GE Predix AI application in action, processing historical performance data of digitized equipment to forecast potential failures with remarkable accuracy. This predictive capability empowers businesses to conduct timely preventive maintenance and effectively averting machinery downtime. Such proactive management is instrumental in ensuring seamless operations and safeguarding against potential financial losses.

CHAPTER 7   RISING EMERGING INFORMATION TECHNOLOGIES: CORE

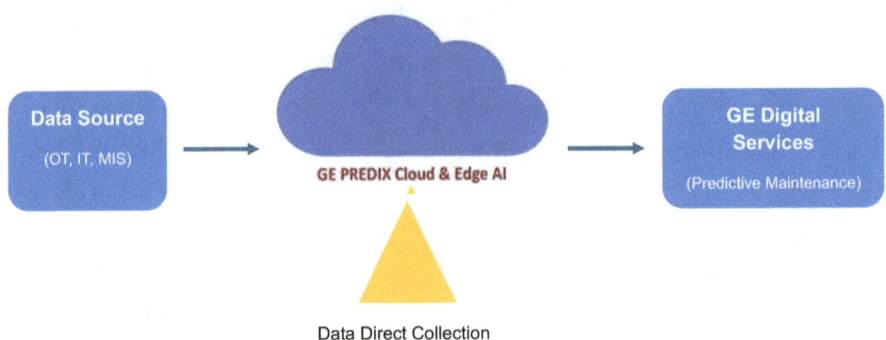

Figure 7-9. GE Predix AI platform for predictive maintenance (source: author's development based on the General Electric website[6])

In the transformative landscape of digital twin metaverse cities, artificial intelligence (AI) is proving to be an irreplaceable force. It enhances logistics efficiency, bolsters security with advanced intrusion detection systems, refines customer behavior predictions for targeted engagement, and powers digital marketing with responsive chatbots. AI's role in translation services is equally transformative, eradicating language barriers to smooth the path for global business and travel.

For instance, in the logistics and delivery sector, AI-driven robots are now staples in warehouse operations, expediting the picking, packing, and shipping processes to meet customer demands. Companies like Amazon deploy fleets of these intelligent machines, processing millions of shipments with precision daily. In the realm of security, AI systems establish baseline operational patterns for IT networks, swiftly detecting and neutralizing deviations to preempt threats and prevent network compromises.

---

[6]https://www.ge.com/digital/applications/analytics

CHAPTER 7   RISING EMERGING INFORMATION TECHNOLOGIES: CORE

In predicting consumer behavior, AI algorithms analyze vast arrays of data—from product preferences to purchasing habits—providing businesses with actionable insights to enhance customer experiences and drive sales. The advent of AI has also revolutionized digital marketing with chatbots like Amelia, a remarkably human-like digital assistant who tirelessly serves customers around the clock, without the need for breaks or salaries.[7]

In the realm of language translation, AI has been a pivotal force, propelling the creation of a multitude of applications that simplify international business expansion and enhance the travel experience for explorers. These innovative tools enable seamless communication across language divides, fostering truly global city experiences. Take, for instance, the recently launched ChatGPT-4 mobile app—a versatile companion that supports major global languages such as English, Spanish, Chinese, Japanese, Arabic, and more. Carried on any mobile device, it acts as a personal interpreter, navigating language barriers with ease. Such AI-driven applications are not merely facilitators but are transformative agents, integral to the operations of digital twin metaverse cities, providing an interconnected and accessible urban environment for all.

Yet, AI is not without its challenges. AI technology demands substantial investment and skilled professionals to harness its full potential. Concerns about AI malfunctioning—potentially catastrophic in fields like autonomous driving and healthcare—necessitate rigorous testing and safeguards. Social implications, particularly the risk of widespread technical unemployment, prompt urgent discussions on policy and retraining programs.

---

[7] https://amelia.ai/

To sum up, as big data propels AI forward, our envisioned digital twin metaverse cities stand to benefit from AI-driven automation, enhancing urban life with innovations like self-driving vehicles, robotic chefs, and intimate companionship. In fact, AI will become an integral architectural part of building digital twin metaverse cities, empowering people and things in the physical cities and creating intelligent services in the digital cities through the digital twinning process, discussed in Chapters 5 and 6 of this book. However, we must navigate AI's complexities with foresight, ensuring substantial investment, addressing potential failures, and mitigating social impacts to realize the promise of AI in shaping the metaverse smart cities of the future.

Cloud Computing

Cloud computing has become an indispensable part of modern Information and Communication Technology systems, seamlessly integrating into both business and personal computing environments at an unprecedented speed. For instance, government and business employees commonly rely on trusted third-party cloud providers like Amazon Web Services (AWS) and Microsoft Azure for daily operations, encompassing cloud storage, operating systems, and cloud-based applications. Similarly, mobile OS providers such as Google Android and Apple iOS automatically store our personal communications, like emails and text messages, on their private clouds, making these services integral to our daily lives.

The concept of cloud computing has evolved alongside computer history since the 1950s [42]. John McCarthy's 1955 initiation of the time-sharing concept marked the beginning, allowing multiple users to simultaneously share expensive mainframe resources. This idea significantly influenced the creation of the Internet. The subsequent decades saw the cloud evolve rapidly, from large server rooms filled with supercomputers to today's versatile cloud services. The turning point for cloud computing came with Amazon's introduction of the Elastic Compute Cloud in 2006, which popularized the term. Since then, cloud computing has expanded to encompass a variety of services, including database services and cloud storage.

Cloud computing can be defined as "the supply of computer services over the Internet (the cloud), such as servers, storage, database, networking, software, analytics, and intelligence [43]," highlights its departure from traditional IT resource management. Cloud computing offers several advantages over traditional MIS, including cost reduction, fast speed, global scalability, and increased productivity and reliability.

Cloud architecture, shown in Figure 7-10, encompassing various components like databases, software capabilities, and applications, is categorized into private, public, hybrid, and community (or social) clouds based on distribution and location. These infrastructures cater to specific needs, from serving a single organization in private clouds to offering IT resources to all enterprises and governments in public clouds. Hybrid clouds combine elements of both public and private clouds, while community clouds are shared among several organizations with similar core businesses or infrastructure needs.

Figure 7-10. *Cloud computing architecture (source: author's development)*

Cloud computing services are broadly classified into Software as a Service (SaaS), Platform as a Service (PaaS), and Infrastructure as a Service (IaaS) [44]. SaaS offers users access to software and applications hosted on the Internet. PaaS provides an environment for software development without the hassle of managing hardware and software infrastructure. IaaS, exemplified by Amazon Web Services, offers processing resources and other infrastructure components. These services vary in their applications, with IaaS anticipated to be a major market player due to its flexibility and economic benefits.

Three leading cloud computing providers—Amazon AWS, Microsoft Azure, and Google Cloud Platform (GCP)—offer varied features and services. AWS is renowned for its extensive services, advanced security, and cost-effectiveness [45]. Azure, known for its deep integration with Microsoft tools, offers broad features and hybrid cloud capabilities [46]. GCP, though later to the market, focuses on high-performance computing products and is renowned for its efficiency in data streaming and productivity. They can be chosen to build the digital twin metaverse cities shown in Figure 5-1 (digital cities), Chapter 5.

Cloud computing's evolution has brought new challenges, such as unreliable latency and lack of mobility support. Fog or edge computing shown in Figure 7-11 addresses these by providing cloud resources and services closer to end users on ground. Fog computing (FC) benefits include low latency, scalability, business agility, lower operating expenses, distributed architecture, and real-time interactions.

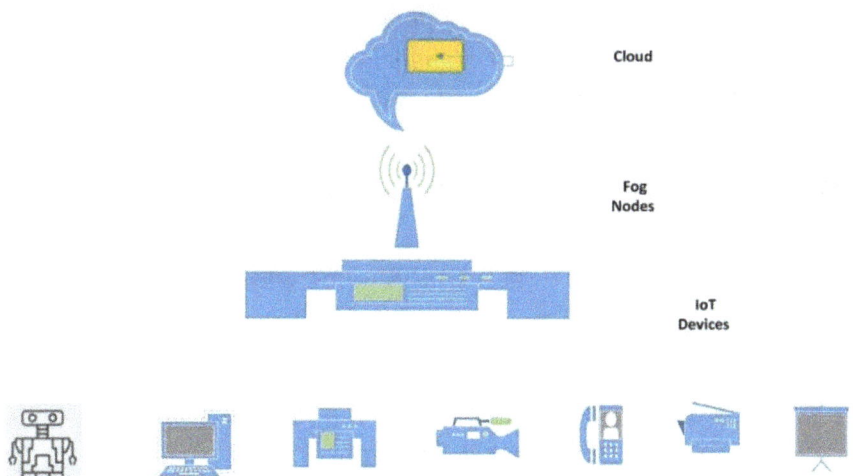

Figure 7-11. Fog computing environment (source: author's development based on [47])

In brief, cloud computing's ongoing evolution plays a pivotal role in providing ICT infrastructure for digital twin smart metaverse cities. Its various service models, such as SaaS, PaaS, and IaaS, along with the advent of fog computing, offer diverse solutions for building data platforms in digital twin metaverse cities, addressing security and privacy concerns. Leading providers like AWS, Azure, and GCP present distinct options for choosing the most suitable cloud service provider for these futuristic urban constructs.

Blockchain

Blockchain technology, increasingly popular and essential in mainstream industries globally, is poised to become a core technology in constructing digital twin metaverse cities. Initially introduced by cryptographer David Chaum and later developed by Stuart Haber and W. Scott Stornetta, blockchain technology gained prominence with Satoshi Nakamoto's launch of Bitcoin [48]. Today, it is rapidly growing, with broad applications beyond digital currencies.

Defined by Crosby et al. as a technology based on a distributed ledger, blockchain ensures that records are chronologically organized, immutable, and shared among participants in a network [49]. This setup guarantees that transactions are secure, tamper-proof, and consistent across all network databases.

The main components of blockchain include a distributed ledger, cryptocurrencies, and its structure [50]. The distributed ledger is a shared database accessible to network participants, allowing instant reflection of transaction changes. Cryptocurrencies, like Bitcoin and Ethereum, are digital currencies recorded in the ledger using robust cryptography. The structure of blockchain pictured in Figure 7-12 involves a network of computers where transactions are encoded and linked in a chain format, ensuring chronological order and immutability.

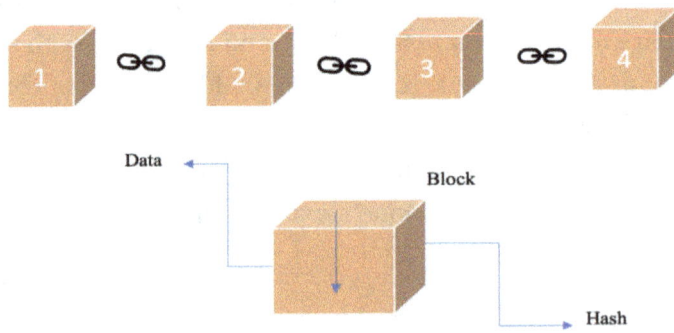

Figure 7-12. *The structure of blockchain (source: author's development based on [51])*

Five major elements of the blockchain network are decentralization, encryption, immutability, distribution, and tokenization, as shown in Figure 7-13. Decentralization shifts decision-making power to the network, creating a trustless environment for anonymous participants. Encryption safeguards personal and transactional data, while immutability ensures ledger entries are permanent and tamper-proof. Tokenization secures asset exchanges, and distribution enables transparent and autonomous ledger management across the network.

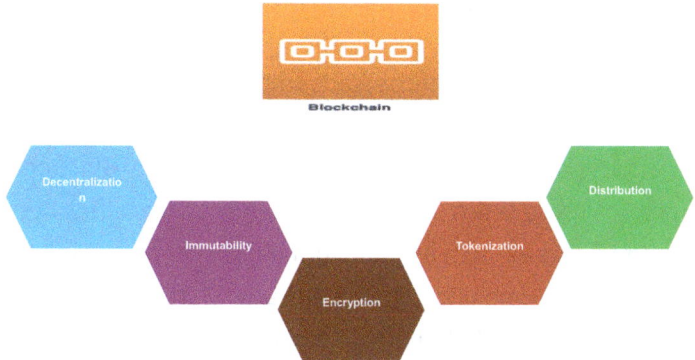

Figure 7-13. *Blockchain's five main components (source: author's development)*

Blockchain technology offers significant benefits, such as reduced transaction costs, enhanced security, fast and reliable transactions, irreversibility, and data loss prevention. These features make blockchain ideal for transforming traditional operations, like supply chain management, into more efficient, transparent, and sustainable systems. IBM Food Trust is a prime example, leveraging blockchain to ensure food safety, traceability, and sustainability in the food industry.[8]

---

[8] https://www.ibm.com/products/supply-chain-intelligence-suite/food-trust

CHAPTER 7   RISING EMERGING INFORMATION TECHNOLOGIES: CORE

In digital twin metaverse cities, blockchain can revolutionize various aspects, from securing massive IoT device transactions to improving data privacy in the Data Collection layer (Figure 5-1, Chapter 5). It can also be instrumental in the digital twinning process (Figure 6-5, Chapter 6), applying smart contracts, cryptocurrency transactions, and cybersecurity mechanisms to safeguard against fraudulent activities and cyber threats.

In closing, blockchain technology stands as a cornerstone in building digital twin metaverse cities, offering advanced features like traceability, real-time transactions, and robust security, crucial for the seamless integration of physical and digital urban infrastructures. Blockchains can be a core technology to build the digital twin metaverse cities because of the advanced features such as traceability, non-localization, real-time transactions, and security. For example, in Data Collection layer in Figure 5-1, Chapter 5, blockchain technology helps organize massive IoT devices to secure data transactions and improve data privacy without human involvement. In the digital twinning process in Figure 6-5, Chapter 6, blockchain technology can be applied for algorithms for smart contracting, cybercurrency-based transactions, and cybersecurity mechanism to prevent fraudulent transactions and cyber-attacks.

Digital Platform

The Internet or digital platform serves as a dynamic conduit for people and machines to communicate and exchange value, encompassing information, merchandise, and currency. Platforms such as Amazon connect buyers and sellers in a virtual marketplace, Facebook facilitates social interactions and information sharing, Airbnb links global guests to hosts for accommodation-sharing services, while Uber's mobile software allows for a diverse range of services, including shared rides, meal delivery, and logistical solutions. The significance of digital platforms has been magnified amid the Covid-19 pandemic due to social distancing mandates, compelling individuals to rely heavily on these platforms for work, travel, education, shopping, healthcare, and entertainment. This shift has led to a notable increase in the stock value of major digital platforms like Amazon, Apple, Facebook, Google, Netflix, Spotify, Airbnb, and Uber, contrasting the overall downward trend in S&P stocks since the pandemic's onset in March 2020.[9]

Central to the operation of digital platforms is the concept of two-sided markets, wherein two distinct agents engage through an intermediary platform, facilitating peer-to-peer (P2P) transactions. This model is characterized by the mutual impact of each agent group's decisions on the other, often through externalities. Nobel laureate Jean Tirole has explored a variety of two-sided market examples, ranging from video games and streaming media to real estate and the Internet [52].

The structure of the Internet market or digital platform, shown in Figure 7-14, distinctly diverges from that of traditional linear, product-centric businesses. In a conventional business model, a manufacturer sources materials, assembles products, bundles them with complementary components, and distributes them through channels like wholesalers and retailers. This linear approach results in extended product life cycles and significant costs in logistics, distribution, and inventory management. Digital platforms, however, directly connect producers and consumers over the Internet, enabling immediate economic value exchange. This model not only accelerates transaction speeds and reduces intermediary costs but also facilitates the creation of more personalized products and services. Additionally, digital platforms capitalize on the "network effect"—the extensive global reach of the Internet—allowing them to target a vast customer base worldwide.

---

[9] https://www.schroders.com/en/global/individual/

CHAPTER 7   RISING EMERGING INFORMATION TECHNOLOGIES: CORE

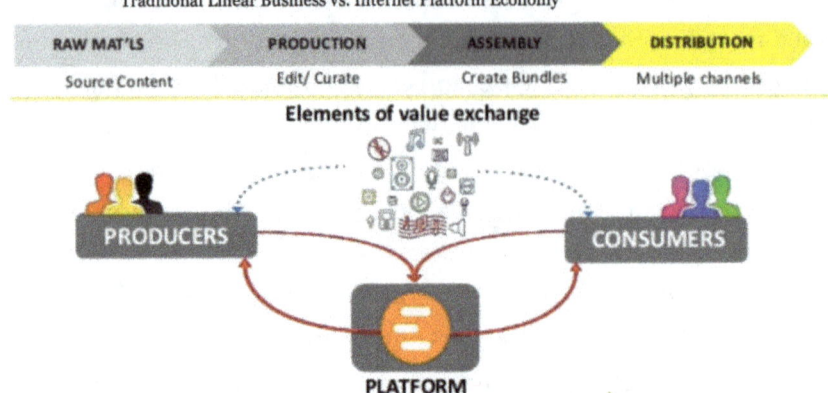

Figure 7-14. Two-sided digital platform vs. traditional linear business (source: author's development based on his PhD dissertation)

The concept of network effects, also known as network externalities, is critical in understanding the economic power behind digital platforms. This concept is derived from Metcalfe's Law, originally applied to telecommunications networks [53]. Metcalfe's Law posits that the value of a network is proportional to the square of the number of its users. Mathematically, the network effects can be represented as $\frac{n(n-1)}{2}$, which simplifies to n^2 as n grows very large. To illustrate, consider the world's first telephone, which on its own was merely a technological novelty with no communicative value. As the number of telephones grew, forming a vast global network, the value of the network didn't just increase linearly but approximately squared with the number of connected phones. Hence, each additional phone exponentially increased the network's utility, allowing every user to potentially connect with any other user across the globe, thereby magnifying the network's communicative value.

In the realm of business and economics, network effects refer to the phenomenon where the value of a product or service increases as more people use it [54]. This concept is analogous to "economies of scale," where increased production volumes lead to lower costs per unit, potentially reducing prices for consumers.

In a traditional business model, economies of scale are balanced by diseconomies of scale, which occur when increasing production leads to higher unit costs due to factors like management challenges or operational bottlenecks. This relationship is typically depicted as a U-shaped cost curve, shown in Figure 7-15a, where the curve's lowest point represents the optimal production volume. To the left of this point, economies of scale are realized, while to the right, diseconomies of scale set in.

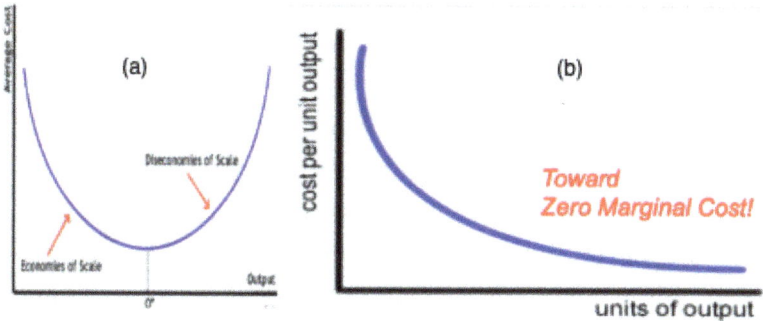

Figure 7-15. *The network effects in digital platform, resulting in almost zero marginal cost (source: author's development)*

Digital platforms, however, operate differently due to the network effects. A seller on a digital platform can reach a virtually unlimited global customer base, sharing production and trading costs over a larger number of sales and continually decreasing the unit cost. Thus, the cost per unit output for the digital platform trends downward, forming a "hockey stick" shape shown in Figure 7-15b, and can approach nearly zero marginal cost as the product scale increases.

For instance, on the Amazon ecommerce platform, a seller can set up an online store with minimal marginal cost to Amazon. Despite Amazon not owning the inventory, it charges a fee (about 15%) on each sales transaction. The fixed costs of establishing the Amazon platform are distributed across millions of products sold, leveraging network effects to offer a vast variety of products at lower prices compared to traditional retailers like Walmart, Target, Carrefour, H&M, Zara, and Eaton. These traditional stores are under increasing pressure from digital platforms like Amazon and Alibaba, leading to the unfortunate closure of some physical stores.

The burgeoning influence of network effects on the Internet is compelling numerous traditional businesses to undertake a digital transformation, also known as digitalization. For instance, Apple has expanded beyond manufacturing iPhones to create an integrated digital ecosystem. This ecosystem includes iTunes, iPods, iPads, iWatch, a vast array of third-party accessories, and millions of applications within the App Store, all designed to enhance the overall value of Apple's offerings for its customers. Consequently, Apple has transitioned from being merely an iPhone manufacturer to becoming a comprehensive platform for user experience, thereby generating significant value for both its customers and shareholders, reaching the milestone of becoming the first three trillion-dollar company in history.[10] Similarly, Nike, renowned as a leading global brand for athletic footwear, has embraced digitalization by developing applications like Nike+iPod that serve as virtual personal trainers. This initiative transforms Nike from a simple retailer of shoes and apparel into a holistic platform provider that also offers fitness and healthcare advisory services. The trend toward digital transformation has accelerated during

---

[10] https://fortune.com/2023/06/30/apple-history-3-trillion-market-value/

the Covid-19 pandemic, as firms with digital platform-based models have been able to not only survive but also thrive amid social distancing measures implemented by governments worldwide.

To establish a successful digital platform, five essential components must be designed and built, as depicted in Figure 7-16. Firstly, the platform requires a suite of core software tools for pricing, payment processing, logistics, store management, and online engagement, which can be developed in-house or outsourced to third-party providers. Secondly, an effective search and matching engine powered by AI and machine learning algorithms is vital for enhancing user search capabilities. Thirdly, the platform should incorporate a trust and reputation system, relying on historical data or third-party datasets, to facilitate secure and honest exchanges between buyers and sellers [55][56]. Fourthly, platform management must implement rules and regulations that ensure fair and secure transactions, safeguarding all participants. Lastly, to ensure long-term sustainable growth, the platform should cultivate a large and engaged user community through various promotional activities and campaigns, thereby establishing a trustworthy brand.

Figure 7-16. Digital platform main components (source: author's development)

CHAPTER 7   RISING EMERGING INFORMATION TECHNOLOGIES: CORE

Summary

This chapter provided an in-depth exploration of the core emerging technologies underpinning digital twin metaverse cities. It emphasized the transformative impact of 5G networks, Internet of Things (IoT), big data analytics, artificial intelligence (AI), cloud computing, blockchain, and digital platform in shaping smart and interconnected urban ecosystems. This chapter highlighted how these technologies enhance infrastructure and functionality, from facilitating seamless M2M communication and IoT integration to harnessing AI and big data for advanced urban analytics. Additionally, it discussed the pivotal role of cloud computing and blockchain in building up smart city digital platforms and securing data transactions. Chapter 8 will dive into various enabling technologies like robotics, AR, VR, 3D printing, autonomous driving, drone, and cybersecurity, which serve as enablers in constructing our digital twin metaverse cities.

CHAPTER 8

Rising Emerging Information Technologies: Enablers

In this chapter, I will examine a range of burgeoning enabling technologies such as robotic automation, augmented reality (AR), virtual reality (VR), 3D printing, autonomous driving, drones, and cybersecurity. These technologies are pivotal enablers for building digital twin metaverse cities, making our urban environments more efficient, sustainable, and livable.

Robotic Automation

In Chapter 7, we delved into artificial intelligence (AI) as the domain that endows machines with capabilities such as logic, reasoning, learning, perception, and even elements of creativity and self-awareness. This intelligence, however, is distinct from physical manipulation, residing purely within computational realms [57]. Robotics, conversely, serves as the physical extension of AI technology and automating tangible tasks. While distinct, AI and robotics often intersect, with AI enhancing robotic functions and vice versa. The term "robot," rooted in the Czech language and meaning "forced labor," was coined by playwright Karel Capek in 1921 to describe humanlike machines. The trajectory of robotics saw a significant milestone in 1950 with George C. Devol's invention of Unimate, the first reprogrammable robot, later commercialized by Joseph Engelberger [58].

Robotics, as we've established, is a multidisciplinary arena focused on the design, enhancement, operation, and evaluation of electromechanical devices, which take on tasks traditionally performed by humans [59]. Commonplace in industrial settings, robots execute a myriad of repetitive tasks and are integral to the operation of advanced military vehicles. Additionally, in the medical field, they assist with complex surgeries. While some robots are humanoid, resembling humans, industrial robots are typically machine-like. Comprising mechanical components, sensors, and processors, robots interact with their environment to carry out physical tasks: sensors gather external data, and processors translate this data into actionable instructions. Incorporating AI, robots can mirror human sensory faculties such as sight and touch, enabling them to adapt to new environments and even understand human language in customer service applications, routing calls effectively based on voice recognition.

The operation of robotics entails a three-step process: data collection, processing, and execution. Initially, sensors play a pivotal role in environmental assessment, capturing various physical metrics from the robot's surroundings. This data is subsequently processed using sophisticated algorithms that facilitate spatial awareness and motion planning. The robot's actions are then choreographed using a specialized motion-description language, which utilizes symbol sets for defining movements, allowing for standardization and reusability in programming. Finally, the spectrum of robot control spans from manual to fully

CHAPTER 8 RISING EMERGING INFORMATION TECHNOLOGIES: ENABLERS

autonomous systems, as illustrated by the cloud-based robot example, which integrates sensory input, data processing, and actuation with cloud computing resources to enhance functionality and adaptability illustrated in Figure 8-1a and b [60][61].

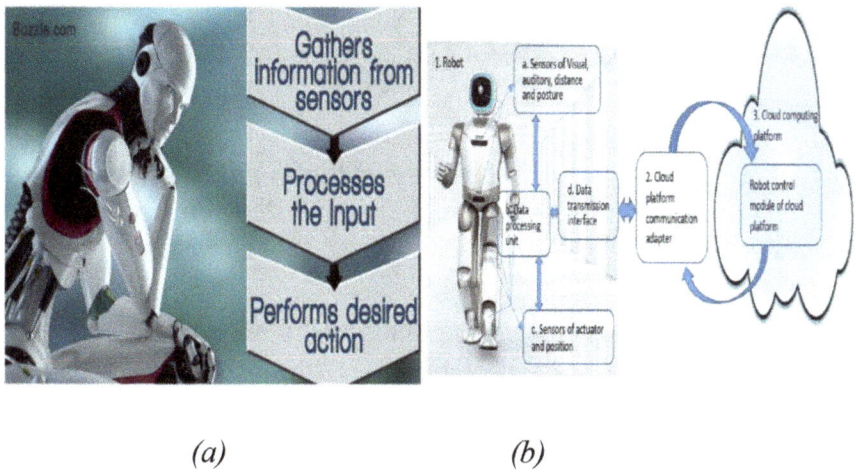

(a) (b)

Figure 8-1. *General robotics process (a) and a cloud-based robot (b) (author's development)*

The increasing integration of robotic automation in manufacturing, geared toward tasks such as vehicle assembly and chemical processing, is driving costs down and simplifying complexity. According to recent IFR World Robotics Report 2020, industrial robots,[1] starting from 2011, as of 2021, the adoption of industrial robots in the world increased from about 166,000 units per year to around 517,000 units per year. And the estimated annual growth rate of the industrial robot market based on the chart is over 12% year after year, shown in Figure 8-2.

---

[1] https://ifr.org/ifr-press-releases/news/wr-report-all-time-high-with-half-a-million-robots-installed

CHAPTER 8   RISING EMERGING INFORMATION TECHNOLOGIES: ENABLERS

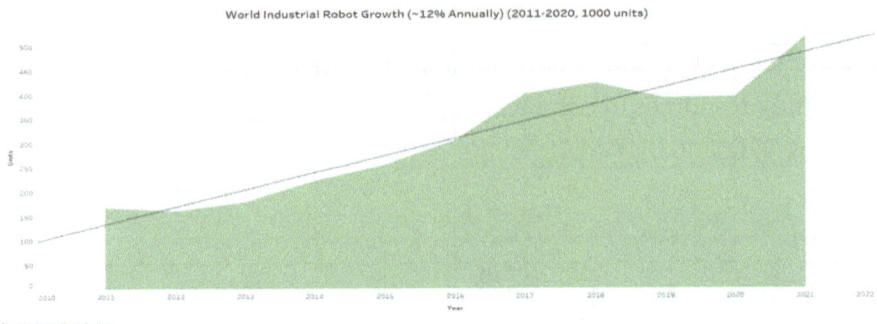

Figure 8-2. *Annual industrial robot installation with ~12% annual growth (source: author's development using Tableau based on World Robotics 2022 Report[2])*

In the pulsing heart of a metaverse city, a symphony of AI, robotics, and communication technology orchestrates a future of sustainable urban living. Picture this: vending machines engaging in conversation, serving your favorite lunch pack or snacks with a simple voice command. Airports and train stations are abuzz with digital assistants, offering guidance with the warmth of human interaction sans the desk. In the realm of education, robots are playing an increasingly integral role, both in classrooms and at home, by engaging and teaching children to enhance their educational outcomes. Meanwhile, in the medical field, robots are revolutionizing care by performing remote surgeries, saving lives in emergency situations, and bringing vital services to remote villages.

For example, amid the Covid-19 pandemic, the reliance on robotics and automated systems has surged, particularly for managing social distancing and quarantine measures.[3] Significantly, robots have replaced human roles in diverse fields, offering enhanced efficiency and reliability. A remarkable example from China includes the first-ever remote

---

[2] https://ifr.org/downloads/press2018/2022_WR_extended_version.pdf
[3] https://www.nature.com/articles/s42256-020-00238-2

brain surgery on a Parkinson's patient, executed using a robot and 5G networking.[4] This technological breakthrough not only marks a milestone in telehealth but also indicates the potential for remote elderly care in digital twin metaverse cities, addressing healthcare worker shortages and improving life quality during global crises.

Growing ethical concerns stand out with AI and robotics proliferation. Privacy is paramount, especially with the need for extensive data in AI, raising issues about the protection of sensitive personal information. Security and weaponization are also critical, as AI technology can be used in warfare, necessitating awareness and regulation. The economic impact, particularly in terms of job displacement by automation, requires thoughtful regulation to balance human and robotic roles. Lastly, biases inherent in AI algorithms can lead to discriminatory outcomes, underlining the need for continuous oversight and improvement in these technologies.

In retrospect, robotic automation (RA), as a vital emerging technology, plays a pivotal role in the development of digital twin metaverse cities. Its influence has expanded beyond production to areas like autonomous vehicles, medical imaging, educational assistance, senior care, vertical farming, food services, and smart city management. This expansion, however, raises ethical concerns, including privacy, potential weaponization, job displacement, and AI biases. Addressing these issues is crucial to harness the benefits of RA while maintaining societal balance and safety.

---

[4] http://www.chinadaily.com.cn/a/201903/18/WS5c8f0528a3106c65c34ef2b6.html

Augmented Reality (AR) and Virtual Reality (VR)

Augmented reality (AR) and virtual reality (VR) are the keystones of the digital twin metaverse cities, without which the metaverse remains an unfulfilled promise. Imagine stepping into a city where the boundaries between physical and virtual realms blur seamlessly, where every element of urban life is enhanced by a digital overlay, creating experiences beyond imagination.

Virtual reality (VR) offers a computer-generated, three-dimensional environment that users can interact with using electronic devices, creating an immersive experience where the virtual world feels real [62]. Conversely, augmented reality (AR) enhances the real world by overlaying computer-generated information, affecting various senses such as sight and sound [63]. Unlike VR's complete immersion, AR adds digital elements to reality. This continuum of digital reality, from actual reality to complete virtuality, including AR, VR, mixed reality (MR), and augmented virtuality (AV), is demonstrated in Figure 8-3 as the AR and VR continuum, from reality (R) to augmented reality (AR), virtual reality (VR), mixed reality (MR), augmented virtuality (AV), to complete virtuality (V).

CHAPTER 8   RISING EMERGING INFORMATION TECHNOLOGIES: ENABLERS

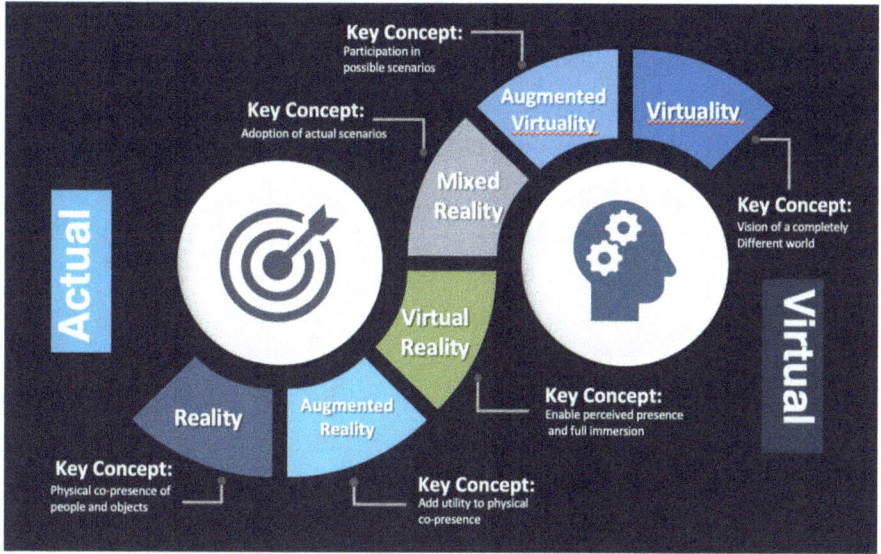

Figure 8-3. *The AR and VR continuum (author's development based on [63])*

The history of VR dates to 1950s, when filmmaker Morton Heilig designed the Sensorama was the beginning of VR [64]. Sensorama was a cabinet-shaped device with third display, vibrating seat, and audio player. Until 1968, computer scientist Ivan Sutherland made the first VR headset. In 1990, NASA designed gloves and a suite to examine the VR headset [65]. The year 2014 was the turning point for VR technology highlighted by a few milestone events. Facebook acquired the Oculus VR company for $2 billion, and it defined a moment in the VR history.[5] And Facebook's VR products are Oculus Quest 2 (2020), Oculus Quest (2018), Oculus Rift S (2019), Oculus Go (2017), Oculus Rift (2016), and Meta Quest Pro (2022), and Meta has released the most advanced VR handset: Meta Quest 3 in

---

[5] https://about.fb.com/news/2014/03/facebook-to-acquire-oculus/

CHAPTER 8　RISING EMERGING INFORMATION TECHNOLOGIES: ENABLERS

2023. Meanwhile, Sony announced that they were working on Project Morpheus, a VR headset for the PlayStation 4 (PS4), and Google released the Cardboard—a low-cost and do-it-yourself stereoscopic viewer for smartphones.[6] Samsung announced its Gear VR, a headset that uses a Galaxy smartphone as a viewer.

The recent developments in AR/VR technology, particularly Apple's unveiling of Apple Vision Pro on June 6, 2023,[7] mark a significant leap toward bringing these technologies into mainstream use as various digital twin metaverse applications. This device, acclaimed as a spatial computer, promises to blend virtual and physical environments seamlessly. Such advancements have sparked wider interest in VR's potential, leading to creative applications and the integration of innovative accessories. For instance, the pairing of Oculus Rift with a Wii's balance board by Cratesmith to recreate a scene from *Back to the Future* exemplifies this trend.[8] Figure 8-4 illustrates the intricate design of the typical VR headset, a marvel of modern technology, which consists of intricate components like lenses, housing, liquid crystal displays, backlights, and driver electronics, each playing a crucial role in crafting immersive virtual experiences.

---

[6] https://virtualspeech.com/blog/history-of-vr
[7] https://www.apple.com/newsroom/2023/06/introducing-apple-vision-pro/
[8] https://www.gmw3.com/2014/04/back-futures-hoverboard-turned-vr-experience-wii-balance-board%e2%80%8f/

An example of VR device structure

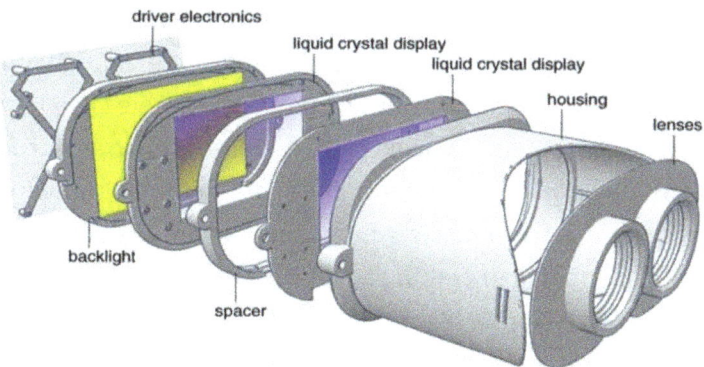

Figure 8-4. *VR headset structure (source: an open source design from the Internet[9])*

AR and VR technologies have made significant strides in industries like gaming, film, TV, education, and social media, with projections showing immense growth in user base and market size. According to Statista,[10] the market size of the AR and VR was about $6.1 billion dollars in the year 2016 and $12.1 billion in 2018, and expected market growth to $72.8 billion by 2026 speaks to their potential for mass-market adoption. The versatility of these technologies is evidenced by their diverse applications—from immersive gaming experiences like *Pokémon Go* to innovative uses in amusement parks and tourism. As AR and VR continue to evolve, they are set to redefine our everyday experiences, offering new ways to interact with the world around us and enhancing various aspects of life, from education to entertainment [66].

---

[9] https://wiki.opensourceecology.org/wiki/Open_Source_VR_Headset
[10] https://www.statista.com/statistics/591181/global-augmented-virtual-reality-market-size/

CHAPTER 8   RISING EMERGING INFORMATION TECHNOLOGIES: ENABLERS

In the realm of digital twin metaverse cities, AR and VR technologies transcend their roles as mere tools, emerging as the foundational elements of a new urban landscape. These technologies enable residents to interact with their cities, access services, and experience urban life in ways previously confined to science fiction. Imagine the possibilities: AR providing real-time navigation and VR enabling intricate city planning and disaster management. Educational experiences are transformed as students virtually explore distant terrains, while architects and medical professionals utilize VR for design and telemedicine. Moreover, AR/VR technologies are pivotal in crafting advanced user interfaces for comprehensive monitoring of a city's digital twin. In purely digital metaverse cities, AR/VR headsets become portals to explore virtual worlds, from gaming to global travel, revolutionizing everyday experiences like shopping and socializing.

Integrating AR and VR into digital twin metaverse cities, though thrilling, is not devoid of hurdles. This journey requires groundbreaking hardware and software advancements, a focus on delivering enriched user experiences, and addressing privacy and ethical issues. These challenges are steppingstones in leveraging human creativity and foresight, shaping a promising future for our digital twin metaverse cities.

3D Printing

3D printing (3DP), or additive manufacturing (AM), stands as a cornerstone in the creation of digital twin metaverse cities, revolutionizing urban development by enhancing construction methodologies, speeding up the building process, and reducing costs. This innovative technology allows for the digital drafting and physical realization of complex structures through a computer-aided design (CAD) process [67][68]. By employing a layer-by-layer fabrication approach, 3DP can utilize various materials, including liquids, powders, or even melted metals and plastics, to produce products with remarkable accuracy, intricate detail, and complex geometries.[11]

3D printing (3DP) offers diverse technologies like selective laser sintering and poly-jet, leading to cost-effective and resource-efficient production compared to conventional methods [69]. Unlike traditional manufacturing that often results in material waste, 3DP optimizes material usage, reducing both production costs and the likelihood of product failures. This efficiency shortens production time, enabling firms to competitively price mass-produced goods. 3DP, encompassing techniques like stereolithography (SL1) and fused deposition modeling (FDM), is increasingly replacing traditional methods in sectors such as automotive and healthcare, as illustrated in Figure 8-5.

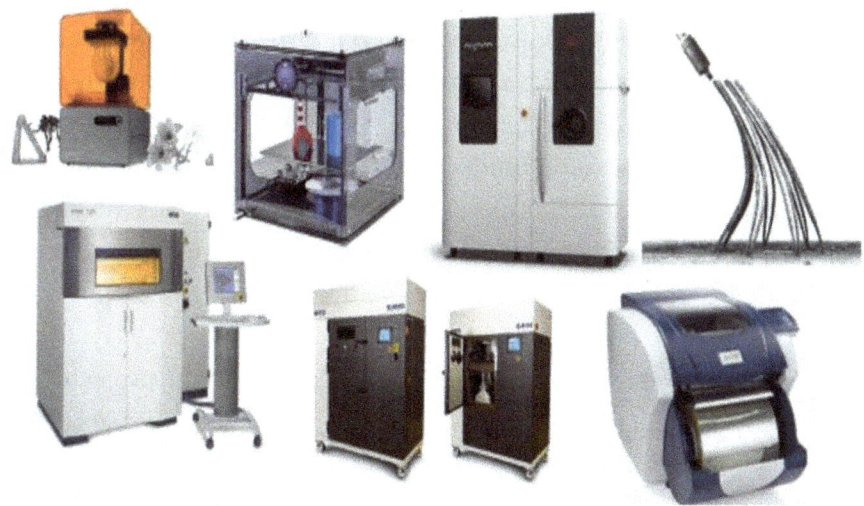

Figure 8-5. *Different types of 3D printers (source: author's development based on pictures from source[12])*

---

[11] https://www.techzone360.com/topics/techzone/articles/2019/09/09/443185-3-types-manufacturing-additive-subtractive-forming.htm
[12] https://3dinsider.com/

The genesis of 3DP traces back to the 1970s, with significant developments occurring in the mid-1980s. Charles W. Hull, credited with inventing the first 3D printer, patented his Stereolithography (SL1) technology in 1986 [70]. Scott Crump further advanced 3DP in 1989 with the introduction and patenting of Fused Deposition Modeling (FDM) [71]. The expiration of these early patents has democratized 3DP, leading to innovations in biomedical printing and the prototyping of automotive and aerospace components, enhancing both product efficiency and detail [72].

3D printing encompasses six primary methods, and each distinct in material use, mechanism, and accuracy requirements. Material extrusion, a widely used method, involves melting filament through a nozzle to form objects, ideal for form and fit testing due to its accuracy [73]. VAT polymerization uses lasers in a liquid photopolymer tank to create precise, yet brittle, 3D objects [74]. Powder bed fusion, particularly selective laser sintering (SLS), fuses powdered materials layer by layer, yielding functional items with complex geometries [75]. Material jetting, involving droplet deposition and hardening by light, is suitable for multi-material and detailed prototypes [76]. Binder jetting, binding powdered material with a liquid agent, is used for metal products and offers cost efficiency for large volumes. Finally, powder bed jetting, utilizing metal powder and laser, produces extremely durable items for applications like dentistry and aerospace.

The 3DP market is on a trajectory of remarkable growth, projected to reach a staggering $51.77 billion by 2026, with an annual increase of 25.8% during the forecast period.[13] This growth is particularly pronounced in the healthcare sector, which is expected to be a major driver. North America's early adoption of 3DP in manufacturing has garnered it a significant

---

[13] https://www.prnewswire.com/news-releases/3d-printing-market-to-reach-usd-51-77-billion-by-2026-rising-demand-for-customized-consumer-products-to-fuel-the-market-fortune-business-insights-300982483.html

market share. The market expansion encompasses various segments, including materials and products, with consumer and electronics sectors showing substantial involvement as of 2015. This rapid growth underlines 3DP's potential in revolutionizing multiple industries.

3DP technology is revolutionizing the construction of the digital twin metaverse cities across various sectors. In aerospace, companies like Boeing and Airbus utilize 3DP for lighter aircraft designs, enhancing manufacturing efficiency [77]. The medical field benefits significantly from 3DP in creating prosthetics, bioprinting organs, and producing dental aligners with unprecedented speed and precision. This technology was crucial during the Covid-19 pandemic, rapidly producing essential medical equipment. In construction, 3DP introduces sustainable building practices, allowing architects to print entire structures or components. The food industry is not left behind, with advancements like 3D printed Wagyu beef,[14] showcasing the technology's potential in culinary innovation.

To sum up, 3D printing is an enabling technology in constructing digital twin metaverse cities, significantly impacting the speed and quality of our smart cities. It offers numerous advantages over traditional manufacturing methods, including material efficiency, cost-effectiveness, and the ability to create complex structures. The market for 3DP is rapidly growing, with diverse applications ranging from lightweight aircraft parts to medical prosthetics and even culinary innovations like 3D printed food. This technology not only enhances manufacturing processes but also plays a crucial role in emergency responses. The versatility and efficiency of 3DP make it an essential tool in developing advanced, sustainable, and interconnected urban environments.

---

[14] https://screenrant.com/3d-printed-wagyu-beef-japan/

CHAPTER 8   RISING EMERGING INFORMATION TECHNOLOGIES: ENABLERS

Autonomous Driving (AD)

Autonomous driving (AD) technology is pivotal in shaping the transportation and mobility landscape of digital twin metaverse cities. It encompasses self-driving vehicles like robotaxi services[15] that offer transformative impacts, particularly in enhancing safety and accessibility. AD technology is poised to significantly decrease traffic accidents, attributed largely to human error, with potential reductions of up to 90% [78]. Furthermore, its integration in electric vehicles (EVs) positions it as a key contributor to environmental sustainability, potentially halving traffic on streets and substantially reducing congestion and travel time [79]. This shift toward AD not only improves quality of life but also advances urban eco-friendliness.

The Society of Automotive Engineers (SAE) defines five levels of driving automation for autonomous vehicles. These levels range from basic driver support systems at Level 1, like adaptive cruise control, to complete vehicle autonomy at Level 5, where no human intervention is required under any driving condition. Levels 2 and 3 involve increasing degrees of automation but still require human oversight. Level 4 offers high automation but may be limited to specific areas or conditions. For detailed specifications and technical details on each level of autonomous driving, please refer to the SAE's update on their website: SAE J3016 Update.[16]

As of the current writing, fully autonomous Level 4 and 5 vehicles are not yet commercially available. Tesla, a leader in autonomous driving technology, operates predominantly at Level 2 although the latest FSD version 11.1 has been quite impressive in its AD capabilities.[17] However,

---

[15] https://www.latimes.com/business/story/2023-08-10/cpuc-vote-on-robotaxi
[16] https://www.sae.org/blog/sae-j3016-update
[17] https://www.forbes.com/sites/jamesmorris/2021/03/13/why-is-teslas-full-self-driving-only-level-2-autonomous/?sh=6db772ab6a32

CHAPTER 8   RISING EMERGING INFORMATION TECHNOLOGIES: ENABLERS

the industry is witnessing an increase in Level 3 and 4 test vehicles. Companies like Cruise, backed by General Motors, are nearing the commercial launch of driverless taxi services.[18] Waymo, a subsidiary of Google, has introduced Level 4 autonomous taxi services in Phoenix, Arizona.[19] In China, companies such as AutoX, Baidu, and Didi are testing robotaxi services, aiming to meet stringent public safety and regulatory requirements.[20] This competitive landscape in AD technology includes major automotive players like GM, Ford, Volvo, BMW, and Toyota.

Achieving autonomous driving in complex urban environments relies on integrating IoT devices like cameras and sensors, including lidar and radar [80][82]. These technologies gather critical information about dynamic traffic conditions and pedestrian movements, feeding this data into machine learning models. Convolutional neural networks (CNNs) play a crucial role in processing this information. CNNs use layers such as convolutional, pooling, and fully connected layers to analyze traffic data, refining it from basic image features to detailed object recognition, illustrated in Figure 8-6. In detail, CNNs in autonomous driving (AD) use a hierarchical structure to process traffic imagery. Initially, they focus on low-level features, which are then abstracted into more complex representations in subsequent layers. This multilayer processing effectively reduces data dimensions for enhancing object recognition accuracy. A pretrained classifier interprets these features, assigning probabilities to identify objects like cars or trucks. The classifier's accuracy improves as it "learns" from more traffic data, advancing the vehicle's autonomous

---

[18] https://www.motorauthority.com/news/1132494_cruise-opens-up-driverless-taxi-service-to-public-in-san-franciscosrc=feed_Google

[19] http://www.franglish.fr/NRC/2018_google_waymo.pdf

[20] https://techcrunch.com/2022/01/14/2021-robotaxi-china/:~:text=As%20of%20today%2C%20no%20city,driverless%20tests%20on%20public%20roads

capabilities. This sophisticated data processing is integral to the development of higher-level AD technologies. This advanced processing is key to enhancing the accuracy and capability of autonomous driving systems.

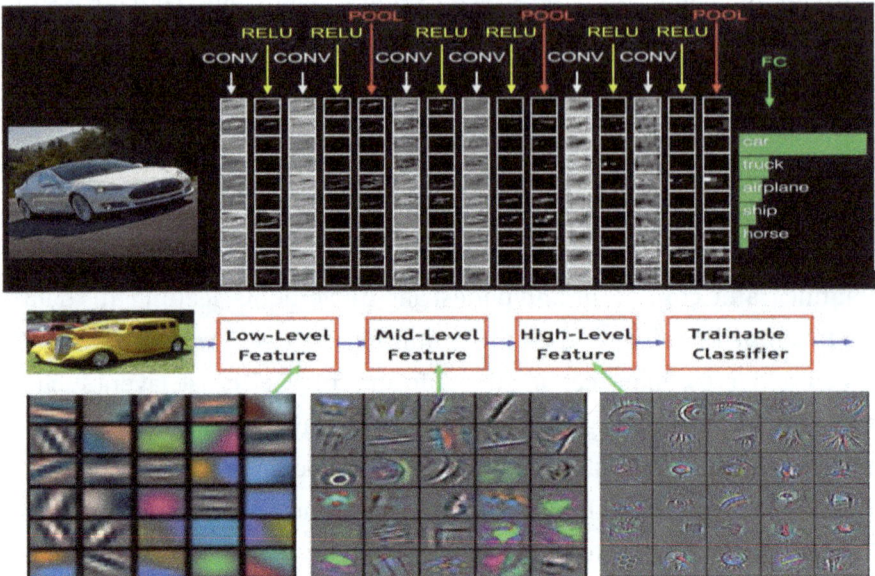

Figure 8-6. *Convolutional neural networks (CNNs) for autonomous driving (source: author's development based on [81])*

To guarantee the safety of autonomous driving (AD) vehicles, several real-time systems, including localization, environment perception, planning, and automatic control, need to function in unison. A robust hardware platform equipped with IoT sensors, 5G connectivity, and advanced computing capabilities like Edge or fog computing is essential. The "nuScenes" project by Caesar et al. [82], for example, demonstrates this with a setup of six cameras, five radars, and one lidar, providing comprehensive views and extensive data for improved AD performance. This integrated approach is key to advancing AD technology.

CHAPTER 8   RISING EMERGING INFORMATION TECHNOLOGIES: ENABLERS

Autonomous driving (AD) technology faces several challenges in its application to various vehicles, from car, bus, to truck. First is the technological complexity of navigating diverse and unpredictable environments, necessitating advanced learning by AD systems like CNN and generative AI. Incidents like the Uber accident in Arizona highlight the risks and the need for continuous improvement in AD technology.[21] Another concern is the potential for significant job loss for driving professions, underscoring the need for worker retraining programs. Additionally, legal issues surrounding liability in AD-related incidents present a complex challenge, as traditional traffic laws are based on human error and technical failures. These factors collectively make obtaining governmental permits for AD technology a demanding process [83][84].

To wrap up, autonomous driving (AD) technology reshapes urban mobility in digital twin metaverse cities, promising a revolution in transportation efficiency and safety. This technology, encompassing self-driving vehicles, has the potential to significantly reduce traffic accidents and congestion. With the integration of electric vehicles, AD also contributes to environmental sustainability. The future of AD, including advanced robotaxi services, could lead to a decrease in personal vehicle ownership, freeing up city spaces and further reducing traffic issues. While still facing challenges in technology, job displacement, and legal frameworks, AD's integration into city infrastructures offers a smarter and more efficient urban living environment.

---

[21] https://www.bbc.com/news/technology-54175359

CHAPTER 8   RISING EMERGING INFORMATION TECHNOLOGIES: ENABLERS

Drone and UAV

Drone, or unmanned aerial vehicle (UAV), is another enabling technology to building digital twin metaverse cities. Drone is an unmanned aerial vehicle (UAV) equipped with multispectral imaging cameras and various IoT sensors such as humidity, temperature, moisture, and light [85][86]. In fact, drone can be regarded as a flying autonomous driving UAV in sky to achieve a specific mission like urgent medical delivery, firefighting, or forest wildfire surveillance. For example, Toronto hospitals notably became the first to use drone for delivering transplant lungs, marking a significant advancement in medical logistics.[22] Similarly, drones have been pivotal in distributing medical supplies to remote communities during the Covid-19 pandemic.[23] Amazon's Prime Air service revolutionized package delivery, leveraging drones for rapid, efficient transportation. DroneSeed's collaboration with the US government for forest reforestation using drones demonstrates their environmental applications. Additionally, drones aid in agriculture and military operations, enhancing efficiency and effectiveness in diverse fields [87][88]. Figure 8-7 illustrates various drone applications in military, delivery, smart farming, and environmental monitoring. These examples underscore drone versatility and their transformative impact on various sectors in digital twin metaverse cities.

---

[22] https://www.cbc.ca/news/canada/toronto/first-lung-transplant-drone-1.6208057

[23] https://research.ubc.ca/drones-will-deliver-medical-supplies-remote-first-nations-during-Covid-19-pandemic

CHAPTER 8   RISING EMERGING INFORMATION TECHNOLOGIES: ENABLERS

Figure 8-7. *Drone applications in military, delivery, environmental monitoring, and smart farming (author's development based on public pictures on the Internet)*

Ding et al. [89] developed Dragnet, an innovative amateur surveillance drone system. This system, as depicted in Figure 8-8, operates on a joint fog computing framework comprising cameras, sensors, radars, and the human input. It utilizes cloud computing for data aggregation, analysis, and decision-making. Dragnet's capabilities include environmental sensing, advanced data analytics for surveillance, semantic processing for intelligent interpretation, and decision-making for actions like drone control. These functions highlight its sophisticated approach to surveillance by combining technology and human intelligence for enhanced security and monitoring.

CHAPTER 8 RISING EMERGING INFORMATION TECHNOLOGIES: ENABLERS

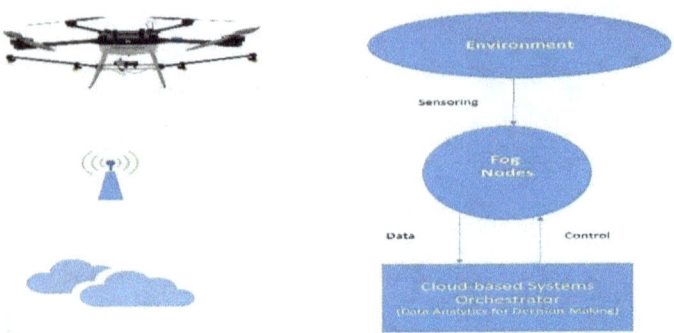

Figure 8-8. Dragnet—an amateur surveillance drone (source: author's development based on [89])

The burgeoning use of drones within smart metaverse cities introduces a host of compelling challenges. Foremost among these is cybersecurity: How do we protect drones from cyber-attacks, particularly when they could be hijacked for nefarious purposes? The ethical quandaries surrounding autonomous military drones—equipped to identify and engage targets with no human intervention—are particularly sobering and warrant serious reflection.

Furthermore, the prospect of city skies thronged with commercial drones, buzzing about to deliver packages, raises significant concerns about the safety and regulation of urban airspace. Also, the utilization of drones for critical medical supplies triggers a debate on the need for stringent regulatory frameworks and robust safety protocols. These pressing challenges underscore the necessity for a nuanced dialogue on finding a judicious equilibrium between technological progress and its ramifications on society.

In sum, drones, as unmanned aerial vehicles (UAVs), are a pivotal technology in constructing digital twin metaverse cities, with a broad spectrum of uses ranging from medical deliveries to environmental monitoring. Equipped with advanced imaging capabilities and IoT sensors, they can undertake a variety of missions across both bustling urban centers and isolated areas. However, to fully integrate drones into urban infrastructures, challenges pertaining to cybersecurity, ethical consideration, and regulatory compliance must be meticulously navigated. Supported by the infrastructure of 5G and intelligent algorithms, drones have the capacity to considerably optimize city operations, establishing them as an indispensable facet of smart city frameworks.

Cybersecurity

Cybersecurity represents an organization's efforts to protect its information assets from a spectrum of cyber threats, which include cyber-attacks, data espionage, breaches, ransomware, cloud attacks, and IoT intrusions [90]. Thus, various cybersecurity policies are needed. Organizations must employ defensive strategies to maintain confidentiality, integrity, and availability of information [91]. Figure 8-9 conceptualizes organizational cybersecurity capabilities as detective, to identify potential threats, and preventive, to implement actions that mitigate the risk of cybercrimes. These actions encompass deploying technology solutions, establishing organizational policies and procedures, adhering to public laws, and following industry standards [92]. For example, the NIS2 (Network and Information Systems Directive 2) is a significant legislative update aimed at enhancing cybersecurity across the EU. It builds upon the original NIS directive, which was the first piece of EU-wide legislation on cybersecurity.

CHAPTER 8   RISING EMERGING INFORMATION TECHNOLOGIES: ENABLERS

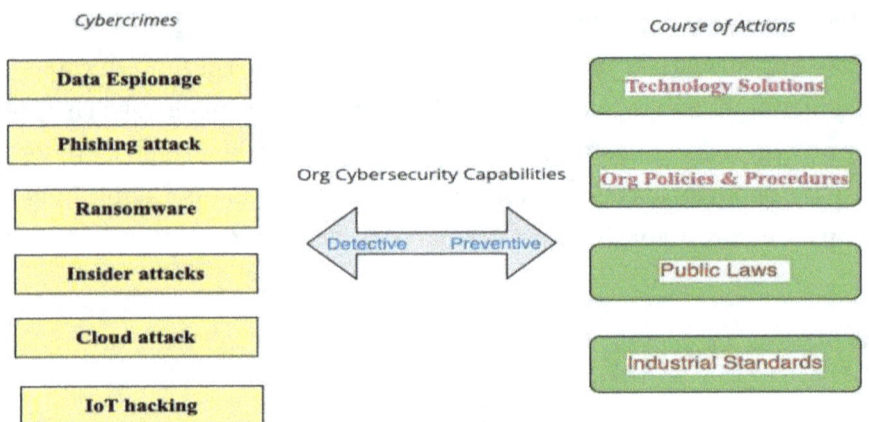

Figure 8-9. An organizational cybersecurity capacity—detective and preventive (author's development)

Cybercrimes can be delineated into the following major categories.

Data espionage involves unauthorized surveillance aimed at accessing sensitive information from private corporations or government databases [93]. Companies need to responsibly embrace cloud innovations, enact stringent security practices, and consistently monitor their cloud environments to shield against espionage. Gartner underscores the significance of cloud-based solutions for fortified cybersecurity, emphasizing scalability, integration, and automation as key to effectively tackling these challenges.

Phishing attack is a common form of cybercrime, where fraudsters trick individuals into revealing sensitive information, such as login credentials and credit card numbers, posing significant risks to personal data security. These attacks can adversely affect an organization's financial status and reputation. Countermeasures include securing email communications with SSL certificates, which encrypt data transmissions and prevent unauthorized interceptions.

Ransomware is a critical threat, deploying malware to lock or encrypt crucial organizational data and demanding a ransom, typically in cryptocurrency, for its release. These attacks can lead to substantial data and financial loss. Organizations should consistently back up important data and deploy strong anti-spam filters to fend off such threats. Furthermore, training employees on the dangers of social engineering and phishing is paramount for ensuring a secure digital landscape.

Insider attack originates from within the organization, where individuals exploit their access to sensitive data for personal gain, resulting in fraud, data breaches, and security sabotage. For an instance, Tesla encountered an internal sabotage in 2018 when an employee altered product code and leaked sensitive information [94]. Mitigating such risks necessitates a focus on internal security, including comprehensive cybersecurity education, diligent monitoring of employee activities, and robust encryption practices. A zero-trust security model can also provide additional protection against breaches, which often occur from trusted insiders.

Cloud attack sees cybercriminals targeting data on cloud platforms, capitalizing on user inattention or security flaws in interfaces and APIs [95]. To counteract such threats, it is crucial to employ IT professionals proficient in secure configurations and strong authentication methods, alongside continuous surveillance of end-user actions through automated detection systems.

IoT hacking is an escalating concern with the proliferation of IoT devices, leading to heightened data exposure [96]. Insufficient security protocols, like subpar password practices and lack of device maintenance, allow for unauthorized access and potential breaches. To shield their digital ecosystem, firms should utilize VPNs to secure online activity and the transmission of data across their networks, thus safeguarding the organization and its stakeholders.

Organizations enhance their cybersecurity defenses with advanced technology solutions, deploying encryption, SSL/TLS, VPNs, and secure Wi-Fi to ensure protected communications. Firewalls, intrusion detection systems (IDS)/intrusion prevention systems (IPS), and antivirus tools are employed to shield networks and endpoints. The role of machine learning algorithms is becoming increasingly critical in identifying and mitigating cyber threats. The substantial investments by firms in cybersecurity measures underscore the imperative to strengthen defenses.

Management policies and procedures form the backbone of comprehensive cybersecurity frameworks, which encompass risk management, security policies, and thorough audit processes. Legislation such as the EU NIS2 Directive, USA Patriot Act, and Canada's PIPEDA support legal actions against cybercrimes. Industry-specific standards, including various ISO/IEC, NERC, NIST, and PCI DSS norms, offer specific guidance to safeguard the digital ecosystem from cyber-attacks. These coordinated efforts, spanning technology, policy, and standards, are essential for a resilient cybersecurity posture.

Returning to the digital twin metaverse city proposed in Chapter 5, the Data Collection layer, rich with IoT devices, presents a notable vulnerability in digital twin metaverse cities. These extensive networks of sensors, actuators, and mobile devices traverse complex urban environments, protecting various assets and community functions. Yet, their uniformity and infrequent updates present substantial security risks. Research into IoT security, such as the work by Shafiq et al. [97], is vital, utilizing machine learning algorithms like Bayes Net and Random Forest to identify and neutralize cyber threats.

Cybersecurity emerges as a crucial intelligent service within the service delivery platform of digital twin metaverse cities, as introduced in Chapter 5, Figure 5-1. This layer actively monitors and counters threats within the urban digital framework, harnessing advanced machine learning algorithms. It acts as a vigilant guardian, orchestrating preventative measures such as data recovery and software patches to bolster city defenses against cyber threats. This critical service highlights the complexity and interconnectedness required to secure the digital twins of urban centers.

CHAPTER 8   RISING EMERGING INFORMATION TECHNOLOGIES: ENABLERS

In summary, this chapter's exploration of emerging enabling technologies underscores their indispensable role in the development of digital twin metaverse cities. Key enablers such as robotics, AR and VR, 3D printing, autonomous vehicles, drones, and cybersecurity are identified as revolutionizing elements of urban life. These technologies drive improvements in efficiency, sustainability, and livability across various sectors, including transportation, healthcare, infrastructure, and environmental monitoring. Moreover, the fusion of IoT with advanced data analytics provides the foundational intelligence for these cities' operations. While highlighting the transformative potential of these technologies, this chapter also recognizes the challenges and ethical considerations inherent in their integration into urban ecosystems.

As we advance to Part 4 of this book, prepare to delve into exciting showcases of smart city implementations, energized by the forefront of emerging ICTs. These real-world examples span an array of urban services, from fluid transportation networks to pioneering green energy initiatives. Chapter 9 will guide you through the quintessential aspects of digital twin metaverse cities, showcasing the seamless integration of advanced emerging technologies within critical city operations. Following this, Chapter 10 will broaden our exploration into how these urban landscapes deliver intelligent services that enhance healthcare, education, and more, thus enriching the fabric of daily life. These chapters will not only shed light on the transformative effects of technologies like AI and IoTs but will also address the detailed needs of urban life, from senior care to disaster response strategies. Prepare to witness the unfolding future of urban living in the ensuing chapters.

PART IV

Showing Me Real Examples: Smart City Showcases

Part 4 of this book invites readers on an exploratory journey into the real-world applications of state-of-the-art ICTs for the creation of digital twin metaverse cities. In Chapter 9, we will embark on an insightful tour of cutting-edge implementations within essential urban services. From transformative transportation systems to innovative energy solutions and intuitive home automation, this chapter offers a dynamic presentation of how emerging technologies are shaping our urban centers into intelligent, sustainable, and high-functioning ecosystems.

Progressing to Chapter 10, the focus will shift from infrastructure to the transformative services that define a smart city. This segment vividly demonstrates how the principles of digital twin metaverses are integrated into superior healthcare, educational, and disaster management services, with highlighted innovations, including telemedicine and AI-facilitated care for the elderly. Through these illustrations, readers will grasp the significant influence of these ICTs on both the quality of urban life and the efficacy of city services.

Each example is meticulously selected to inspire and exhibit the vast potential of these technologies in fostering interconnected, thriving, and more inhabitable digital twin metaverse cities.

CHAPTER 9

Showcases of Emerging ITs for Digital Twin Metaverse Cities: *Core*

In this chapter, we will explore dynamic examples of how emerging technologies, as discussed in Chapters 7 and 8, are instrumental in building the digital twin metaverse cities outlined in Chapters 5 and 6. We'll delve into the core functions of smart city services, ranging from transportation to ocean cleaning, underlining their contributions to creating cities that are not just more efficient but also sustainably and holistically improved for living.

Smart Transportation

Public transportation, pivotal for urban commuting, grapples with congestion, a challenge highlighted in TomTom's 2023 report,[1] which lists Mexico City, Los Angeles, and Vancouver as North America's most

---

[1] https://www.tomtom.com/traffic-index/ranking/

CHAPTER 9   SHOWCASES OF EMERGING ITS FOR DIGITAL TWIN METAVERSE CITIES: CORE

congested cities. To address these issues, emerging technologies like 5G, AI, and big data analytics play a crucial role. AI's deep learning technologies, utilizing neural networks, empower self-driving cars to navigate in real time, enhancing efficiency and safety while reducing congestion and accidents. Key industry players like Tesla and Google Waymo employ distinct technologies for autonomous driving. Tesla uses advanced camera systems, whereas Waymo relies on Lidar sensor technology. These systems are designed to collect and analyze environmental data, enabling the autonomous operation of vehicles.

Vehicular networks, or VANETs, foster a cohesive communication system within the urban infrastructure, streamlining traffic and aiding emergency services [98]. This integration facilitates the smooth operation of traffic and enhances public transportation efficiency, potentially reducing the need for costly traditional transit services during off-peak hours.

The vehicular network architecture encompasses a diverse array of components strategically distributed to enhance traffic management. This sophisticated integration enables adaptive traffic light systems to modulate vehicular flow effectively. Emergency response vehicles benefit from instantaneous routing, expediting their critical services. Additionally, electric vehicles are prompted to adjust speeds in areas with high foot traffic, bolstering pedestrian safety.

Moreover, this advanced network infrastructure supports the functionality of autonomous vehicles from leading innovators like Tesla, Google's Waymo, and Uber. Such vehicles have the potential to supplement or even substitute for traditional subway services during quieter hours, offering economic and environmental benefits. The outcome is a more serene and cleaner city environment.

The deployment of 5G and IoT technologies is critical to the seamless operation of these autonomous systems. Vehicles equipped with an array of sensors necessitate swift data processing, a task adeptly handled by the high-speed, low latency 5G networks. This facilitates essential communication between vehicles (V2V) and between vehicles and infrastructure (V2I), enabling instantaneous sharing of traffic updates and navigational guidance.

In the assessment of smart transportation frameworks, factors such as time and cost efficiency, congestion and pollution mitigation, and accident frequency reduction are crucial metrics. These indicators are key to gauging the success of intelligent transport innovations in fostering sustainable, efficient, and safer digital twin metaverse cities, as envisioned in this book.

Smart Green Energy

Global governments are actively adopting renewable energy sources such as wind and solar to combat global warming and diminish greenhouse gas emissions.[2] For instance, Germany has committed to a significant reduction in carbon dioxide emissions, with plans to shut down nuclear power plants and source at least 80% of its electricity from renewables by 2050. A primary challenge with renewable energy is its variability since wind and solar outputs are inherently inconsistent. As highlighted in *Nature*,[3] Germany's expansive wind farms and solar arrays are not just symbolic of its energy transition but also manifest the country's move away from nuclear and high-carbon sources.

Solar panels, for example, only generate maximum energy output during certain daylight hours, which requires supplemental energy sources to meet demand spikes. To overcome these fluctuations, Germany has adopted solutions such as the rapid-response capabilities of natural

---

[2] https://www.economist.com/films/2021/11/14/was-cop26-a-success?fsrc=core-app-economist
[3] https://www.nature.com/articles/535212a

CHAPTER 9   SHOWCASES OF EMERGING ITS FOR DIGITAL TWIN METAVERSE CITIES: CORE

gas-fired power plants, as illustrated in Figure 9-1. These plants offer several advantages, including operational flexibility, cost-effectiveness, and lower carbon emissions, especially when compared to traditional coal, oil, and nuclear energy sources.

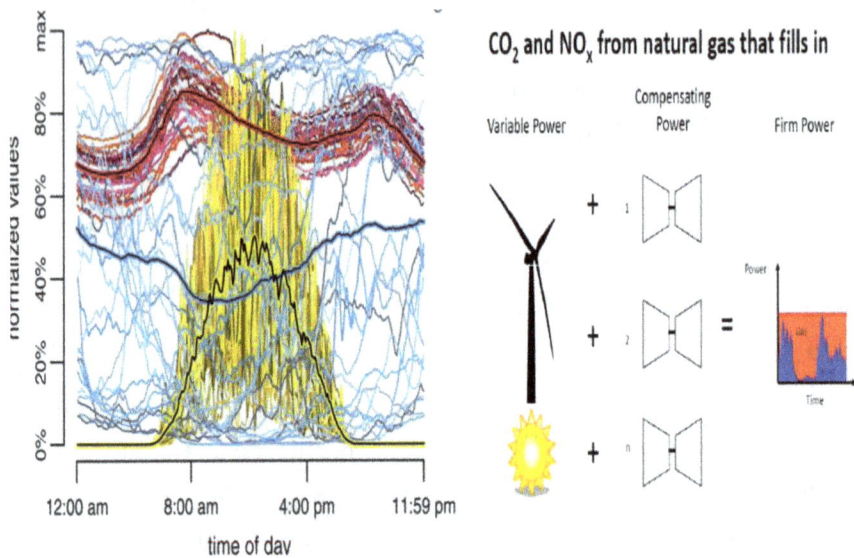

Figure 9-1. *Wind and solar energy intermittent problems and flexible gas turbine compensations (author's development based on public pictures on the Internet)*

Emerging ICTs explored in Chapters 7 and 8 of this book hold significant promise in overcoming the challenges associated with the intermittent nature of wind and solar energies. These advanced technologies are crucial in fostering their seamless incorporation into intelligent grid systems. Wind turbines, endowed with IoT capabilities, are now able to accurately gauge wind velocities, while solar panels are equipped with sophisticated sensors that diligently evaluate the intensity of sunlight. The data amassed from these sources, when synthesized with meteorological information, feeds into complex machine learning algorithms. These algorithms are designed to adeptly predict energy output, thus enabling grid operators to manage the unpredictable nature of renewable energy with unprecedented precision.

The efficacy of this approach extends beyond mere prediction; it equips grid operators with the tools to meticulously control the influx of renewable energy into the grid, obviating the reliance on extensive energy storage infrastructures. Precise forecasting emerges as a linchpin in the realm of grid management, granting those at the helm the ability to meticulously orchestrate energy generation, schedule system operations, and steer energy storage strategies, all while optimizing the delicate balance of supply and demand [99].

At the heart of this modernized approach is the Data Analytics Flywheel (DAFW), a concept introduced in Chapter 6. The DAFW is a testament to the power of integration, bringing together machine learning models that meticulously analyze an array of data streams. These streams flow from IoT devices and sensors embedded within the energy-generating fabric of our smart cities, providing pivotal insights that drive smarter, more effective energy solutions. Figure 9-2 encapsulates this holistic approach, illustrating the central role that accurate renewable energy forecasts play in actualizing the vision of a smart, sustainable grid operation.

This technological evolution, underpinned by the DAFW, ensures that the grids of tomorrow are not only more intelligent but also significantly more sustainable, fostering a future where green energy is not a mere supplement to our energy needs but a cornerstone of our energy generation arsenal. The narrative that unfolds within these chapters is not only informative but also a clarion call to action—a beacon guiding us toward a future where our cities breathe in synergy with the environment, powered by the very forces of nature they seek to protect.

CHAPTER 9 SHOWCASES OF EMERGING ITS FOR DIGITAL TWIN METAVERSE CITIES: CORE

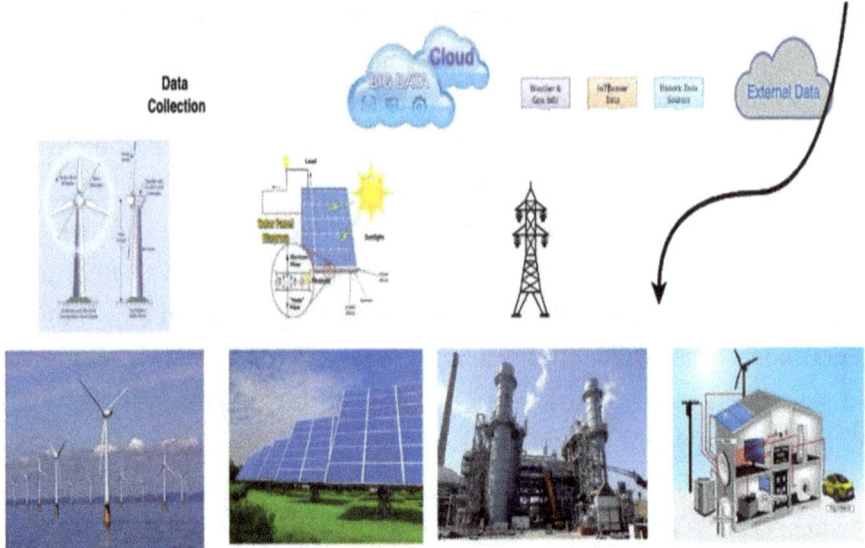

Figure 9-2. *Data Analytics Flywheel (DAFW) powered digital twinning process for smart energy (author's development based on public pictures on the Internet)*

In summary, the progression of ICTs is critical for transforming conventional electrical grids into intelligent and efficient smart grids. This change deeply influences grid management and user engagement. Within digital twin metaverse cities, such innovations are essential, enabling an integrated digital twinning process. Enhanced renewable energy forecasting through ICTs streamlines energy efficiency and cuts down on fossil fuel dependency, thereby decreasing greenhouse gas emissions and promoting sustainable energy within smart grids.

Smart Home

The smart home concept elevates the standard living space into an integrated and advanced network, as explored in Chapters 7 and 8. Figure 9-3 presents a smart home as a comprehensive ecosystem that seamlessly integrates energy systems, devices, and services to enhance the daily experiences of residents. This ecosystem is a harmonious arrangement of energy-efficient management systems, user-friendly automated appliances, and adaptable environmental controls such as lighting and climate.

It also includes the customization of personal comfort with intelligent furniture like beds and tables that adapt to individual preferences, atmospheric mood lighting for every occasion, and rigorous cleanliness protocols, including advanced waste sorting and disposal. Furthermore, smart homes cater to health and well-being with in-house monitoring systems, provide immersive learning and working environments through metaverse integration, and offer sophisticated home entertainment options [100].

Figure 9-3 depicts the multifaceted nature of smart home systems, indicating their role in digital twin metaverse cities. This illustration underscores how each component—from security to wellness—contributes to a comfortable, convenient, and sustainable living environment. The smart home is the embodiment of modern living, where every element is designed to anticipate and meet the needs of its inhabitants, creating an unparalleled living experience powered by technology.

CHAPTER 9 SHOWCASES OF EMERGING ITS FOR DIGITAL TWIN METAVERSE CITIES: CORE

Figure 9-3. Smart home systems within digital twin metaverse cities (author's development)

Smart homes represent the zenith of contemporary security and convenience, evolving into sophisticated networks of surveillance and alert systems that deliver tranquility and protection. Leading companies like Amazon, Google, Apple, and Samsung are at the forefront of this secure revolution, introducing innovative platforms such as Amazon Echo, Google Home, Apple HomeKit, and Samsung SmartThings. These platforms transcend the role of mere devices to become essential fixtures of the home, allowing occupants to manage their environment with ease. They adjust lighting, control media streams, and regulate temperature, often through simple voice commands or a streamlined app interface.

In a smart home, convenience is just the beginning. You could, for instance, remotely initiate your home's heating or cooling system, guaranteeing a welcoming, climate-controlled environment upon your arrival. If an unexpected downpour strikes while you are out, your intelligent system autonomously secures your home by closing windows, thereby maintaining the integrity of your living space. The smart home's foresight doesn't stop there; envision your refrigerator alerting you to replenish supplies or warning about expiring items, thus revolutionizing grocery management [101].

The potential of smart homes extends into becoming your interactive culinary consultant, courtesy of advanced AI. Such a system could offer step-by-step guidance on preparing gourmet dishes or tips for preserving the crunchiness of last night's pizza, elevating the simplicity and enjoyment of meal preparation.

When it comes to security, the integrity of your data and personal information holds utmost importance in a smart home network. The implementation of blockchain technology, detailed in Chapter 7, introduces a resilient safeguard to your home's interconnected system. It secures your devices and the data they exchange, providing a solid defense against unauthorized access and breaches, hence fortifying your confidence in the smart ecosystem of your home.

Smart systems also play a pivotal role in environmental stewardship by using data analytics to enhance energy efficiency and minimize waste, aligning with a sustainable lifestyle. Each device, whether it's a sensor-equipped thermostat or an AI-driven entertainment system, serves as a cog in the vast IoT machinery that harmonizes digital amenities with physical comfort.

As we venture deeper into the realm of digital twinning and metaverse cities, the smart home emerges as a microcosm of this tech-driven union. It epitomizes an advanced lifestyle that is marked by personalized efficiency, rigorous security, and a nuanced, environmentally conscious living experience. This is the promise of the smart home: a bespoke, secure, and sustainable haven within the pulsating heart of the digital twin metaverse city.

CHAPTER 9   SHOWCASES OF EMERGING ITS FOR DIGITAL TWIN METAVERSE CITIES: CORE

Smart Housing

In today's urban landscapes, escalating housing costs have precipitated an acute crisis of homelessness, challenging city administrators and social structures alike. The critical research by Quigley et al. [102] establishes a direct empirical connection between housing accessibility, affordability, and the burgeoning homeless populations across US cities. The striking example of Vancouver—often cited among the globe's costliest urban areas to reside in—unveiled a distressing tally of 2,095 individuals without homes in 2020, a statistic confirmed by the city's own records.[4] Such stark figures not only tarnish Vancouver's global reputation but also perpetuate complex social challenges. The disenfranchised homeless, stripped of a fundamental human need for shelter, frequently endure profound psychological turmoil, including eroded self-esteem and an acute sense of detachment from society. Moreover, heightened susceptibility to substance dependence and a proclivity for minor criminal activities intensify security issues within urban districts.

In this context, the pioneering application of 3D printing (3DP) technology, comprehensively discussed in Chapter 8, emerges as a seminal strategy to combat the worldwide homelessness predicament by facilitating the rapid construction of cost-effective dwellings. This innovative manufacturing process, which synthesizes solid objects via the methodical layering of materials, has markedly disrupted the construction sector with its operational swiftness and economic efficiency. It enables the expeditious assembly of habitable structures, dramatically reducing traditional construction timelines and costs, thus becoming a critical instrument for urban planning and humanitarian aid.

---

[4] https://council.vancouver.ca/20201007/documents/pspc1presentation.pdf

CHAPTER 9 SHOWCASES OF EMERGING ITS FOR DIGITAL TWIN METAVERSE CITIES: CORE

The versatility of 3DP in the realm of construction is unmatched. It can be applied directly at construction sites, with colossal printers and robotic arms methodically erecting buildings in real time, or, alternatively, utilized within industrial settings for the prefabrication of components that are subsequently transported and assembled on-site. Such operational flexibility profoundly expedites the creation of residential units, meticulously adapted to the unique specifications and limitations inherent to each housing project. Additionally, this approach significantly curtails the generation of building waste, advancing the cause of sustainable development, and fosters the exploration of architectural designs previously deemed too avant-garde or cost-prohibitive under traditional construction paradigms.

Moreover, houses materialized through 3D printing can incorporate integrated systems geared toward the optimization of energy usage, water conservation, and waste minimization, thereby aligning with the overarching goals of environmental stewardship. Amid the dual crises of housing scarcity and global climate change, 3DP is recognized as a dual-purpose innovation capable of concurrently tackling both challenges. Its application is especially salient in the construction of rapid deployment shelters, offering a robust response to the housing deficit. Urban areas plagued by exorbitant living costs and acute accommodation shortfalls might employ armadas of 3D printers to forge whole communities designed for transitional habitation. These structures can swiftly provide the homeless with a safe and honorable abode, furnishing a transitional sanctuary as they navigate toward more enduring housing solutions.

For instance, by leveraging cost-efficient materials, specifically chosen to suit the demands of each project, 3D printing allows for the erection of modestly proportioned homes on urban peripheries, substantially diminishing the aggregate construction outlay. The innovative method capitalizes on continuous, automated operation, thereby reducing labor costs dramatically. A prime example of such an initiative is the endeavor by Icon, a trailblazing enterprise specializing in 3DP technology. Icon has

CHAPTER 9   SHOWCASES OF EMERGING ITS FOR DIGITAL TWIN METAVERSE CITIES: CORE

successfully established a community of 200 humble yet functional houses in a Texas village, United States, confronting the homelessness crisis, as vividly depicted in Figure 9-4. By utilizing low-cost raw materials, Icon has showcased the capacity of 3D printing to fabricate a compact residence, measuring 8.5 feet in height and 28 feet in width, within an astounding timeframe of just 24 hours.

Figure 9-4. *3D printed house by Icon (source[5])*

Icon's endeavors transcend beyond mere provision of immediate housing solutions. They resonate with the potential for substantial societal transformation, offering a firm foundation from which individuals can reconstruct their lives. The integration of this disruptive technology within the schema of smart city planning seamlessly dovetails with the strategic objectives of elevating living standards and fostering sustainability within the digital twin metaverse cities as envisioned in our architectural blueprints.

---

[5] https://www.businessinsider.com/tiny-home-village-in-austin-3d-printed-for-the-homeless-2020-3the-400-square-foot-homes-in-austin-will-each-have-a-bedroom-bathroom-kitchen-and-living-room-3

CHAPTER 9   SHOWCASES OF EMERGING ITS FOR DIGITAL TWIN METAVERSE CITIES: CORE

Smart Streetlight

The quintessential urban streetlight stands at the brink of an intelligent revolution, transitioning from a simple source of light to a sophisticated, integrated element of the smart city network. Traditional streetlights are criticized for their inefficiency and insensitivity to the nuanced ebb and flow of city life, exemplifying a bygone era of excessive energy consumption. Moreover, their inability to meld with advanced smart city technologies—such as 5G, IoTs, big data analytics, and artificial intelligence (AI)—exposes an urgent call for innovative upgrades that embody the ethos of digital twin metaverse cities.

Charting the course to smart urban illumination, smart LED lamps emerge as frontrunners, supplanting the obsolete sodium halide lamps with their superior energy efficiency and longevity. In this envisioned lighting network, each lamp is a beacon of connectivity, seamlessly interfacing with adjacent fixtures and a centralized data nexus through the arteries of 5G connectivity, signaling for maintenance and reacting adaptively to environmental stimuli. Motion sensors, an integral component of these lamps, modulate luminance instantaneously diminishing in quiescence to conserve power while augmenting public safety with strategic and context-aware lighting.

But the aspirations of smart streetlights extend beyond the realm of energy savings. These luminaires assume a multifaceted role within the 5G infrastructure, serving both as illuminators and conduits of data transmission. This multifunctionality gracefully reconciles the functional necessity of 5G technology with urban aesthetic aspirations, allowing for the discreet integration of 5G apparatus within streetlight structures, thereby preserving the visual integrity of the cityscape.

The utility of smart streetlights is anticipated to significantly influence urban traffic systems. In this interconnected IoT landscape, traffic indicators, empowered by embedded sensors, transform from passive

CHAPTER 9   SHOWCASES OF EMERGING ITS FOR DIGITAL TWIN METAVERSE CITIES: CORE

markers to active agents of change, delivering instantaneous traffic updates and navigational suggestions, thus alleviating congestion and refining the flow of vehicles.

In the visionary system delineated by Yoshiura et al. [103], the smart streetlight shown in Figure 9-5 is a symphony of components working in unison: a lamp unit equipped with a versatile LED array for variable lighting, a sensor unit that not only detects movement but also communicates with its network, and an access point that orchestrates data exchange over extensive distances. This design represents an intelligent fusion of illumination, security, and data communication, laying the foundation for the sophisticated infrastructure of an urban setting.

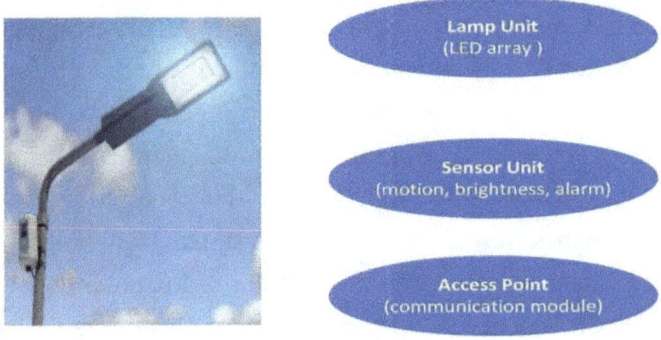

Figure 9-5. *Anatomy of a smart streetlight system (source: author's development based on [103])*

When married with renewable energy technologies, the capabilities of smart streetlight systems reach new heights. As demonstrated by El-Faouri et al. [104], a cutting-edge prototype capitalizes on solar power, integrating energy storage batteries, responsive motion sensors, and even self-maintenance features, epitomizing the union of efficiency and environmental consciousness.

These advanced systems gain further versatility through the addition of ultra-high-definition surveillance capabilities, transforming streetlights into vigilant sentinels of the urban landscape, supporting real-time traffic observation and incident response initiatives coordinated by central traffic management hubs. The convergence of rapid 5G connectivity with intricate digital twinning methodologies catalyzes a transformation in urban navigation and safety strategies, marking a pivotal advancement of emergent technologies in fostering a city's operational and navigational finesse.

The efficacy of these sophisticated streetlight networks is measurable through discernible improvements in energy conservation, traffic management, and public security enhancement. Marked reductions in crime, heightened community satisfaction, and the city's renown as a haven of safety and security serve as palpable affirmations of the system's profound influence. Nonetheless, the deployment of these technologies must judiciously weigh the variables of success, ensuring active law enforcement collaboration, civic participation, governmental facilitation, equitable public access, and the uncompromised protection of individual privacy.

Smart Environment

The notion of a smart environment is anchored in the meticulous weaving of ICTs into the urban tapestry, elevating the natural habitat to enhance city livability for both inhabitants and sojourners. It encompasses robust initiatives aiming at pollution reduction, waste minimization, water preservation, and energy optimization, which form the cornerstone of sustainable urban development as highlighted in Chapter 2. A pressing contemporary issue is marine pollution, extensively classified by the Intergovernmental Oceanographic Commission (IOC) as the harmful dissemination of anthropogenic substances and energies in our oceans. Such pollution gravely afflicts aquatic ecosystems, human health, and the vitality of marine-based economies, like fisheries.

CHAPTER 9 SHOWCASES OF EMERGING ITS FOR DIGITAL TWIN METAVERSE CITIES: CORE

The World Economic Forum [105] paints a stark future: if the current trajectories persist, plastics in the ocean will outweigh fish by 2050. Cities nestled along coastlines, such as Boston and Vancouver, bear the brunt of this pollution. Reports by the Ocean Legacy Foundation are alarming, with vast amounts of daily waste tumbling into the sea, inflating this ecological blight. The repercussions are profound, extending from the marine biosphere to the human sphere, as microplastics percolate through the food web. The mounting pressures of tourism and urban expansion only serve to escalate waste production, despite legislative attempts to promote ecological consciousness.

A cogent response entails mobilizing AI, drone fleets, and robotic cleaners, state-of-the-art tech delineated in Chapters 7 and 8. Drones, arrayed with sophisticated sensory apparatus, operate as vigilant custodians of the sea, offering exhaustive assessments of marine pollution over sprawling areas. With a harmonious blend of high-altitude observation and meticulous low-altitude scrutiny, these drones are poised to identify hotspots of marine debris, thereby directing cleanup operations with precision. The employment of multispectral imaging facilitates the segregation of waste, differentiating pollutants from benign materials—a critical process spearheaded by AI's analytical prowess. This enhances the efficiency of marine preservation while yielding cost savings.

Kim et al. [106] propose a captivating multilayered drone system, displayed in Figure 9-6, comprising diverse UAV classes, each with a specified function in oceanic surveillance. The structure's base comprises C-UAVs gathering data from floating debris and surface buoys, with M-UAVs situated in the middle, enhancing communication and powering C-UAVs. At the pinnacle, S-UAVs synthesize the accumulated data and issue commands down the hierarchy. This system guarantees continuous operation through intelligent replenishment and data synthesis, vital for potent marine oversight.

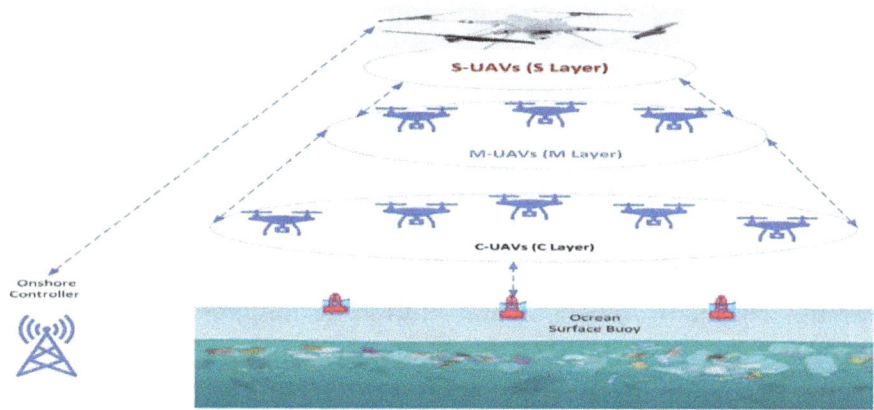

Figure 9-6. *Hierarchical ocean surveillance drone/UAV system (source: author's development based on [106])*

Subsequent to pinpointing pollutants, robotic operatives like BeBot, active on Florida's shores, embark on cleanup tasks, using solar power to sift through beach sand, discerning trash from natural sediment.[6] Additionally, Akib et al. [107] detail a pioneering marine waste-collecting robot, affirming the tangible impact such innovations can have on mitigating the ocean's plastic predicament.

The impact of this smart environmental venture is measurable through metrics such as the decline of marine pollution proximate to smart cities, the vitality of marine fauna unburdened by plastic entrapment or ingestion—information garnered from local environmental science institutions. These indicators of intelligent marine pollution management must be integrated within the service delivery platform of the digital twin metaverse cities shown in Figure 5-1, Chapter 5 of this book, ensuring robust environmental oversight and simulation capabilities.

---

[6] https://www.keeptahoeblue.org/combat-pollution/beach-cleaning-robot/#:~:text=The%20BEBOT%20is%20a%20solar,and%20fauna%2C%20or%20generating%20emissions

CHAPTER 9   SHOWCASES OF EMERGING ITS FOR DIGITAL TWIN METAVERSE CITIES: CORE

To conclude this chapter, reflecting upon the progression within this volume, we have witnessed the transformative influence of burgeoning ICTs on the anatomy of digital twin metaverse cities. This chapter has illustrated the profound ways smart transportation systems, advanced energy solutions, and integrated environmental strategies are redefining the very essence of urban existence. We've delved into the realm of smart homes, explored the potential of 3D-printed housing solutions, seen the integration of smart streetlights, and addressed complex environmental concerns—all through the lens of technology-enhanced sustainability and living standards.

Chapter 10 awaits, ready to unfold a series of riveting showcases of smart city services. These narratives will traverse the realms of healthcare, senior care, education, recycling, disaster preparedness, and vertical farming—each embodying a fragment of the holistic vision for digital twin smart cities. Here, we will witness the seamless incorporation of the advanced technologies discussed prior, culminating in a panoramic portrayal of enhanced urban life quality within the digitally twinned metropolis.

CHAPTER 10

Showcases of Emerging ITs for Digital Twin Metaverse Cities: *Services*

Welcome to Chapter 10, where we embark on an insightful exploration into the service-oriented heartbeat of digital twin metaverse cities, illuminated by the transformative power of emerging ICTs. Here, we delve into the dynamic interplay between cutting-edge tech and everyday life, showcasing how these advancements are not only reshaping our urban environments but also revolutionizing the very manner in which we live, learn, and engage within these vibrant spaces. This chapter promises a deep dive into a world where technology seamlessly integrates into the fabric of daily existence, enriching our experiences and opening new doors to possibilities that once resided only in the realm of imagination.

CHAPTER 10   SHOWCASES OF EMERGING ITS FOR DIGITAL TWIN METAVERSE CITIES: SERVICES

Smart Healthcare

The smart healthcare sector in our proposed digital twin metaverse cities represents an area where emerging ICTs are not merely influencing but fundamentally transforming the landscape of personal healthcare. In these visionary urban spaces, the application of advanced technologies extends beyond mere enhancement; it redefines the very essence of medical care. This shift heralds a new era marked by precision, efficiency, and patient-centric services, signaling a significant leap forward in how we approach health and wellness.

The healthcare system is a crucial element in a smart city, primarily responsible for protecting the health and well-being of its citizens. Yet, contemporary urban healthcare systems are besieged with several challenges. These include the scarcity of qualified doctors and specialists, resulting in prolonged waiting times for medical procedures, including surgeries. Complications are further aggravated by limited remote access to medical services, the prohibitive costs of treatments like prostheses, and insufficient follow-up care for existing patients. The Covid-19 pandemic intensified these issues, leading to severe disruptions in healthcare services and an uptick in mortality rates. The lack of prompt and effective medical support has a significant impact on the lives of city residents, an issue that becomes more pressing with an increasing aging population. Moreover, the city is also battling acute problems related to drug addiction and homelessness, both of which have been officially recognized as public health crises. These multifaceted issues highlight the critical need for innovative and adaptable solutions in urban healthcare.

Baker et al. [108] propose an IoT-based healthcare system, as illustrated in Figure 10-1, comprising four main components:

- Wearable Sensors: These sensors are crucial for measuring physiological conditions and vital signs, including pulse, respiratory rate, body temperature, blood pressure, and blood oxygen levels. The system can also incorporate specialized sensors for monitoring specific conditions, such as blood glucose levels, fall detection, and joint angle monitoring. A central node is designated to collect and process information from these medical sensors.

- Short-Range Communications: This layer is responsible for transmitting the data collected by medical sensors to healthcare service providers, such as nurses and doctors. It plays a critical role in ensuring that patient data is promptly and accurately relayed for immediate attention.

- Long-Range Communications: This component aggregates critical patient data to be stored in a healthcare database. Key requirements for this communication include security, error correction, robustness, low latency, and high reliability, ensuring that patient data is transmitted securely and efficiently.

- Cloud Storage and Machine Learning: This final component involves storing medical data from various sensors and patients' medical histories. The data, sent by the communication systems, is then analyzed to discover patterns and trends. This analysis aids in providing diagnostics and developing treatment plans, which healthcare professionals can tailor to individual patients.

CHAPTER 10   SHOWCASES OF EMERGING ITS FOR DIGITAL TWIN METAVERSE CITIES: SERVICES

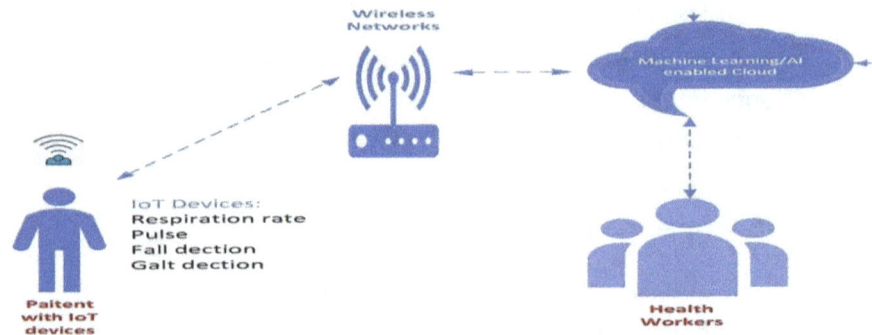

Figure 10-1. IoT-based smart healthcare systems (source: author's development based on [108])

The integration of these components in the IoT-based healthcare system signifies a major advancement in patient care, offering a more personalized, responsive, and efficient approach to health management.

The integration of emerging technologies, as discussed in Chapters 7 and 8, is paving the way for the creation of sophisticated smart healthcare systems in digital twin metaverse cities. These advanced systems harness the power of 5G networks, not only enhancing communication quality but also providing the high-speed, reliable connectivity crucial for life-saving healthcare applications. Imagine a world where 3D printing technology is routinely used to create temporary or permanent human organs, such as hearts and livers, potentially saving countless lives. This is not science fiction; it's a rapidly approaching reality.[1]

Furthermore, the combined prowess of AI and robotics is revolutionizing surgical procedures, enabling healthcare professionals to perform faster and more precise surgeries, even from remote locations. This leap in technology greatly improves patient outcomes and overall life quality. For instance, AI, robotics, and wearable IoT devices are being synergistically used to develop innovative healthcare systems like

---

[1] https://www.medicaldevice-network.com/analyst-comment/3d-printing-human-organs/

telemedicine. Telemedicine, a vital component of healthcare in digital twin metaverse cities, leverages the rapid 5G networks and reliable data transfer systems to provide medical care to patients remotely, reducing the need for hospital or clinic visits.

The Covid-19 pandemic underscored the importance of such technological advancements in healthcare. During this unprecedented public health crisis, telemedicine emerged as a crucial tool in protecting health workers from direct exposure to the deadly virus. For example, doctors now practice teleconsultations more frequently, saving precious time and allowing them to reach a greater number of patients. Patients, on their end, benefit from the convenience of booking appointments with their doctors using smart telemedicine devices, which display all available dates and times, eliminating the need for back-and-forth communication with clinics and lengthy wait times for responses.

The virtual meetings facilitated by this smart telemedicine system save time and expenses for both doctors and patients. Moreover, when integrated with wearable health gadgets, this system can continuously monitor vital signs and critical health parameters from the comfort of the patient's home. In emergencies, the intelligent telemedicine system is designed to send instant notifications or alerts to both the doctor and emergency services like 911.

An innovative facet of smart telemedicine is the application of 3D printing technology. This includes creating custom 3D printed walker canes to assist senior citizens and post-surgery patients, available for order and pickup at walk-in clinics. Additionally, in medical education, 3D printing is used to produce detailed replicas of human organs. These models allow medical professionals to simulate surgical procedures, enhancing training without the need for real organs. This integration of 3D printing, as discussed in Chapter 8, not only advances patient care but also revolutionizes medical training, demonstrating the transformative impact of technology in healthcare within digital twin metaverse cities.

This vision of smart healthcare in the digital twin metaverse cities represents more than just technological advancement; it embodies a new era of patient-centric care, where efficiency, accessibility, and safety are paramount. It's a future where healthcare transcends physical boundaries, bringing quality medical care to the doorstep of every individual, regardless of their location.

In the vanguard of medical innovation, telesurgery stands as a groundbreaking application, harnessing the prowess of cutting-edge ICTs. This remarkable system safeguards the patient's private information through a secured network, instantly available to smart ambulances or any physician requiring access to clinical records and examinations. Going one step further, the integration of blockchain with a 5G network has paved the way for the possibility of conducting telesurgeries—surgeries where the physical presence of a surgeon with the patient isn't required. This advancement is particularly poignant in the era of Covid-19, allowing for physical distancing measures to be upheld, thereby protecting both surgeons and patients from potential viral transmission.

The low latency characteristic of 5G technology is critical here, as it provides surgeons with real-time feedback. Such responsiveness is crucial during complex procedures and has shown excellent results, particularly in a study involving patients undergoing spine surgery. Moreover, this technology enables surgeons from different geographical locations to perform operations remotely, presenting a solution to reduce the long waiting lists for surgeries in many cities.

A striking illustration of this technology in action is the RAVEN telesurgery system, presented by Lum et al. [109]. The RAVEN system is comprised of three main components: (1) the patient site, equipped with two surgical manipulators poised over the patient; (2) the surgeon site, featuring two control devices and a live video feed from the operative site; (3) the communication layer, which utilizes any TCP/IP network, including a local private network, the Internet, or even a wireless network.

CHAPTER 10 SHOWCASES OF EMERGING ITS FOR DIGITAL TWIN METAVERSE CITIES: SERVICES

This robust system can teleoperate via a single bidirectional UDP socket controlled by a remote master device, capable of operating under extreme conditions and across various network configurations.

This innovative approach not only epitomizes the pinnacle of telemedical technology but also signifies a leap forward in global healthcare delivery, offering high-quality medical services that transcend geographical boundaries. The RAVEN telesurgery system is not just a technological marvel; it is a beacon of hope, a means to democratize surgical expertise and provide life-saving procedures to those in dire need, wherever they may be.

In recent years, the integration of robotics into the global healthcare system has marked a revolutionary shift in medical practices. Notably, robots have been instrumental in enhancing hospital maintenance and sanitation, a critical aspect in the fight against infectious diseases like the Covid-19 pandemic. One of the primary roles of these robots is in performing cleaning tasks, traditionally handled by hospital staff. Equipped with advanced sensors and specialized tools, these robots meticulously navigate hospital corridors and rooms, ensuring the air quality is free from harmful viruses and bacteria.[2] By continuously monitoring air quality levels, they can autonomously detect areas needing extra sanitization and dispense the necessary cleaning agents, thereby maintaining a consistently sterile environment.

Beyond air sanitization, these robots also manage other crucial tasks such as handling and laundering contaminated linens from patients with infectious diseases. This function is particularly vital in minimizing the risk of cross-contamination, a significant concern in healthcare settings. Perhaps most importantly, the advent of healthcare robots has been a boon for medical staff. By taking over routine and risk-laden tasks, robots reduce healthcare workers' exposure to hazardous environments. This is especially pertinent in areas where face-to-face patient interaction is not

---

[2] https://gausium.com/2023/02/03/robolution-in-healthcare/

critical. Moreover, these robotic systems can assist in other areas, such as delivering medications, transporting supplies, or even aiding in surgical procedures with precision and consistency unattainable by human hands.

Thus, the incorporation of robotics in healthcare not only streamlines operational efficiency but also significantly enhances patient safety and staff well-being. As technology continues to advance, the potential of robotics in transforming healthcare is boundless, promising a future where medical professionals can focus more on patient care and less on ancillary tasks.

In evaluating the efficacy of smart healthcare systems within the context of digital twin metaverse cities, several critical indicators emerge as benchmarks for success. These indicators not only reflect the system's operational efficiency but also its impact on patient care and medical practice. (1) Time and Commuting Efficiency: A primary measure is the time and commuting saved for both patients and physicians through telemedicine, compared to traditional in-person consultations. This metric assesses the convenience and efficiency of remote healthcare delivery. (2) Patient Satisfaction: The quality of healthcare service received through these systems is pivotal. Patient satisfaction surveys can provide valuable insights into the system's effectiveness in meeting patients' needs and expectations. (3) Diagnostic Accuracy: The precision and reliability of diagnoses made using the system are crucial. This indicator reflects the technological sophistication and practical utility of the smart healthcare system in clinical decision-making. (4) System Usability and Quality: The overall quality and user-friendliness of the system are vital for its adoption and effectiveness. This encompasses the interface design, ease of navigation, and the integration of various functionalities. (5) Physician Learning and Adaptation: The extent to which these advanced systems contribute to physicians' learning and practice development is another significant indicator. This measures how well healthcare professionals adapt to and enhance their skills through the use of advanced digital tools.

CHAPTER 10   SHOWCASES OF EMERGING ITS FOR DIGITAL TWIN METAVERSE CITIES: SERVICES

To sum up, the ultimate goal of such smart healthcare systems in the realm of the digital twin metaverse cities transcends operational metrics. The safety and satisfaction of caregivers, alongside the happiness and well-being of citizens, stand as overarching key performance indicators. These elements collectively define the success of these innovative healthcare models, pointing toward a future where technology harmoniously blends with human-centric care to create more efficient, effective, and empathetic healthcare experiences.

Smart Senior Caring

In the landscape of our rapidly aging world, the advent of "smart senior caring" within the digital twin metaverse cities emerges as a beacon of hope and innovation. The World Health Organization (WHO) underscores this demographic shift, projecting that the population of people over 60 years old will double from 12% to 22% between 2015 and 2050. By 2020, the number of seniors had already begun to surpass the number of children under 5 years old.[3] Taking Vancouver, Canada, as a microcosm, the senior population witnessed a 20% increase from 2010 to 2016, positioning seniors as a significant societal segment, with one in five Vancouverites now over the age of 65. This trend, mirrored globally, presents unique challenges, particularly as many seniors live alone, grappling with health issues, a reality exacerbated by the Covid-19 pandemic. Research from the BC Office of the Seniors Advocate reveals that over 46% of Vancouver's senior population lives solo, often unable to timely seek health assistance, leading to preventable adverse outcomes.[4]

---

[3] https://www.who.int/news-room/fact-sheets/detail/ageing-and-health
[4] https://www.seniorsadvocatebc.ca/reports/

CHAPTER 10 SHOWCASES OF EMERGING ITS FOR DIGITAL TWIN METAVERSE CITIES: SERVICES

The digital twin metaverse cities stand at the forefront of addressing these challenges. They offer innovative healthcare solutions, transforming how we protect and serve our senior citizens. Enabling seniors to seamlessly access city healthcare systems enhances the quality of their living, thereby reshaping the landscape of senior care. For instance, doctors can now recommend wearable sensors or IoT devices for seniors, targeting specific health concerns. A compelling example is the sensor-powered pacemaker, which, upon detecting a cardiac event, automatically alerts healthcare professionals and loved ones, ensuring swift medical response. This integration of technology into healthcare, validated by blockchain technology for security and reliability, is redefining emergency response and treatment protocols. As we venture further into the realm of smart senior caring, we realize it's not just about reactive measures but also about proactive, dignified, and independent living for our seniors. This section delves into the myriad ways the digital twin metaverse cities are revolutionizing senior care, embodying a blend of compassion, innovation, and efficiency.

Charlon et al. [110] propose a senior home elderly monitoring system for smart senior caring, shown in Figure 10-2. It depicts a local and remote network setup that facilitates the monitoring of elderly residents through various components:

1) Local Environment: The retirement home is equipped with IR sensors and electronic patches that are worn by the seniors. These devices collect movement data, such as detecting falls, and communicate with a local computer within the facility. The local computer acts as an anchor point, collecting data from the sensors.

2) Nursing Staff: On-site medical personnel are integrated into the system, receiving immediate alerts if an incident is detected. They can respond promptly to emergencies within the home.

CHAPTER 10   SHOWCASES OF EMERGING ITS FOR DIGITAL TWIN METAVERSE CITIES: SERVICES

3) Remote Access: The data collected is sent to remote servers via the Internet. This includes a web server and a database server, which process and store the information securely.

4) Medical Staff with Remote Access: Healthcare professionals outside the retirement home can access the data through clients like laptops and mobile devices. They can review the senior movements and other collected data to take corresponding actions, such as providing remote medical advice or directing on-site staff during emergencies.

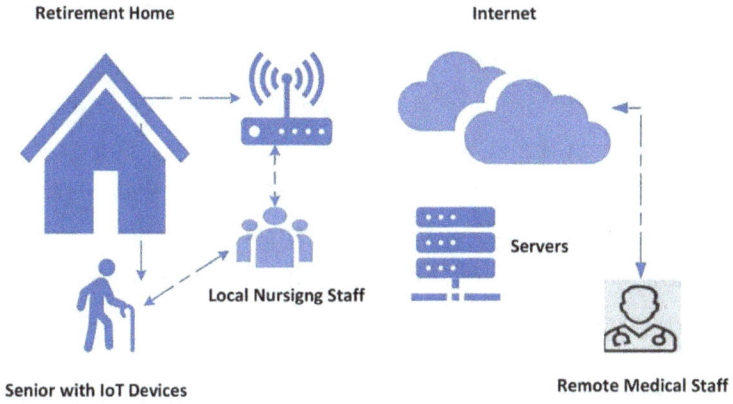

Figure 10-2. *A home monitoring system for smart senior caring (source: author's development based on [110])*

This system exemplifies the interconnectivity between local monitoring devices and remote medical support, enabling a comprehensive care environment for seniors. It allows for real-time data analysis and prompt emergency response and supports the overarching goal of maintaining seniors' independence while ensuring their safety and well-being.

CHAPTER 10   SHOWCASES OF EMERGING ITS FOR DIGITAL TWIN METAVERSE CITIES: SERVICES

Integrating Charlon et al.'s design into the broader context of the digital twin metaverse cities involves scaling the system to an urban level while maintaining the precision of care characteristic of home monitoring systems. This integration transforms local and remote monitoring capabilities into a cohesive network of smart city health services, leveraging IoT and advanced data analytics.

Imagine a metaverse city where each senior's home is equipped with infrared sensors and wearable technologies. These devices continuously monitor vital signs and activities, detecting anomalies and alerting medical teams. The synergy of fog and edge computing networks, complemented by 5G connectivity, forms the backbone of our digital twin metaverse cities. The remote unit, acting as an advanced command center (Figure 5-1, Chapter 5), enables healthcare professionals to take proactive measures based on real-time data.

Central to this system is its intelligence (Figure 6-5, Chapter 6), powered by machine learning algorithms that adapt to individual behavior patterns, enhancing predictive accuracy for health risks. Fog computing ensures rapid response, promoting a proactive healthcare model that adjusts living conditions to optimize residents' well-being.

This vision of smart senior care transcends traditional caregiving, fostering an ecosystem that supports senior independence and health, personalized to each senior's profile. In this digital twin metaverse, the integration of physical and digital realms forges a dynamic and empathetic healthcare landscape.

As a key component of the service delivery platform in digital twin metaverse cities, this smart senior caring system employs digital twinning to create a responsive care environment. Seniors with critical health conditions are provided with advanced sensors and IoT devices for continuous monitoring. The real-time data triggers the digital twinning process, ensuring prompt medical intervention for emergencies.

The effectiveness of this service is evaluated through key performance indicators (KPIs), such as the extension of life expectancy for city seniors, reflecting the system's efficacy in providing continuous care. Satisfaction surveys among seniors offer insights into the qualitative impact of these services, measuring changes in satisfaction and well-being.

To conclude, the integration of smart senior care within the digital twin metaverse cities is a forward-thinking approach to elder care. It combines advanced technology with compassionate service delivery, creating a supportive, safe, and independent living environment for seniors.

Smart Education

The onset of the Covid-19 pandemic marked a watershed moment in the history of education, ushering in an era where traditional classroom-based systems were compelled to pivot dramatically to online learning. This shift, necessitated by the stringent social distancing rules imposed by governments worldwide, transformed the educational landscape. Students, educators, and institutions navigated this new reality, leveraging platforms like Teams, Zoom, and other video conferencing tools for classes, assignments, exams, and group projects.

In this crucible of change, the concept of "smart education" emerged as a beacon of progress. Defined by the use of intelligent ICTs, smart education transcends the boundaries of time and space, enabling students to master 21st-century knowledge and skills crucial for a better society.

This new educational paradigm is characterized by its intelligence, personalization, and adaptability, catering to the unique learning context, personality, and needs of each student. Whether on campus or online, smart education represents a radical shift toward a more responsive, individualized, and forward-thinking approach to learning, setting the stage for an educational revolution that promises to reshape how we conceive of and engage with the pursuit of knowledge and skill development [111].

CHAPTER 10   SHOWCASES OF EMERGING ITS FOR DIGITAL TWIN METAVERSE CITIES: SERVICES

Tikhomirov et al. offer a multidimensional view of smart education, captured eloquently in Figure 10-3. It maps these dimensions into a conceptual framework for smart education, highlighting the interconnected strategies, technologies, and materials that define a smart educational environment. It is within this intelligently designed framework that smart education can truly thrive, delivering education that is not only effective but also adaptive and personalized to the needs of each student. At its core, smart education is delineated into three critical dimensions: educational outcomes, ICT, and organizational aspects:

1) Educational Outcomes: This component is the foundation of the smart education framework. It focuses on the objectives of educational systems which include enabling students to learn and master a wide array of skills, competences, and knowledge. Beyond academic prowess, it encompasses the understanding of cultures and the internalization of values, preparing students to contribute meaningfully to society.

2) ICT Dimension: This facet involves the deployment of various Information and Communication Technologies to elevate the educational experience. It aims to enhance social interaction, integrity, interactivity, and the flexibility of educational systems. Through these technologies, students can engage in a more collaborative, interactive, and mobile learning process, which is integral to achieving the desired educational outcomes.

3) Organizational Aspect: This dimension relates to the structural elements of education, including the curriculum, learning modes, and teaching

methodologies. It supports the notion of educational customization, where students are given the freedom to choose specific courses that align with their personal educational aspirations and career trajectories. This component acknowledges the need for education systems to adapt to the individual pathway of the students.

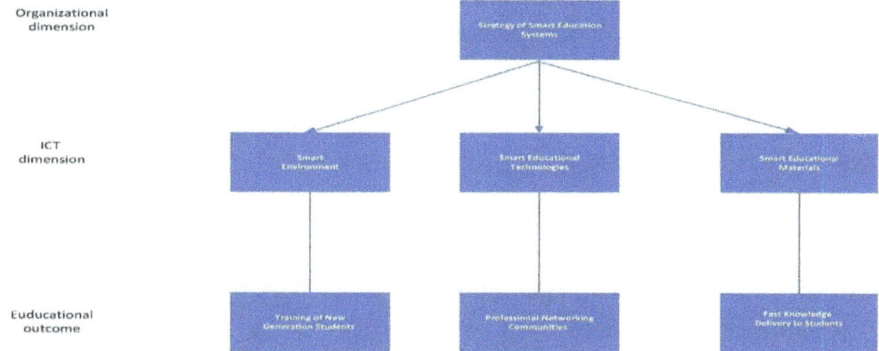

Figure 10-3. *A conceptual framework of smart education (source: author's development based on [112])*

In the digital twin metaverse cities, the role of education transcends traditional boundaries, becoming an immersive, interactive, and highly personalized experience. AR and VR serve as the twin pillars of this revolutionary approach. As elucidated in Chapter 8, AR brings a new dimension to learning by superimposing digital information onto the physical world, enabling computers and smartphones to enhance real-world objects with data and visuals through advanced AI analytics. Conversely, VR offers a dive into a simulated world, where learners can interact with 3D objects and environments in a fully immersive fashion. In classrooms dedicated to biology, chemistry, history, and computer science, students with AR headsets connected to computing systems via HDMI, embarking on educational journeys that bring complex concepts to life.[5] These high-quality 3D video streaming apps, bespoke to educational institutions, are used by teachers to present and dissect intricate topics, thereby fostering a deep and lasting understanding in the student's memory.

Blockchain technology, introduced in Chapter 7, fortifies this educational ecosystem by providing a secure, decentralized platform for e-learning. It acts as a guardian of digital integrity, making unauthorized alteration of records practically impossible due to its peer-to-peer network that distributes data across numerous nodes. The transparency and immutability inherent in blockchain technology make it an ideal candidate for managing the e-learning process. This is particularly crucial in the wake of the Covid-19 pandemic, which saw a hasty migration to online learning platforms that often left security as an afterthought. Blockchain ensures that educational materials are secure and verifiable, offering a robust defense against illicit activities and attacks on the system.

When students participate in online classes, blockchain technology facilitates the verification process, establishing a secure and transparent channel for data exchange. Upon completion of a course, blockchain records the details, creating an indelible and trusted record of educational achievements. This serves as a verifiable credential that students can present to future employers, reducing the risk of degree fraud and enhancing the credibility of the certification. The collaboration between MIT and the Learning Machine Company exemplifies this, where blockchain-based digital signatures provide a secure and transparent record of student achievements [113].

Within the metaverse, these technologies coalesce to form a vibrant tapestry of smart education, where learning is not a static activity confined to textbooks and classrooms but a dynamic, sensory-rich experience. AR and VR turn education into a multidimensional exploration, engaging

---

[5] https://online.maryville.edu/blog/augmented-reality-in-education/

CHAPTER 10   SHOWCASES OF EMERGING ITS FOR DIGITAL TWIN METAVERSE CITIES: SERVICES

students through visuals, sounds, and even tactile feedback. They are not merely passive recipients of information but active participants in a learning adventure that spans the virtual and the real, the current and the historical, the micro and the macro.

The digital twin metaverse cities represent an educational utopia where every learner has a front-row seat to the unfolding of knowledge. It is here that the educational paradigms of the future are being written, and the promise of a fully integrated, technologically empowered learning environment is realized. In this world, education is not just about knowledge acquisition; it's about experiencing and living through the lessons that prepare students for the challenges of the future.

Evaluating the efficacy of smart education within the digital twin metaverse cities involves a nuanced approach that transcends traditional metrics. The digital twinning process offers a unique opportunity to mirror the educational journey, allowing for real-time assessment and adjustments. To conclude this visionary educational model, let's explore the multifaceted KPIs that capture the essence of this transformative experience.

In the seamlessly integrated world of digital twin metaverse cities, evaluating the success of smart education systems requires a comprehensive suite of KPIs that reflect the depth and breadth of the educational experience. These KPIs need to account for both quantitative and qualitative aspects of learning:

1) Success Rate: Beyond the binary measure of pass or fail, success rates must consider the mastery of subject matter, critical thinking, and problem-solving skills. Advancements in digital assessment tools within the metaverse allow educators to track these competencies through interactive and adaptive testing.

2) Engagement Hours: The number of hours students engage in educational activities is not merely a measure of time but the quality of interaction. In the metaverse, this includes participation in virtual labs, collaborative projects, and interactive simulations that bring theoretical concepts to life.

3) Document Processing: Efficiency in document processing, including the submission of assignments and dissemination of educational materials, is enhanced by blockchain's secure and expedited verification process. The reduction in processing time indicates a streamlined workflow, allowing students and educators to focus more on learning and less on bureaucracy.

4) Instructor Workload: Smart education aims to optimize the workload of instructors through AI-powered assistance and automation, providing them with more time to engage directly with students, thus enhancing the overall quality of education.

5) Intellectual Development: Perhaps the most significant KPI is the intellectual growth of students, which can be evaluated through longitudinal tracking of their critical thinking, creativity, and innovation. Digital twin technology enables the creation of a digital footprint that captures each student's learning path, allowing for personalized educational strategies and insights into cognitive development.

To conclude, smart education within the digital twin metaverse cities is a bold reimagining of traditional learning paradigms. It's an educational symphony that harmonizes technology with pedagogy, personalized learning with collaborative exploration, and security with accessibility. As we evaluate this innovative system, our KPIs reflect not only academic achievement but the holistic development of students, preparing them for a world where the boundaries between the physical and digital are increasingly blurred. The ultimate goal is a learning ecosystem that is as dynamic and multifaceted as the students it serves, fostering a generation of learners who are equipped to navigate and shape the future with confidence and creativity.

Smart Retailing

The evolution of retail in the digital age has been nothing short of revolutionary. A burgeoning online shopping megatrend, driven by the allure of convenience, customization, and personalization, has steadily shifted consumer preferences toward virtual marketplaces. This transition reflects not only in the Z-Generation's inclination toward digital consumption but also in the growing expectation for on-demand services across all demographics. The metaverse cities, with their digitally native infrastructure, stand at the forefront of this transformation, offering a seamless integration of virtual and physical retail experiences.

In the pursuit of convenience, consumers have embraced the digital landscape, which promises a shopping experience liberated from the constraints of time and space. Online shopping has become a mainstay, with personalization algorithms and AI-enhanced interfaces crafting uniquely tailored experiences. AR and VR technologies have further enriched this by allowing customers to visualize products within their personal spaces or simulate the try-on experience from the comfort of their homes.

CHAPTER 10 SHOWCASES OF EMERGING ITS FOR DIGITAL TWIN METAVERSE CITIES: SERVICES

The modern consumer seeks not just products but personalized experiences that reflect their individual preferences and lifestyle. Smart retailing caters to this by harnessing data analytics and IoT to offer bespoke product recommendations and services. Furthermore, the on-demand economy has recalibrated expectations, with consumers accustomed to the immediate fulfillment of goods and services. Smart retailing infrastructure facilitates this by enabling precise, real-time inventory management and efficient home delivery systems.

The Z-Generation, digital natives by birth, navigate online spaces with unprecedented fluency, and their shopping habits have spurred the growth of ecommerce and the integration of retail within the metaverse. The digital twin metaverse cities become the ideal playground for this new generation of shoppers, blending interactive digital experiences with the tangibility of physical products.

While these trends have been steadily advancing, the onset of the Covid-19 pandemic acted as a catalyst, accelerating the adoption of smart retailing solutions. The pandemic underscored the necessity for a retail model that is resilient, adaptive, and capable of meeting the needs of consumers in a rapidly changing world.

Step into the world of Amazon Go, the paragon of smart retailing that promises a shopping experience as seamless and intuitive as online browsing. Picture yourself walking into the bustling Seattle store, the first of its kind, opened in 2017.[6] As you step through the doors, you enter a realm where the friction of checkout lines and cash transactions has vanished, replaced by a fluid, tech-driven shopping journey.

The magic begins the moment you enter. A quick scan of the Amazon Go app on your phone at the gateways registers your presence. Inside, a network of sensors, cameras, and RFID tags works in concert to create a symphony of data with every step you take. Each shelf is equipped with

---

[6] https://www.cnbc.com/2020/02/24/amazon-opens-its-first-full-size-cashierless-grocery-store-in-seattle.html

CHAPTER 10   SHOWCASES OF EMERGING ITS FOR DIGITAL TWIN METAVERSE CITIES: SERVICES

weight sensors and pressure detectors that can discern the slightest change when an item is picked up or placed back. The shelves are not just storage; they are smart hubs that communicate with the cloud in real time.

As you move through the aisles, cameras above track your movement while algorithms churn in the background, making sense of your shopping behavior. These are not ordinary cameras; they are the eyes of the store, powered by deep learning algorithms capable of distinguishing between different customers and their chosen items, even in a crowded space. RFID tags attached to items couple with this visual data, providing a fail-safe to ensure your virtual cart reflects your physical one with precision.

The store's intelligence extends beyond its physical space, tapping into the rich vein of Amazon's big data. Every choice you've made in the past, every online purchase feeds into predictive analytics that tailor the store around you. Perhaps you'll receive a notification on your phone about a deal on your favorite coffee blend as you pass by the café section or a suggestion for a new snack that aligns with your dietary preferences.

When your shopping is complete, there's no need to queue or unpack your basket. You simply walk out the door, and the system tallies your items, charging your Amazon account as you pass through the exit sensor gates. In moments, a receipt pops up on your phone, detailing your purchases, while behind the scenes, the inventory system has already updated to reflect the stock changes.

Figure 10-4 shows the Amazon Go Store where the intricate network makes it possible. Computing resources, network systems, and inventory management are all components of a vast, interconnected structure that underpins the Amazon Go experience [114]. This is where the digital twin concept materializes in retail, replicating the physical store in a digital dimension, allowing unparalleled efficiency and analysis.

1) Pressure Detectors and Weight Measures:
   Embedded within each shelf, these sensors detect when an item is removed or returned. The precise

change in weight or pressure signals to the system exactly which product has been picked up, allowing the store to keep track of the items in real time and update the shopper's virtual cart instantaneously.

2) RFID Tags: Each product is tagged with an RFID chip that carries unique information. As customers shop, RFID readers throughout the store continually scan these tags, facilitating an additional layer of item identification. This ensures that the system accurately records each customer's selections, even in cases where items are moved or returned to different locations.

3) Distance/Dimension Measurement: To distinguish between similar items and ensure the correct product is identified, sensors capable of measuring distance and dimensions are utilized. These measurements help the system to differentiate between a small and large version of the same product, for instance.

4) Camera Systems: Overhead cameras are a critical element in the Amazon Go Store layout. They are equipped with computer vision technology to monitor the movement of both products and customers. These cameras can track a product as it moves from shelf to cart and identify which customer is making the selection. This technology works in crowded environments and distinguishes between individuals even in close proximity.

5) Big Data Analytics: Amazon Go taps into Amazon's extensive reservoir of customer purchase history to enhance the in-store experience. By analyzing past

online behaviors, the system can predict shopping patterns and preferences, allowing Amazon Go to customize the shopping experience for each individual.

6) Predictive and Prescriptive Data Analytics: These analytics tools process the wealth of data collected to anticipate customer needs and manage inventory intelligently. Predictive analytics can forecast product demand, while prescriptive analytics may suggest strategic decisions, such as personalized product placements and promotions.

7) Deep Learning Algorithms: Amazon Go's system employs deep learning to refine its understanding of customer behavior and product recognition over time. These algorithms can learn from every interaction, continually improving the system's accuracy and the customer's experience.

8) IoT Integration: The Internet of Things (IoT) forms the backbone of communication between the diverse array of sensors, tags, and cameras. This interconnectedness allows for the seamless exchange of data and the orchestration of all the system components to function as a cohesive whole.

9) Digital Twinning: By mirroring the physical space within a digital framework, Amazon Go can simulate and analyze the entire retail operation. This digital twin allows for sophisticated modeling and adjustment of the retail environment, ensuring that the physical store remains optimally organized and stocked.

CHAPTER 10   SHOWCASES OF EMERGING ITS FOR DIGITAL TWIN METAVERSE CITIES: SERVICES

Figure 10-4. *Amazon Go Store (source: Amazon company website)*

This complex layering of technologies transforms Amazon Go from a mere physical store into a dynamic, responsive environment. It is a testament to the convergence of retail and technology, where the shopping experience is not just about the products but about the innovative interaction between people, space, and data.

Amazon Go's pioneering technology showcases what is possible when retail is reimagined for the digital age. It exemplifies a future where smart retailing in the digital twin metaverse cities delivers not just goods but a personalized, efficient, and satisfying shopping experience that feels less like an errand and more like a glimpse into the future of commerce [115].

In the blueprint of digital twin metaverse cities, smart retailing takes center stage, reflecting a future where stores like Amazon Go become the norm. The integration of emerging ICTs, as explored in Chapters 7 and 8, enables the creation of retail spaces where convenience and technology converge to offer an unprecedented shopping experience.

- Seamless Connectivity and Intelligent Operations: 5G technology lays the groundwork for this new retail era, offering the necessary infrastructure to support stores without the need for personnel, all monitored in real time thanks to its expansive bandwidth. Coupled with AI, these stores can operate continuously, providing round-the-clock service to customers. The journey begins with a simple scan of an ID barcode from an exclusive app, granting the customer access to the store.

- Interactive Shopping Experience: Inside, intelligent baskets equipped with sensors and micro-cameras recognize and log items as they are placed inside by shoppers. This integration feeds information back to the customer's mobile app in real time, detailing product prices and descriptions. Upon exiting, there is no traditional checkout; the system has already calculated the total, promptly sending a detailed electronic receipt to the customer's phone.

- Augmented Reality in Retail: The smart retail experience is further enhanced by augmented reality (AR) for those wishing to try on apparel. AR goggles eliminate the wait for fitting rooms, allowing customers to virtually try on clothes, altering colors and sizes with ease. This technology extends beyond clothing to other departments, such as food, cosmetics, and housewares, providing customers with a vivid preview of the products, interactive information, and usage instructions without the need to unbox.

- Automated Warehousing Solutions: Beyond the storefront, smart retailing warehouses act as centralized hubs for goods distribution, situated near the metaverse cities to capitalize on space and reduce rental costs. Modeled after Amazon Fulfillment Centers (AFCs), these warehouses are fully automated, operated by AI and robotics to minimize human error and maximize efficiency. Such machines are tasked with precise picking and storage, ensuring that all products are readily available for swift transport to retail outlets.

- Cloud Computing and Inventory Management: The application of cloud computing and big data analytics serves to maintain real-time stock levels for each company. This system symbolizes a unique smart city concept where inventory is not just stored but managed intelligently by AI, providing a dynamic supply chain solution. Retail managers are kept abreast of inventory levels, ensuring that stock shortages are preemptively managed.

In digital twin metaverse cities, smart retailing's triumph is measured by KPIs that track sales performance across store sections, customer return rates, queue and return item reductions, and financial indicators like ROI, operational savings, and customer acquisition costs. Together, these metrics offer a comprehensive view of a smart store's operational efficiency, customer satisfaction, and economic success, encapsulating the full impact of integrating advanced retail technologies into the urban fabric.

To conclude, smart retailing in the digital twin metaverse cities represents a profound shift in the consumer shopping paradigm. As these cities embrace the digital twin concept, the retail sector must adapt by adopting and integrating advanced technologies that not only streamline operations but also enhance the customer experience. The success of such systems is not measured by technology implementation alone but by how they translate into increased sales, customer loyalty, and cost efficiencies.

By consistently monitoring these KPIs, smart retailing can evolve and adapt, ensuring it remains at the forefront of the retail revolution, offering unmatched convenience, personalization, and engagement to the consumers of tomorrow.

Smart Recycling

Recycling and waste separation are critical yet challenging tasks for urban households, compounded by daily issues that affect the efficiency and effectiveness of garbage collection systems.[7] Common problems include improper sorting of recyclables from general waste, leading to contamination and the devaluation of recyclable materials. Furthermore, the presence of nonrecyclable items in blue bins often results in the entire contents being sent to landfills. Overfilled bins are a frequent sight, causing spillage and attracting pests, while inadequate frequency of collection services can lead to accumulation and unsanitary conditions. Additionally, lack of public awareness and insufficient incentives for proper waste segregation exacerbate the issue, making the goal of a recycling-driven community far more difficult to achieve. These daily hurdles in waste management highlight the need for a smarter, more efficient recycling system in the fabric of digital twin metaverse cities.

Expanding on the issue of smart recycling, municipalities face a multifaceted set of challenges that extend beyond basic collection and sorting. Among the most significant hurdles are the confusion and lack of education around recycling practices. Many residents are aware that recycling is beneficial but remain uncertain about which items are recyclable, leading to low participation rates. Additionally, the cost of recycling services can be prohibitive, deterring individuals and communities from engaging with recycling programs.

---

[7] https://www.colorado.edu/ecenter/2022/02/04/challenges-recycling

Inadequate recycling services further complicate matters, exemplified by cities with insufficient resources to provide residents with necessary recycling bins or facilities, leading to ineffective recycling programs. The complexity of managing diverse waste types—from household refuse to construction debris—adds another layer of difficulty, making a one-size-fits-all approach impractical.

Addressing these issues calls for a combination of innovative technology to track and analyze waste streams, better planning for recycling facilities and equipment, and more effective education to promote sustainable practices. Technology-driven solutions such as on-demand waste collection and optimized routing can improve efficiency and reduce the environmental footprint of waste management. Moreover, analytics play a crucial role in monitoring and evaluating waste streams to divert materials away from landfills and encourage responsible waste management habits across all sectors.[8]

Hong et al. [116] present an IoT-based smart garbage recycling system for food waste management, illustrated in Figure 10-5, which is installed in apartment buildings and residential houses and communicates via 5G wireless networks.

---

[8] https://www.rts.com/blog/municipal-recycling-and-waste-management-challenges-how-can-tech-help/

CHAPTER 10   SHOWCASES OF EMERGING ITS FOR DIGITAL TWIN METAVERSE CITIES: SERVICES

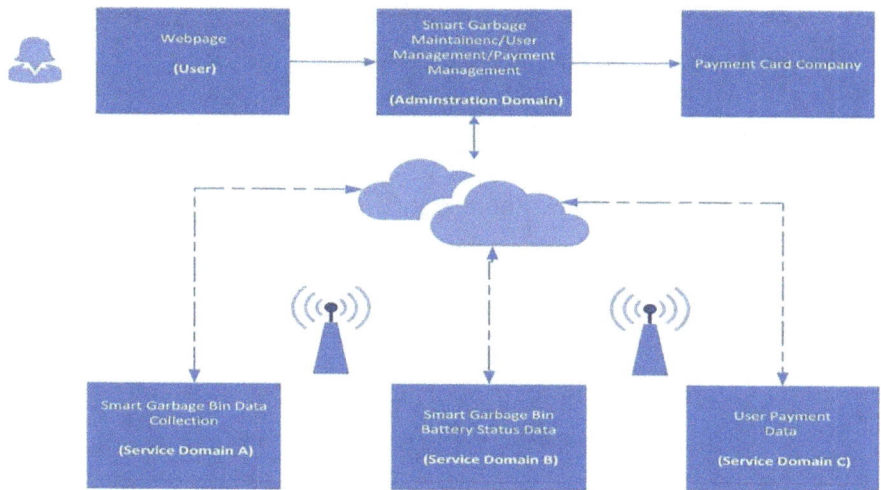

Figure 10-5. *Smart garbage management systems for food waste (source: author's development based on [116])*

Let's delve into the technological components and workflow of this system:

1) Interface: Residents interact with the system through a user-friendly interface, likely a web page or a mobile app, where they can view their waste management information, such as disposal history or schedules.

2) Administration Domain: This domain comprises several servers that manage different aspects of the system:

    • Smart Garbage Maintenance Server: Central to the system, it collects and processes data from the IoT sensors in the garbage bins.

    • User Management Server: Handles user-related data, likely including account information, usage patterns, and possibly user feedback.

- Payment Management Server: Processes payments, which could involve pay-as-you-throw models or other financial transactions related to waste disposal services.

- Card Company: Represents the financial institutions or payment gateways that facilitate secure transactions within the system.

3) Service Domains (A, B, C): These are the physical locations, such as apartment complexes or individual homes, where the waste is collected.

 - Smart Garbage Bins: Equipped with IoT sensors that monitor waste levels, identify the type of waste, and even assess the bin's battery status to ensure uninterrupted service.

 - Garbage Pickup Data: Information related to waste collection schedules and actual pickup events.

 - Discharge Data and Bin Capacity Data: Details regarding how much waste is disposed of and the current capacity of the bins, which is crucial for scheduling collections.

4) Waste Collection Infrastructure: Includes waste collectors who are notified by the system when a pickup is needed. There's a clear indication of potential issues such as malfunctions or low battery states in the bins, triggering maintenance actions.

5) Communication Network: The wireless network, possibly 5G for its high speed and low latency, connects all physical components with the administration domain, allowing real-time data transfer and immediate responsiveness.

6) Integrated Workflow: The system's workflow suggests that when users dispose of waste, the smart bins transmit this data to the maintenance server. The administration then analyzes the data and communicates with service providers to execute timely waste collection. This integration ensures optimal coordination, avoids overflow, and streamlines the collection process.

7) Payment and Charge System: After waste disposal, users may be charged based on the amount or type of waste, with the payment management server handling these transactions securely.

This smart garbage management system exemplifies a closed-loop solution that leverages IoTs for efficiency and user convenience. It's a sophisticated network that not only automates waste collection but also integrates financial transactions, user management, and predictive maintenance into a cohesive smart city service.

The principal advantage of a smart recycling system lies in its capacity for real-time coordination between service providers, which allows for dynamic scheduling of garbage collection based on actual need rather than rigid preset routes. Traditional methods often fail to accommodate the variable rates of waste production in different areas, leading to inefficiencies. By integrating sensor data, an IoT-based platform ensures that all stakeholders have access to current information, enabling them to adjust their operations for maximum efficiency. This system not only optimizes collection routes and schedules, enhancing the recycling process, but also reduces operational costs for cities. A successful implementation of such a system in Chennai, India, underscores its viability [117]. Smart waste management systems are particularly crucial in densely populated urban areas, where they can significantly improve the quality of life and economic conditions by streamlining waste management practices.

CHAPTER 10   SHOWCASES OF EMERGING ITS FOR DIGITAL TWIN METAVERSE CITIES: SERVICES

In our digital twin metaverse cities, smart recycling services are revolutionized by the innovative integration of emerging ICTs, as detailed in Chapters 7 and 8 of this book. Our systems harness the power of AI to intelligently automate the sorting process in recycling plants, using machine learning and an array of sensors to accurately distinguish between different types of materials on the conveyor belt, such as separating plastics from aluminum and glass. AR is deployed to visualize the life cycle and environmental impact of products, thereby encouraging consumers to reduce waste generation. Blockchain technology is crucial for its real-time tracking capabilities, providing a transparent record of waste quantities, collection activities, and the logistics of recycling or disposal.

IoT solutions focus on optimizing waste collection routes, effectively reducing fuel consumption and carbon emissions. Smart bins, integrated with AI and IoT sensors, are pivotal in measuring waste levels, facilitating timely collection, and further streamlining the recycling process. Robotics plays a transformative role in our waste management strategy. AI-powered robots are equipped to sort waste with precision, reducing the need for human contact and increasing both the speed and accuracy of waste processing. Additionally, intelligent robots are employed to address littering by promptly collecting discarded waste in public spaces.

The use of Waste Robotics Autonomous Recycling (WAR) technology epitomizes the advanced waste management process.[9] This technology merges computer vision and deep learning to enhance the efficiency of recycling services, offering a cost-effective solution that aligns with the environmental and economic goals of smart cities. These technologies, when synchronized within the digital twin infrastructure of metaverse cities, lead to a cleaner environment, improved public health, and a robust, sustainable waste management ecosystem.

---

[9] wasterobotic.com

To gauge the effectiveness of our smart recycling system in digital twin metaverse cities, we adopt KPIs that reflect the multifaceted benefits of the system. A significant KPI is the reduction in complaints regarding recycle bin overflow from both residential and commercial entities. A decrease in such grievances would signify a more efficient collection process, attuned to the actual waste generation rates.

Another critical KPI is the alleviation of traffic congestion on collection days, particularly in the service alleys of high-rise buildings. This indicator points to improved scheduling and routing of collection services, leading to less disruption in urban life. From the perspective of service providers, a valuable metric is the reduction in overtime hours necessitated by inefficient routes. Optimizing collection paths through intelligent systems should translate to a balanced workload for employees. Success hinges on several key factors: collaboration among service providers facilitated by secure information sharing, government-led initiatives to develop robust and secure platforms for data management, and comprehensive training for operators to adeptly handle the smart system. Additionally, resident participation in proper waste sorting is crucial to avoid triggering sensors mistakenly and maintaining system integrity.

Thus, the success of our smart recycling system in the digital twin metaverse cities can be measured by the system's operational efficiency, stakeholder collaboration, and the active engagement of residents. By achieving these benchmarks, the system promises not only to enhance environmental sustainability but also to contribute to the overall quality of life and operational smoothness within the metropolis.

To conclude, in our digital twin metaverse cities, smart recycling is a holistic approach to waste management, addressing challenges from improper sorting to inefficient collection schedules. The system, powered by IoT, AI, AR, blockchain, and robotics, enables real-time monitoring, intelligent sorting, and predictive waste management. It embodies a high-tech solution where residents actively participate, service providers operate efficiently, and governments foster sustainable

CHAPTER 10   SHOWCASES OF EMERGING ITS FOR DIGITAL TWIN METAVERSE CITIES: SERVICES

practices. The success of this smart ecosystem is measured by reduced complaints, better traffic management, and optimized provider schedules, leading to a cleaner environment and enhanced urban living.

Smart Disaster Response

The escalating severity of climate change poses a stark reality for residents in global cities, increasingly vulnerable to catastrophic events such as wildfires, floods, windstorms, earthquakes, landslides, tsunamis, and severe winter storms. For example, San Francisco, United States, faces up to a 75% chance of experiencing a major earthquake within the next 30 years, posing a substantial risk with the potential to cause widespread devastation along the Pacific coast, including loss of life and the triggering of massive tsunamis,[10] a threat that looms large with its ability to wreak havoc across the Pacific coast, claiming lives and triggering towering tsunamis. These environmental calamities underscore the urgent need for robust disaster management strategies. While local governments have endeavored to establish risk mitigation and swift response frameworks, the integration of ICTs stands to revolutionize disaster readiness and response. These technological advancements offer critical, scalable solutions to safeguard populations against the spectrum of natural hazards.

The smart disaster response system [118] proposed by Boukerche and Coutinho in Figure 10-6, integrated into digital twin metaverse cities, encompasses a sophisticated network of components designed to predict, detect, and respond to natural disasters efficiently.

---

[10] https://www.earthquakeauthority.com/blog/2020/san-francisco-bay-area-earthquake-prediction-risk:~:text=There%20is%20a%203%20out,earthquake%20and%20weeks%20of%20aftershocks

CHAPTER 10 SHOWCASES OF EMERGING ITS FOR DIGITAL TWIN METAVERSE CITIES: SERVICES

1) Smart Sensing: Utilizing IoT devices, this component gathers data on potential hazards. It employs both crowdsourced information via online social networks and sensors embedded in the environment and personal devices, creating a comprehensive sensing network.

2) Processing: Leveraging big data analytics, including data filtering, indexing, and machine learning. This stage processes the collected data to identify patterns that predict impending disasters.

3) Smart Response: This element activates emergency services, like firefighters and medical facilities, and community response efforts like mass evacuation planning, ensuring a swift and effective response to disasters.

4) Communication Networking Systems: Underpinning the system is a robust mobile network that ensures seamless communication between all components, essential for the coordination of disaster response efforts.

5) Privacy and Security: This crucial aspect safeguards the integrity and confidentiality of data throughout the disaster prediction and response process.

CHAPTER 10   SHOWCASES OF EMERGING ITS FOR DIGITAL TWIN METAVERSE CITIES: SERVICES

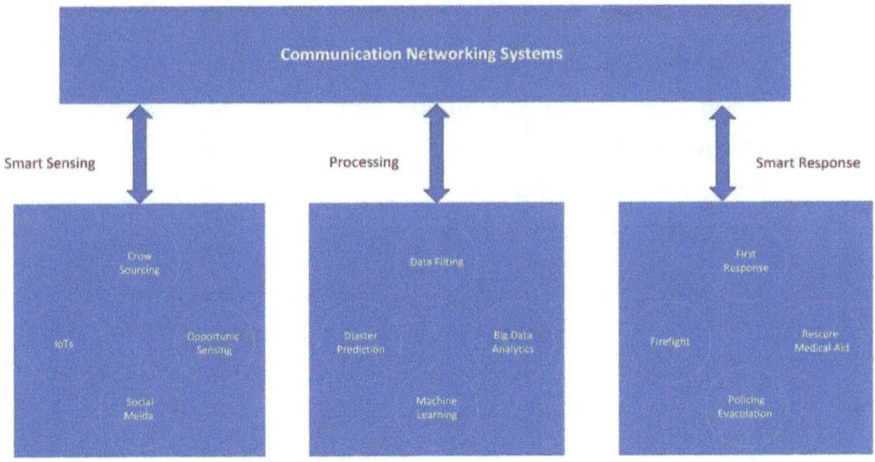

Figure 10-6. *Smart disaster prediction, discovery, and response (source: author's development based on [118])*

The system, operational within the interconnected fabric of a digital twin city, is designed to enhance the safety and resilience of urban environments against the increasing threats posed by natural disasters.

In Takamatsu City, Japan, a prototype of a smart disaster response system showcases the capabilities of ICTs within a digital twin metaverse framework.[11] The system integrates geo-located sensors, satellites, drones, and other devices to monitor environmental and climatic changes for early disaster detection. This networked ecosystem, powered by 5G and IoTs, feeds into a big data platform, allowing for real-time analysis and predictive insights. Professionals and local authorities can then access a unified dashboard displaying this data, facilitating prompt, informed decision-making to safeguard residents against natural calamities such as earthquakes, tsunamis, and wildfires. This example demonstrates how advanced technology can be utilized for comprehensive environmental surveillance and proactive disaster management.

---

[11] https://www.fiware.org/2020/12/01/collaborating-municipalities-for-disaster-resiliency-and-sustainable-growth/

CHAPTER 10   SHOWCASES OF EMERGING ITS FOR DIGITAL TWIN METAVERSE CITIES: SERVICES

In the event of a disaster, these interconnected technologies allow for rapid data gathering, analysis, and dissemination of information, ensuring that the city's response is both efficient and effective. The digital twin reflects the city's physical state in real time, allowing for quick adjustments and deployment of resources to the areas most in need. It's this seamless integration of physical and digital, underpinned by cutting-edge technologies, that exemplifies the strength of the digital twin metaverse cities in disaster management and response.

To effectively measure the success of a smart disaster response system in a digital twin metaverse city, it's essential to track a range of metrics that reflect both the system's efficiency and its impact on the community. Citizen satisfaction surveys are a direct way to gauge public opinion on the timeliness and quality of the disaster response services. Furthermore, assessing the community's level of preparedness for potential disasters can indicate the effectiveness of the system's communication and educational efforts.

Engagement on the platform, such as the frequency and quality of citizen feedback and suggestions, can provide insights into the system's usability and the community's involvement. Other quantitative measures could include response times to disaster events, the accuracy of predictions, and the reduction in disaster-related damages and casualties. These metrics, together with citizen input, can paint a comprehensive picture of the system's performance and areas for improvement.

To sum up, in the face of escalating climate threats, smart disaster response systems, as a part of the Intelligent Services layer in the digital twin metaverse cities, represent a transformative approach to crisis management. These systems, underpinned by the digital twinning process and technologies like IoTs, AI, and cloud computing, predict and respond to emergencies, enhancing urban resilience. The system's success hinges on its real-time capabilities, community engagement, and feedback, with metrics such as response times and predictive accuracy serving as benchmarks. This holistic strategy not only ensures efficient disaster management but also fosters a proactive, informed, and safe community in the digital twin metaverse cities.

Smart Vertical Farming

In the heart of bustling metropolises, where glass and steel stretch skyward and the concrete sprawl leaves little room for greenery, the health-conscious urbanite's craving for fresh, organic produce grows ever stronger. Yet, this hunger collides with the reality of shrinking green spaces, as Adl et al. [119] highlight the detrimental impact of conventional agriculture on both health and the environment, with its reliance on chemical fertilizers that taint our natural resources. This sets the stage for the rise of vertical farming, a beacon of sustainability in the urban landscape [120].

Envision layers upon layers of lush greenery, not spread across vast fields, but ascending within the very skeleton of the city's architecture. Vertical farming is not just a method; it's a transformative vision for urban agriculture, promising year-round produce free from the blemishes of disease and harmful substances. It's a countermovement to food waste and environmental degradation, offering solutions that harmonize with the rhythms of nature while enhancing urban resilience against climate change and its cascading effects.

This vertical revolution in farming is poised to redefine our relationship with food, turning every urban center into a potential oasis of nourishment and health. As we pivot from the old paradigms of resource-intensive agriculture, smart vertical farming stands as a testament to innovation, delivering not just sustenance but also a blueprint for a sustainable, health-focused future within our cities.

Vertical farming is the practice of cultivating plants in stacked layers within a controlled environment, such as inside buildings, mobile containers, or underground spaces. This method utilizes precision in regulating light, temperature, and nutrients, diverging from traditional horizontal farming that uses soil and open land. The structure of a vertical farm typically involves the arrangement of plants in vertical layers, optimizing space and resource use.

Figure 10-7 illustrates a hydroponics vertical farming technique. It employs sophisticated hydroponics systems, where plants are nourished with a mineral-rich water solution instead of soil. The roots are immersed in this nutrient solution, which is meticulously managed to maintain the ideal balance of chemical elements essential for growth.

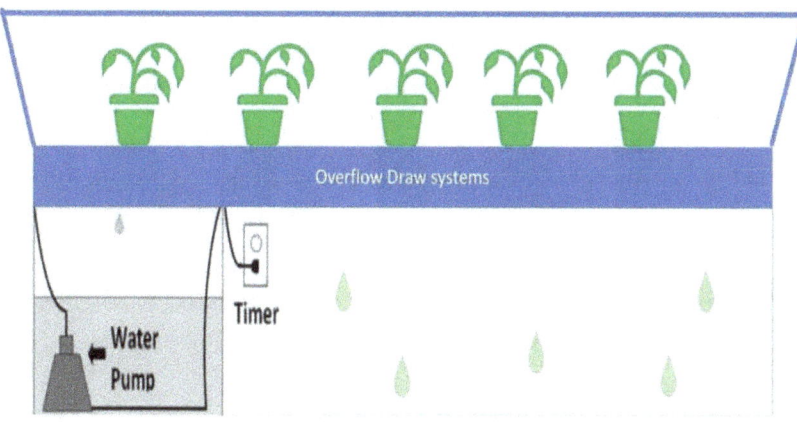

Figure 10-7. Hydroponics vertical farming (source: author's development based on [120])

Different techniques of vertical farming include hydroponics, aeroponics, and aquaponics. *Hydroponics* is a common approach in vertical farming, where plants grow in a soilless nutrient solution, allowing for close monitoring and adjustment of the necessary chemical components for plant growth. *Aeroponics*, developed by NASA, allows plants to grow in an air or mist environment with minimal water usage. *Aquaponics* combines this system with aquaculture, circulating nutrient-rich water from fish tanks to hydroponically grown plants, which in turn purify the water for the fish.

CHAPTER 10   SHOWCASES OF EMERGING ITS FOR DIGITAL TWIN METAVERSE CITIES: SERVICES

These systems can offer year-round crop production without reliance on weather conditions, reduce pesticide and herbicide use, and enhance water and land efficiency. They can also integrate automation for greater efficiency. Despite these benefits, vertical farming requires significant energy for artificial lighting and climate control and can involve substantial initial investment costs, which currently limits its viability to certain crops that yield a quick turnover.

In our digital twin metaverse cities, smart vertical farming is an essential intelligence service, promising a sustainable and health-centric future for urban agriculture. Embracing the digital twinning process articulated in Chapter 6 and powered by the emerging technologies explored in Chapters 7 and 8, smart vertical farming represents a paradigm shift in how we conceive of food production within city landscapes.

At its core, this innovative approach employs IoT sensors for a myriad of critical functions, including nutrient balance, climate control, and resource allocation, ensuring that crops thrive in their vertically aligned habitats. Drones, equipped with advanced imaging technology, patrol the aerial domain of these urban farms, collecting data that is as diverse as it is vital for the meticulous monitoring and management of plant health and growth patterns.

The power of big data analytics lies in its ability to synthesize these vast data streams, transforming them into actionable insights for optimizing farming cycles and enhancing yield. Blockchain technology introduces an unprecedented level of traceability and trust to the urban food chain, ensuring that any produce reaching the city's populace is fresh, safe, and sustainably sourced.

AI and robotics represent the vanguard of smart vertical farming, offering precise and autonomous interventions that not only conserve resources but also elevate the quality of produce. These robotic agents, guided by AI, are the tireless laborers of the vertical farms, tending to the crops with a precision that marries the art of agriculture with the science of technology.

CHAPTER 10 SHOWCASES OF EMERGING ITS FOR DIGITAL TWIN METAVERSE CITIES: SERVICES

In the digital twin metaverse cities, smart vertical farming transcends being merely a component of the urban fabric. It is deeply interwoven with the "Life in the Physical City" layer, as described in Chapter 5, with data flowing seamlessly from the farms through the Data Collection layer, analyzed and visualized by the DAFW models. This integrated approach ensures that every aspect of the vertical farming process is optimized, from seeding to harvesting, making each city a self-sustaining oasis of greenery.

City governance plays a pivotal role not just in oversight but in fostering the growth of these smart farming ecosystems. Their support is essential for ensuring the long-term viability of vertical farming operations, contributing to a vision of smart cities where technology and nature coexist in a symbiotic relationship, nurturing not just the body with wholesome food but also the soul with the verdant bounty of nature integrated into the urban expanse.

The success of Smart Vertical Farming within the digital twin metaverse cities will likely be measured by its impact on urban food supply, sustainability, and quality of life. KPIs may include the reduction in the carbon footprint of food supply chains, improvements in the nutritional quality of urban diets, and the economic viability of farming within a metropolitan context. The integration of such farming with city life is a step toward a greener, healthier future, reflecting a commitment to innovation and well-being in the urban landscape of tomorrow.

In conclusion, this chapter offers more than a glimpse into the future—it presents a vivid blueprint of urban innovation where smart services converge with digital twinning to revolutionize the fabric of city living. It's a realm where immersive education springs to life through augmented and virtual realities, where retail experiences are intuitively personalized by artificial intelligence, and where the cycles of recycling and vertical farming reflect a commitment to sustainability. Here, smart disaster response networks become bastions of resilience, ready to meet the challenges of a changing climate head-on.

CHAPTER 10   SHOWCASES OF EMERGING ITS FOR DIGITAL TWIN METAVERSE CITIES: SERVICES

But this is just the prologue to an even grander narrative. As we venture forth into Part 5 of this seminal work, we prepare to delve into the very act of creation—crafting digitally twinned metaverse cities from the ground up. Armed with cutting-edge engineering tools and inspired by a vision of global urban transformation, we stand on the cusp of turning these innovative concepts into tangible realities. The chapters ahead are more than just words on a page; they are the keys to unlock a new dimension of smart city development, one where technology and humanity synergize to forge environments that are sustainable, intelligent, and deeply interconnected.

Join us as we embark on this exhilarating journey, charting a course through the intricate process of digital twinning. Let's navigate the complexities of architectural innovation, decode the language of smart city engineering, and breathe life into the digital twin smart cities that will define our collective urban future. The path ahead is charged with potential and promise—a testament to the transformative power of the digital twin metaverse cities in sculpting a resilient, efficient, and vibrant world.

PART V

Showing Me How: The Development Tools and Prototypes

In Part 5, we delve into an exploration of a compendium of state-of-the-art digital twin metaverse development tools, sharpening practical skills for the construction of various prototypes that are pivotal in shaping the future of the digital twin metaverse cities. This part meticulously guides you through the use of advanced tools, including Ansys, AWS IoT, Azure Digital Twins, Bosch IoT Suite, PTC ThingWorx, GE Digital Predix, IBM Maximo Asset Monitor, Meta Spark, Unity, Unreal Engine (UE), Nvidia Omniverse, Roblox Studio, Blender, ZBrush, SpatialOS, Decentraland SDK, and the ChatGPT large language AI model. This segment aims not only to introduce these innovative tools but also to demonstrate their applications in building an array of digital twin metaverse prototypes step by step. From sustainable smart homes, virtual healthcare clinics, and smart education centers to urban vertical farming, augmented reality training modules, AI-powered virtual assistances, metaverse concert arenas, interactive public art installations, metaverse theme parks, digital twin museums, smart sports complexes to the comprehensive construction of a complete metaverse city prototype, this part is dedicated to equipping you with the necessary skills to employ these sophisticated tools in crafting smart city application prototypes that contribute significantly to the development of digital twin metaverse cities.

CHAPTER 11

Harnessing Digital Twin Development Tools to Build Digital Twin Cities

Building upon the foundation established in the first ten chapters, this chapter ushers in a new discussion on the practical aspects of creating the envisioned digital twin metaverse cities. This chapter marks a pivotal transition from theoretical discussions to actionable applications, specifically tailored for professionals leading the charge in urban digital transformation. It aims to equip them with a comprehensive suite of advanced digital twin development tools, vital for constructing the future digital twin metaverse cities. We explore the functionalities, applications, and integration methods of key digital twin development tools, preparing readers for the intricate process of building these sophisticated urban environments. Following this, Chapter 12 delves into the latest metaverse development technologies, offering guidance through the intricate landscape of digital twin technologies. This introduction serves as a bridge between theoretical insights and practical application, guiding professionals in leveraging these tools to shape the digital twin metaverse cities of the future.

CHAPTER 11   HARNESSING DIGITAL TWIN DEVELOPMENT TOOLS TO BUILD DIGITAL TWIN CITIES

1. AWS IoT TwinMaker

1) **What Is This Tool?**

    AWS IoT TwinMaker is a service provided by Amazon Web Services designed to simplify the creation of digital twins for the physical world. Digital twins are virtual representations of physical objects or systems, used for monitoring, simulation, and analysis. AWS IoT TwinMaker enables developers to create rich digital twins of real-world systems, combining live data from various sources, including IoT sensors, video feeds, and existing business applications, to create immersive and interactive experiences.

2) **This Tool URL**

    For detailed information and resources and to get started with AWS IoT TwinMaker.

3) **Brief History**

    AWS IoT TwinMaker was announced and launched by Amazon Web Services in late 2021. It was introduced to address the growing need for more accessible and integrated digital twin technologies in various industries, such as manufacturing, healthcare, and smart cities. By leveraging AWS's cloud infrastructure and IoT capabilities, IoT TwinMaker aims to streamline the digital twin development process, making it easier for organizations to innovate and enhance their operational efficiency.

4) **Smart City Application Examples**

- Manufacturing Plant Optimization: Creating digital twins of manufacturing equipment to monitor performance, predict maintenance needs, and optimize production processes.

- Smart Building Management: Developing virtual models of buildings to manage energy consumption, space utilization, and security systems efficiently.

- Healthcare Facility Simulation: Simulating hospital environments to improve patient flow, resource allocation, and emergency response protocols.

5) **Main Strengths**

- Integration with AWS Services: Seamless integration with other AWS services, such as IoT Core and Lambda, enhancing data collection, processing, and analysis capabilities.

- Ease of Use: Provides a user-friendly interface and tools that simplify the complex process of digital twin creation, making it accessible to developers and organizations without deep expertise in IoT or 3D modeling.

- Scalability: Leverages AWS's scalable infrastructure, allowing for the development of digital twins that can grow and evolve with the organization's needs.

6) **Limitations**

    - Learning Curve: Despite its ease of use, there's still a learning curve associated with understanding how to best leverage the service and integrate it with existing systems and data sources.

    - Dependence on AWS Ecosystem: While integration with AWS services is a strength, it also means organizations are further tied into the AWS ecosystem, which may not suit all businesses.

7) **Integrative Strategies**

    - Cross-Industry Collaborations: Encourage collaborations between different industries to share best practices and innovative uses of digital twin technology.

    - Education and Training: Develop comprehensive educational programs and certifications to help developers and businesses effectively utilize IoT TwinMaker and related AWS services.

AWS IoT TwinMaker is a transformative service that empowers organizations to create detailed and actionable digital twins of physical systems and environments. Its integration with the AWS ecosystem, ease of use, and scalability make it a powerful tool for enhancing operational efficiency, innovation, and decision-making across various industries. While there is a learning curve, the potential benefits and applications of leveraging IoT TwinMaker for digital twin development are vast and varied, offering significant value to businesses looking to embrace digital transformation.

2. Microsoft Azure Digital Twins

1) **What Is This Tool?**

   Microsoft Azure Digital Twins is an Internet of Things (IoT) platform that enables users to create comprehensive digital models of physical environments. It leverages the power of cloud computing to build next-generation IoT solutions that connect the physical and digital worlds. The platform allows developers to model entire environments, including people, places, and devices, to create rich, interconnected ecosystems with deep insights and analytics.

2) **This Tool URL**

   For more information, resources, and access to the Microsoft Azure Digital Twins platform, visit the official website.

3) **Brief History**

   Microsoft Azure Digital Twins was officially announced in 2018 as part of Microsoft's Azure IoT platform. It was designed to extend the capabilities of traditional IoT solutions by enabling a comprehensive virtual representation of real-world environments. Since its launch, Azure Digital Twins has evolved to support a wider range of scenarios, including smart buildings, smart cities, and industrial IoT applications, facilitating complex scenario modeling and advanced analytics.

4) **Smart City Application Examples**

- Smart Buildings: Implementing IoT solutions for energy management, security, and occupancy tracking to optimize resource use and enhance occupant comfort.

- Smart Cities: Modeling urban environments to monitor and control infrastructure, traffic, public services, and environmental conditions.

- Industrial IoT: Creating digital twins of manufacturing processes and supply chains to improve efficiency, predict maintenance needs, and optimize production.

5) **Main Strengths**

- Flexibility and Scalability: Supports a wide range of IoT applications, from small-scale deployments to extensive, city-wide models.

- Advanced Analytics and AI Integration: Offers deep insights into the modeled environments by leveraging Azure's analytics and AI capabilities.

- Real-Time Updates and Interactions: Enables dynamic interaction with and between digital twins, reflecting real-world changes in near real time.

6) **Limitations**

- Complexity in Deployment: The initial setup and configuration of Azure Digital Twins can be complex, requiring a steep learning curve for those unfamiliar with Azure's ecosystem.

CHAPTER 11   HARNESSING DIGITAL TWIN DEVELOPMENT TOOLS TO BUILD DIGITAL TWIN CITIES

- Cost: Depending on the scale and complexity of the deployment, costs can escalate, making it potentially prohibitive for smaller projects or organizations.

7) **Integrative Strategies**

- Partnerships with Solution Providers: Collaborating with specialized IoT solution providers to offer tailored implementations for specific industries.

- Educational Programs and Certifications: Developing comprehensive training materials and certification programs to help developers and IT professionals master the platform.

- Open Source SDKs and Tools: Providing open source software development kits (SDKs) and tools to encourage innovation and ease integration with other systems and platforms.

Microsoft Azure Digital Twins is a powerful platform for creating digital representations of physical environments, bridging the gap between the tangible and digital worlds. Its strengths in scalability, analytics, and real-time interactions make it an ideal choice for a variety of IoT applications, from smart buildings and cities to complex industrial scenarios. While challenges exist in terms of deployment complexity and potential costs, the platform's integrative strategies and ongoing development promise to expand its accessibility and applicability across industries.

3. Siemens MindSphere

1) **What Is This Tool?**

   Siemens MindSphere is a leading industrial IoT as a service solution developed by Siemens. It provides a powerful platform for connecting physical infrastructure to the digital world, enabling businesses to harness big data from their operations to drive efficiency, productivity, and innovation. MindSphere collects, analyzes, and visualizes data from connected devices and systems in real time, offering actionable insights that can help in optimizing processes and predicting maintenance needs.

2) **This Tool URL**

   For more information, resources, and access to Siemens MindSphere.

3) **Brief History**

   Siemens MindSphere was launched in 2016 as part of Siemens' digital business strategy. It was designed to provide industries with a robust cloud-based platform to implement IoT solutions easily. Over the years, MindSphere has evolved, incorporating advanced analytics, machine learning capabilities, and extensive connectivity options to support a wide range of industrial applications.

4) **Smart City Application Examples**

- Predictive Maintenance: Using IoT data to predict when machinery or components are likely to fail or require maintenance, minimizing downtime and repair costs.

- Energy Management: Monitoring and analyzing energy consumption across facilities to identify savings opportunities and optimize usage.

- Asset Tracking and Monitoring: Keeping track of physical assets in real time, providing insights into their usage, location, and condition.

5) **Main Strengths**

- Scalability: MindSphere can scale from small IoT projects to enterprise-wide solutions, accommodating the growing data needs of businesses.

- Openness and Flexibility: Offers an open API, allowing for the integration of custom applications and third-party services.

- Global Connectivity: Supports connections to a wide range of devices and systems, facilitating global operations.

6) **Limitations**

- Complexity: The platform's extensive capabilities can be complex to navigate for beginners or small businesses without dedicated IT support.

CHAPTER 11   HARNESSING DIGITAL TWIN DEVELOPMENT TOOLS TO BUILD DIGITAL TWIN CITIES

- Cost: While powerful, the cost of implementation and operation may be prohibitive for smaller organizations.

7) **Integrative Strategies**

- Partner Ecosystem: Collaborating with a wide range of partners to offer specialized applications and integrations that extend the platform's capabilities.

- Training and Support: Providing comprehensive training resources and support to help users maximize the value of MindSphere.

Siemens MindSphere is a powerful industrial IoT platform that enables businesses to connect their physical infrastructure to the digital realm, unlocking valuable insights and efficiencies. Its strengths lie in its scalability, openness, and global connectivity, making it suitable for a wide range of industrial applications. While the platform's complexity and cost may pose challenges, its potential to drive digital transformation and innovation in industrial operations is significant.

4. PTC ThingWorx

1) **What Is This Tool?**

PTC ThingWorx is an end-to-end IoT (Internet of Things) platform designed to enable the rapid development and deployment of smart, connected solutions. It provides a comprehensive set of tools for building and managing IoT applications, including connectivity, analytics, application development, and integration services. ThingWorx aims to simplify the process of creating IoT solutions, making it easier for businesses to collect, analyze, and act on data from various devices and sensors in real time.

2) **This Tool URL**

   For more information, resources, tutorials, and access to PTC ThingWorx, visit the official website.

3) **Brief History**

   PTC ThingWorx was launched in 2011 by ThingWorx, Inc., a company that aimed to pioneer the next generation of technology for the connected world. PTC, a global provider of technology platforms and solutions, acquired ThingWorx in 2013, integrating it into its broader portfolio of offerings. Since its acquisition, ThingWorx has evolved to become a leading platform in the IoT space, continually expanding its capabilities to meet the growing demands of the industry.

4) **Smart City Application Examples**

   - Smart Manufacturing: Automating production lines and monitoring equipment health in real time to optimize manufacturing processes and reduce downtime.

   - Connected Health: Enhancing patient care through connected medical devices that monitor patient health and provide actionable insights to healthcare providers.

   - Smart Cities: Managing urban services such as lighting, waste management, and traffic control systems to improve efficiency and sustainability.

5) **Main Strengths**

    - Comprehensive IoT Solution: Offers a complete suite of tools for IoT application development, from data collection and analytics to visualization and execution.

    - Flexible and Scalable: Supports a wide range of use cases and scales from small deployments to enterprise-level solutions.

    - Robust Security Features: Provides advanced security measures to protect data and ensure the integrity of IoT systems.

6) **Limitations**

    - Complexity for Beginners: The breadth of features and capabilities can be overwhelming for newcomers to IoT development.

    - Cost: The platform's comprehensive offerings and enterprise focus may represent a significant investment for smaller businesses or startups.

7) **Integrative Strategies**

    - Partner Ecosystem Development: Collaborating with a wide range of partners to offer integrated solutions that extend the platform's capabilities across different industries.

    - Education and Training Programs: Providing extensive documentation, online courses, and certification programs to help users maximize the platform's potential.

- Open Innovation Initiatives: Encouraging the development of custom extensions and applications by the community to address niche needs and enhance platform versatility.

PTC ThingWorx is a powerful IoT platform that facilitates the creation of smart, connected solutions across a variety of industries. It stands out for its comprehensive suite of development tools, scalability, and security features, making it a preferred choice for businesses looking to leverage IoT technology. While it offers extensive capabilities, the platform's complexity and cost may require careful consideration by newcomers and smaller entities. Nonetheless, ThingWorx's commitment to innovation, coupled with its strong partner ecosystem and support resources, positions it as a key enabler of IoT-driven transformation.

5. IBM Maximo Asset Monitor

1) **What Is This Tool?**

    IBM Maximo Asset Monitor is an AI-powered asset monitoring solution designed to help organizations across various industries manage and optimize their physical assets. This tool leverages IoT (Internet of Things) data and advanced analytics to provide real-time insights into asset performance, predict potential failures, and recommend preventive maintenance actions. It aims to improve asset reliability and availability while reducing operational costs and downtime.

2) **This Tool URL**

   For more information, resources, and access to IBM Maximo Asset Monitor, visit the official website.

3) **Brief History**

   IBM Maximo Asset Monitor builds upon the legacy of IBM Maximo, a leader in enterprise asset management (EAM) software, which has been in development for several decades. IBM's acquisition of Maximo in 2006 expanded its portfolio into asset management. Over the years, IBM has infused Maximo with AI and IoT capabilities, culminating in the launch of Maximo Asset Monitor, which specifically focuses on real-time monitoring and analytics of assets across industries.

4) **Smart City Application Examples**

   - Manufacturing: Monitoring machinery and equipment in real time to predict failures and schedule maintenance, thus reducing unplanned downtime and extending asset life.

   - Energy and Utilities: Tracking the performance of energy distribution networks to ensure reliability and efficiency, identifying issues before they lead to service interruptions.

   - Transportation and Logistics: Enhancing fleet management through real-time vehicle tracking, condition monitoring, and predictive maintenance to improve operational efficiency and safety.

5) **Main Strengths**

    - Predictive Analytics: Utilizes AI and machine learning to analyze asset data, predict potential issues, and suggest preventive measures.

    - Scalability: Can monitor thousands of assets across multiple locations, providing a comprehensive view of asset health and performance.

    - Integration Capabilities: Easily integrates with existing systems and IoT devices, allowing for a seamless flow of data and insights.

6) **Limitations**

    - Complexity: The initial setup and integration may require significant technical expertise and resources.

    - Cost: The investment in IBM Maximo Asset Monitor might be substantial, especially for small- to medium-sized enterprises.

7) **Integrative Strategies**

    - Partnering with IoT Device Manufacturers: To ensure seamless integration and data collection from a wide range of assets.

    - Developing Industry-Specific Solutions: Tailoring the platform to meet the unique needs of different industries, enhancing its applicability and effectiveness.

    - Offering Training and Support: Providing comprehensive training programs and robust technical support to help users maximize the tool's potential.

CHAPTER 11   HARNESSING DIGITAL TWIN DEVELOPMENT TOOLS TO BUILD DIGITAL TWIN CITIES

IBM Maximo Asset Monitor represents a sophisticated solution for real-time asset monitoring and management, leveraging AI and IoT technologies to enhance operational efficiency and reliability. Its predictive analytics capabilities and scalability make it a valuable asset across multiple industries. Despite challenges related to complexity and cost, strategic integrations and support can unlock its full potential, making it a cornerstone in the digital transformation of asset management.

6. Dassault Systèmes 3DEXPERIENCE

1) **What Is This Tool?**

   Dassault Systèmes' 3DEXPERIENCE platform is an extensive suite of software solutions designed to facilitate product design, analysis, simulation, and management in a collaborative virtual environment. It integrates various applications and tools into a single, unified environment, enabling companies across a wide range of industries—from aerospace and defense to fashion and retail—to innovate and bring complex products to market more efficiently. The platform emphasizes collaboration, allowing teams to work together seamlessly, regardless of geographical location.

2) **This Tool URL**

   For more information, resources, and access to the 3DEXPERIENCE platform, visit the official website.

CHAPTER 11   HARNESSING DIGITAL TWIN DEVELOPMENT TOOLS TO BUILD DIGITAL TWIN CITIES

3) **Brief History**

   The 3DEXPERIENCE platform was launched by Dassault Systèmes, a French software company known for its CAD and simulation software, in 2012. The platform was developed as part of the company's vision to provide a comprehensive digital environment that supports the entire life cycle of a product, from conception to manufacturing and beyond. Over the years, it has evolved to include a broader range of tools and capabilities, catering to the ever-growing needs of various industries.

4) **Smart City Application Examples**

   - Product Lifecycle Management (PLM): Companies in the automotive and aerospace sectors use the platform to manage the entire life cycle of complex products, from initial design to maintenance and recycling.

   - Simulation and Virtual Testing: Engineers use the platform's simulation tools to test and validate the performance of products under various conditions, reducing the need for physical prototypes.

   - Collaborative Design: Design teams across different locations collaborate in real time on the platform, sharing ideas, models, and feedback to accelerate the design process.

5) **Main Strengths**

   - Comprehensive Integration: Combines CAD, CAM, PLM, and more into a single platform, streamlining workflows and improving efficiency.

- Collaboration: Facilitates seamless collaboration among stakeholders, enhancing teamwork and innovation.

- Industry Versatility: Offers tailored solutions for a wide range of industries, addressing specific challenges and requirements.

6) **Limitations**

- Learning Curve: The platform's extensive capabilities and sophistication can present a steep learning curve for new users.

- Cost: The comprehensive nature and advanced features of the platform may represent a significant investment, potentially limiting access for smaller enterprises.

7) **Integrative Strategies**

- Developing targeted training programs and resources to help new users navigate the platform's complexities more effectively.

- Offering flexible pricing models or modular access to make the platform more accessible to startups and smaller companies.

The 3DEXPERIENCE platform by Dassault Systèmes represents a groundbreaking approach to collaborative product development and life cycle management. By integrating a wide range of tools and capabilities into a single environment, it enables industries to innovate, design, and bring products to market more efficiently. While its advanced features and cost may pose challenges for some, the platform's emphasis on

CHAPTER 11   HARNESSING DIGITAL TWIN DEVELOPMENT TOOLS TO BUILD DIGITAL TWIN CITIES

collaboration and industry-specific solutions make it a powerful asset for companies looking to navigate the complexities of modern product development.

7. GE Digital Predix

1) **What Is This Tool?**

    GE Digital's Predix is an industrial IoT platform designed to collect, analyze, and leverage data from industrial equipment. It enables developers to create applications that can monitor, optimize, and predict operational issues in industrial environments. Predix is built to handle the massive volumes of data generated by industrial assets, providing powerful analytics and machine learning capabilities to improve efficiency, reduce downtime, and enhance performance.

2) **This Tool URL**

    For more information about GE Digital Predix, resources, and documentation, visit the official website.

3) **Brief History**

    Launched by General Electric in 2015, Predix was developed to address the growing need for digital solutions in industrial operations. It was designed as a cloud-based Platform as a Service (PaaS) to support the development of applications focused on operational efficiency and asset performance management. Over the years, Predix has evolved,

CHAPTER 11   HARNESSING DIGITAL TWIN DEVELOPMENT TOOLS TO BUILD DIGITAL TWIN CITIES

incorporating more advanced analytics, machine learning, and data management capabilities to serve a wide range of industries, including aviation, power generation, and manufacturing.

4) **Smart City Application Examples**

- Asset Performance Management (APM): Companies use Predix to monitor and analyze the performance of industrial equipment, predicting failures before they occur and scheduling maintenance to prevent downtime.

- Operational Efficiency: Predix applications help optimize industrial processes by analyzing operational data in real time, identifying inefficiencies, and suggesting improvements.

- Energy Management: Utilizing data from smart sensors and equipment, Predix can optimize energy consumption across industrial facilities, reducing costs and environmental impact.

5) **Main Strengths**

- Scalability: Designed to handle the vast data volumes from industrial operations, making it suitable for enterprises of all sizes.

- Advanced Analytics and Machine Learning: Offers powerful tools for data analysis, helping predict and prevent equipment failures and optimize operations.

- Ecosystem and Integration: Supports a wide range of industrial applications and easily integrates with existing systems and equipment.

CHAPTER 11   HARNESSING DIGITAL TWIN DEVELOPMENT TOOLS TO BUILD DIGITAL TWIN CITIES

6) **Limitations**

    - Complexity: The platform's extensive capabilities can be daunting for beginners, requiring a steep learning curve.

    - Cost: The comprehensive features and enterprise-level solutions might represent a significant investment for smaller companies.

7) **Integrative Strategies**

    - Developing targeted training programs and certifications for developers and engineers to build expertise in using Predix for industrial applications.

    - Partnering with academic institutions and research centers to explore new use cases and innovations in industrial IoT and digital twin technologies.

GE Digital's Predix platform stands at the forefront of industrial IoT, offering robust tools for data analysis, machine learning, and operational optimization. While it primarily targets industrial applications, its principles of connectivity, data management, and predictive analytics are integral to developing complex systems within the metaverse, especially those simulating real-world industrial environments or smart infrastructure. Despite its complexity and cost, Predix's contribution to enhancing operational efficiency and sustainability in industries is undeniable.

8. Ansys Twin Builder

1) **What Is This Tool?**

    Ansys Twin Builder is a powerful software tool designed for the creation and deployment of digital twins. It enables users to build, validate, and deploy simulation-based digital twins efficiently. Ansys Twin Builder combines multi-domain systems simulation, 3D component modeling, and IoT data integration to offer a comprehensive platform for developing digital twins that closely replicate physical assets. It's used across various industries for optimizing the performance and maintenance of products throughout their life cycle.

2) **This Tool URL**

    For more information, resources, and access to Ansys Twin Builder, visit the official website.

3) **Brief History**

    Ansys Twin Builder emerged from Ansys' extensive experience in engineering simulation and its strategic focus on digital transformation technologies. As part of Ansys' portfolio, Twin Builder was developed to meet the growing demand for digital twin solutions across industries, leveraging Ansys' advanced simulation capabilities to model and analyze real-world phenomena in a virtual environment accurately.

4) **Smart City Application Examples**

- Predictive Maintenance: Industries use Twin Builder to create digital twins of machinery and equipment for predictive maintenance, reducing downtime and extending asset life.

- Energy Systems Optimization: Utility companies implement digital twins to simulate and optimize the performance of energy systems, including renewable energy sources, to enhance efficiency and reliability.

- Automotive Systems Simulation: Automotive manufacturers utilize Twin Builder to model and simulate vehicle systems for design optimization, performance testing, and integration of smart, connected features.

5) **Main Strengths**

- Comprehensive Simulation Capabilities: Offers advanced simulation tools that cover a wide range of physics and engineering disciplines, enabling detailed and accurate modeling of complex systems.

- Integration with IoT Data: Allows for the integration of real-time data from IoT devices, enhancing the fidelity and utility of digital twins with up-to-date operational insights.

- Scalability: Suitable for projects of various sizes, from individual components to entire systems, facilitating scalability in digital twin development.

6) **Limitations**

    - Learning Curve: The sophisticated nature of the tool and its broad capabilities can present a steep learning curve for new users unfamiliar with advanced simulation software.

    - Hardware Requirements: High-fidelity simulations demand significant computational resources, which may require substantial hardware investments.

7) **Integrative Strategies**

    - Educational Partnerships: Collaborating with universities and educational institutions to integrate Twin Builder into engineering and simulation curricula, preparing the next generation of engineers.

    - Industry-Specific Solutions: Developing templates and preconfigured models for specific industry applications to simplify the digital twin development process for users.

Ansys Twin Builder stands out as a leading solution for developing digital twins, offering robust simulation capabilities integrated with IoT data to mirror real-world assets accurately. It supports a wide range of applications from predictive maintenance to system optimization, providing significant value across industries. While the tool's complexity and hardware requirements may pose challenges, its potential to enhance product life cycle management and operational efficiency makes it a critical asset in the digital transformation toolkit.

9. Bosch IoT Suite

1) **What Is This Tool?**

    The Bosch IoT Suite is a flexible, open, and comprehensive software platform designed to provide the foundational tools needed for building and deploying scalable, secure, and sustainable Internet of Things (IoT) solutions. It supports a wide range of IoT applications, from managing devices and analyzing data to integrating various IoT components. The suite is aimed at businesses and developers looking to digitalize processes, enhance operational efficiencies, and develop new business models around connected devices.

2) **This Tool URL**

    For more information, resources, and access to the Bosch IoT Suite, visit the official website.

3) **Brief History**

    Developed by Bosch Software Innovations, the software and systems unit of the global Bosch Group, the Bosch IoT Suite was introduced to meet the growing needs of the IoT market. Bosch has been at the forefront of IoT technology development, leveraging its expertise in engineering and technology. Over the years, the suite has evolved, incorporating advanced technologies like AI and blockchain to further enhance IoT solutions.

4) **Smart City Application Examples**

- Smart City Solutions: Implementing IoT-enabled infrastructure management for traffic control, public safety, and environmental monitoring to improve urban living.

- Industrial IoT (IIoT): Enabling predictive maintenance, asset tracking, and factory automation to increase efficiency and reduce downtime in manufacturing processes.

- Connected Mobility: Supporting the development of connected vehicle solutions, including fleet management, telematics, and autonomous driving technologies.

5) **Main Strengths**

- Comprehensive IoT Toolkit: Offers a wide range of services for device management, analytics, and connectivity, providing a one-stop solution for IoT projects.

- Scalability and Security: Designed to scale from small to large IoT deployments while ensuring high levels of security for devices and data.

- Industry Expertise: Benefits from Bosch's extensive experience in engineering and technology, making it a reliable platform for industrial IoT solutions.

6) **Limitations**

- Complexity for Beginners: The breadth of features and capabilities might be overwhelming for newcomers to IoT development.

- Integration Challenges: While it's designed to be open and flexible, integrating with existing systems and technologies might require additional effort and expertise.

7) **Integrative Strategies**

- Partner Ecosystem Development: Establishing partnerships with technology providers, system integrators, and industry specialists to enhance the platform's capabilities and ease of integration.

- Education and Training: Offering comprehensive training programs, documentation, and support to help users effectively utilize the suite and overcome initial learning barriers.

The Bosch IoT Suite stands as a robust and versatile platform for the development and deployment of IoT solutions across various domains, including smart cities, industrial automation, and connected mobility. Its comprehensive set of tools, combined with scalability and security features, positions it as a key enabler of digital transformation. While the platform's complexity may pose a challenge for beginners, its potential to drive innovation and efficiency in IoT projects makes it an invaluable asset for businesses and developers looking to harness the power of connected devices.

CHAPTER 11 HARNESSING DIGITAL TWIN DEVELOPMENT TOOLS TO BUILD DIGITAL TWIN CITIES

10. SAP Digital Twin

1) **What Is This Tool?**

    SAP Digital Twin could be envisioned as an integrated digital replica of physical assets, systems, or processes managed through SAP's software ecosystem. This concept would leverage real-time data, analytics, and machine learning to mirror the life cycle of physical entities, offering insights, predicting outcomes, and facilitating decision-making.

2) **This Tool URL**

    For more information on SAP's solutions that might support digital twin technology, you can visit the SAP official website.

3) **Brief History**

    SAP has a long history of providing comprehensive ERP solutions to businesses worldwide. The concept of a digital twin has gained prominence in recent years, aligning with SAP's push toward digital transformation and the Internet of Things (IoT). While SAP does not offer a stand-alone digital twin product, it integrates digital twin capabilities into its software, particularly within its IoT and digital supply chain solutions, evolving these features as part of its broader enterprise technology offerings.

4) **Smart City Application Examples**

- Manufacturing Process Optimization: Creating digital replicas of manufacturing equipment to monitor performance, predict maintenance needs, and optimize production processes.

- Supply Chain Management: Enhancing supply chain visibility and efficiency by simulating logistics networks and operations, allowing for scenario planning and risk management.

- Asset Lifecycle Management: Managing the entire life cycle of physical assets from procurement to retirement, enabling companies to maximize asset utilization and reduce costs.

5) **Main Strengths**

- Integration with SAP Ecosystem: Seamless integration with SAP's extensive suite of business applications, offering a unified approach to enterprise resource planning and management.

- Real-Time Data Analysis and Prediction: Leveraging IoT data to provide real-time insights and predictive analytics for better decision-making.

- Enhanced Operational Efficiency: Improving operational processes through detailed analysis and simulation of physical assets and systems.

6) **Limitations**

- Complexity and Implementation: Integrating digital twin capabilities within large and complex SAP environments can be challenging, requiring significant time and expertise.

- Cost: Implementing and maintaining digital twin technology within the SAP ecosystem might incur substantial costs, potentially limiting accessibility for smaller businesses.

7) **Integrative Strategies**
   - Educational Programs and Partnerships: SAP could offer specialized training programs and partnerships to help businesses understand and implement digital twin technology effectively.
   - Open Innovation and Collaboration: Collaborating with customers, partners, and technology providers to co-innovate and expand the digital twin capabilities within SAP's software suite.

While not a stand-alone tool, the concept of SAP Digital Twin represents the integration of digital twin technology within SAP's comprehensive ERP and IoT solutions, offering businesses advanced capabilities to replicate, analyze, and optimize their physical assets and processes digitally. This approach can significantly enhance operational efficiency, predictive maintenance, and decision-making processes, albeit with considerations around complexity and cost. As digital transformation continues to evolve, SAP's role in enabling digital twin technology is likely to expand, providing valuable insights and efficiencies to enterprises worldwide.

11. Oracle Digital Twin

As of my last update in April 2023, Oracle's specific offerings in the digital twin space are part of their broader suite of cloud solutions and enterprise software products, focusing on enabling businesses to create

CHAPTER 11   HARNESSING DIGITAL TWIN DEVELOPMENT TOOLS TO BUILD DIGITAL TWIN CITIES

virtual representations of physical systems for various purposes, including monitoring, diagnostics, and predictive maintenance. Let's detail Oracle's approach to digital twins based on this context:

1) **What Is This Tool?**

    Oracle Digital Twin provides a comprehensive framework for businesses to create, visualize, and manage digital replicas of physical assets, processes, or systems. Integrated within Oracle's cloud ecosystem, it leverages IoT, AI, and analytics to offer real-time insights and predictive analytics, enhancing decision-making and operational efficiency.

2) **This Tool URL**

    For more information, resources, and insights on Oracle Digital Twin, you can visit Oracle's official website, specifically the sections dedicated to their cloud and IoT solutions.

3) **Brief History**

    Oracle has been a major player in the enterprise software market for decades. Their venture into digital twin technology is part of a natural progression, building on their extensive experience in databases, cloud computing, and enterprise resource planning (ERP) systems. Over the years, Oracle has continuously expanded its cloud offerings, incorporating IoT and AI capabilities to support the development and deployment of digital twins.

4) **Smart City Application Examples**

    - Manufacturing Process Optimization: Manufacturers use Oracle's digital twin technology to simulate and optimize their production lines, reducing downtime and increasing efficiency.

    - Supply Chain Management: Digital twins of supply chains help businesses predict disruptions, optimize logistics, and improve inventory management.

    - Asset Maintenance and Management: Enterprises deploy digital twins for predictive maintenance of physical assets, minimizing repair times and costs.

5) **Main Strengths**

    - Integration with Oracle Ecosystem: Seamless integration with Oracle's cloud services, ERP systems, and data analytics tools.

    - Scalability: Capable of handling complex, large-scale digital twin implementations across various industries.

    - Advanced Analytics and AI: Leverages Oracle's AI and analytics for deep insights, predictive maintenance, and optimized performance.

6) **Limitations**

    - Complexity and Cost: Implementing digital twin solutions can be complex and costly, particularly for small- to medium-sized enterprises.

- Learning Curve: Requires a significant investment of time and resources to fully leverage its capabilities and integrate it into existing workflows.

7) **Integrative Strategies**

- Education and Training Programs: Offering comprehensive training and certification programs to help businesses and IT professionals effectively utilize digital twin technology.

- Partnerships and Collaborations: Collaborating with industry leaders and innovators to expand the application scope and ease of use of digital twins.

Oracle Digital Twin represents a sophisticated approach to bridging the gap between physical assets and digital capabilities. By leveraging the power of IoT, AI, and analytics within Oracle's cloud ecosystem, it offers businesses valuable insights, predictive capabilities, and enhanced operational efficiency. Despite its complexity and the investment required to fully exploit its potential, Oracle Digital Twin stands out for its scalability, integration capabilities, and the strength of its analytics, making it a powerful tool for enterprises looking to innovate and optimize their operations in the digital age.

12. Autodesk Tandem

1) **What Is This Tool?**

Autodesk Tandem is a Virtual Asset Management (VAM) platform designed to create a comprehensive digital twin of any built asset. It allows for the integration and visualization of data from various stages of the asset's life cycle, from planning and design through construction to operation. Tandem enables stakeholders to access, analyze, and manage the information needed to make informed decisions, optimize operations, and enhance the sustainability of the built environment.

2) **This Tool URL**

   For more information, resources, and access to Autodesk Tandem, visit the official website.

3) **Brief History**

   Launched by Autodesk, a leader in 3D design, engineering, and entertainment software, Autodesk Tandem represents the company's foray into the digital twin technology space. It was developed to address the growing need for a more integrated and accessible way to manage the vast amounts of data associated with built assets, facilitating better operational efficiency and asset performance monitoring.

4) **Smart City Application Examples**

   - Facility Management: Leveraging Tandem for ongoing facility management, enabling operators to monitor systems in real time and predict maintenance needs.

   - Construction Project Handover: Simplifying the handover process by providing a comprehensive digital twin that includes all relevant data from the construction phase.

   - Energy Efficiency Optimization: Using the digital twin to analyze and optimize energy consumption patterns for sustainability improvements.

5) **Main Strengths**
    - Integration of Lifespan Data: Tandem excels in integrating data across the asset's entire life cycle, providing a unified view of its history and current status.
    - Enhanced Decision-Making: The accessibility of detailed asset information supports better-informed decision-making processes for maintenance, operations, and sustainability efforts.
    - User-Friendly Interface: Designed with user experience in mind, Tandem offers an intuitive interface that simplifies the complex data management of built assets.

6) **Limitations**
    - Learning Curve: New users may face a learning curve in navigating and fully utilizing the platform's extensive features.
    - Dependence on Data Quality: The effectiveness of the digital twin depends on the quality and completeness of the input data.

7) **Integrative Strategies**
    - Training and Education: Offering comprehensive training programs and resources to users, ensuring they can leverage the full potential of Tandem.
    - Open API for Integration: Encouraging the development of third-party integrations and extensions to enhance Tandem's capabilities and interoperability with other systems.

CHAPTER 11 HARNESSING DIGITAL TWIN DEVELOPMENT TOOLS TO BUILD DIGITAL TWIN CITIES

Autodesk Tandem is a pioneering Virtual Asset Management platform that bridges the gap between physical assets and their digital counterparts. By facilitating the integration, analysis, and management of data throughout an asset's life cycle, Tandem empowers stakeholders to optimize operational efficiency, enhance sustainability, and make more informed decisions. Despite the initial learning curve and the need for high-quality data, Tandem's intuitive design and powerful features position it as a key player in the digital twin and built asset management space.

In summing up Chapter 11, we provide a thorough exploration of a myriad of digital twin development tools that lay the groundwork for constructing digital twin metaverse cities. Beginning with AWS IoT TwinMaker, tailored for industrial scenarios and seamless integration of varied data sources, to the scalable Microsoft Azure Digital Twins, ideal for the physical environment modeling, and extending to Siemens MindSphere's enhancement of industrial processes through its IoT solutions, each tool undergoes a detailed analysis. PTC ThingWorx and IBM Maximo Asset Monitor stand out for their exceptional IoT and AI-powered asset management capabilities, respectively. Furthermore, Dassault Systèmes' 3DEXPERIENCE and GE Digital Predix are acclaimed for offering virtual twin experiences and operational insights. Ansys Twin Builder specializes in simulation-based digital twins, whereas SAP Digital Twin, Oracle Digital Twin, and Autodesk Tandem are recognized for their unique contributions to the digital twin technology in smart city frameworks. This comprehensive synthesis of tools' functionalities, strengths, and how they intertwine underscores their paramount importance in steering the urban environments toward a sustainable, efficient, and technologically forward metaverse cities.

CHAPTER 11 HARNESSING DIGITAL TWIN DEVELOPMENT TOOLS TO BUILD DIGITAL TWIN CITIES

As we transition from the solid groundwork and practical insights provided by exploring digital twin technologies in this chapter, we venture into the broader and equally transformative realm of metaverse development in Chapter 12. Here, we will unfold an array of cutting-edge metaverse development tools, platforms, and innovative strategies pivotal for creating immersive, interconnected digital worlds within the metaverse. Delving into the rich ecosystem of development tools that open the metaverse to creators, architects, and visionaries, the readers will be empowered with the knowledge to not just navigate but also actively contribute to the future of digital twin metaverse cities. Anticipate a comprehensive exploration that melds the digital and physical, pushing the boundaries of what's achievable in urban development and beyond.

CHAPTER 12

Crafting Metaverse Cities: Unveiling the Cutting-Edge Development Tools

In this chapter, we embark on an exhilarating journey into the heart of metaverse city creation, showcasing a treasure trove of innovative tools and platforms that are at the forefront of virtual world development. As we traverse this digital landscape, we uncover the astonishing capabilities of Unreal Engine's high-fidelity environments, Unity's versatile development ecosystem, and Roblox Studio's expansive universe of user-generated content. Furthermore, we dive into the transformative potential of Minecraft as a canvas for creative urban design, offering readers a glimpse into the endless possibilities for crafting personalized and immersive digital cities. Furthermore, we introduce cutting-edge AI tools, including the likes of ChatGPT and Genesis, which promise to revolutionize the metaverse with intelligent interactions and dynamic content creation. These AI powerhouses enable the development of smart, responsive environments that adapt and evolve, bringing the metaverse to life with unprecedented realism and interactivity.

CHAPTER 12   CRAFTING METAVERSE CITIES: UNVEILING THE CUTTING-EDGE DEVELOPMENT TOOLS

This chapter is your gateway to mastering the tools that empower today's visionaries to sculpt the digital cities of tomorrow. From the architectural grandeur enabled by Nvidia's Omniverse to the interactive narratives woven through Meta Spark, we delve into each tool's unique contributions to the metaverse ecosystem. Whether you're a developer, architect, or dreamer, this chapter equips you with the knowledge to navigate the burgeoning world of metaverse development confidently.

As we unravel the capabilities of these development tools, we lay the foundation for readers to not only grasp the technical intricacies but also to unleash their creativity in designing metaverse cities that are as boundless as their imagination. Get ready to step into a realm where digital and physical merge, pushing the boundaries of urban development into new, uncharted territories.

1. Unity

Unity is recognized for its versatility in game development, architectural visualizations, and creating interactive experiences. Unity's strength lies in its broad platform support and extensive asset store, making it ideal for developing immersive metaverse cities with rich interactive elements.

1) **What Is This Tool?**

    Unity is a leading cross-platform game engine and development environment used for creating video games, simulations, and other interactive 3D and 2D content. Its flexibility and ease of use make it accessible to both beginners and professionals, allowing for the development of projects across a wide range of devices, including PCs, consoles, mobile devices, and VR/AR hardware. Unity's comprehensive set of tools supports every stage of the development process, from design and modeling to animation and final deployment.

CHAPTER 12 CRAFTING METAVERSE CITIES: UNVEILING THE CUTTING-EDGE DEVELOPMENT TOOLS

2) **This Tool URL**

   For more information, resources, tutorials, and the Unity community, visit the Unity official website.

3) **Brief History**

   Unity was first launched in 2005 by Unity Technologies. It was initially developed as a game engine for the Mac OS X and has since expanded to support a vast array of platforms. Unity's focus on accessibility and cross-platform capabilities quickly made it popular among game developers. Over the years, Unity has evolved to support not just game development but also industries like film, automotive, architecture, and more, becoming a versatile platform for creating interactive and immersive experiences.

4) **Smart City Application Examples**

   - Video Game Development: Unity is behind many popular indie and mobile games, offering developers a flexible and powerful environment for game creation.

   - Virtual Reality (VR) and Augmented Reality (AR): Unity is widely used for developing immersive VR and AR experiences across various sectors, including entertainment, education, and healthcare.

   - Simulation and Training: Many industries use Unity for creating simulations for training purposes, such as flight simulators for aviation or medical procedure simulations for healthcare professionals.

5) **Main Strengths**

    - Cross-Platform Support: Unity's ability to deploy projects across a wide range of platforms is one of its biggest strengths, making it a go-to choice for developers.

    - Large Community and Asset Store: Unity boasts a massive community and a comprehensive asset store, providing resources and support that facilitate development.

    - User-Friendly Interface: Its intuitive interface and user-friendly tools lower the barrier to entry for new developers and non-programmers.

6) **Limitations**

    - Performance Issues: For very high-end or graphically intense projects, Unity can sometimes lag behind in performance compared to more specialized engines.

    - Learning Curve for Advanced Features: While Unity is accessible for beginners, mastering its more advanced features and optimizing projects can require a significant time investment.

7) **Integrative Strategies**

    - Promoting collaboration and integration with emerging technologies, such as AI and machine learning platforms, to enhance Unity's capabilities in simulation and predictive modeling.

- Expanding educational initiatives and partnerships to provide comprehensive training and resources, making advanced development skills more accessible to a broader audience.

Unity is a versatile and widely used game engine that empowers creators across various industries to bring their visions to life. Its cross-platform support, robust community, and extensive asset store make it an attractive platform for developing a wide range of interactive and immersive content. While challenges exist, particularly in handling very high-end projects, Unity's continuous updates and commitment to accessibility ensure it remains at the forefront of digital content creation tools.

2. Unreal Engine (UE)

Famed for its high-quality visuals and advanced rendering capabilities, Unreal Engine is a powerful tool for creating highly immersive and visually stunning metaverse environments, with strong support for VR and AR experiences.

1) **What Is This Tool?**

Unreal Engine, developed by Epic Games, is a powerful and advanced real-time 3D creation tool widely used across various industries. Renowned for its high-fidelity graphics and robust development environment, Unreal Engine enables creators to design, simulate, and render immersive experiences. Its applications range from video game development to architectural visualization, film and television content production, and beyond, making it a versatile tool for artists, designers, and developers aiming to push the boundaries of digital content creation.

2) **This Tool URL**

   For more information, resources, tutorials, and downloads, visit the Unreal Engine official website.

3) **Brief History**

   Unreal Engine was first developed by Tim Sweeney of Epic Games in 1998, with its debut in the first-person shooter game *Unreal*. Since its inception, it has undergone significant advancements, with several major versions introducing new features and improvements. The engine has evolved to support a wide range of platforms, including consoles, PCs, mobile devices, and VR, making it one of the most widely adopted engines for real-time 3D content creation.

4) **Smart City Application Examples**

   - Video Game Development: From indie titles to blockbuster AAA games, Unreal Engine is the foundation for numerous critically acclaimed video games.

   - Architectural Visualization: Architects and designers use Unreal Engine to create highly detailed and interactive visualizations of buildings and spaces.

   - Film and Television Production: Unreal Engine is utilized in the film and TV industry for virtual production, enabling real-time visual effects and environments.

5) **Main Strengths**

- High-Quality Visuals: Unreal Engine is known for its ability to produce high-fidelity visuals and cinematic-quality graphics.

- Versatility: Its wide range of tools and features supports diverse applications, from game development to simulation and visualization.

- Large Community and Ecosystem: A vast community of developers and creators, along with a rich ecosystem of assets and plugins, supports innovation and ease of development.

6) **Limitations**

- Complexity for Beginners: The extensive capabilities and advanced features of Unreal Engine can be overwhelming for newcomers to 3D development.

- Resource Intensity: High-quality visuals and complex projects can require significant hardware resources, potentially limiting access for individuals or small teams with limited budgets.

7) **Integrative Strategies**

- Encouraging collaboration between industries to explore new applications of Unreal Engine, such as in healthcare simulation or educational tools.

- Developing comprehensive training programs and resources to lower the barrier to entry for new users, ensuring a wider adoption and utilization of the engine.

CHAPTER 12   CRAFTING METAVERSE CITIES: UNVEILING THE CUTTING-EDGE DEVELOPMENT TOOLS

Unreal Engine stands as a cornerstone in the realm of real-time 3D creation, offering unparalleled graphical fidelity and a robust suite of development tools. Its impact extends beyond video game development into architectural visualization, film production, and more, demonstrating its versatility and power as a creative platform. While its complexity may pose challenges for beginners, the supportive community and the ongoing evolution of the engine continue to open up new possibilities for creators across various industries.

3. Nvidia's Omniverse

Nvidia's Omniverse is a platform designed for collaboration in creating and operating metaverse applications, featuring real-time simulation and photorealistic rendering capabilities. It's particularly beneficial for creating interconnected metaverse experiences that require high fidelity and physical accuracy.

1) **What Is This Tool?**

   Nvidia's Omniverse is a platform designed for collaboration and simulation in 3D production workflows. It enables artists, designers, and developers to work together in real-time across various software suites, facilitating a unified and interoperable workflow. Built on Nvidia's RTX technology, Omniverse leverages the power of ray tracing and AI to deliver photorealistic simulation environments. This platform is particularly useful for creating complex virtual worlds, digital twins, and simulations for industries ranging from entertainment and architecture to engineering and autonomous vehicle development.

CHAPTER 12 CRAFTING METAVERSE CITIES: UNVEILING THE CUTTING-EDGE DEVELOPMENT TOOLS

2) **This Tool URL**

For detailed information, resources, and access to Nvidia's Omniverse, visit the official website.

3) **Brief History**

Nvidia announced Omniverse at GTC 2019 as a platform aimed at enhancing collaboration in 3D workflows. It was initially released in beta to select partners and customers, with the goal of addressing the challenges of working across different 3D applications. Nvidia's vision for Omniverse is to create a "metaverse" for engineers, enabling real-time collaboration and simulation on a level previously not possible. Over time, it has evolved with added features, broader access, and integrations with popular 3D tools and engines, emphasizing its utility in creating interconnected virtual worlds.

4) **Smart City Application Examples**

- Architectural Visualization: Architects and designers use Omniverse to create and collaborate on highly realistic simulations of architectural projects.

- Automotive Simulation: The automotive industry utilizes Omniverse for designing, simulating, and visualizing advanced vehicle systems and autonomous driving scenarios.

- Digital Twin Creation: Industries ranging from manufacturing to city planning use Omniverse to build and operate digital twins, offering real-time insights and decision-making capabilities.

5) **Main Strengths**

    - Real-Time Collaboration: Enables seamless collaboration across different software and teams, breaking down traditional workflow barriers.

    - Photorealistic Simulation: Powered by RTX ray tracing and AI, Omniverse delivers high-fidelity visuals and simulations.

    - Extensible and Interoperable: Supports a wide range of 3D applications and tools, making it highly versatile for various industries and use cases.

6) **Limitations**

    - Hardware Requirements: The high-quality simulations and rendering capabilities require powerful hardware, specifically Nvidia RTX GPUs, which may not be accessible to all users.

    - Complexity: The breadth of features and potential applications can make Omniverse complex to navigate for newcomers.

7) **Integrative Strategies**

    - Partnering with software developers and industry leaders to expand Omniverse's ecosystem, ensuring broader compatibility and more integrative use cases.

    - Offering training and resources to help users leverage the full potential of Omniverse, reducing the learning curve and encouraging adoption across industries.

CHAPTER 12   CRAFTING METAVERSE CITIES: UNVEILING THE CUTTING-EDGE DEVELOPMENT TOOLS

Nvidia's Omniverse represents a groundbreaking platform for collaborative creation and simulation within the metaverse and beyond. It stands out for its ability to unify workflows, deliver photorealistic environments, and support real-time collaboration across a multitude of industries. While its advanced capabilities necessitate high-performance hardware, Omniverse's potential to transform 3D content creation, digital twin development, and simulation workflows is unparalleled, marking a significant step toward a more interconnected and immersive digital future.

4. Amazon Sumerian

Amazon Sumerian simplifies the creation of VR, AR, and 3D applications, making it accessible for developers to build educational and training environments within smart cities.

1) **What Is This Tool?**

   Amazon Sumerian is a managed service from Amazon Web Services (AWS) that allows developers to create and run virtual reality (VR), augmented reality (AR), and 3D applications quickly and easily without requiring specialized programming or 3D graphics expertise. With Sumerian, users can build highly immersive and interactive scenes for a variety of uses, including training simulations, virtual concierge services, and interactive product demos, deployable across web and mobile platforms.

2) **This Tool URL**

   For more information and resources and to start building with Amazon Sumerian, visit the official website.

3) **Brief History**

   Amazon Sumerian was announced by AWS in November 2017, aiming to democratize the creation of VR, AR, and 3D content by eliminating the need for specialized skills in 3D graphics. It was designed to integrate seamlessly with other AWS services, offering a comprehensive set of tools for building, hosting, and deploying immersive experiences. Amazon Sumerian was part of Amazon's broader efforts to expand its offerings in the cloud services and emerging technology sectors.

4) **Smart City Application Examples**

   - Education and Training: Educational institutions and corporations use Sumerian to create interactive learning experiences and training simulations.

   - Retail and Ecommerce: Retailers leverage Sumerian to create virtual showrooms and product demonstrations, enhancing online shopping experiences.

   - Hospitality and Service: Companies in the hospitality sector use Sumerian to build virtual concierge services and interactive customer service experiences.

5) **Main Strengths**

   - Ease of Use: Sumerian's user-friendly interface allows for the creation of immersive experiences without deep technical knowledge of VR or AR development.

- AWS Integration: Seamless integration with other AWS services, such as Amazon Lex for natural language understanding and AWS Lambda for serverless computing, enhances the functionality of applications.

- Cross-Platform: Supports deployment across various platforms, including mobile devices, web browsers, and head-mounted displays, without requiring platform-specific adjustments.

6) **Limitations**

- Limited Customization: While accessible, Sumerian might not offer the same level of depth and customization as more specialized or advanced 3D development tools.

- Dependency on AWS Ecosystem: Being tied to the AWS ecosystem could be limiting for developers or organizations that prefer or require a multicloud or different hosting solution.

7) **Integrative Strategies**

- Encouraging the development of plugins and extensions that expand Sumerian's capabilities and integration with non-AWS services and platforms.

- Fostering partnerships with educational institutions and industries to develop tailored applications, driving innovation and practical use cases in VR, AR, and 3D content creation.

CHAPTER 12   CRAFTING METAVERSE CITIES: UNVEILING THE CUTTING-EDGE DEVELOPMENT TOOLS

Amazon Sumerian is a versatile tool designed to simplify the creation of VR, AR, and 3D applications, making immersive and interactive digital experiences more accessible to a broad range of creators. Its strengths lie in its ease of use, integration with AWS services, and cross-platform support, although it faces limitations in customization and a dependence on the AWS ecosystem. Despite these challenges, Sumerian represents a significant step forward in democratizing the development of immersive content, with potential applications spanning education, retail, hospitality, and beyond.

5. Roblox Studio

Roblox Studio enables the creation of multiplayer online experiences, offering potential for educational games and social hubs within the metaverse.

1) **What Is This Tool?**

    Roblox Studio is the development environment provided by Roblox, allowing users to create, share, and monetize immersive 3D games and experiences on the Roblox platform. It offers a comprehensive set of tools for building virtual worlds, scripting game mechanics, and designing interactive content. Aimed at a wide range of users, from beginners to experienced developers, Roblox Studio facilitates the creation of diverse experiences accessible on various devices, including PC, mobile, and VR.

2) **This Tool URL**

    For more information, resources, and tutorials and to download Roblox Studio, visit the official website.

CHAPTER 12 CRAFTING METAVERSE CITIES: UNVEILING THE CUTTING-EDGE DEVELOPMENT TOOLS

3) **Brief History**

   Roblox Studio was launched alongside the Roblox platform in 2006, founded by David Baszucki and Erik Cassel. It was designed to empower users to create their own games and experiences within the Roblox ecosystem. Over the years, Roblox Studio has evolved, incorporating more sophisticated development tools, a more user-friendly interface, and enhanced capabilities for creators to build complex and engaging virtual experiences, contributing to the platform's growth into a vast online community.

4) **Smart City Application Examples**

   - Educational Games: Developers use Roblox Studio to create interactive learning experiences, teaching subjects like math, science, and history through engaging gameplay.

   - Virtual Events: Roblox Studio has been used to host virtual concerts, meetups, and other events, bringing together users in immersive settings.

   - Simulation Games: Many popular Roblox games are simulations, allowing players to experience various careers, adventures, and scenarios.

5) **Main Strengths**

   - Accessibility: Its user-friendly interface makes game development accessible to novices while still offering depth for more experienced developers.

CHAPTER 12 CRAFTING METAVERSE CITIES: UNVEILING THE CUTTING-EDGE DEVELOPMENT TOOLS

- Cross-Platform Functionality: Games created in Roblox Studio can be published and played across multiple platforms, including PC, mobile, and VR.
- Monetization Opportunities: Roblox Studio provides developers with the opportunity to earn revenue through in-game purchases and passes.

6) **Limitations**

- Performance Limitations: Games built with Roblox Studio may not match the graphical fidelity or performance of titles made with more advanced engines like Unreal or Unity.
- Content Restrictions: Being a platform aimed at younger audiences, Roblox imposes strict content guidelines, which can limit creative freedom.

7) **Integrative Strategies**

- Encouraging educational institutions to use Roblox Studio as a tool for teaching coding and game design.
- Partnering with brands and content creators to develop unique virtual experiences and merchandise within the Roblox ecosystem.

Roblox Studio is a powerful and accessible tool that democratizes game development, enabling creators of all ages and skill levels to design, build, and share their own games and experiences within the Roblox platform. Its strengths lie in its ease of use, cross-platform support, and opportunities for monetization, though it faces limitations in terms of performance and creative restrictions. Despite these challenges, Roblox Studio has played a pivotal role in fostering a vibrant and creative community, making it a significant player in the realm of user-generated content and virtual experiences.

CHAPTER 12   CRAFTING METAVERSE CITIES: UNVEILING THE CUTTING-EDGE DEVELOPMENT TOOLS

6. CryEngine

CryEngine is known for its advanced graphics and physics. It supports the development of visually impressive games and simulations for the metaverse.

1) **What Is This Tool?**

   CryEngine is a powerful game engine designed for the development of highly detailed, immersive virtual environments. Known for its cutting-edge graphics, real-time rendering capabilities, and robust physics system, CryEngine enables developers to create visually stunning and interactive experiences. It caters to a wide range of applications, from video games to simulations and beyond, making it a versatile tool for creators aiming to push the boundaries of digital realism.

2) **This Tool URL**

   For detailed information, resources, and the latest updates on CryEngine, visit their official website.

3) **Brief History**

   CryEngine was initially developed by Crytek for the first-person shooter game *Far Cry*, released in 2004. It quickly gained acclaim for its impressive graphics and physics, distinguishing itself in the game development industry. Since then, CryEngine has undergone several iterations, each enhancing its capabilities, including improved rendering techniques, enhanced AI, and more efficient toolsets for developers. Its evolution reflects a commitment to providing a high-fidelity development platform for creating complex, interactive virtual worlds.

4) **Smart City Application Examples**

- Game Development: CryEngine has been used to create several critically acclaimed video games, including the *Crysis* series, known for its groundbreaking visuals and gameplay.

- Simulation Training: Its realistic environmental rendering and physics simulation capabilities make it ideal for military, flight, and emergency response training programs.

- Architectural Visualization: Architects and designers use CryEngine to create detailed, immersive representations of buildings and landscapes, enabling virtual walk-throughs and environment interaction.

5) **Main Strengths**

- Advanced Graphics and Lighting: CryEngine's advanced rendering capabilities produce stunningly realistic visuals, with dynamic lighting and shadows that enhance the immersion of virtual environments.

- Powerful Physics Engine: It offers a sophisticated physics simulation, allowing for realistic interactions within the virtual world, which is crucial for both games and simulations.

- Scalability: CryEngine supports a wide range of hardware, from high-end PCs to consoles, allowing for flexible development and deployment of applications.

CHAPTER 12 CRAFTING METAVERSE CITIES: UNVEILING THE CUTTING-EDGE DEVELOPMENT TOOLS

6) **Limitations**

    - Steep Learning Curve: Due to its advanced features and capabilities, new users may find CryEngine challenging to learn and master, requiring significant time and resources.

    - Limited Community Support: Compared to other engines like Unity or Unreal, CryEngine has a smaller developer community, which can limit resources and support for new developers.

7) **Integrative Strategies**

    - Leveraging its visual and physical simulation strengths, integrating CryEngine into multidisciplinary projects can enhance realism in simulations for urban planning, environmental studies, and interactive media.

    - Collaborating with educational institutions to develop training modules and curricula around CryEngine can help mitigate its steep learning curve and foster a larger, more engaged community of developers.

CryEngine stands out as a robust platform for developing high-fidelity virtual environments, offering unparalleled graphics and physics simulation capabilities. While it presents challenges in terms of usability and community support, its strengths in creating immersive, realistic experiences make it a valuable tool for a wide range of applications, from game development to architectural visualization and simulation training. Its ongoing development and potential for integrative projects highlight its role as a significant contributor to the advancement of virtual and augmented reality technologies.

CHAPTER 12   CRAFTING METAVERSE CITIES: UNVEILING THE CUTTING-EDGE DEVELOPMENT TOOLS

7. Blender

Blender is a free, open source 3D creation suite ideal for asset creation, supporting the design of detailed virtual worlds and animated content.

1) **What Is This Tool?**

   Blender is an open source 3D creation suite that supports the entirety of the 3D pipeline—modeling, rigging, animation, simulation, rendering, compositing, and motion tracking, even video editing and game creation. Highly favored for its versatility, Blender is used by hobbyists and professionals alike, in industries ranging from film and animation to video game development, architectural visualization, and more. It stands out for being entirely free, offering powerful tools that rival those of commercial counterparts.

2) **This Tool URL**

   For comprehensive resources, tutorials, and downloads, the official Blender website is the go-to destination.

3) **Brief History**

   Blender began as an in-house tool for a Dutch animation studio, NeoGeo, in the early 1990s. It was developed by Ton Roosendaal, the studio's founder. In 2002, Blender was released as open source software under the GNU General Public License, thanks to a crowdfunding campaign that helped buy out the rights from investors. Since then, it has grown significantly, supported by a dedicated

CHAPTER 12 CRAFTING METAVERSE CITIES: UNVEILING THE CUTTING-EDGE DEVELOPMENT TOOLS

community and the Blender Foundation. The software has seen continuous improvements and expansions in its functionality, becoming a leading tool in 3D content creation.

4) **Smart City Application Examples**

- Architectural Visualization: Architects and designers rely on Blender for creating detailed 3D models and renderings of architectural projects, allowing for immersive presentations and walk-throughs.

- Film and Animation: Blender is widely used for creating animated short films, feature films, and visual effects. Projects like *Big Buck Bunny* and *Sintel* demonstrate its capabilities in this field.

- Video Game Development: Game developers utilize Blender for creating 3D models, animations, and environments for video games, benefiting from its comprehensive toolset and integration with game engines.

5) **Main Strengths**

- Comprehensive Toolset: Blender offers a wide range of 3D creation tools, covering every aspect of the 3D pipeline without the need for external software.

- Open Source and Free: It is completely free and open source, making high-quality 3D creation accessible to everyone.

- Strong Community Support: A large, active community contributes to Blender's development, providing extensive tutorials, plugins, and support.

6) **Limitations**

    - Learning Curve: While powerful, Blender's comprehensive features can be overwhelming for beginners, requiring a significant investment of time to learn effectively.

    - Performance with Large Projects: Handling large, complex scenes can be challenging, with performance sometimes lagging behind that of some proprietary software.

7) **Integrative Strategies**

    - Encouraging the development and sharing of custom add-ons and plugins can enhance Blender's functionality and usability for specific industries, such as game development or scientific visualization.

    - Partnering with educational institutions to include Blender in digital art and design curricula can help mitigate the learning curve and cultivate a new generation of skilled users.

Blender stands as a beacon in the 3D creation world, offering a versatile, comprehensive suite of tools that cater to professionals and hobbyists across various industries. Its open source nature not only democratizes 3D content creation but also fosters a vibrant community dedicated to its continuous improvement. Despite challenges related to its learning curve and performance with very large projects, Blender's strengths in versatility, accessibility, and community support make it an invaluable tool for anyone looking to explore or expand their 3D creation capabilities.

8. Autodesk Maya

Autodesk is a comprehensive tool for 3D modeling, animation, and rendering, facilitating complex animations and character creation for the metaverse.

1) **What Is This Tool?**

   Autodesk Maya is a highly advanced 3D computer graphics software used for creating interactive 3D applications, including video games, animated film, TV series, and visual effects. Maya is renowned for its comprehensive set of tools that cover the full spectrum of the 3D development pipeline, including modeling, simulation, rendering, and animation. It is particularly noted for its powerful animation tools, which have made it a standard among animation and VFX studios worldwide.

2) **This Tool URL**

   For more information, resources, tutorials, and updates on Autodesk Maya, visit their official website.

3) **Brief History**

   Developed by Alias Systems Corporation (formerly Alias|Wavefront) and currently owned and maintained by Autodesk, Inc., Maya was originally released in 1998. Maya has undergone significant evolution and improvement, incorporating new technologies and functionalities that have kept it at the forefront of the industry. It has played a crucial role in the creation of numerous award-winning films, games, and television projects, cementing its status as a cornerstone tool for 3D artists and animators.

4) **Smart City Application Examples**

- Film and Visual Effects: Maya is extensively used in the film industry to create realistic character animations and visual effects. Movies like *Avatar* and *Frozen* have utilized Maya for their groundbreaking visual effects and animations.

- Video Game Development: Game developers use Maya to model, rig, and animate characters, environments, and in-game assets.

- Television and Advertisements: Maya is a go-to tool for creating animated content for television, including commercials, TV series, and title sequences.

5) **Main Strengths**

- Advanced Animation and Rigging Tools: Maya's sophisticated animation toolkit allows for the creation of complex animations with ease, making it ideal for character animation and cinematic sequences.

CHAPTER 12 CRAFTING METAVERSE CITIES: UNVEILING THE CUTTING-EDGE DEVELOPMENT TOOLS

- Highly Customizable: Maya can be extensively customized through its MEL (Maya Embedded Language) scripting and Python support, allowing studios to tailor the software to their specific project needs.

- Industry Standard: Being an industry standard, Maya offers extensive learning resources, a vast user community, and interoperability with other VFX and animation tools.

6) **Limitations**

- Cost: Compared to some other 3D modeling and animation tools, especially open source options, Maya can be expensive, making it less accessible for independent creators and small studios.

- Complexity: The vast array of features and customization options can make Maya intimidating for beginners, requiring a significant time investment to learn effectively.

7) **Integrative Strategies**

- Developing partnerships with educational institutions to incorporate Maya into their curriculum can help new artists become proficient with the tool.

- Encouraging the development of plugins and extensions can further enhance Maya's capabilities and application in various fields, such as virtual reality and game development.

CHAPTER 12 CRAFTING METAVERSE CITIES: UNVEILING THE CUTTING-EDGE DEVELOPMENT TOOLS

Autodesk Maya stands as a titan in the 3D modeling, animation, and rendering space, offering unparalleled tools for creators in the film, television, and game development industries. Its robust set of features for animation and rigging, combined with its adaptability and status as an industry standard, make it an essential tool for professionals. However, its complexity and cost may pose challenges for beginners and smaller studios. Despite these hurdles, Maya's impact on the digital content creation landscape is undeniable, driving innovation and creativity across multiple media platforms.

9. SketchUp

SketchUp offers intuitive tools for architectural design; it is excellent for urban planning models and visualization projects within the metaverse.

1) **What Is This Tool?**

   SketchUp is a 3D modeling computer program for a wide range of drawing applications such as architectural, interior design, landscape architecture, civil and mechanical engineering, film, and video game design. It is known for its user-friendly interface that simplifies the process of 3D design, making it accessible to both professionals and hobbyists. SketchUp allows users to quickly sketch out 3D models, offering tools for modeling and editing, as well as a vast repository of premade models in its 3D Warehouse.

2) **This Tool URL**

   For more information, resources, tutorials, and the SketchUp community, visit their official website.

3) **Brief History**

   SketchUp was initially developed by @Last Software and released in August 2000. It was designed to offer a more intuitive and flexible approach to 3D modeling than other available tools at the time. Google acquired SketchUp in 2006, integrating it with Google Earth to allow users to model buildings for the Google Earth application. In 2012, Trimble Navigation (now Trimble Inc.) acquired SketchUp from Google, focusing on further developing its capabilities for professional markets.

4) **Smart City Application Examples**

   - Architectural Design: SketchUp is widely used by architects and designers for creating detailed 3D models of buildings, allowing for easy visualization and modification.

   - Interior Design: Interior designers use SketchUp to lay out spaces, experiment with decor, and visualize design concepts for clients.

   - Urban Planning: Urban planners and landscape architects utilize SketchUp for planning and visualizing new developments, landscapes, and public spaces.

5) **Main Strengths**

   - Intuitive Use: SketchUp's user-friendly interface makes it accessible to users of all skill levels, encouraging experimentation and learning.

- Extensive Model Library: The 3D Warehouse provides users with access to a vast library of premade models, significantly speeding up the design process.

- Versatility: It is versatile enough to be used in a wide range of industries, from architecture to video game design.

6) **Limitations**

- Limited Rendering Capabilities: While SketchUp is excellent for modeling, its built-in rendering capabilities are somewhat basic compared to specialized rendering software.

- Performance Issues with Large Models: Users may experience performance lags or difficulties in managing very large or complex models.

7) **Integrative Strategies**

- Enhancing SketchUp's capabilities through plugins and extensions developed by the community or third-party companies can address some of its limitations, particularly in rendering and performance.

- Encouraging collaboration between Trimble and educational institutions can help integrate SketchUp into curriculums, training the next generation of designers and architects.

SketchUp is a powerful yet user-friendly tool for 3D modeling, beloved by professionals and hobbyists alike for its intuitive design and versatility across various industries. While it shines in quick modeling and the ease of

CHAPTER 12   CRAFTING METAVERSE CITIES: UNVEILING THE CUTTING-EDGE DEVELOPMENT TOOLS

use, it faces limitations in rendering and handling large, complex models. Nonetheless, its extensive model library and the potential for expansion through plugins make it a valuable tool in the design process, from conceptualization to visualization.

10. ZBrush

ZBrush specializes in high-detail modeling for character design and complex textures, enhancing the visual quality of metaverse environments.

1) **What Is This Tool?**

    ZBrush is a digital sculpting tool that combines 3D/2.5D modeling, texturing, and painting. It uses a proprietary "pixol" technology which stores lighting, color, material, orientation, and depth information for the points making up all objects on the screen. This unique approach allows for an incredibly intuitive and powerful sculpting experience that feels more like traditional sculpting. ZBrush is widely used in the film, gaming, and illustration industries for its ability to create highly detailed models and textures.

2) **This Tool URL**

    For more information, resources, and tutorials and to join the ZBrush community, visit their official website.

3) **Brief History**

    ZBrush was first introduced by Pixologic in 1999, developed by Ofer Alon, also known as "Pixolator." Initially designed as a software for creating 2.5D pixel-based art, it has evolved into a powerful 3D modeling and sculpting tool. Over the years, ZBrush has become a staple in digital art, particularly in the entertainment industry, for its innovative approach to modeling and sculpting digital and virtual entities.

4) **Smart City Application Examples**

- Character Design: ZBrush is extensively used in the gaming and film industries for character and creature design, enabling artists to sculpt complex models with high levels of detail.

- Concept Art: Concept artists use ZBrush to bring their visions to life, creating detailed 3D models and illustrations for films, video games, and consumer products.

- Jewelry Design: ZBrush is also used in the jewelry design industry, allowing designers to sculpt detailed pieces that can be directly 3D printed or used in the manufacturing process.

5) **Main Strengths**

- High-Detail Sculpting: ZBrush allows for the creation of extremely high-detail models, thanks to its powerful sculpting capabilities and the unique pixol technology.

- Intuitive Interface and Tools: Despite its complexity, ZBrush offers an intuitive set of tools that mimic real-world sculpting techniques.

CHAPTER 12 CRAFTING METAVERSE CITIES: UNVEILING THE CUTTING-EDGE DEVELOPMENT TOOLS

- Dynamic Tessellation: ZBrush's DynaMesh technology dynamically tessellates the model, allowing artists to create complex shapes and details without worrying about the topology.

6) **Limitations**

- Steep Learning Curve: The unique approach and vast array of features in ZBrush can be overwhelming for newcomers, requiring a significant time investment to master.

- Hardware Requirements: High-detail sculpting in ZBrush demands powerful hardware, particularly for models with millions of polygons, which can be a barrier for some users.

7) **Integrative Strategies**

- Encouraging the development of plugins and integrations that enhance ZBrush's functionality in various industries, such as virtual reality and medical visualization.

- Promoting educational programs and online tutorials tailored to different skill levels can help mitigate the steep learning curve associated with ZBrush.

ZBrush is a groundbreaking digital sculpting tool that has revolutionized 3D modeling and texturing in the entertainment industry. Its ability to handle incredibly detailed models with an intuitive set of sculpting tools makes it a favorite among professionals. While it poses challenges for beginners and demands high-performance hardware, ZBrush's capabilities in bringing intricate designs to life are unmatched.

Its continued evolution and the growing ecosystem of plugins and educational resources further cement its status as an indispensable tool for digital artists.

11. Tilt Brush

Tilt Brush enables 3D painting in virtual reality, suitable for creating immersive art and conceptual designs for metaverse spaces.

1) **What Is This Tool?**

   Tilt Brush is a groundbreaking virtual reality (VR) application that enables users to paint in three-dimensional space with virtual reality. Using motion-controlled handheld controllers, artists can create paintings and sculptures with strokes of virtual paint in an immersive environment. This tool opens up new possibilities for artists, designers, and creatives, allowing them to explore spatial compositions, intricate designs, and immersive artworks in a fully 3D space.

2) **This Tool URL**

   For more information, resources, and community projects, visit the official Tilt Brush website, which has been archived by Google.

3) **Brief History**

   Tilt Brush was originally developed by Skillman & Hackett, a small team that Google acquired in 2015. Following the acquisition, Google further developed Tilt Brush, releasing it to the public as a VR painting tool. It became one of the first applications to

CHAPTER 12 CRAFTING METAVERSE CITIES: UNVEILING THE CUTTING-EDGE DEVELOPMENT TOOLS

showcase the potential of creative work in virtual reality, offering an innovative platform for artists and designers to experiment with 3D spatial artwork. In 2021, Google announced it would no longer actively develop Tilt Brush, opting instead to make it open source, allowing the community to continue its development.

4) **Smart City Application Examples**

   - Artistic Expression: Artists use Tilt Brush to create immersive art installations and exhibitions, exploring new forms of artistic expression within virtual spaces.

   - Design and Prototyping: Designers utilize Tilt Brush for spatial design and prototyping, allowing them to visualize and iterate on 3D concepts in real time.

   - Education and Training: Educational institutions incorporate Tilt Brush into their curriculum to teach concepts of 3D design, art, and spatial awareness, offering a hands-on experience with VR technology.

5) **Main Strengths**

   - Intuitive User Interface: Tilt Brush offers an intuitive and user-friendly interface that allows users to easily navigate and create within the 3D space.

   - Creative Freedom: It provides artists and designers with a new level of creative freedom, enabling the creation of artworks that are not possible with traditional mediums.

- Community and Open Source: Since becoming open source, Tilt Brush has benefited from community-driven improvements and integrations, expanding its capabilities and applications.

6) **Limitations**

    - Hardware Dependency: Tilt Brush requires VR hardware to use, which can be a barrier for those without access to VR technology.

    - Learning Curve for Traditional Artists: Artists accustomed to traditional mediums may face a learning curve in adapting to spatial 3D drawing and the virtual environment.

7) **Integrative Strategies**

    - Encouraging collaboration between artists, developers, and educators to create new plugins and tools that expand Tilt Brush's functionality across various fields, such as therapeutic art and virtual exhibitions.

    - Integrating Tilt Brush into VR-based curriculum in schools and workshops to foster creativity and innovation in art and design education.

Tilt Brush stands as a pioneering tool in the realm of virtual reality, offering artists and designers a unique platform for exploring and creating 3D art in an immersive environment. Its intuitive design and open source status encourage ongoing innovation and application across various fields, from artistic expression to education. While the requirement for VR hardware may limit accessibility, Tilt Brush's impact on the creative process and its potential for future applications in virtual and augmented reality spaces are undeniable.

CHAPTER 12   CRAFTING METAVERSE CITIES: UNVEILING THE CUTTING-EDGE DEVELOPMENT TOOLS

12. ChatGPT for Metaverse

ChatGPT potentially enhances metaverse development by enabling dynamic content generation, AI-driven character interactions, and complex narrative scripting, providing a foundation for engaging and interactive virtual worlds.

1) **What Is This Tool?**

    ChatGPT for Metaverse refers to the integration of advanced conversational AI, like ChatGPT, into virtual worlds and metaverse platforms. This application of AI technology allows for the creation of interactive, intelligent non-player characters (NPCs), virtual assistants, and automated customer service agents within these digital spaces. By leveraging natural language processing and understanding, ChatGPT can provide users with immersive, engaging interactions, enhance storytelling, and offer practical support in navigating virtual environments.

2) **This Tool URL**

    As ChatGPT for Metaverse involves the integration of AI technology rather than a stand-alone application, there isn't a specific URL for this tool. However, for more information on ChatGPT and its capabilities, one might visit OpenAI's official website.

3) **Brief History**

    ChatGPT, developed by OpenAI, represents a significant advancement in AI, particularly in natural language understanding and generation.

Since its inception, it has been adapted and integrated into various applications, including the metaverse, where its ability to process and generate human-like text transforms user interaction within virtual environments. The integration of such AI into the metaverse is a more recent development, coinciding with the growth of virtual worlds and the increased demand for intelligent, interactive content.

4) **Smart City Application Examples**

- Interactive NPCs: Creating NPCs that can engage in meaningful conversations, provide quests, or offer guidance within virtual worlds.

- Virtual Assistants: Assisting users in navigating the metaverse, providing information, or facilitating transactions and interactions.

- Automated Customer Service: Offering customer support within virtual marketplaces, events, or platforms, handling inquiries, and providing assistance.

5) **Main Strengths**

- Enhanced User Interaction: ChatGPT can significantly improve the interactivity and engagement of virtual environments, making them more dynamic and responsive to user input.

- Scalability: It can be deployed at scale, providing consistent and intelligent interactions to countless users simultaneously.

CHAPTER 12 CRAFTING METAVERSE CITIES: UNVEILING THE CUTTING-EDGE DEVELOPMENT TOOLS

- Customizability: The responses and behavior of ChatGPT-powered entities can be tailored to fit the specific needs and themes of different virtual worlds or applications.

6) **Limitations**

    - Contextual Understanding: While highly advanced, ChatGPT may sometimes struggle with understanding complex, nuanced, or domain-specific queries.

    - Dependency on Training Data: The quality of interactions can depend heavily on the breadth and quality of the training data, potentially limiting the scope of its understanding.

7) **Integrative Strategies**

    - Collaborating with metaverse developers to seamlessly integrate ChatGPT into virtual environments, ensuring natural and contextually appropriate interactions.

    - Developing specialized training programs or models tailored to specific metaverse applications, enhancing the AI's ability to understand and engage with domain-specific content.

ChatGPT for Metaverse represents a cutting-edge application of conversational AI, offering the potential to revolutionize how users interact within virtual worlds. Its integration can lead to more immersive and engaging experiences, supporting a wide range of functionalities from interactive storytelling to automated support services. While challenges remain in achieving perfect contextual understanding, the ongoing development and customization of AI models promise to expand its capabilities and applications within the metaverse.

CHAPTER 12   CRAFTING METAVERSE CITIES: UNVEILING THE CUTTING-EDGE DEVELOPMENT TOOLS

13. Gemini for Metaverse

Gemini for Metaverse acts as a creative assistant in the metaverse development process, offering capabilities in content generation, research assistance, and narrative development to enrich the storytelling and user experience in virtual environments.

1) **What Is This Tool?**

   While not a development tool itself, Gemini serves as a valuable creative partner throughout the metaverse development process. It assists with various tasks, fostering creativity, content generation, research, and refinement at various stages of development.

2) **This Tool URL**

   Here is the public Gemini URL. Moreover, you can access and interact with it through various Google products and platforms that leverage its capabilities.

3) **Brief History**

   Gemini is a large language model created by Google AI. It has been under development since 2017, with ongoing advancements in its capabilities for text generation, translation, writing different kinds of creative content, and answering your questions in an informative way.

4) **Smart City Application Examples**

   - Research and Information Gathering: Need to understand user experience design trends in the metaverse or research best practices for building virtual environments? Gemini can summarize

CHAPTER 12 CRAFTING METAVERSE CITIES: UNVEILING THE CUTTING-EDGE DEVELOPMENT TOOLS

complex topics, analyze user feedback, and provide relevant information to guide your development decisions.

- Scriptwriting and Storyboarding: Provide a basic plot outline and ask Gemini to generate dialogue snippets or script ideas for your metaverse experience. You can also use it to flesh out storyboards by describing scenes and requesting detailed descriptions of the virtual environment.

- User Testing and Feedback Analysis: After playtesting your metaverse experience, ask Gemini to analyze the feedback from users. It can help identify recurring themes, areas for improvement, and refine your project based on real user experiences.

5) **Main Strengths**

- Versatility: Applicable across various stages of metaverse development, from brainstorming to content creation and user feedback analysis.

- Creativity: Sparks creative inspiration and assists with generating various creative text formats, narratives, and ideas.

- Information Access: Provides access to and analysis of vast information resources, aiding research and knowledge gathering.

6) **Limitations**

- Limited Direct Development: Cannot directly code or build applications for the metaverse.

- Accuracy and Factual Verification: Requires careful review and fact-checking of generated content as factual accuracy cannot be guaranteed.

- Bias and Fairness: As with any AI model, potential biases in the training data can influence the outputs. It's crucial to be mindful of potential biases and use Gemini responsibly.

7) **Integrative Strategies**

- Combine with Other Development Tools: Use Gemini alongside other metaverse development tools like Unity or Unreal Engine for a comprehensive workflow.

- Utilize for Specific Tasks: Integrate Gemini into specific stages of the development process where its strengths, like creative brainstorming or content generation, can be most beneficial.

- Provide Clear Prompts and Instructions: Ensure clear and specific prompts to guide Gemini toward the desired outputs and minimize the risk of irrelevant or inaccurate responses.

While not a metaverse development tool in the traditional sense, Gemini acts as a valuable creative partner, aiding in brainstorming, content generation, research, and refinement throughout the development process. Its strengths lie in its versatility, creativity, and access to information, but it's essential to be aware of its limitations and integrate it strategically alongside other tools and critical human oversight.

14. SpatialOS

SpatialOS is designed for creating vast, complex, and persistent virtual worlds that can scale dynamically. It's particularly well suited for developing MMORPGs, large-scale simulations, and other metaverse applications that require a high degree of interactivity and scalability.

1) **What Is This Tool?**

    SpatialOS is a cloud-based platform designed to create vast, complex, and persistent virtual worlds that go beyond the capabilities of traditional game servers or development platforms. Developed by Improbable, SpatialOS allows developers to build massively multiplayer online games (MMOs), simulations, and other large-scale virtual environments. It integrates with popular game engines like Unity and Unreal Engine, enabling the creation of detailed and dynamic worlds where thousands of players can interact simultaneously within the same space.

2) **This Tool URL**

    For more information, resources, and documentation on SpatialOS, visit their official website.

3) **Brief History**

    SpatialOS was developed by Improbable Worlds Limited, a British multinational technology company founded in 2012. The platform was created with the vision of enabling developers to build more ambitious online worlds than were previously possible, leveraging cloud computing to handle complex simulations and large numbers of concurrent players. Over the years, SpatialOS has seen adoption in various projects, from gaming to urban planning simulations, showcasing its versatility and power.

4) **Smart City Application Examples**

- Massively Multiplayer Online Games (MMOs): Games like *Worlds Adrift* utilized SpatialOS to create a vast, persistent world where players could interact with each other and the environment in real time.

- Simulation and Training: Used by organizations to simulate complex, real-world environments for training purposes, such as urban planning or emergency response drills.

- Virtual Events: Hosting large-scale virtual events, conferences, or concerts, where thousands of participants can interact within a shared virtual space.

5) **Main Strengths**

- Scalability: Allows for the creation of large-scale, persistent worlds with thousands of simultaneous users, thanks to its cloud-based infrastructure.

- Integration: Compatible with popular game engines, offering developers the flexibility to use familiar tools while leveraging the unique capabilities of SpatialOS.

- Dynamic World Simulation: Supports complex simulations, including physics and AI-driven entities, enabling rich, interactive environments.

6) **Limitations**

- Complexity: The development on SpatialOS can be complex, requiring a good understanding of both the platform and distributed systems.

- Cost: Running large-scale simulations on cloud infrastructure can become costly, especially for prolonged or extensive projects.

- Dependency on Third-Party Infrastructure: Being cloud-based, projects are dependent on the stability and availability of SpatialOS's infrastructure.

7) **Integrative Strategies**

- Partnerships with Educational Institutions: Offering resources and access to SpatialOS for educational purposes could help train the next generation of developers.

- Expanded Developer Resources and Support: Providing comprehensive documentation, tutorials, and community support can lower the barrier to entry for new developers.

- Collaboration with Industry: Working closely with industries that could benefit from large-scale simulations, such as urban planning or defense, to tailor solutions to their needs.

SpatialOS by Improbable represents a significant leap forward in the development of virtual worlds, offering unparalleled scalability and complexity in creating persistent, dynamic environments. While it presents challenges in terms of complexity and cost, its integration with popular game engines and the ability to host thousands of users in rich, simulated worlds make it a powerful tool for a wide range of applications, from MMOs to professional simulations. As the platform continues to evolve, its potential applications in the metaverse and beyond are only limited by the imagination of the developers who use it.

15. Decentraland SDK

Decentraland SDK is another strong contender for building metaverse experiences, particularly those focused on virtual land and user-generated content.

1) **What Is This Tool?**

   The Decentraland SDK (Software Development Kit) is a comprehensive toolset designed for developers to create, deploy, and manage interactive content and applications within the Decentraland virtual world. Decentraland is a decentralized virtual reality platform powered by the Ethereum blockchain, allowing users to create, experience, and monetize content and applications. The SDK enables developers to build immersive experiences using a scripting language that controls the behavior of the virtual scenes, assets, and interactions within Decentraland.

CHAPTER 12   CRAFTING METAVERSE CITIES: UNVEILING THE CUTTING-EDGE DEVELOPMENT TOOLS

2) **This Tool URL**

   For more information, resources, and developer guides and to access the Decentraland SDK, visit the official Decentraland developer portal.

3) **Brief History**

   Decentraland was conceptualized in 2015 and officially launched to the public in February 2020. The development of the Decentraland SDK was integral to the platform, providing the necessary tools for creators to contribute to the virtual world from its inception. The SDK has evolved alongside the platform, incorporating feedback from the community and adapting to the growing needs of developers and content creators within the Decentraland ecosystem.

4) **Smart City Application Examples**

   - Virtual Real Estate Development: Developers use the SDK to design and construct unique virtual spaces, buildings, and environments on parcels of land owned within Decentraland.

   - Interactive Games and Experiences: Creators build engaging games and interactive experiences that users can explore and enjoy, ranging from puzzles and adventures to casinos and social hubs.

   - Educational and Artistic Installations: The SDK is utilized to create educational content, art galleries, and exhibitions, showcasing digital art and hosting virtual lectures and workshops.

5) **Main Strengths**

    - Blockchain Integration: Leveraging the Ethereum blockchain, the Decentraland SDK provides a secure and transparent way to manage ownership and transactions within the virtual world.

    - Creative Freedom: The SDK offers extensive tools and capabilities for creating a wide range of interactive content, from simple scenes to complex, multiplayer games.

    - Community and Ecosystem: A strong community of developers and creators supports the platform, fostering collaboration and the exchange of ideas and assets.

6) **Limitations**

    - Technical Barrier: The need for understanding blockchain concepts and familiarity with the SDK's scripting language can pose challenges for new developers.

    - Performance Optimization: As with any large-scale virtual world, ensuring optimal performance and user experience across different devices and connections can be difficult.

7) **Integrative Strategies**

    - Offering comprehensive documentation, tutorials, and support forums to lower the entry barrier for new developers and encourage community growth.

    - Developing partnerships with educational institutions and organizations to promote the use of Decentraland SDK for academic and professional projects.

CHAPTER 12   CRAFTING METAVERSE CITIES: UNVEILING THE CUTTING-EDGE DEVELOPMENT TOOLS

The Decentraland SDK is a powerful tool that enables developers and creators to build rich, interactive content within a blockchain-based virtual world. Its strengths lie in its integration with the Ethereum blockchain, offering a level of security and transparency in content ownership and transactions. While there are challenges related to the technical complexities of blockchain and content optimization, the supportive community and ongoing developments in the SDK aim to make Decentraland an accessible and innovative platform for virtual reality experiences.

16. Meta Spark

Meta Spark is a suite of tools from Meta (formerly Facebook) for building AR/VR experiences. It includes Spark AR for creating augmented reality filters, Spark Core for building VR applications, and Oculus tools for developing Meta's VR headsets.

1) **What Is This Tool?**

Meta Spark (formerly known as Facebook's Spark AR Studio) is a platform developed by Meta Platforms that enables creators and developers to build augmented reality (AR) experiences for Instagram, Facebook, and other platforms within the Meta ecosystem. It provides a comprehensive suite of tools and features that allow for the creation of interactive, immersive AR effects, such as face filters, animated backgrounds, and interactive games that can be experienced through the camera on smartphones.

2) **This Tool URL**

   For more information, resources, tutorials and to download Meta Spark, visit the official website.

3) **Brief History**

   Meta Spark was launched in 2017 as Spark AR Studio, with the aim of democratizing AR creation and enabling a wider range of creators to design and share AR experiences across Meta's platforms. Since its inception, the platform has seen significant growth and expansion, introducing new features and capabilities that leverage the latest in AR technology. The rebranding to Meta Spark reflects the company's broader focus on building immersive, interactive experiences in the metaverse.

4) **Smart City Application Examples**

   - Interactive Marketing Campaigns: Brands use Meta Spark to create engaging AR filters and games that promote products and events on Instagram and Facebook.

   - Educational Content: Educators and organizations design AR experiences to provide interactive learning opportunities, such as virtual museum tours or anatomy lessons.

   - Social Media Engagement: Individuals and influencers create unique, shareable AR effects to enhance their content and engage with their followers.

5) **Main Strengths**

- Accessibility: Meta Spark's user-friendly interface and extensive documentation make it accessible to creators of all skill levels, from beginners to advanced developers.

- Integration with Meta Platforms: Seamless integration with Instagram and Facebook allows for the wide distribution and easy sharing of AR experiences.

- Community and Support: A robust community of creators and comprehensive support resources, including tutorials and forums, support the development and sharing of AR projects.

6) **Limitations**

- Platform Limitations: AR experiences created with Meta Spark are primarily limited to Meta's own platforms, potentially restricting reach outside the Meta ecosystem.

- Performance Constraints: The complexity and performance of AR effects may be limited by the capabilities of users' devices and the technical specifications of the Meta Spark platform.

7) **Integrative Strategies**

- Encouraging collaboration between AR creators and brands to develop innovative marketing solutions and interactive content.

- Offering educational programs and resources to teach AR development skills, expanding the community of Meta Spark creators.

CHAPTER 12 CRAFTING METAVERSE CITIES: UNVEILING THE CUTTING-EDGE DEVELOPMENT TOOLS

Meta Spark is a powerful and accessible platform for creating augmented reality experiences, designed to integrate closely with Meta's social media platforms. It democratizes AR creation, enabling a wide range of creators to design interactive, immersive effects. Despite some limitations related to platform exclusivity and device performance, Meta Spark fosters a vibrant community of AR developers and offers significant opportunities for engagement and creativity within the Meta ecosystem.

To sum up, in this chapter, we've explored a comprehensive range of cutting-edge development tools that are pivotal in shaping the metaverse cities of tomorrow. We discussed the cutting-edge metaverse development tools like Unreal Engine, known for its high-fidelity visuals; Unity, celebrated for its versatility; and emerging AI technologies like ChatGPT that offer potential for dynamic interactions within metaverse environments. Each tool was analyzed for its unique capabilities, applications, and transformative impact on metaverse development. From creating immersive digital cities with Unreal Engine and Unity to leveraging Roblox Studio for user-generated universes and enhancing virtual interactions with AI-driven tools like ChatGPT and Bard/Genesis, this chapter provided a thorough examination of the technological foundations essential for constructing the virtual worlds of the future. Additionally, the chapter delved into platforms like Nvidia's Omniverse for collaborative creation, Amazon Sumerian for accessible VR/AR development, and specialized tools such as CryEngine and Blender for high-detail modeling. Autodesk Maya was highlighted for animation and character creation, SketchUp for architectural design, ZBrush for high-detail sculpting, and Tilt Brush for 3D painting in VR. Furthermore, it mentioned SpatialOS for creating scalable virtual worlds, Decentraland SDK for blockchain-based virtual land development, and Meta Spark for building AR/VR experiences.

CHAPTER 12 CRAFTING METAVERSE CITIES: UNVEILING THE CUTTING-EDGE DEVELOPMENT TOOLS

The culmination of this exploration is not merely academic; it equips developers with the insights to judiciously choose and adeptly wield the ideal tools for their metaverse projects, navigating the ever-expanding universe of digital twin city development. As we proceed to Chapters 13–15, prepare to be enthralled by a series of captivating prototype applications. These sections promise a hands-on guide to realizing digital twin metaverse cities, from conceptualization to creation, using the diverse array of development tools unveiled in this chapter. Join us as we transition from theoretical exploration to practical application, setting the stage for a future where digital and physical realms converge in harmony.

CHAPTER 13

Digital Twin Metaverse Prototypes: *Smart Living*

It is time to do it! Dive into this chapter where the concepts and tools from earlier chapters materialize into tangible, interactive experiences. This chapter is not just a continuation of our journey; it's the embodiment of our digital dreams. Envision your creative impulses coming alive as we meticulously craft six smart living prototypes that will revolutionize urban life within the digital twin metaverse. Each prototype weaves together the advanced functionalities of the 28 tools we've discussed, from Unreal Engine's unrivaled rendering capabilities to the intuitive design elements of Unity and the intelligent interaction layers of ChatGPT. Imagine stepping into a metaverse city where your living space responds to your touch, where virtual healthcare is a swipe away, and where AI-powered environments learn and adapt to your preferences.

Here, we construct prototypes that are not only technologically impressive but are also tailored to enhance convenience, comfort, and connectivity. You'll witness firsthand how these prototypes are intricately designed with detailed attention to the nuances of smart living. From homes that adapt to your mood with lighting and temperature to gardens that whisper the health of each plant to your smartphone, we delve into a new realm where every corner of your digital twin city responds to the beat of modern life.

We invite you to roll up your sleeves as we embark on this hands-on journey to shape living spaces that are as smart as they are stylish. Get ready to be inspired, to learn, and to lead the way in the evolution of smart living in the metaverse cities. This is not just the next chapter of the book; it's the next chapter of our shared future.

Sustainable Smart Homes

We will harness the power of Unity and Unreal Engine for our immersive 3D visualizations, crafting a prototype that brings sustainable smart homes to life. These homes will integrate IoT devices for sophisticated energy management, feature solar panels for renewable energy, and include rainwater recycling systems for sustainable living. Figure 13-1 presents a conceptual design of a sustainable smart home—the blueprint we aspire to replicate in our prototype. This prototype will illustrate the interaction between residents and home automation systems, showcasing how technology can optimize energy usage and significantly reduce the carbon footprint.

Creating a sustainable smart home prototype involves several steps, especially for beginners. We'll break down the process into manageable parts, first using Unity and then Unreal Engine, focusing on key aspects like importing assets, basic scripting for interactions, and simulating IoT devices for energy management. Let's start with Unity and then Unreal Engine (UE).

CHAPTER 13   DIGITAL TWIN METAVERSE PROTOTYPES: SMART LIVING

Figure 13-1. Conceptual design of a ***sustainable smart home*** *(author's development with Dall-E)*

Using Unity for Sustainable Smart Homes
Step 1: Setting Up Unity

- Download and Install Unity Hub: Visit the (https://unity.com/downloa4) and download Unity Hub. Install it on your computer.

- Install Unity Editor: Through Unity Hub, install the latest version of the Unity Editor. Select a version that's appropriate for your project needs.

- Create a New Project: Open Unity Hub, go to the "Projects" tab, and click "New." Choose the "3D" template and name your project "Sustainable Smart Homes."

CHAPTER 13   DIGITAL TWIN METAVERSE PROTOTYPES: SMART LIVING

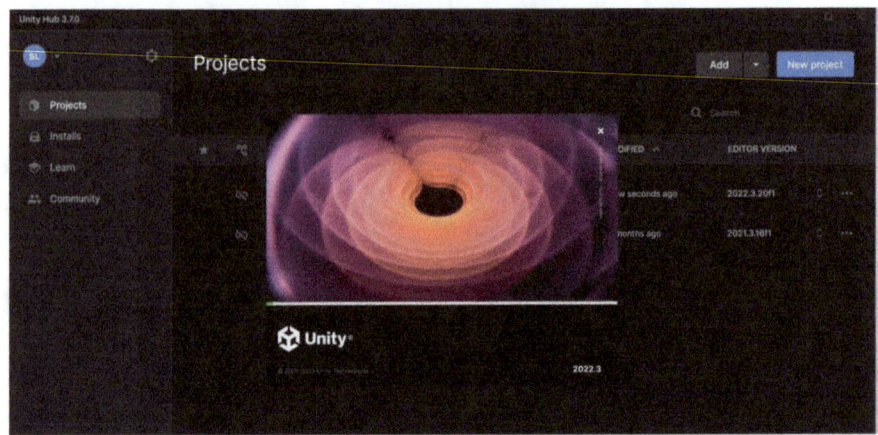

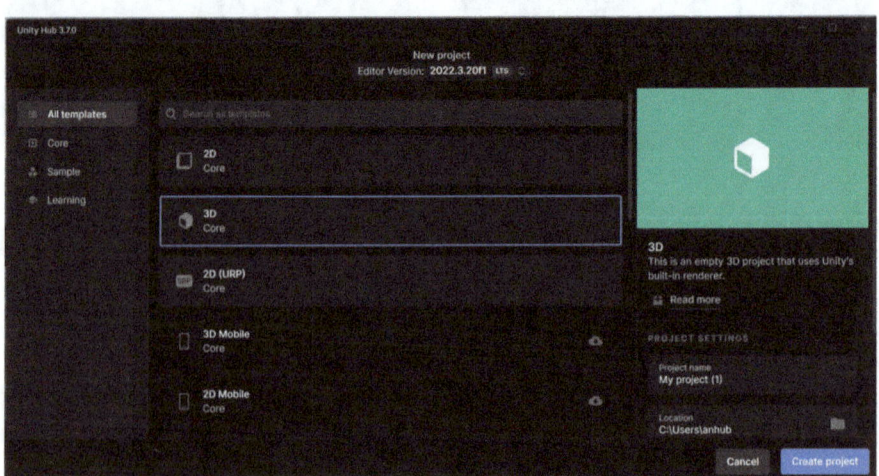

CHAPTER 13 DIGITAL TWIN METAVERSE PROTOTYPES: SMART LIVING

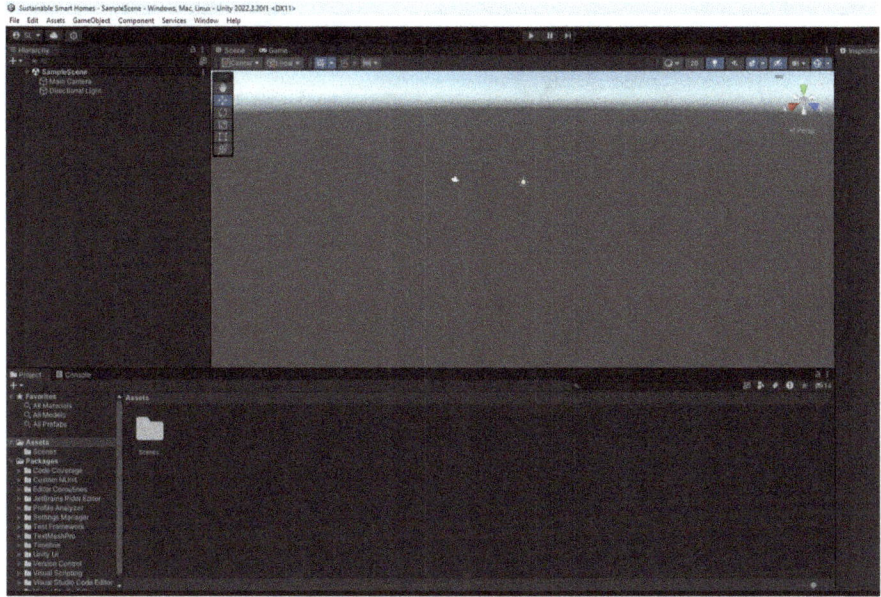

Step 2: Importing Assets

- Unity Asset Store: Access the Unity Asset Store from within the Unity Editor or via a web browser. Look for free assets for houses, furniture, solar panels, and IoT devices. Download and import them into your project.

- Custom Assets: If you have custom 3D models (e.g., from Blender), you can import them by dragging the files into the "Assets" folder in your Unity project.

CHAPTER 13   DIGITAL TWIN METAVERSE PROTOTYPES: SMART LIVING

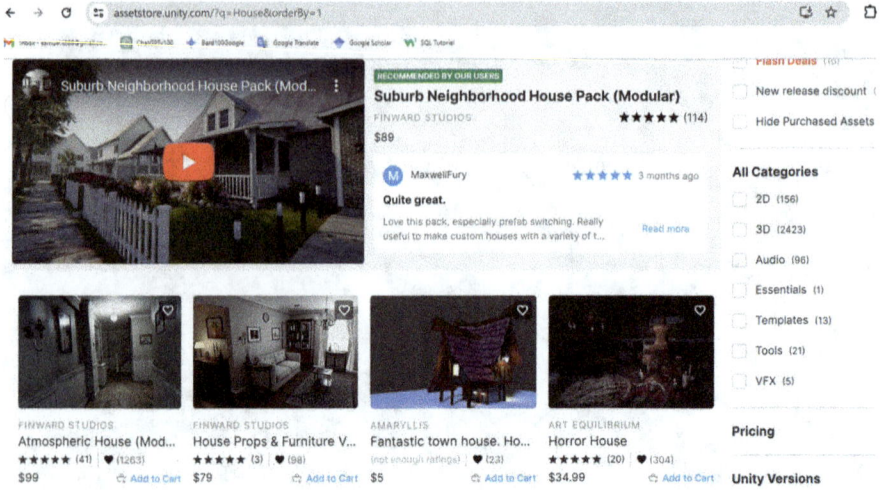

Step 3: Setting Up the Scene

- Create Your Home: Using the imported assets, start creating your smart home in the Unity scene view. Drag and drop items like walls, roofs, solar panels, and furniture to assemble your house.

- Add Lighting: Go to the "GameObject" menu, select "Light," and choose "Directional Light" to simulate sunlight. Adjust its position and intensity to illuminate your home effectively.

CHAPTER 13   DIGITAL TWIN METAVERSE PROTOTYPES: SMART LIVING

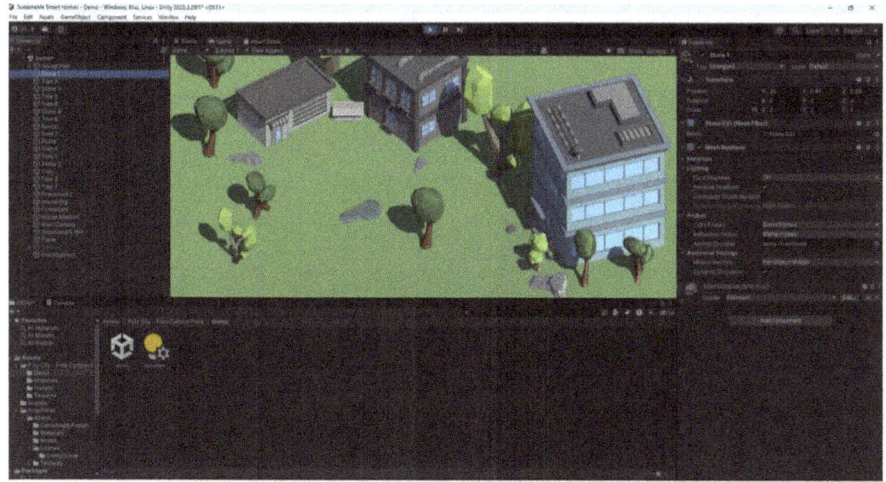

Step 4: Adding Interactivity

- Scripting Basics: Learn basic C scripting in Unity to add functionality. For instance, create a script to turn lights on/off when clicking a switch. Unity's (https://docs.unity3d.com/ScriptReference/) and tutorials will be invaluable.

- Simulate IoT Devices: Write scripts to simulate IoT devices, for example, a script that adjusts the indoor temperature based on external weather conditions or one that tracks energy generated by solar panels.

Step 5: Testing and Iteration

- Play Mode: Use Unity's Play Mode to test your smart home's functionality. Interact with the IoT devices and observe how they affect your home's energy management.

- Iterate: Based on testing, make necessary adjustments to improve functionality and user experience.

CHAPTER 13   DIGITAL TWIN METAVERSE PROTOTYPES: SMART LIVING

Now it's your turn   *As you venture further into the realm of digital twin metaverse city development, I encourage you to continue the remaining steps and enhance your prototype by adding rich, realistic scenery, fine-tuning materials, and weaving in greater interactivity. Your engagement and dedication to this work are invaluable—embrace this chance to innovate and hone your expertise in crafting the digital landscapes of tomorrow...*

Using Unreal Engine for Sustainable Smart Homes
Step 1: Setting Up Unreal Engine

- Download and Install: Download the Epic Games Launcher from the (https://www.unrealengine.com/download), install it, and navigate to the Unreal Engine tab.

- Create a New Project: Click "Launch" on the version you want to use, then select "New Project," and choose the "Blank" template. Name your project "Sustainable Smart Homes UE."

CHAPTER 13　DIGITAL TWIN METAVERSE PROTOTYPES: SMART LIVING

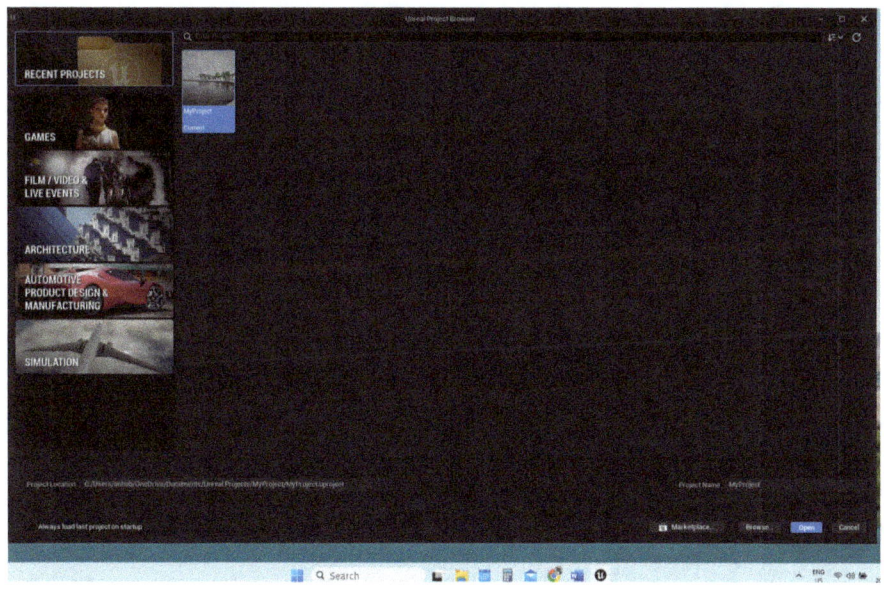

271

Step 2: Importing Assets

- Unreal Marketplace: Use the Unreal Engine Marketplace to find assets for your smart home. Import assets directly into your project.

- Using Custom Models: If you have custom models, import them by clicking "Import" in the "Content Browser" and selecting your files.

Step 3: Building Your Home

- Assemble Your Home: Drag and drop assets from the "Content Browser" into your scene to build your home. Position elements like solar panels and IoT devices strategically.

- Environmental Setup: Add a "Directional Light" for the sun and adjust the "Sky Sphere" to enhance the realism of your scene.

Step 4: Blueprint for Interactivity

- Introduction to Blueprints: Unreal Engine's Blueprint system allows for creating interactivity without deep coding knowledge. Start with simple Blueprints to control lights or simulate energy consumption.

- IoT Device Simulation: Create Blueprints that represent the functionality of IoT devices, such as adjusting energy usage based on solar panel input or managing water recycling.

Step 5: Testing and Refinement

- Simulate and Test: Use the "Play" button to enter your scene and interact with the elements you've created. Test the functionality of your IoT devices.

- Refine Your Prototype: Make adjustments based on your observations during testing to improve the efficiency and realism of your smart home.

Now it's your turn *As you venture further into the realm of digital twin metaverse city development, I encourage you to continue the remaining steps and enhance your prototype by adding rich, realistic scenery, fine-tuning materials, and weaving in greater interactivity. Your engagement and dedication to this work are invaluable— embrace this chance to innovate and hone your expertise in crafting the digital landscapes of tomorrow...*

Both Unity and Unreal Engine offer robust platforms for creating a sustainable smart home prototype. Unity might be more accessible for beginners due to its extensive documentation and supportive community. Unreal Engine, with its powerful Blueprint system, can offer more visually stunning results with less emphasis on traditional coding. Whichever tool you choose, the key is to experiment, learn, and iterate as you bring your sustainable smart home to life in the digital twin metaverse.

Virtual Healthcare Clinic

Leveraging Meta Spark and ChatGPT, we will develop a virtual healthcare clinic where users can interact with AI-powered healthcare assistants for preliminary diagnoses, mental health support, and wellness advice. Figure 13-2 presents a conceptual design of a virtual healthcare clinic— the blueprint we aspire to replicate in our prototype. This prototype would showcase the potential for remote healthcare services within the metaverse, providing accessible and immediate care.

CHAPTER 13   DIGITAL TWIN METAVERSE PROTOTYPES: SMART LIVING

To develop a prototype of a virtual healthcare clinic using Meta Spark and ChatGPT, here's a step-by-step guide tailored for beginners. This prototype aims to create an interactive, AI-powered virtual clinic within the metaverse, offering services like preliminary diagnoses, mental health support, and wellness advice.

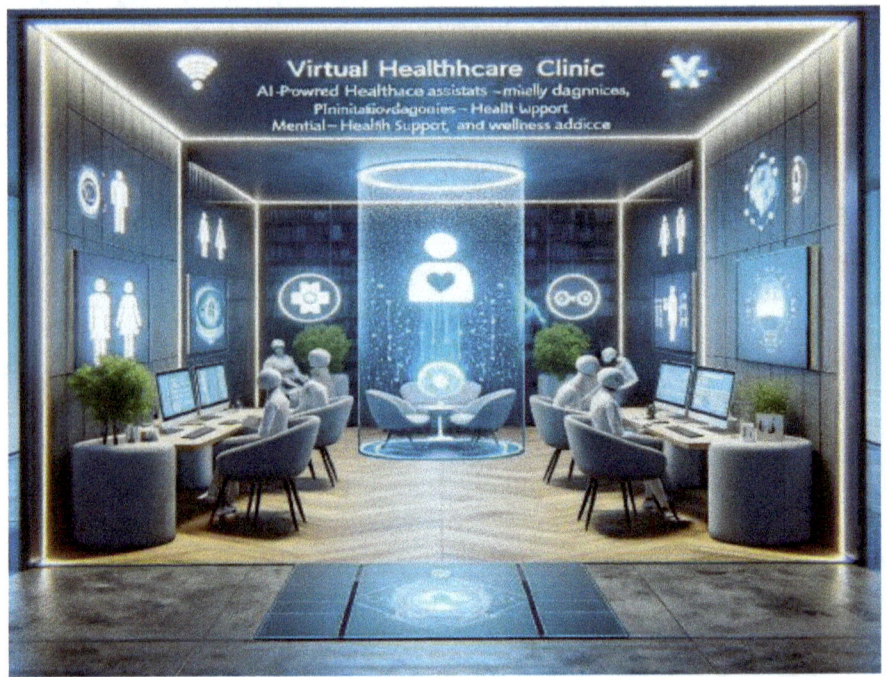

Figure 13-2. *Conceptual design of a virtual healthcare clinic (author's development with Dall-E)*

Step 1: Familiarizing Yourself with the Tools

- Meta Spark: A platform for creating augmented reality (AR) experiences on Facebook and Instagram. Learn the basics of AR creation on Meta Spark by exploring the official documentation and tutorials on the (https://sparkar.facebook.com/ar-studio/).

CHAPTER 13   DIGITAL TWIN METAVERSE PROTOTYPES: SMART LIVING

- ChatGPT: An AI developed by OpenAI that can generate humanlike text responses. Understand how ChatGPT works and how it can be integrated into applications by reviewing documentation on the (https://www.openai.com/).

Step 2: Setting Up Your Development Environment

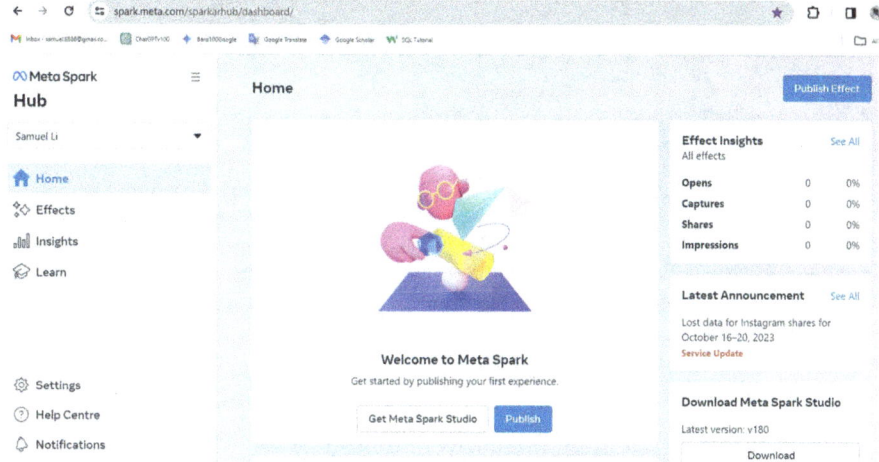

- Download Meta Spark Studio: Install Meta Spark Studio on your computer to start creating AR experiences.

275

CHAPTER 13   DIGITAL TWIN METAVERSE PROTOTYPES: SMART LIVING

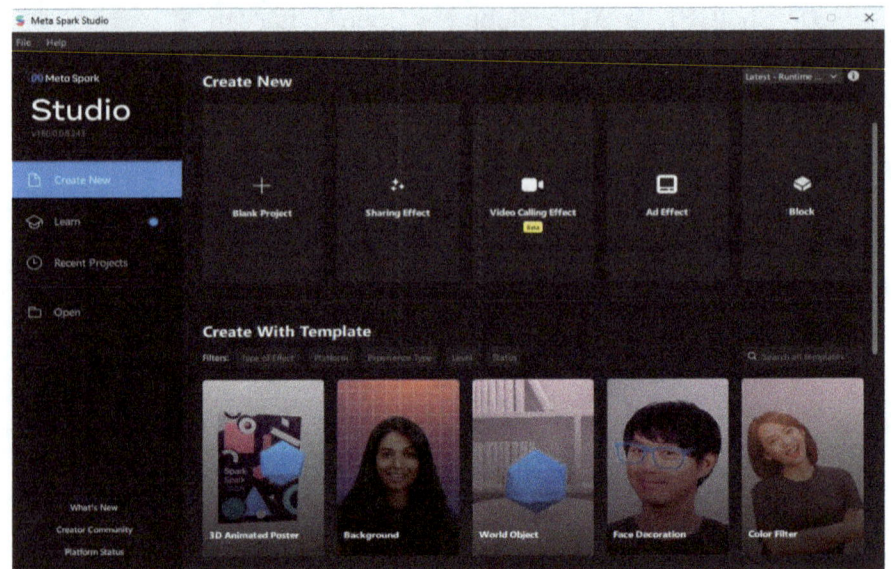

- Access ChatGPT API: Register for access to the ChatGPT API through OpenAI's platform. This will allow you to integrate conversational AI into the virtual clinic.

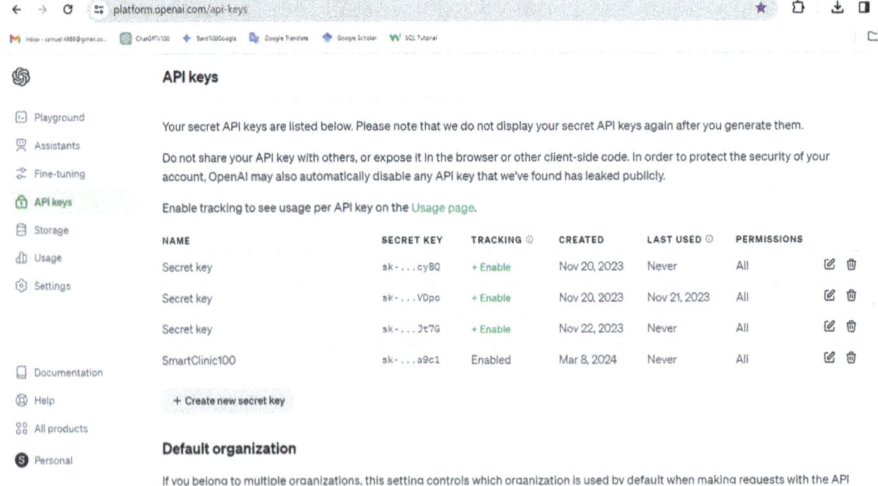

CHAPTER 13   DIGITAL TWIN METAVERSE PROTOTYPES: SMART LIVING

Step 3: Designing the Virtual Clinic Experience

- Sketch Your Ideas: Start by sketching out the layout and key features of your virtual clinic. Consider including a waiting area, consultation rooms, and interactive health kiosks.

- Create AR Elements: Use Meta Spark Studio to create AR elements that patients can interact with, such as informational pop-ups about health practices or navigational aids within the clinic.

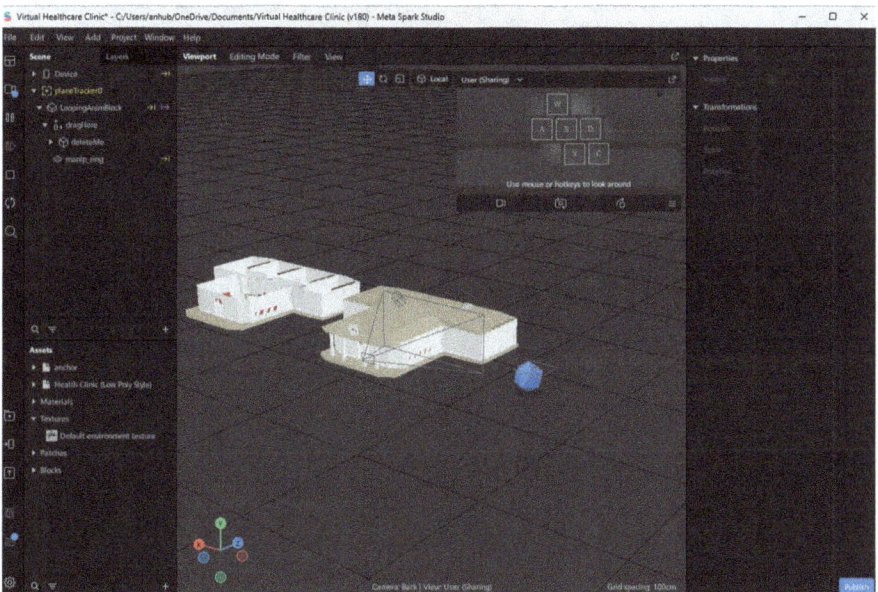

Step 4: Integrating ChatGPT for Interactive Services

- Set Up ChatGPT Integration: Use the ChatGPT API to enable real-time interaction between users and the virtual healthcare assistants. This involves coding, so you may need to follow specific API integration guides provided by OpenAI.

- Design Conversational Flows: Create scripts for common healthcare inquiries that users might have, and design conversational flows for ChatGPT to follow, ensuring responses are informative and empathetic. The following steps helps to create ChatGPT AI Services for the health clinic:

1) Setting Up Your Server-Side Environment

```
// Import necessary libraries
const express = require('express');
const axios = require('axios');
const app = express();

// Body parser middleware to handle JSON payloads
app.use(express.json());

// Replace with your actual OpenAI API key
const OPENAI_API_KEY = 'YOUR-API-KEY-HERE';
```

2) Defining Your Conversational Flow

Before writing code, outline the conversational flows in a document. For example:

If a user asks about symptoms of the common cold, ChatGPT should provide a list of symptoms and advise rest and hydration.

If a user inquires about booking an appointment, ChatGPT should explain the booking process.

3) Creating Endpoint for ChatGPT Interaction

```javascript
// Endpoint to receive user input and return ChatGPT response
app.post('/chat', async (req, res) => {
    // Extract the message from the request body
    const { message } = req.body;

    try {
        // Make the API call to OpenAI's ChatGPT
        const response = await axios.post('https://api.openai.com/v1/engines/davinci-cod
            prompt: message,
            max_tokens: 150,
        }, {
            headers: {
                'Authorization': `Bearer ${OPENAI_API_KEY}`
            }
        });

        // Send the ChatGPT response back to the client
        res.json({ response: response.data.choices[0].text });
    } catch (error) {
        console.error('Error calling the OpenAI API', error);
        res.status(500).json({ error: 'Error calling the OpenAI API' });
    }
});

// Start the server
const PORT = process.env.PORT || 3000;
app.listen(PORT, () => console.log(`Server running on port ${PORT}`));
```

Handling Conversational Logic

```javascript
app.post('/chat', async (req, res) => {
    // Extract the message from the request body
    const { message } = req.body;

    let responseText = '';

    // Handle specific cases
    if (message.includes('symptoms of the common cold')) {
        responseText = 'Common symptoms of a cold include sneezing, sore throat, cough,
    } else if (message.includes('book an appointment')) {
        responseText = 'To book an appointment, please visit our booking page or call ou
    } else {
        // Fallback to OpenAI API call for general inquiries
        try {
            const response = await axios.post('https://api.openai.com/v1/engines/davinci-co
                prompt: message,
                max_tokens: 150,
            }, {
                headers: {
                    'Authorization': `Bearer ${OPENAI_API_KEY}`
                }
            });

            responseText = response.data.choices[0].text;
        } catch (error) {
            console.error('Error calling the OpenAI API', error);
            return res.status(500).json({ error: 'Error calling the OpenAI API' });
        }
    }

    // Send the response back to the client
    res.json({ response: responseText });
});
```

Step 5: Testing and Iteration

- Prototype Testing: Test your AR elements and ChatGPT integration within Meta Spark Studio. You can use the preview feature to simulate user interactions and adjust as needed.

- Gather Feedback: Share your prototype with a small group of users for feedback. Pay attention to their experience with the AR features and the helpfulness of the AI-powered healthcare assistants.

Step 6: Deployment and Sharing

- Publish Your AR Experience: Once you're satisfied with the prototype, follow Meta Spark's guidelines to publish your AR experience. Ensure it's accessible to your intended audience, whether it's through a specific link or directly on Facebook/Instagram.

- Promote Your Virtual Clinic: Use social media or other digital platforms to inform potential users about your virtual healthcare clinic. Include instructions on how to access the clinic and what services are available.

Step 7: Continuous Improvement

- Monitor User Interactions: Keep an eye on how users are engaging with your virtual clinic and the types of inquiries they're making.

- Iterate Based on Feedback: Continuously improve the virtual clinic based on user feedback and emerging healthcare needs. Update the AR experiences and conversational AI scripts as necessary to keep the service relevant and useful.

> **Now it's your turn** *As you venture further into the realm of digital twin metaverse city development, I encourage you to continue the remaining steps and enhance your prototype by adding rich, realistic scenery, fine-tuning materials, and weaving in greater interactivity. Your engagement and dedication to this work are invaluable—embrace this chance to innovate and hone your expertise in crafting the digital landscapes of tomorrow...*

This guide provides a foundation for beginners to start creating a virtual healthcare clinic prototype. Remember, building interactive and immersive experiences requires patience and iteration, so don't be discouraged by initial challenges.

Eco-Friendly Urban Transportation Hub

Using Unity for its high-quality visuals and physics simulation capabilities, we will create a prototype of an eco-friendly urban transportation hub. Figure 13-3 presents a conceptual design of an eco-friendly urban transportation hub—the blueprint we aspire to embody in our prototype.

This hub could include electric vehicle charging stations, solar-powered public transport systems, and AR navigation aids for efficient urban mobility, emphasizing sustainability and convenience.

To create a prototype of an eco-friendly urban transportation hub using Unity, follow these detailed steps designed for beginners. This guide will help you understand how to utilize Unity's capabilities for developing immersive environments and simulations.

CHAPTER 13   DIGITAL TWIN METAVERSE PROTOTYPES: SMART LIVING

Figure 13-3. *Conceptual design of an eco-friendly urban transportation hub (author's development with Dall-E)*

Step 1: Setting Up Unity

- Download Unity Hub: Visit the (https://unity.com/downloa4) and download Unity Hub. Unity Hub is a management tool that allows you to manage Unity projects and installations.

- Install Unity Editor: Through Unity Hub, install the latest version of the Unity Editor. Opt for the Unity version that best suits your system and requirements. For beginners, the recommended version is the latest stable release.

- Create a New Project: Open Unity Hub, go to the "Projects" tab, and click "New." Choose the "3D" template as your project base for the transportation hub.

Step 2: Basic Scene Setup

- Understand the Interface: Familiarize yourself with the Unity Editor interface, focusing on the scene view (where you'll build your world), the Game View (where you'll see the game as players would), and the Inspector (where you'll adjust the properties of your game objects).

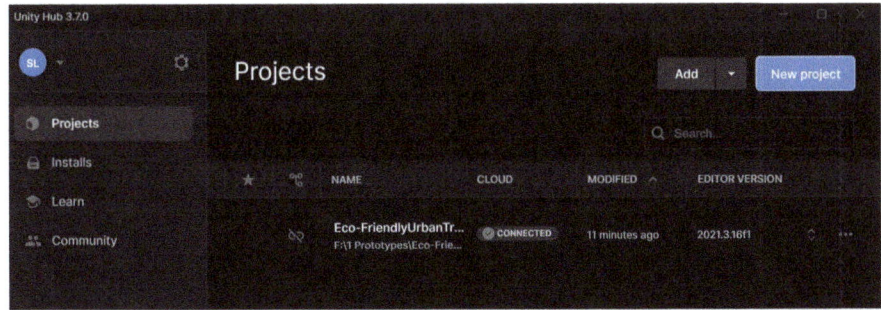

CHAPTER 13   DIGITAL TWIN METAVERSE PROTOTYPES: SMART LIVING

- Create Terrain: Go to the Hierarchy panel, right-click, select 3D Object ➤ Terrain. This terrain will serve as the ground for your transportation hub.

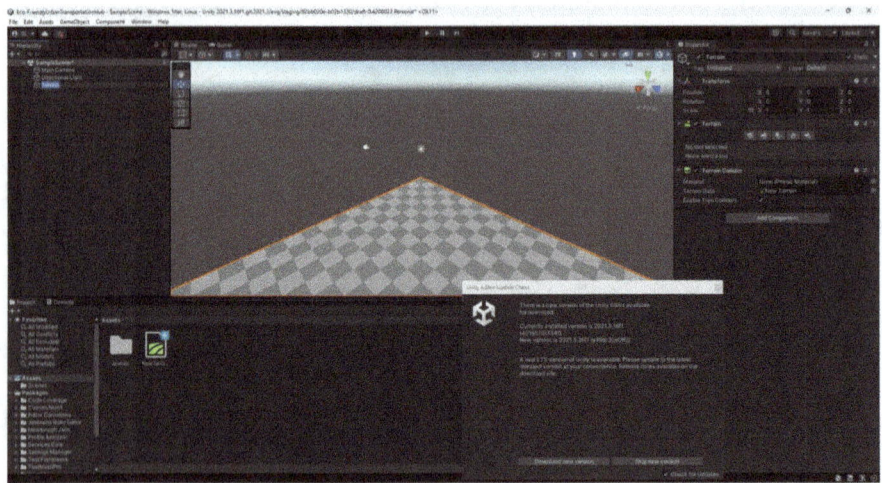

- Adjust Terrain: Use the Terrain Tools in the Inspector panel to sculpt the terrain. Add hills, valleys, or flat areas where your transportation hub and related infrastructure will be located.

CHAPTER 13 DIGITAL TWIN METAVERSE PROTOTYPES: SMART LIVING

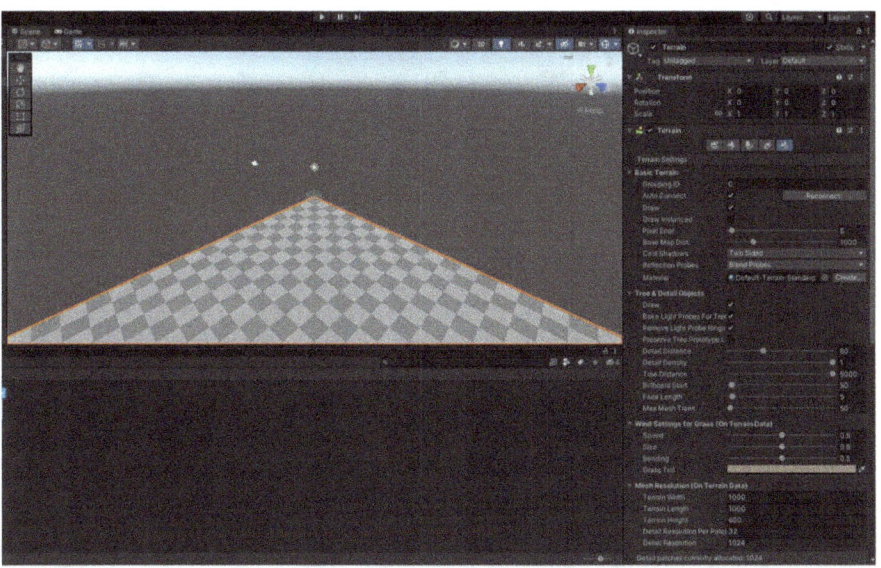

Step 3: Building the Hub

- Import Assets: Unity Asset Store offers a wide range of free and paid assets. For this project, you might need assets for electric vehicle charging stations, solar panels, and public transport vehicles. Download and import these into your project.

285

CHAPTER 13 DIGITAL TWIN METAVERSE PROTOTYPES: SMART LIVING

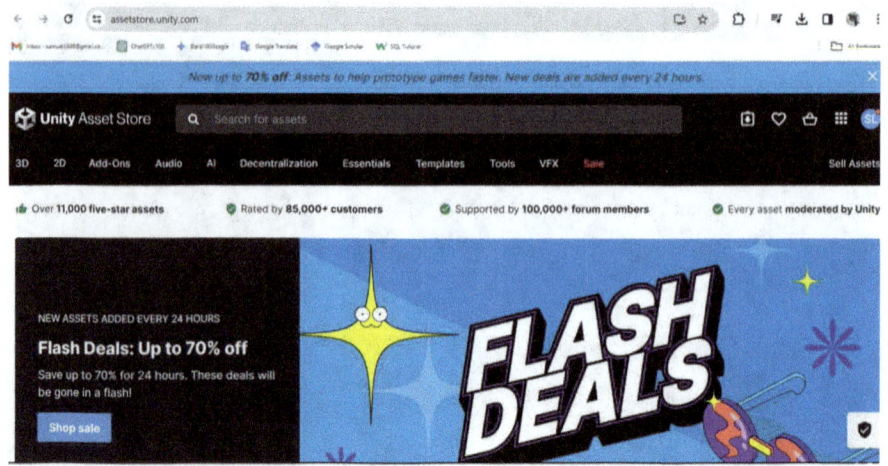

- Place Assets: Drag and drop assets onto your terrain to start building your transportation hub. Position electric vehicle charging stations, solar panels, and other elements according to your design.

- Customize Assets: Use the Inspector to adjust the scale, rotation, and position of your assets to fit the scene perfectly.

CHAPTER 13 DIGITAL TWIN METAVERSE PROTOTYPES: SMART LIVING

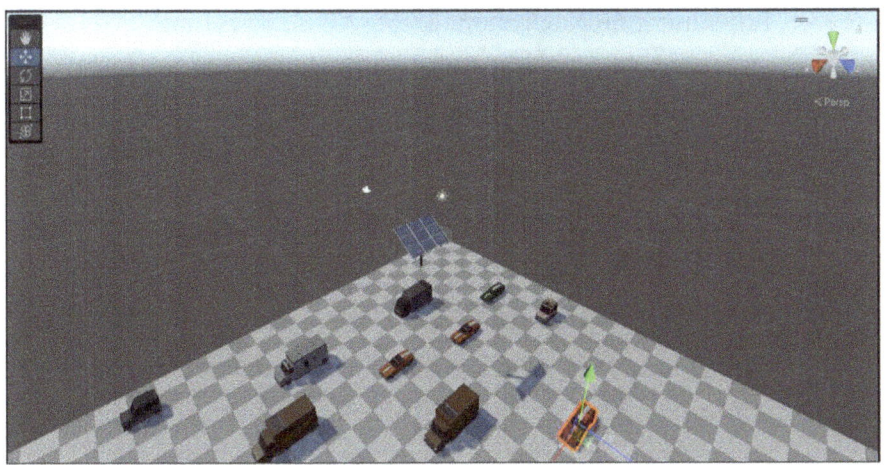

Step 4: Adding Interactivity with C Scripts

- Learn Basic C: Unity uses C for scripting. If you're a complete beginner, consider following a basic C tutorial to grasp variables, functions, and classes.

- Create a Script: Right-click the Project panel; select Create ➤ C Script. Name it "InteractiveElement." This script can be attached to any object you want to make interactive, like charging stations.

- Edit the Script: Double-click the script to open it in Unity's script editor. You might write a simple script to display a message when a player approaches a charging station, using OnTriggerEnter and OnTriggerExit methods.

Step 5: Adding Navigation Aids

- AR Integration: For an augmented reality (AR) navigation system, explore Unity's AR Foundation, a cross-platform framework. Start by installing AR Foundation from the Package Manager and follow tutorials specific to AR setup.

287

CHAPTER 13   DIGITAL TWIN METAVERSE PROTOTYPES: SMART LIVING

- Implement AR Navigation: Create AR markers that guide users through the hub, showing directions to different sections like charging stations or bus stops.

Step 6: Testing and Iteration

- Playtest: Regularly click the Play button in Unity to enter Play Mode and experience your transportation hub from a user's perspective.

- Iterate: Based on playtesting feedback, make an adjustment. This might involve moving assets, changing the terrain, or modifying scripts to improve the user experience.

Step 7: Building the Project

- Build Settings: Once satisfied with your prototype, go to File ➤ Build Settings. Select your target platform (e.g., Windows, Mac, Android, iOS) and click "Build."

- Follow Prompts: Choose a location for your built application and wait for Unity to compile everything.

CHAPTER 13   DIGITAL TWIN METAVERSE PROTOTYPES: SMART LIVING

Now it's your turn   *As you venture further into the realm of digital twin metaverse city development, I encourage you to continue the remaining steps and enhance your prototype by adding rich, realistic scenery, fine-tuning materials, and weaving in greater interactivity. Your engagement and dedication to this work are invaluable— embrace this chance to innovate and hone your expertise in crafting the digital landscapes of tomorrow...*

By following these steps, you will have created a basic prototype of an eco-friendly urban transportation hub in Unity. Remember, game development is an iterative process. Continuously test, receive feedback, and improve your prototype. Explore Unity's vast documentation and tutorials to expand your skills and add more complex features to your transportation hub.

CHAPTER 13   DIGITAL TWIN METAVERSE PROTOTYPES: SMART LIVING

Smart Education Centers

Employing Roblox Studio and Meta Spark, we will prototype interactive and gamified smart education centers that offer virtual reality and augmented reality learning experiences. Figure 13-4 presents a conceptual design of smart education centers—the blueprint we aspire to replicate in our prototype. These centers could focus on STEM education, language learning, and history, providing engaging and immersive educational content for students of all ages.

Creating interactive and gamified smart education centers within a digital twin metaverse city can greatly enhance the learning experience for students of all ages. Here's a step-by-step guide to developing these centers using Roblox Studio for the virtual environment and Meta Spark for augmented reality (AR) experiences, tailored for beginners.

CHAPTER 13   DIGITAL TWIN METAVERSE PROTOTYPES: SMART LIVING

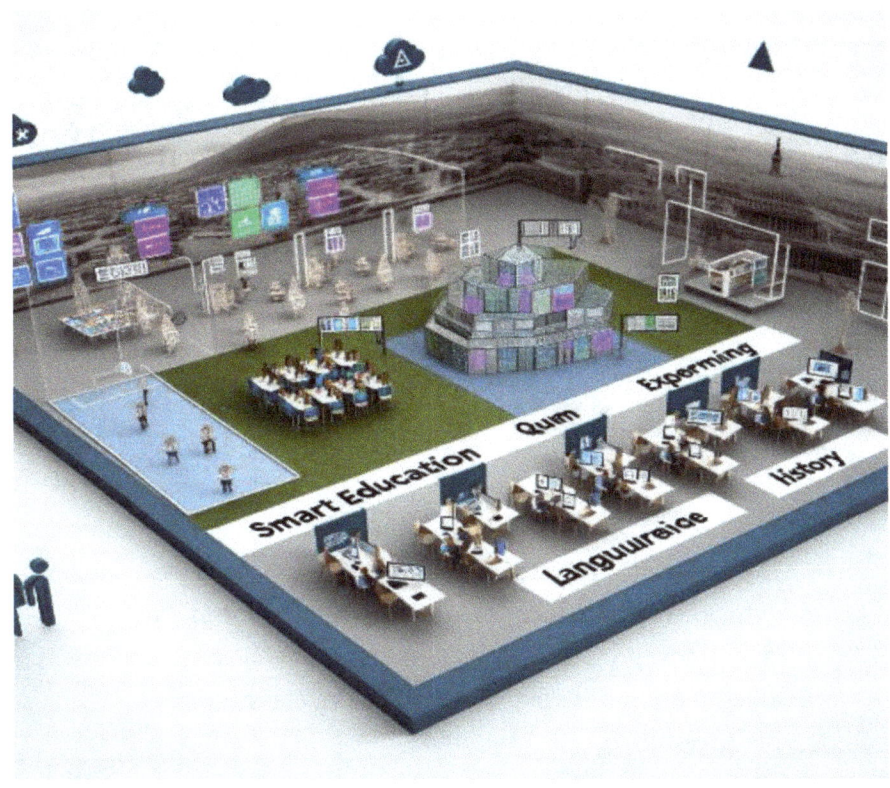

Figure 13-4. Conceptual design of smart education centers (author's development with Dall-E)

Step 1: Getting Started with Roblox Studio

- Download and Install Roblox Studio: Go to the Roblox Studio website (https://create.roblox.com/landing), download the latest version, and install it on your computer.

CHAPTER 13   DIGITAL TWIN METAVERSE PROTOTYPES: SMART LIVING

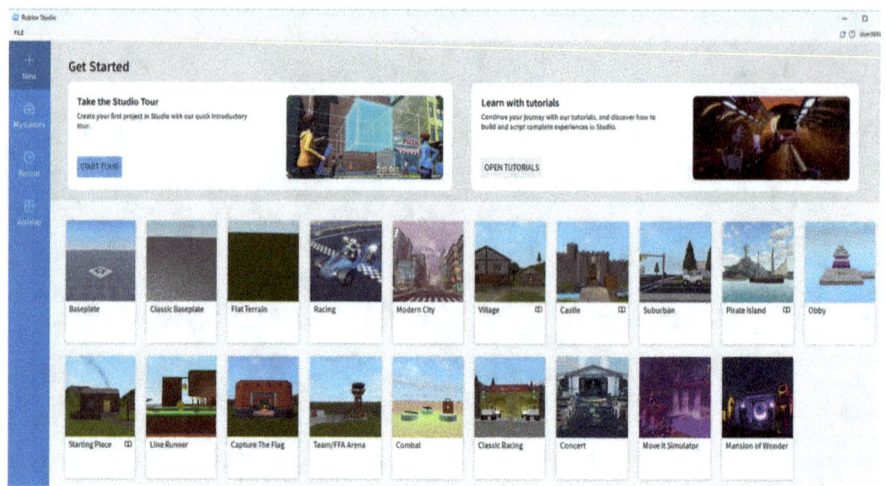

- Create a New Project: Open Roblox Studio, sign in with your Roblox account, and select "Create New" to start a new project. Choose a template that best suits an educational environment, such as a classroom or a playground.

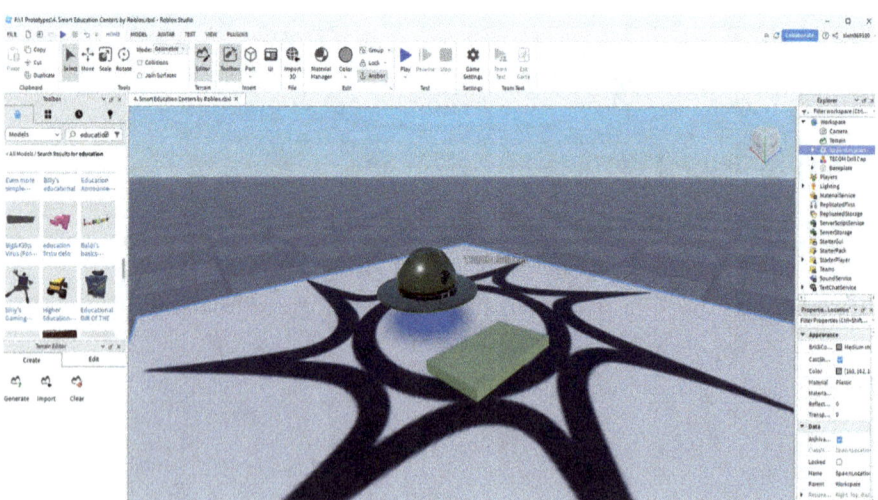

CHAPTER 13   DIGITAL TWIN METAVERSE PROTOTYPES: SMART LIVING

Step 2: Building the Virtual Environment

- Learn the Basics: Familiarize yourself with the Roblox Studio interface. Understand the essential tools: Select, Move, Scale, Rotate, and the Properties and Explorer panels.

- Design the Layout: Use the tools to create the basic layout of your education center. This includes classrooms, laboratories, and common areas for social interaction.

- Import Assets: Visit the Roblox Library to find and import premade assets like desks, chairs, equipment, and decorative items to enhance your space.

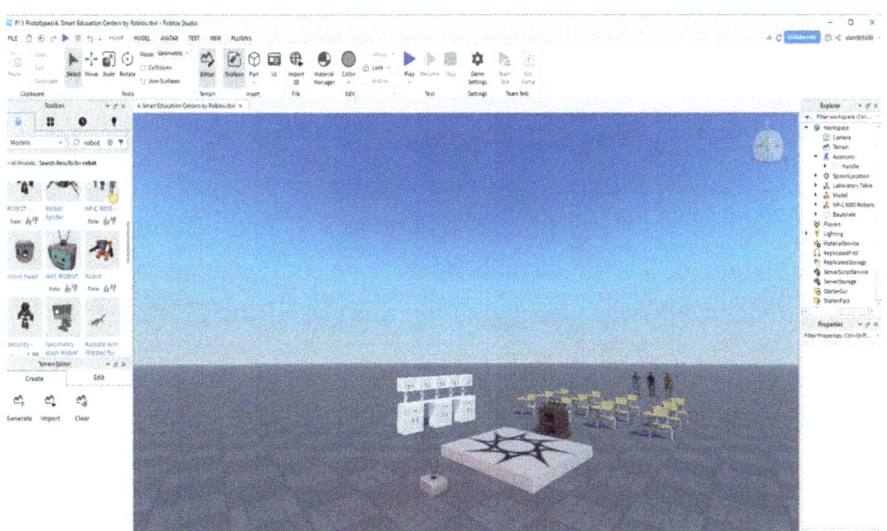

CHAPTER 13   DIGITAL TWIN METAVERSE PROTOTYPES: SMART LIVING

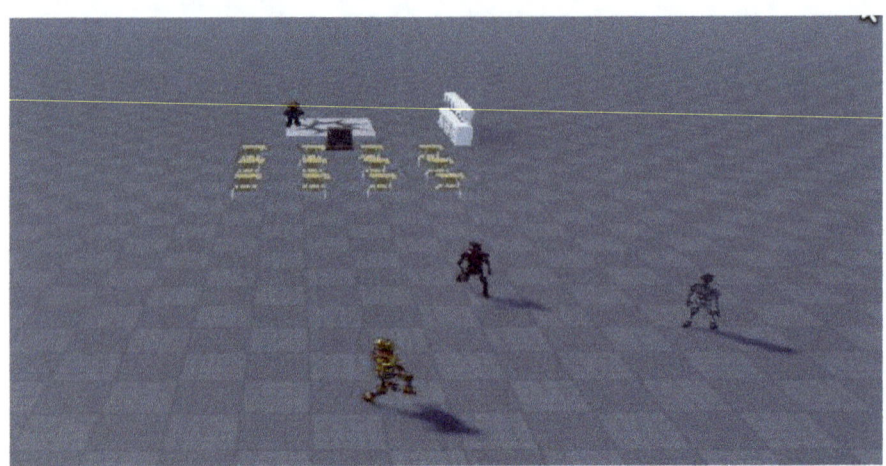

Step 3: Adding Interactive Elements

- Scripting Basics: Learn Lua, the scripting language used in Roblox. Start with simple scripts to create interactive elements. Tutorials on the Roblox Developer Hub can help you begin.

- Create Interactive Lessons: Script interactive quizzes, experiments, and puzzles related to STEM education, language learning, and history. For example, create a science l2) where students can mix virtual chemicals to see reactions.

Step 4: Incorporating VR and AR with Meta Spark

- Introduction to Meta Spark: While Roblox Studio creates the virtual environment, Meta Spark will allow you to add AR elements. Download Meta Spark Studio from the official website.

- Create AR Experiences: Follow Meta Spark's tutorials to create simple AR projects, such as 3D models of historical monuments or interactive AR books that bring stories and educational content to life.

CHAPTER 13 DIGITAL TWIN METAVERSE PROTOTYPES: SMART LIVING

- Integrate AR into Roblox: Although direct integration might be complex, you can create QR codes in Roblox Studio that, when scanned with a smartphone, lead users to AR experiences created in Meta Spark. Place these QR codes around your educational center for an enhanced learning experience.

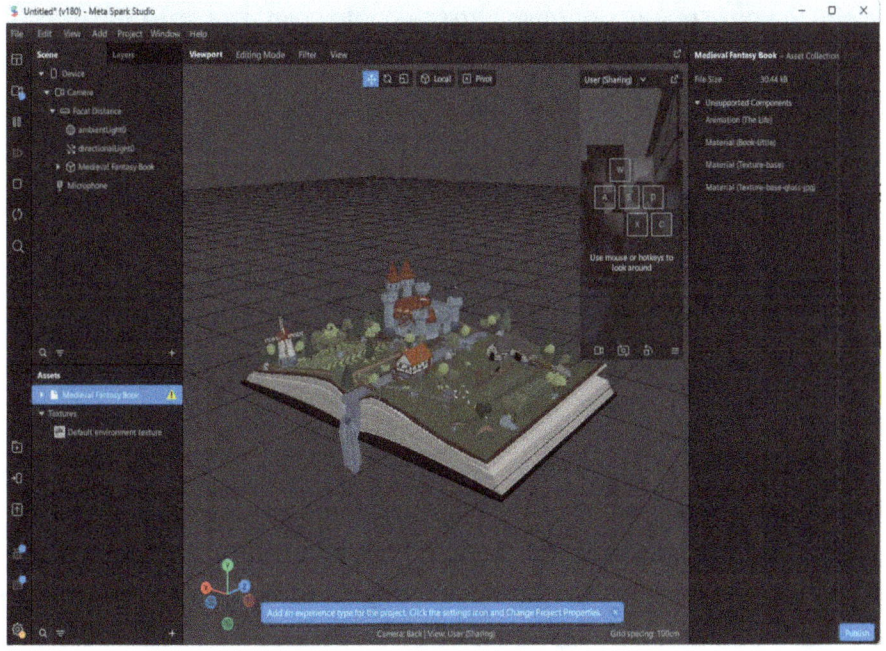

Now it's your turn   *As you venture further into the realm of digital twin metaverse city development, I encourage you to continue the remaining steps and enhance your prototype by adding rich, realistic scenery, fine-tuning materials, and weaving in greater interactivity. Your engagement and dedication to this work are invaluable—embrace this chance to innovate and hone your expertise in crafting the digital landscapes of tomorrow...*

Step 5: Testing and Publishing

- Test Your Project: Use Roblox Studio's testing features to playtest your educational center. Ensure all interactive elements work as intended and adjust based on feedback.

- Publish Your Education Center: Once satisfied with your creation, publish it to the Roblox platform, making it accessible to users worldwide. Share it with schools, teachers, and educational organizations.

Step 6: Gathering Feedback and Iteration

- Collect User Feedback: Encourage users to provide feedback on their learning experience.

- Iterate and Improve: Use feedback to make iterative improvements to your education center, adding new content, refining existing lessons, and enhancing interactivity.

By following these steps, beginners can embark on creating engaging and immersive smart education centers within the digital twin metaverse city, leveraging the unique capabilities of Roblox Studio and Meta Spark to offer innovative learning experiences.

Public Safety and Emergency Response Simulation

With Unreal Engine's advanced rendering capabilities and SpatialOS's scalability, we will develop a prototype simulation for public safety and emergency response in the metaverse city. Figure 13-5 presents a conceptual design of a public safety and emergency response simulation—the blueprint we aspire to replicate in our prototype. This could include virtual training environments for firefighters, police, and emergency medical services, enhancing preparedness and response strategies through realistic simulations.

Creating a prototype for a public safety and emergency response simulation that utilizes Unreal Engine's advanced rendering capabilities and SpatialOS's scalability involves several steps. This guide is tailored for beginners, explaining each step to help readers develop a basic understanding of how to use these tools to build an immersive simulation.

Figure 13-5. *Conceptual design of public safety and emergency response simulation (author's development with Dall-E)*

CHAPTER 13   DIGITAL TWIN METAVERSE PROTOTYPES: SMART LIVING

Step 1: Familiarizing Yourself with Unreal Engine

- Download Unreal Engine: Visit the (`https://www.unrealengine.com/`) and download the Epic Games Launcher. Install Unreal Engine through the launcher.

- Explore the Interface: Open Unreal Engine and create a new project using the First Person template. This gives you a simple starting point with a character that can move and look around.

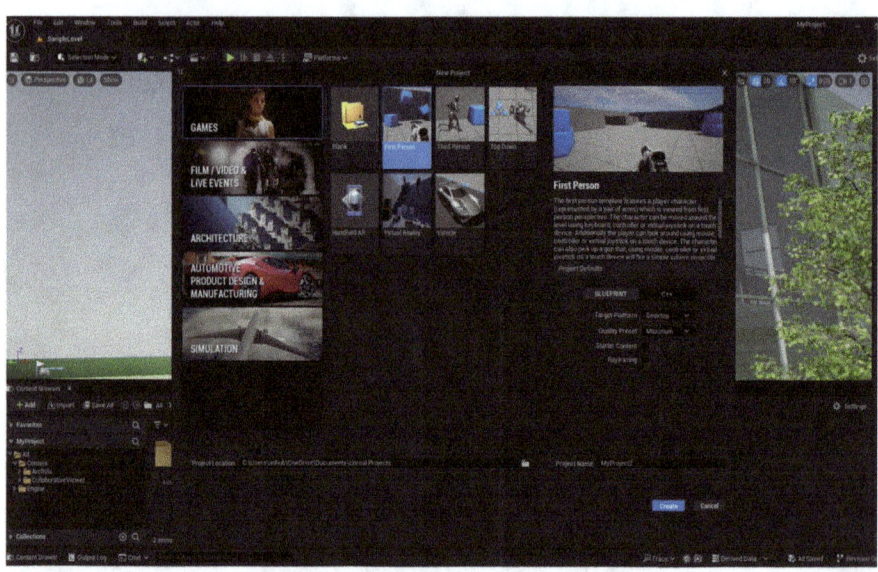

- Learn Basic Navigation: Familiarize yourself with navigating the Unreal Editor. Learn to navigate the viewport, use the Content Browser, and understand the basics of the Blueprint visual scripting system, which allows for programming without traditional coding.

CHAPTER 13   DIGITAL TWIN METAVERSE PROTOTYPES: SMART LIVING

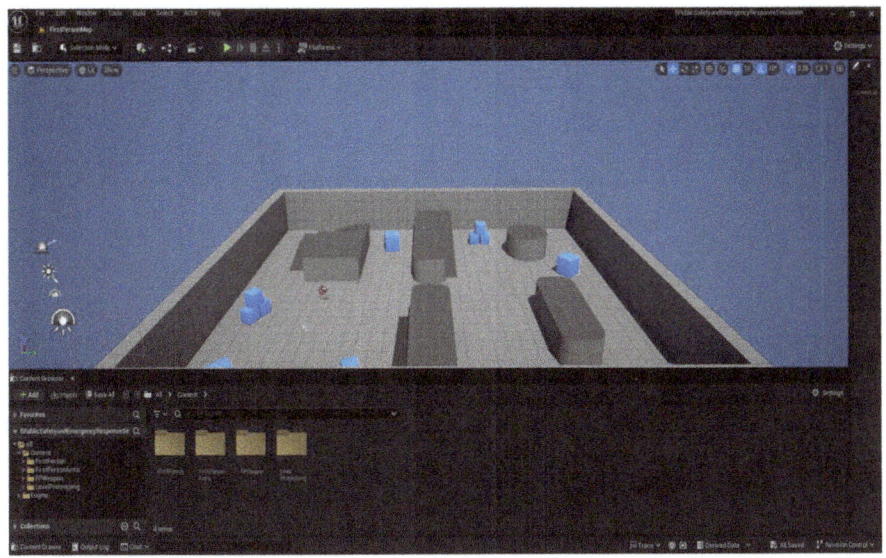

Step 2: Introduction to SpatialOS

- Understanding SpatialOS: Visit the (https:// improbable.io/) to learn about SpatialOS. It's a platform that allows you to create massive, persistent virtual worlds. While Unreal Engine handles the rendering, SpatialOS manages the simulation on a large scale.

CHAPTER 13 DIGITAL TWIN METAVERSE PROTOTYPES: SMART LIVING

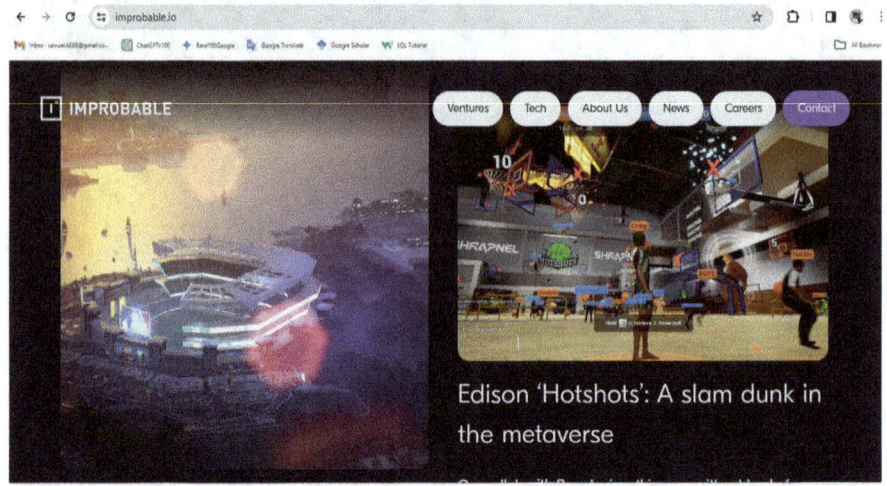

- SpatialOS GDK for Unreal: Download the SpatialOS GDK (Game Development Kit) for Unreal from the Improbable website. This GDK integrates SpatialOS with Unreal Engine, allowing you to build scalable, multiplayer simulations.

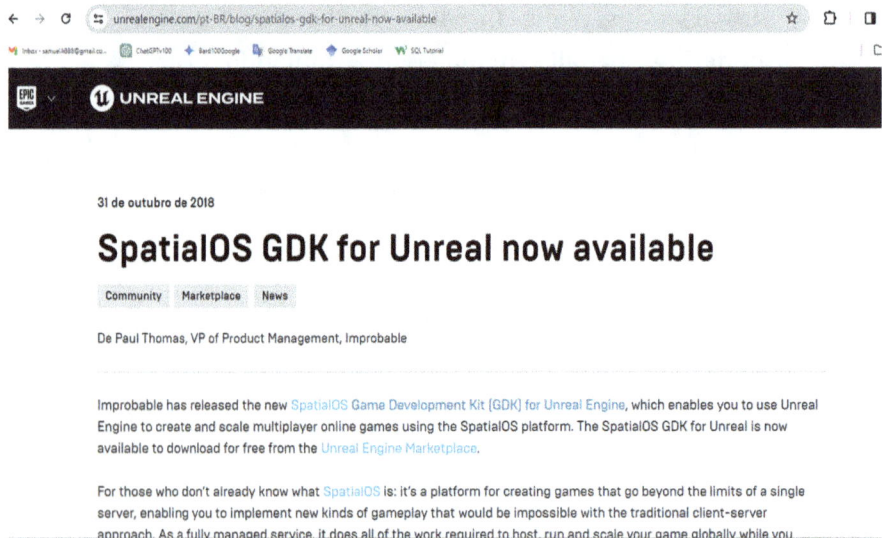

Step 3: Creating the Environment

- Design the Environment: Use Unreal Engine's level design tools to create the basic layout of your city. Include streets, buildings, and other urban elements. Focus on creating a realistic environment where emergency scenarios can take place.

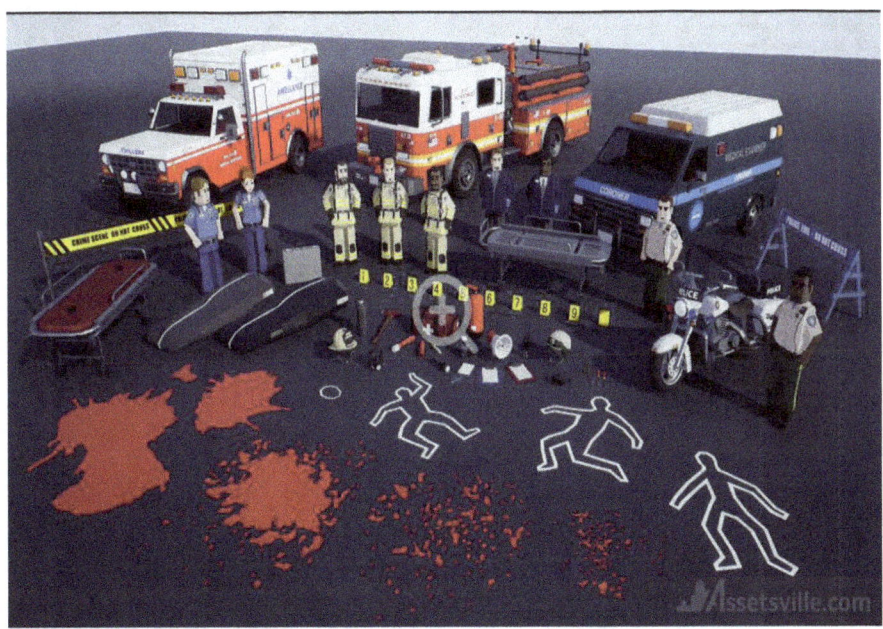

- Import Assets: Utilize the Unreal Engine Marketplace to find and import assets that fit a public safety and emergency theme, such as fire trucks, police cars, and medical equipment.

CHAPTER 13   DIGITAL TWIN METAVERSE PROTOTYPES: SMART LIVING

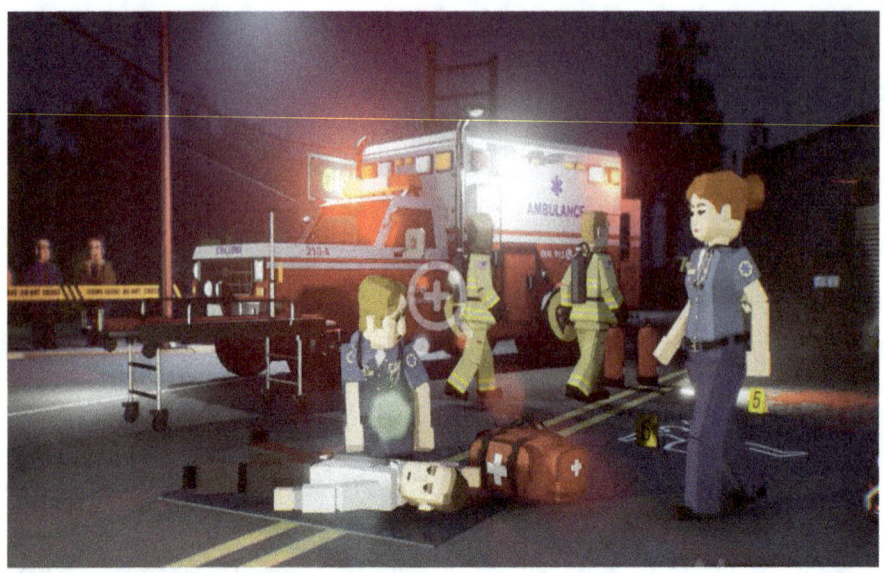

Step 4: Integrating SpatialOS

- Set Up SpatialOS: Follow the GDK setup guide to integrate SpatialOS with your Unreal project. This involves configuring your project settings to use SpatialOS for networking and simulation.

- Define Entities: In SpatialOS, define entities for different aspects of your simulation, such as vehicles, NPCs (non-player characters), and environmental hazards. Entities are objects in your world that have their own behavior and can interact with other entities.

Now it's your turn *As you venture further into the realm of digital twin metaverse city development, I encourage you to continue the remaining steps and enhance your prototype by adding rich, realistic scenery, fine-tuning materials, and weaving in greater interactivity. Your engagement and dedication to this work are invaluable— embrace this chance to innovate and hone your expertise in crafting the digital landscapes of tomorrow…*

Step 5: Programming Logic and Scenarios

- Use Blueprints: Start with simple scenarios, such as a building fire or a traffic accident. Use Unreal Engine's Blueprints to program the logic behind each scenario. This might include triggering an alarm, dispatching emergency vehicles, and managing NPC behaviors.

- Multiplayer Setup: Use SpatialOS to manage the multiplayer aspect of your simulation. This includes synchronizing the state of the simulation across multiple clients and handling the logic for multiplayer interactions.

Step 6: Testing and Iteration

- Local Testing: Use Unreal Engine's built-in tools to test your simulation locally. Debug any issues and make an adjustment as needed.

- Deploy with SpatialOS: Once you're satisfied with the local version, use SpatialOS to deploy your simulation to the cloud. This allows you to test the scalability and performance of your simulation with potentially thousands of simultaneous users.

Step 7: Iterate and Expand

- Gather Feedback: After testing, gather feedback from users to identify areas for improvement.

- Expand Scenarios: Gradually introduce more complex scenarios into your simulation, incorporating a wider range of public safety and emergency response situations.

Creating a public safety and emergency response simulation as a beginner may seem daunting, but by breaking down the process into manageable steps and gradually building up your skills in Unreal Engine and SpatialOS, you can create an engaging and educational simulation. Remember, the key to success is to start simple, iterate based on feedback, and continuously expand your knowledge and capabilities.

Urban Farming and Green Spaces

Utilizing Blender for asset creation and Unity for interactive experiences, we will prototype urban farming solutions and green spaces within the digital twin metaverse city. Figure 13-6 presents a conceptual design of urban farming and green spaces—the blueprint we aspire to embody in our prototype. This prototype could explore vertical farming technologies, community gardens, and interactive educational tours about sustainability and local food production, promoting environmental awareness and community engagement.

CHAPTER 13 DIGITAL TWIN METAVERSE PROTOTYPES: SMART LIVING

Figure 13-6. *Conceptual design of urban farming and green spaces (author's development with Dall-E)*

To create a prototype of urban farming solutions and green spaces within a digital twin metaverse city using Blender for asset creation and Unity for interactive experiences, follow these step-by-step instructions tailored for beginners:

Work 1: Asset Creation with Blender

Step 1: Installing Blender

- Download Blender from the (https://www.blender.org/download/).

- Install Blender on your computer by following the installation prompts.

305

CHAPTER 13   DIGITAL TWIN METAVERSE PROTOTYPES: SMART LIVING

Step 2: Basic Navigation

- Open Blender and familiarize yourself with the interface: the 3D viewport (where you model and view your scene), the timeline (for animations), and the properties panel (for modifying object properties).

- Learn Basic Navigation: Use the middle mouse button to rotate the view, scroll to zoom in and out, and Shift + middle mouse button to pan the view.

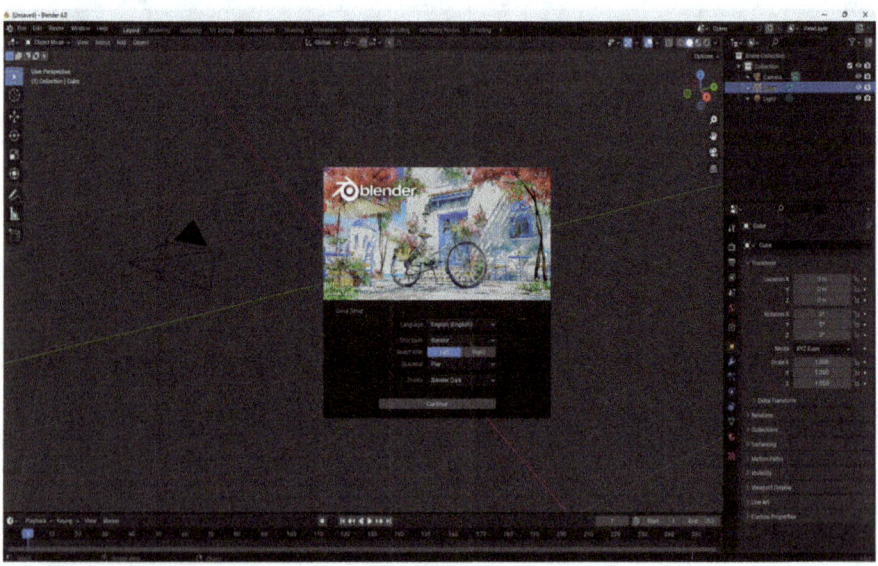

Step 3: Creating Basic Models

- Start with simple models to represent your urban farming assets, like planters, vertical farms, and greenhouses.

- Use the "Add" menu (Shift + 1) to create basic shapes (cubes, cylinders) that can be modified to represent your assets.

CHAPTER 13   DIGITAL TWIN METAVERSE PROTOTYPES: SMART LIVING

- Modify these shapes using Edit Mode (T2) to toggle. Use tools like Extrude (E), Scale (S), and Move (G) to shape your objects.

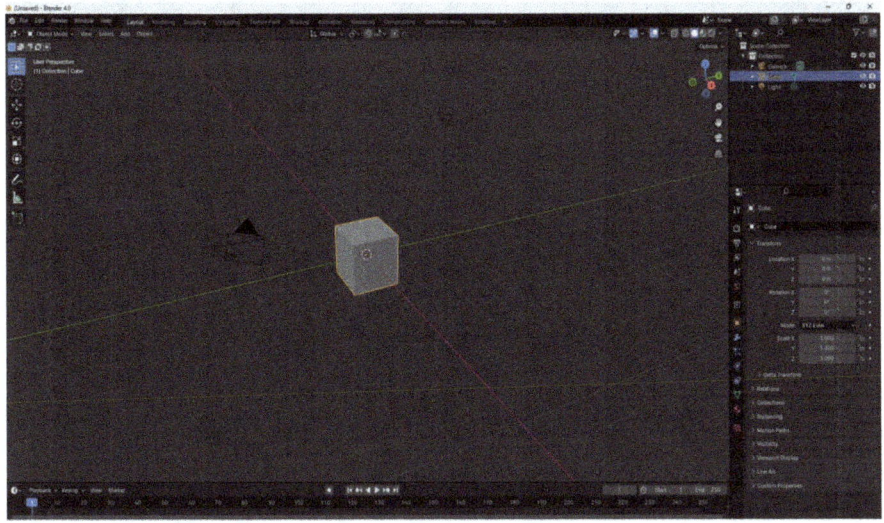

Step 4: Adding Details

- Apply materials and colors to your models in the Material Properties to make them visually distinct.

- Optional: Learn to apply textures for more realistic appearances. You can find free textures online or create your own.

CHAPTER 13   DIGITAL TWIN METAVERSE PROTOTYPES: SMART LIVING

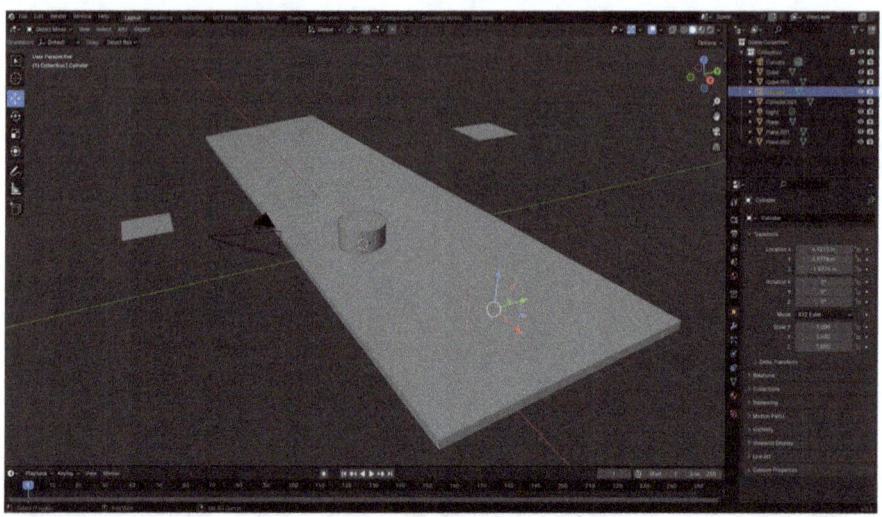

Step 5: Exporting Models

- Once satisfied with your models, export them as FBX files, a format compatible with Unity. Go to File ➤ Export ➤ FBX (.fbx).

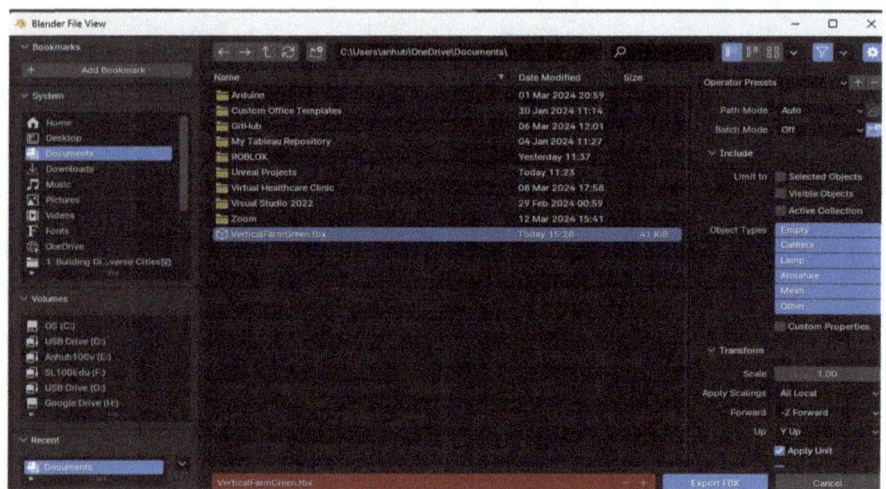

Work 2: Creating Interactive Experiences with Unity

CHAPTER 13   DIGITAL TWIN METAVERSE PROTOTYPES: SMART LIVING

Step 1: Installing Unity Hub and Unity

- Download and install Unity Hub from the (https://unity.com/download).

- Use Unity Hub to install a version of Unity. For beginners, the latest stable version is recommended.

Step 2: Creating a New Project

- Open Unity Hub, go to the Projects tab, and click "New Project."

- Choose the 3D template and name your project "Urban Farming Metaverse."

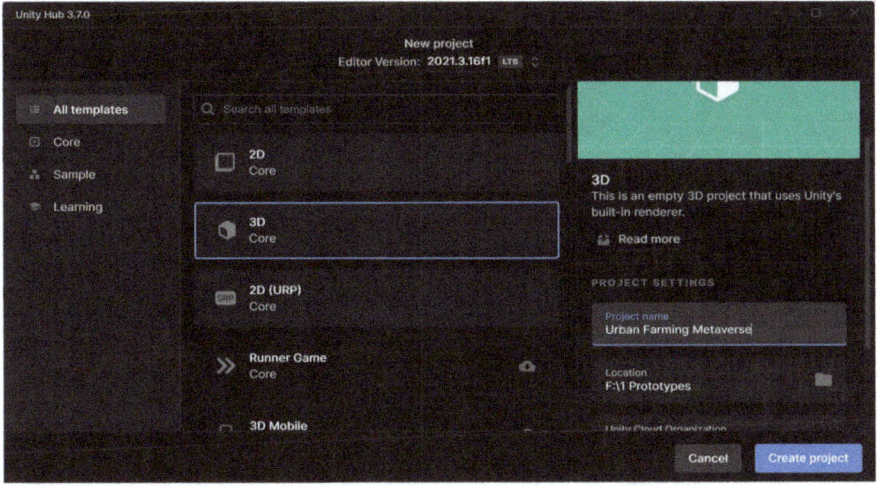

Step 3: Importing Blender Assets

- In Unity, go to Assets ➤ Import New Asset, and navigate to where you saved your FBX files from Blender. Select and import them.

CHAPTER 13   DIGITAL TWIN METAVERSE PROTOTYPES: SMART LIVING

- Drag and drop the imported models from the Assets panel into the scene to place them in your virtual environment.

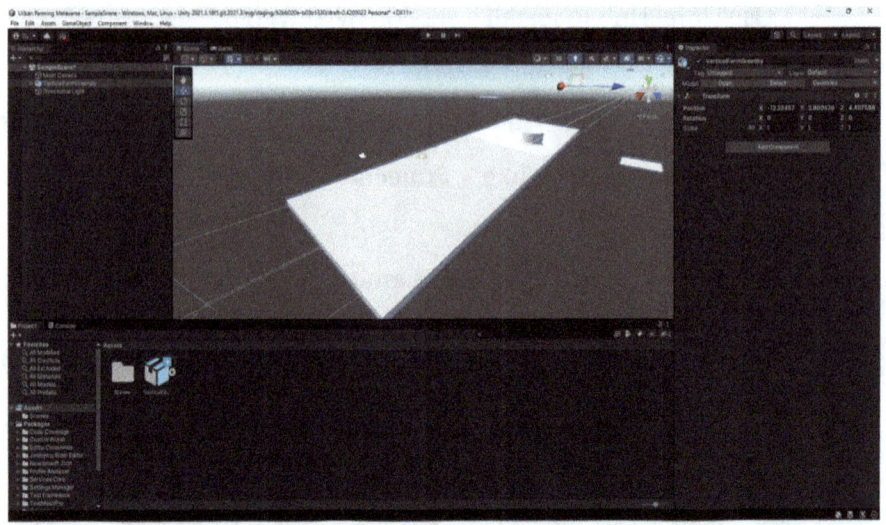

Now it's your turn   *As you venture further into the realm of digital twin metaverse city development, I encourage you to continue the remaining steps and enhance your prototype by adding rich, realistic scenery, fine-tuning materials, and weaving in greater interactivity. Your engagement and dedication to this work are invaluable—embrace this chance to innovate and hone your expertise in crafting the digital landscapes of tomorrow…*

Step 4: Adding Interactivity

- To make your urban farming scene interactive, you can start by creating a simple script. Right-click the Assets panel, choose Create ➤ C Script, and name it "InteractiveElement."

CHAPTER 13   DIGITAL TWIN METAVERSE PROTOTYPES: SMART LIVING

- Double-click the script to open it in Unity's script editor. You can start with something simple, like printing a message to the console when an object is clicked.

- Attach the script to one of your farming assets by selecting the asset in the scene and dragging the script onto the Inspector panel:

```csharp
using UnityEngine;
public class InteractiveElement: MonoBehaviour
{
    void OnMouseDown()
    {
        Debug.Log("Object Clicked!");
    }
}
```

Step 5: Building the Environment

- Use Unity's Terrain tool to create land for your urban farm. Access it via the Terrain menu in the Hierarchy panel.

- Add trees, grass, and paths to make your green space more realistic. Unity's Asset Store offers free assets for additional decorations.

Step 6: Playtesting

- Click the Play button at the top of Unity to enter Play Mode. Interact with your scene to test the functionality.

- Make adjustments as needed based on your observations.

CHAPTER 13 DIGITAL TWIN METAVERSE PROTOTYPES: SMART LIVING

Step 7: Learning and Expanding

- Unity offers extensive documentation and tutorials. Explore topics like lighting, camera controls, and advanced interactivity to enhance your prototype.

This guide provides a foundation for creating a basic urban farming and green spaces prototype. As you become more comfortable with Blender and Unity, continue to explore their vast capabilities to add complexity and depth to your digital twin metaverse project.

In summary, each of these prototypes represents a facet of smart living in a digital twin metaverse city, demonstrating how the integration of advanced development tools can lead to innovative solutions for sustainable and efficient urban living.

CHAPTER 14

Digital Twin Metaverse Prototypes: *Smart Working*

Embarking on a journey to the workplace of the future, this chapter invites readers to discover the innovative prototypes of smart working environments. This chapter unfolds a series of pioneering projects that merge the realms of virtual and augmented reality with AI-powered solutions, heralding a new era for workspaces. As we venture through the intricacies of virtual coworking spaces, we envision a world without borders, where collaboration transcends physical barriers, fostering global connectivity and innovation. The prototypes presented will demonstrate how smart office management systems can streamline workflows, amplify productivity, and usher in unprecedented levels of efficiency.

Delving deeper, we encounter transformative examples such as AI-powered virtual assistants—sophisticated digital companions that provide tailored support and insights, optimizing day-to-day operations. Augmented reality training modules emerge as another focal point, offering immersive experiences that enhance skill development and knowledge retention, thus reshaping professional growth and learning. These cutting-edge tools serve not just as showcases of technological prowess but as harbingers of a profound shift in how we perceive and engage with our work environments.

CHAPTER 14 DIGITAL TWIN METAVERSE PROTOTYPES: SMART WORKING

Our aim with this chapter is to delineate a future where the workplace transcends traditional confines, emerging as a digitally enhanced landscape that we thoughtfully construct and inhabit. It's a future where digital twins and metaverse technologies are not mere adjuncts but core components that define the fabric of our professional lives. As you immerse yourself in the detailed expositions of each prototype, you're encouraged to visualize and anticipate the boundless possibilities that await in the digitized paradigm of work.

Virtual Coworking Spaces

Using Unity for its broad platform support, we will create a prototype of virtual coworking spaces where remote workers from different parts of the metaverse can collaborate in real time. Figure 14-1 presents a conceptual design of virtual coworking spaces—the blueprint we aspire to replicate in our prototype. These spaces could feature virtual meeting rooms, communal work areas, private booths, and interactive whiteboards, all designed to enhance productivity and foster community among digital nomads.

Creating a prototype for "virtual coworking spaces" in Unity for beginners involves several steps, from initial setup to deploying a basic interactive environment. This guide will walk you through the process, assuming no prior experience with Unity or Unreal Engine (UE). We'll focus on Unity for its user-friendly interface and broad platform support, ideal for developing immersive virtual environments.

CHAPTER 14   DIGITAL TWIN METAVERSE PROTOTYPES: SMART WORKING

Figure 14-1. *Conceptual design of virtual coworking spaces (author's development with Dall-E)*

Step 1: Download and Install Unity

- Visit the Unity official website (https://unity.com/download) and download the Unity Hub installer.

- Install Unity Hub on your computer. Unity Hub is a management tool that allows you to manage Unity versions and projects easily.

- Through Unity Hub, install the latest version of Unity

CHAPTER 14   DIGITAL TWIN METAVERSE PROTOTYPES: SMART WORKING

Editor. Choose the version that is recommended for new users, ensuring it includes the Unity WebGL build support for deploying projects online.

Step 2: Set Up a New Project

- Open Unity Hub and go to the "Projects" tab.

- Click the "New Project" button.

- Select the "3D" template as your starting point.

- Name your project "Virtual Co-Working Spaces" and choose a location to save it on your computer.

- Click "Create" to initialize your new project.

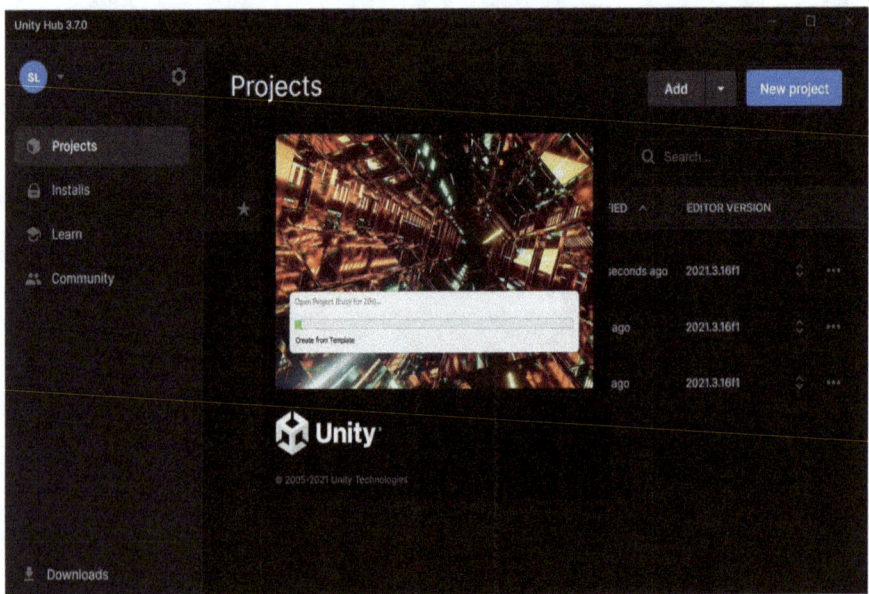

Step 3: Familiarize Yourself with the Unity Interface

- Scene View: This is where you'll design and preview your coworking space.

- Game View: Shows you what your scene will look like from the perspective of a player or camera.

- Hierarchy: Lists all the objects in your current scene.

- Inspector: Displays properties of the selected object, where you can modify them.

- Project: Organizes all your assets, including models, materials, scripts, etc.

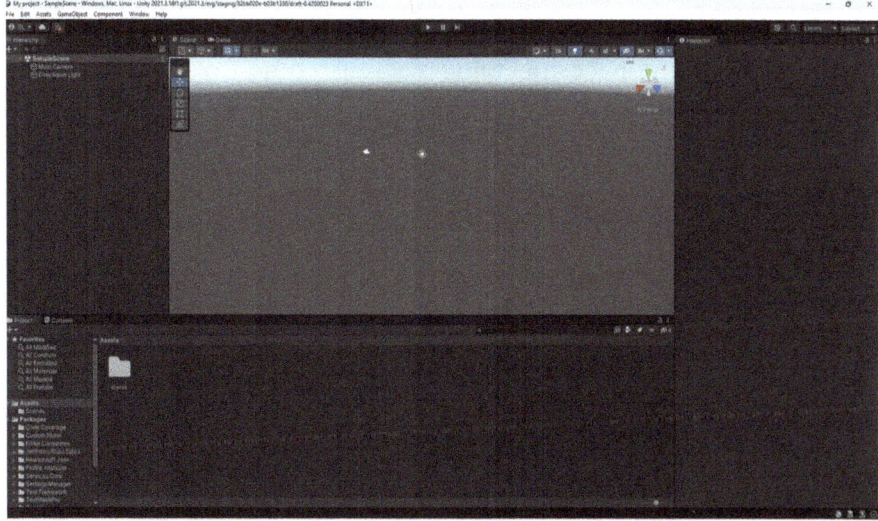

Step 4: Create Your Virtual Environment

- Use the "GameObject" menu to create basic shapes (Cube, Sphere, Plane) that will serve as your space's structure (walls, floors, tables).

CHAPTER 14   DIGITAL TWIN METAVERSE PROTOTYPES: SMART WORKING

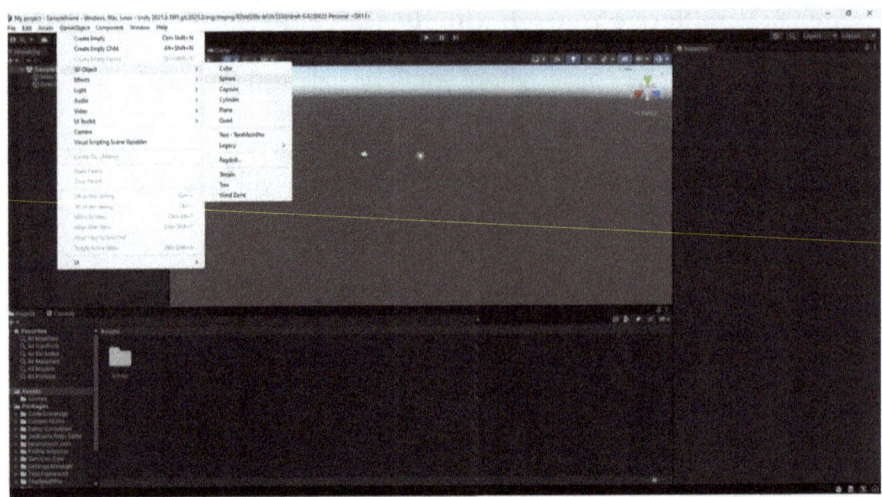

- Arrange these objects to form the layout of your coworking space, including meeting rooms, work areas, and booths.

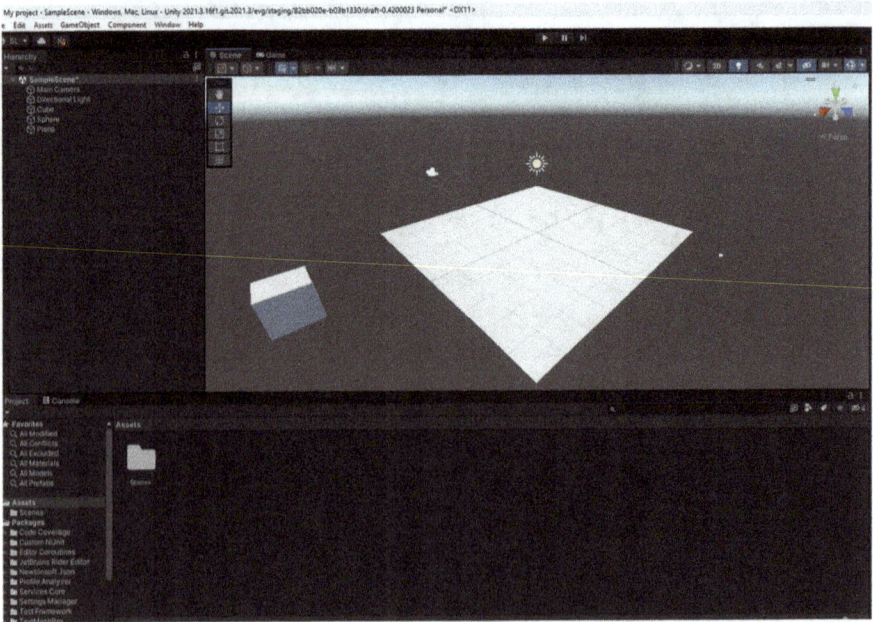

CHAPTER 14   DIGITAL TWIN METAVERSE PROTOTYPES: SMART WORKING

- Import textures that resemble real-life materials (wood, glass, fabric) by dragging and dropping them into the "Assets" folder.

- Apply these textures to your objects to enhance the realism of your space.

- Use the "Light" option under the "GameObject" menu to add light sources, simulating natural and artificial lighting.

Now it's your turn   *As you venture further into the realm of digital twin metaverse city development, I encourage you to continue the remaining steps and enhance your prototype by adding rich, realistic scenery, fine-tuning materials, and weaving in greater interactivity. Your engagement and dedication to this work are invaluable— embrace this chance to innovate and hone your expertise in crafting the digital landscapes of tomorrow…*

Step 5: Add Interactivity

- Create separate rooms and use Unity's "Cinemachine" package to set up virtual cameras that players can switch between, simulating the experience of moving through different meeting rooms.

- Create a flat surface with a white material for the whiteboard.

- Implement simple drawing mechanics using Unity's "Input System" package, allowing users to draw or write on the whiteboard with their cursor or VR controllers.

Step 6: Implement Multiplayer Functionality

- To enable real-time collaboration, explore Unity's "Photon Unity Networking (PUN)" package, which simplifies the process of adding multiplayer features. Follow the package's documentation to set up basic multiplayer functionality, allowing remote workers to see and interact with each other in the virtual space.

Step 7: Build and Deploy Your Prototype

- Once your virtual coworking space is ready, go to "File" ➤ "Build Settings."

- Select "WebGL" as the platform to enable your project to be accessible online.

- Click "Build and Run" to compile your project. Unity will prompt you to choose a location to save the compiled files.

- After the build process, Unity opens your default web browser to run your project, allowing you to explore your virtual coworking space.

This guide provides a foundation for creating a basic prototype. As you become more familiar with Unity, you can explore advanced features, add custom assets from the Unity Asset Store, and refine your virtual coworking space to better suit the needs of digital nomads.

Augmented Reality Training Modules

Leveraging Meta Spark, we will develop AR training modules for various industries, allowing employees to gain hands-on experience with equipment and procedures in a safe, virtual environment. Figure 14-2 presents a conceptual design of augmented reality training modules—the blueprint we aspire to embody in our prototype. These modules could be used for onboarding new employees, upskilling current staff, or simulating emergency response drills.

Developing augmented reality (AR) training modules with Meta Spark for various industries involves a step-by-step process that beginners can follow. Meta Spark enables creators to design immersive AR experiences accessible via smartphones, which can simulate real-world equipment and scenarios for training purposes. Here's a beginner-friendly guide to creating AR training modules:

CHAPTER 14   DIGITAL TWIN METAVERSE PROTOTYPES: SMART WORKING

Figure 14-2. Conceptual design of augmented reality training modules (author's development with Dall-E)

Step 1: Get Familiar with Meta Spark

- Download Meta Spark Studio: Visit the (https://sparkar.facebook.com/ar-studio/) and download Meta Spark Studio for your operating system.

- Explore the Interface: Open Meta Spark Studio and spend some time getting familiar with the interface. Look for the Project Templates, which can provide a quick start to your project.

CHAPTER 14   DIGITAL TWIN METAVERSE PROTOTYPES: SMART WORKING

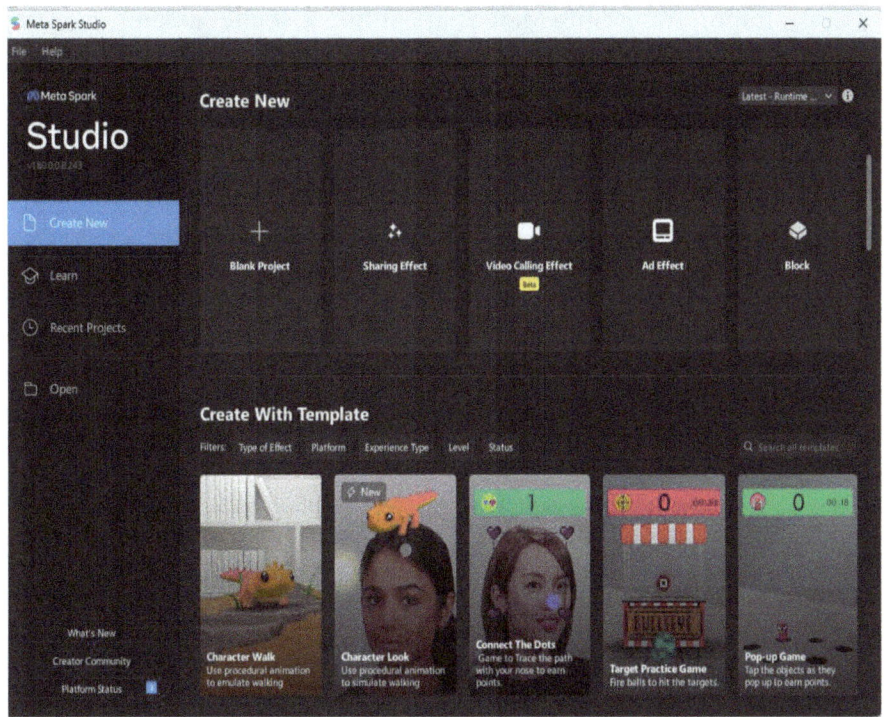

Step 2: Start a New Project

- Create a New Project: In Meta Spark Studio, select "Create New" to start a new project. Choose a blank project or a template that closely matches the type of training module you want to create.

Step 3: Import Assets

- Gather Assets: Collect or create 3D models, textures, and any other assets you will need for your training module. Websites like Sketchf or TurboSquid can be good sources for 3D models.

323

CHAPTER 14   DIGITAL TWIN METAVERSE PROTOTYPES: SMART WORKING

- Import Assets into Meta Spark Studio: Use the "Assets" panel to import your 3D models and textures. Ensure they are optimized for AR to maintain performance on mobile devices.

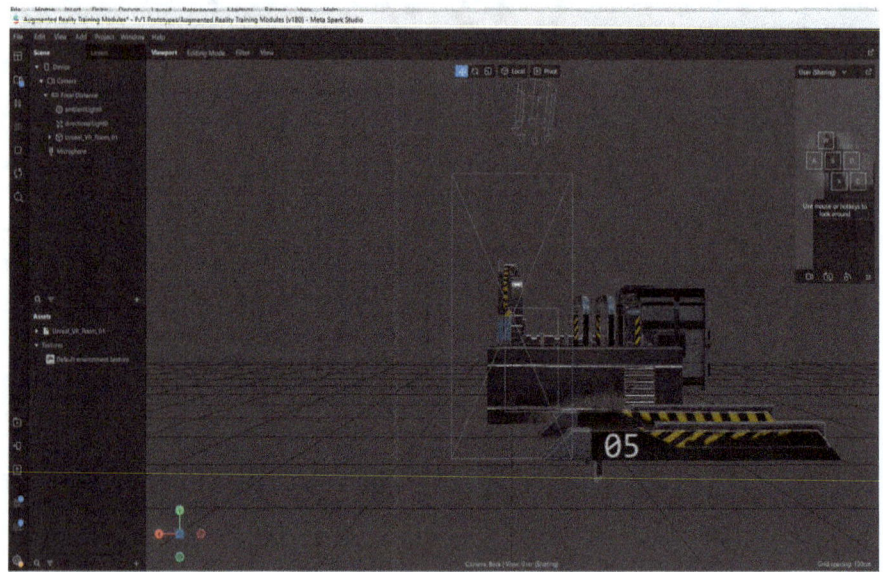

Step 4: Create the AR Experience

- Place Your Assets: Drag and drop your 3D models into the scene. Use the transform tools (move, rotate, scale) to position them appropriately.

- Add Interactivity: Utilize the "Patch Editor" to create interactivity without coding. For example, you can make a machine model animate or disassemble when a user taps on it.

- Simulate Procedures: Break down complex procedures into steps. Use animation and interactive patches to guide the user through each step, simulating the operation of machinery or execution of tasks.

CHAPTER 14   DIGITAL TWIN METAVERSE PROTOTYPES: SMART WORKING

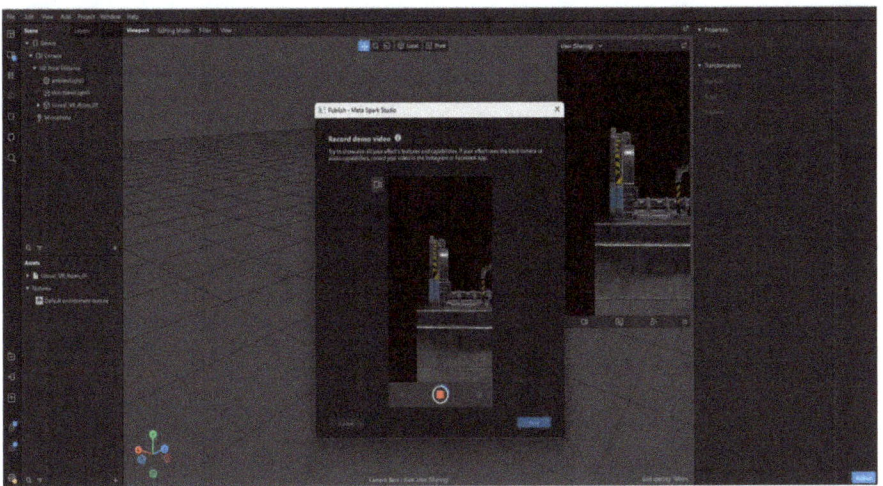

Now it's your turn   *As you venture further into the realm of digital twin metaverse city development, I encourage you to continue the remaining steps and enhance your prototype by adding rich, realistic scenery, fine-tuning materials, and weaving in greater interactivity. Your engagement and dedication to this work are invaluable— embrace this chance to innovate and hone your expertise in crafting the digital landscapes of tomorrow...*

Step 5: Test Your AR Experience

- Preview Your Project: Use the Meta Spark Player app (available for iOS and Android) to test your AR experience on a real device. Make adjustments based on performance and user experience.

- Iterate and Improve: Based on testing, iterate on your design. Consider user feedback to make the experience as intuitive and informative as possible.

Step 6: Publish Your AR Training Module

- Review Meta's Policies: Before publishing, ensure your AR module complies with Meta's content policies.

- Publish: Once satisfied, use Meta Spark Studio to publish your AR training module. You can share it directly on Instagram or Facebook or distribute it through a link.

Step 7: Integrate and Deploy

- Integration: Discuss with your IT department or AR platform how to integrate the AR module into your training curriculum or LMS (Learning Management System).

- Deployment: Deploy the AR training module for employee training. Use QR codes or direct links for easy access.

Step 8: Collect Feedback and Iterate

- Feedback: Collect feedback from users to understand the effectiveness of the training module.

- Iterate: Make necessary adjustments to the module based on feedback to enhance the learning experience.

By following these steps, even beginners can leverage Meta Spark to create engaging and educational AR training modules for various industries. This hands-on approach allows employees to gain valuable experience in a controlled, virtual environment, enhancing learning outcomes and operational safety.

CHAPTER 14 DIGITAL TWIN METAVERSE PROTOTYPES: SMART WORKING

Smart Office Management System

Utilizing the Decentraland SDK and smart contract capabilities of the Ethereum blockchain, we will prototype a smart office management system. Figure 14-3 presents a conceptual design of smart office management system—the blueprint we aspire to replicate in our prototype. This system could automate tasks such as booking meeting rooms, managing resource allocation, and maintaining office security, all within a digital twin of a physical office environment.

To develop a "smart office management system" prototype using the Decentraland SDK and smart contract capabilities of the Ethereum blockchain, follow these steps. This guide is tailored for beginners with no prior experience in these tools.

Figure 14-3. *Conceptual design of smart office management system (author's development with Dall-E)*

CHAPTER 14   DIGITAL TWIN METAVERSE PROTOTYPES: SMART WORKING

Step 1: Understanding the Tools

- Decentraland SDK: A set of tools for creating, deploying, and managing interactive content within the Decentraland virtual world, a decentralized VR platform built on the Ethereum blockchain.

- Ethereum Blockchain and Smart Contracts: A decentralized platform that runs smart contracts—applications that run exactly as programmed without any possibility of downtime, fraud, or third-party interference. These are used for managing transactions and automating processes in a secure manner.

Step 2: Setting Up Your Development Environment

- Install Node.js: Decentraland requires Node.js to run. Download and install Node.js from (https://nodejs.org/).

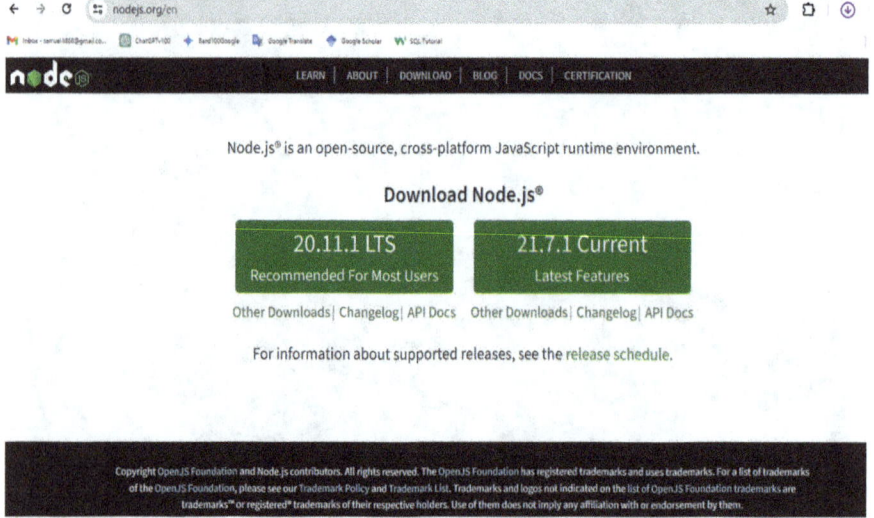

CHAPTER 14   DIGITAL TWIN METAVERSE PROTOTYPES: SMART WORKING

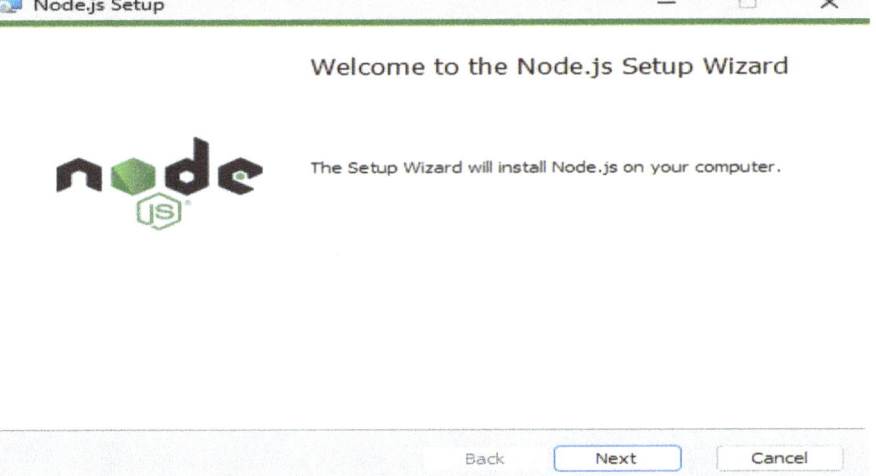

- Install Decentraland SDK.

- Open a terminal or command prompt.

- Run `npm install -g decentraland` to install the Decentraland CLI.

CHAPTER 14   DIGITAL TWIN METAVERSE PROTOTYPES: SMART WORKING

- Set up Metamask.

- Install the Metamask browser extension from [https://metamask.io/].

- Create an account. You'll use this to interact with the Ethereum blockchain.

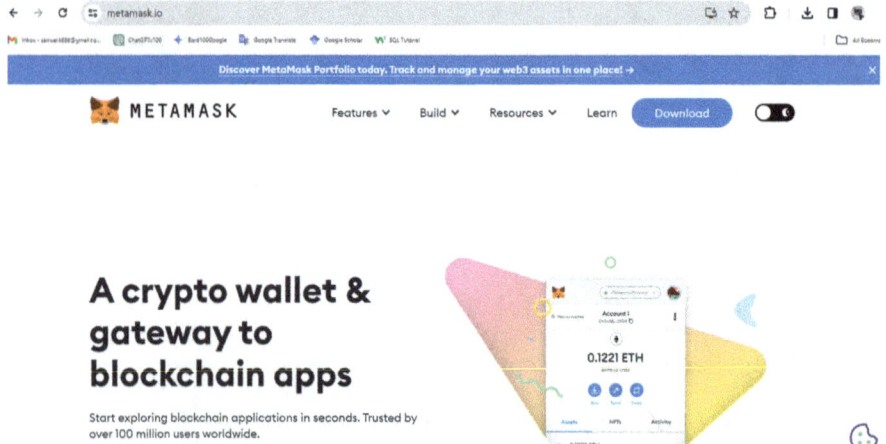

Step 3: Creating Your Smart Office Space in Decentraland

- Initialize your project.

- In the terminal, navigate to the folder where you want to create your project.

- Run `dcl init` and follow the prompts to initialize a new Decentraland scene.

Now it's your turn *As you venture further into the realm of digital twin metaverse city development, I encourage you to continue the remaining steps and enhance your prototype by adding rich, realistic scenery, fine-tuning materials, and weaving in greater interactivity. Your engagement and dedication to this work are invaluable—embrace this chance to innovate and hone your expertise in crafting the digital landscapes of tomorrow…*

- Design your office.

- Use the Decentraland SDK to design your office space. Start with basic shapes and then add more complex structures.

- Edit the `scene.json` file and the TypeScript files in the `src` directory to add objects and functionalities. Decentraland's documentation (https://docs.decentraland.org/) provides guides and examples.

- Test Your Scene Locally: Run `dcl start` in your project directory to preview your scene in a local development server.

Step 4: Integrating Smart Contracts with Ethereum

- Learn Solidity: Solidity is the programming language for writing smart contracts on Ethereum. Visit [https://soliditylang.org/] to learn the basics.

- Write Smart Contracts for Office Management Tasks

CHAPTER 14   DIGITAL TWIN METAVERSE PROTOTYPES: SMART WORKING

1) Use a code editor to write smart contracts that handle tasks like booking meeting rooms or managing resource allocations.

2) Example:

```solidity
pragma solidity ^0.5.0;
contract MeetingRoomBooking {
    // Your smart contract code here
}
```

- **Deploy Your Smart Contracts**

- Use Remix (an online IDE at (https://remix.ethereum.org/)) to compile and deploy your smart contracts to the Ethereum blockchain.

- Connect Metamask to Remix to deploy from your account.

Step 5: Connecting Your Decentraland Scene with Smart Contracts

- **Interact with Smart Contracts**

- In your Decentraland scene's TypeScript files, use the `eth-connect` library to interact with your deployed smart contracts.

- Example:

```typescript
import { abi, contractAddress } from './contractInfo';
import { EthConnect } from 'eth-connect';
async function bookMeetingRoom() {
```

```
    // Example function to interact with a
    smart contract
}
```

- **Finalize and Deploy Your Scene**
- Once your smart office management system is functional and tested, use `dcl deploy` to publish your scene to Decentraland.

Step 6: Testing and Iteration

- Invite users to test the functionalities within Decentraland and gather feedback.
- Iterate on your design and smart contract functionalities based on user feedback.

This guide provides a basic overview. Each step involves substantial learning and experimentation, especially for beginners. Utilize resources like Decentraland's documentation, Solidity tutorials, and Ethereum development forums to deepen your understanding and troubleshoot issues as you progress.

Professional Development and Networking Hub

With Roblox Studio's user-generated content capabilities, we will create a prototype of professional development and networking hub. Figure 14-4 presents a conceptual design of a professional development and networking hub—the blueprint we aspire to embody in our prototype. This space could host virtual career fairs, workshops, and panel discussions, allowing professionals to learn, grow, and connect with peers across the metaverse.

Creating a "professional development and networking hub" in a digital twin metaverse city using Roblox Studio involves several steps, designed to guide beginners through the process. This prototype aims to host virtual career fairs, workshops, and panel discussions, facilitating professional growth and networking. Here's a step-by-step guide:

Figure 14-4. *Conceptual design of professional development and networking hub (author's development with Dall-E)*

Step 1: Downloading and Installing Roblox Studio (Getting Started with Roblox Studio)

- Go to the (https://www.roblox.com/creat5) and click the "Start Creating" button.

CHAPTER 14   DIGITAL TWIN METAVERSE PROTOTYPES: SMART WORKING

- Download and install Roblox Studio on your computer.
- Open Roblox Studio and log in with your Roblox account. If you don't have an account, you'll need to create one.

Step 2: Familiarizing Yourself with the Interface

- Spend some time exploring the Roblox Studio interface. Key areas include the Viewport (where you'll see your creation), the Explorer (listing all elements in your project), and the Properties panel (showing details about the selected element).

Step 3: Starting a New Project

- Click "New" or "Create New" to start a new project.
- Choose a template that suits a networking event space, such as the "Baseplate" for a blank canvas.

CHAPTER 14 DIGITAL TWIN METAVERSE PROTOTYPES: SMART WORKING

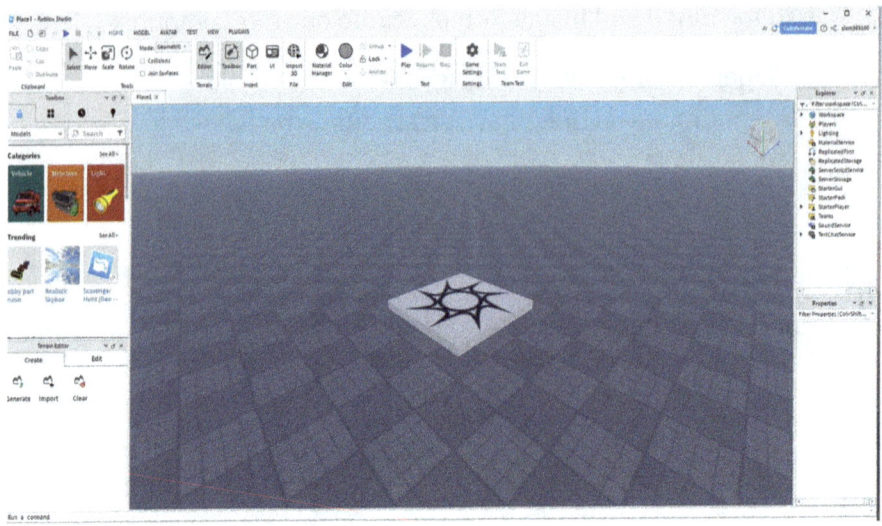

Step 4: Designing the Environment (Building the Hub)

- Use the Terrain Editor to create natural landscapes or urban settings for your hub.

- Select the Part tool to create basic structures like buildings, stages, or booths for career fairs and workshops.

CHAPTER 14   DIGITAL TWIN METAVERSE PROTOTYPES: SMART WORKING

Now it's your turn   *As you venture further into the realm of digital twin metaverse city development, I encourage you to continue the remaining steps and enhance your prototype by adding rich, realistic scenery, fine-tuning materials, and weaving in greater interactivity. Your engagement and dedication to this work are invaluable—embrace this chance to innovate and hone your expertise in crafting the digital landscapes of tomorrow…*

Step 5: Adding Interactivity

- Utilize the Toolbox to add interactive elements. Search for items like chairs, tables, or presentation screens and drag them into your scene.

- To create custom scripts for interactions (e.g., joining a workshop), select a part (like a button) and insert a script. Use simple Lua code, like opening a GUI when the part is clicked.

337

Step 6: Scripting for Networking Features

- Learn basic Lua scripting to enable networking features, for example, scripts to exchange virtual business cards or initiate private chat rooms. Roblox's Developer Hub provides excellent (https://developer.roblox.com/en-us/learn-roblox/coding-scripts).

Step 7: Testing Your Hub

- Click "Play" within Roblox Studio to enter playtest mode. Interact with your environment to ensure everything works as intended.
- Invite friends or colleagues to test the networking features and provide feedback.

Step 8: Publishing Your Hub

- Once you're satisfied with the hub, click "File" ➤ "Publish to Roblox As…" to publish your project.
- Fill in the details for your project, such as name and description, ensuring it's clear as a professional development and networking hub.
- Set the appropriate privacy and access settings, then publish.

Step 9: Promoting Your Hub (Engaging the Community)

- Share your hub on social media, professional forums, and within the Roblox community to attract professionals.
- Consider hosting scheduled events or workshops to kick-start engagement.

Step 10: Iterating Based on Feedback

- Gather feedback from users and iterate on your design. Adding new features or refining existing ones based on user interactions will keep your hub relevant and engaging.

This guide is designed to help beginners take their first steps in Roblox Studio toward creating a professional development and networking hub, emphasizing learning, networking, and professional growth within the digital twin metaverse city.

AI-Powered Virtual Assistants

Integrating ChatGPT for dynamic content generation and AI-driven interactions, we will prototype AI-powered virtual assistants tailored for various professional needs. Figure 14-5 presents a conceptual design of AI-powered virtual assistants—the blueprint we aspire to attempt prototyping. These assistants could help with scheduling, email management, project tracking, and providing instant information, all designed to streamline workflow and increase efficiency.

To create a prototype for AI-powered virtual assistants tailored for various professional needs using ChatGPT, let's break down the process into beginner-friendly steps. This prototype will demonstrate how AI-driven interactions can assist with tasks like scheduling, email management, project tracking, and providing instant information to streamline workflow and increase efficiency.

CHAPTER 14   DIGITAL TWIN METAVERSE PROTOTYPES: SMART WORKING

Figure 14-5. *Conceptual design of AI-powered virtual assistants (author's development with Dall-E)*

Step 1: Understanding ChatGPT and Its Capabilities

- What is ChatGPT? ChatGPT is an advanced language model developed by OpenAI capable of understanding and generating humanlike text. It can answer questions, simulate conversation, generate content, and perform specific tasks based on textual instructions.

- Capabilities: For our virtual assistant, ChatGPT's capabilities can include understanding natural language queries, generating responses or actions based on those queries (like drafting emails, creating schedules, and tracking projects), and pulling in relevant information from a predefined database or the Internet (if integrated).

Step 2: Setting Up Your Development Environment

- Create an OpenAI Account: Visit OpenAI's official website and sign up for an account to access ChatGPT and the API.

- API Key: Obtain an API key from OpenAI, which will allow you to integrate ChatGPT into your application.

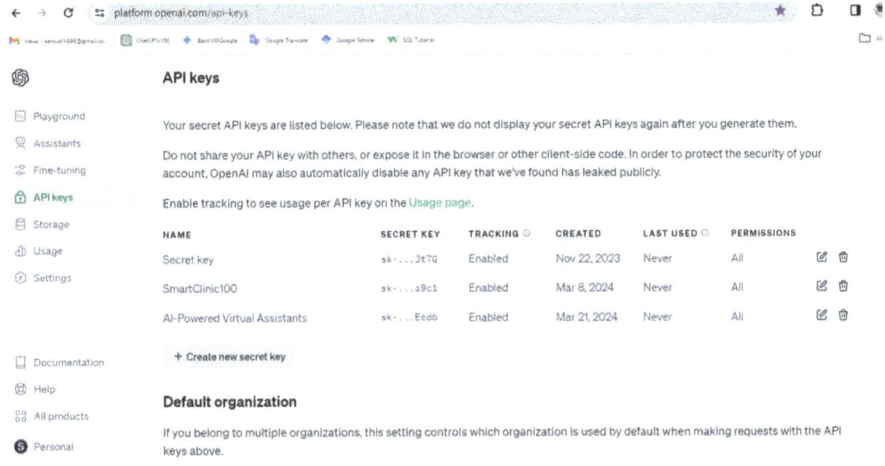

Step 3: Basic ChatGPT Integration

- Choose Your Development Platform: Decide if you want to create a web-based, mobile, or desktop application for the virtual assistant. For beginners, creating a web-based application using JavaScript might be the most accessible approach.

- Install API Client: Depending on your platform, install the necessary OpenAI API client. For web applications, you might use JavaScript or Python for back-end communication.

- API Request: Learn how to make an API request to ChatGPT with your API key. OpenAI's documentation provides examples that you can follow.

Step 4: Designing the Virtual Assistant's Features

- Define Tasks: List the tasks your virtual assistant needs to perform, such as managing schedules, handling emails, or providing project updates.

- Interaction Design: Plan how users will interact with your assistant. Will it be text based, voice activated, or both? Design a simple user interface (UI) that allows users to input their queries.

Step 5: Implementing ChatGPT Responses

- Processing Queries: Use the API to send user queries to ChatGPT and receive responses. This involves coding the logic to capture user input, sending it to ChatGPT via the API, and handling the response.

CHAPTER 14   DIGITAL TWIN METAVERSE PROTOTYPES: SMART WORKING

- Custom Responses: Customize responses based on specific tasks. For example, for scheduling, you might format ChatGPT's responses to fit a calendar view. The following is an example of a response interface:

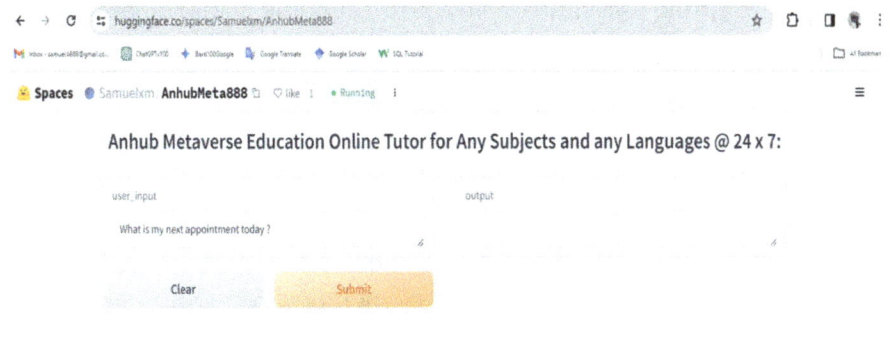

Now it's your turn   *As you venture further into the realm of digital twin metaverse city development, I encourage you to continue the remaining steps and enhance your prototype by adding rich, realistic scenery, fine-tuning materials, and weaving in greater interactivity. Your engagement and dedication to this work are invaluable—embrace this chance to innovate and hone your expertise in crafting the digital landscapes of tomorrow...*

Step 6: Testing and Iteration

- Test Each Feature: Individually test the scheduling, email management, and project tracking features to ensure ChatGPT's responses are accurate and relevant.
- User Feedback: Allow beta testers to use the virtual assistant and provide feedback on its functionality and user experience.

- Iterate: Use feedback to refine and improve the assistant's capabilities and UI.

Step 7: Deployment and Usage

- Deploy Your Application: Once you're satisfied with the virtual assistant, deploy it on a suitable platform for your target users.

- User Guides: Create comprehensive user guides or tutorials to help users understand how to interact with the virtual assistant effectively.

This outline provides a foundational approach to developing an AI-powered virtual assistant prototype. Remember, developing such a tool requires patience, testing, and continuous learning to incorporate feedback and improve the assistant's capabilities.

Virtual Reality Design and Prototyping Studio

Using Unreal Engine's advanced rendering capabilities and VR support, we will develop a prototype of a virtual reality design and prototyping studio. Figure 14-6 presents a conceptual design of a virtual reality design and prototyping studio—the blueprint we aspire to replicate in our prototype. This studio could enable engineers, architects, and designers to create and iterate on projects in a fully immersive 3D environment, facilitating collaboration and reducing the need for physical prototypes.

Developing a virtual reality design and prototyping studio using Unreal Engine involves a series of steps tailored for beginners. This prototype will enable creators to design, iterate, and collaborate on projects in a fully immersive 3D environment. Let's perform the following step-by-step guide to move forward.

CHAPTER 14   DIGITAL TWIN METAVERSE PROTOTYPES: SMART WORKING

Figure 14-6. *Conceptual design of virtual reality design and prototyping studio (author's development with Dall-E)*

Step 1: Download and Install Unreal Engine

- Action: Go to the (https://www.unrealengine.com/) and sign up for an Epic Games account if you don't already have one. Download the Epic Games Launcher and install it on your computer. Through the launcher, install the latest version of Unreal Engine.

- Explanation: Unreal Engine is a powerful tool for creating 3D content, and having the latest version ensures you have access to the most recent features and updates.

345

CHAPTER 14   DIGITAL TWIN METAVERSE PROTOTYPES: SMART WORKING

Step 2: Familiarize Yourself with the Interface

- Action: Open Unreal Engine and create a new project. Select a template that best suits a virtual environment, such as the "Blank" project with no starter content, to start from scratch.

- Explanation: Understanding the Unreal Engine interface is crucial for navigation and utilizing its tools effectively. Spend some time exploring the various panels and menus.

Step 3: Basic Scene Setup

- Action: In your new project, begin by creating a simple environment that will serve as your VR design studio. Use basic geometric shapes (available in the "Place Actors" menu) to create a room structure.

- Explanation: This initial setup provides a foundation for your virtual studio, where you will later add more complex elements and interactive features.

CHAPTER 14   DIGITAL TWIN METAVERSE PROTOTYPES: SMART WORKING

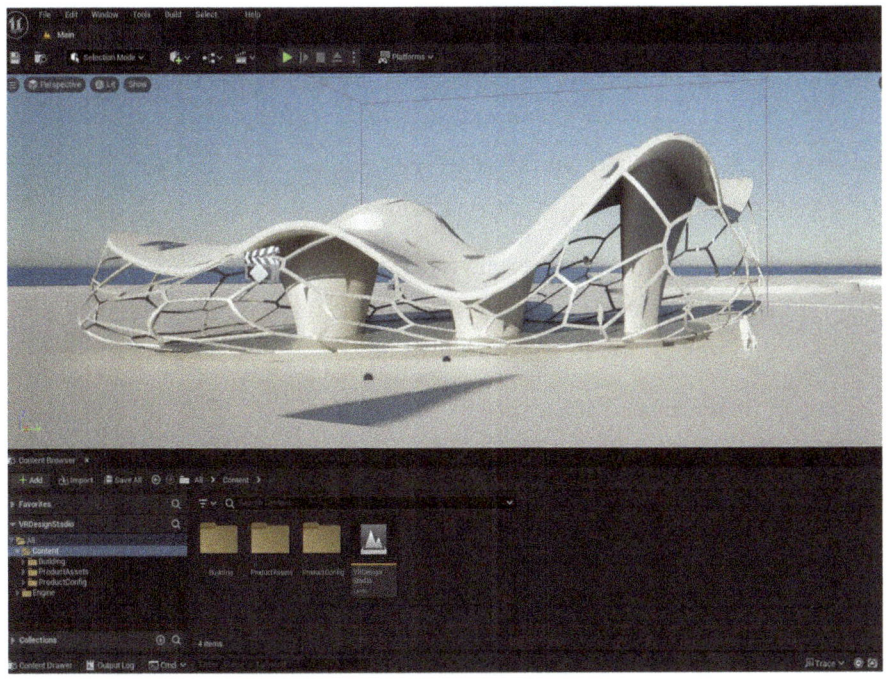

Now it's your turn   *As you venture further into the realm of digital twin metaverse city development, I encourage you to continue the remaining steps and enhance your prototype by adding rich, realistic scenery, fine-tuning materials, and weaving in greater interactivity. Your engagement and dedication to this work are invaluable— embrace this chance to innovate and hone your expertise in crafting the digital landscapes of tomorrow...*

Step 4: Import Assets

- Action: Import 3D models that represent furniture, tools, or any equipment relevant to a design studio. Unreal Engine's Marketplace is a great source for free and paid assets that can enhance your studio.

- Explanation: These assets will populate your studio, making it more realistic and tailored to the needs of engineers, architects, and designers.

Step 5: Implement VR Support

- Action: Go to "Edit" ➤ "Project Settings" ➤ "Platforms" ➤ "VR" and enable the VR plugins compatible with your hardware (e.g., Oculus, HTC Vive). Follow the prompts to configure the basic settings.

- Explanation: Enabling VR support is essential for making your studio fully immersive and interactive in a virtual reality environment.

Step 6: Add Interaction Capabilities

- Action: Using Unreal Engine's Blueprints visual scripting system, create simple interactions, such as the ability to pick up, move, or manipulate objects within the studio.

- Explanation: Blueprints allow you to add functionality without writing code, making it accessible for beginners to implement interactive features.

Step 7: Test in VR

- Action: Connect your VR headset and controllers to your computer. Click the "Play" button in Unreal Engine, selecting the VR preview option to test the studio environment in virtual reality.

- Explanation: Testing in VR allows you to experience the studio from the user's perspective, ensuring that interactions and navigation feel intuitive and natural.

Step 8: Iterate and Improve

- Action: Based on your testing experience, make adjustments to the environment, interactions, or assets as needed. Repeat the testing process to refine the studio.

- Explanation: Iteration is a key part of the design process, enabling you to progressively enhance the user experience and functionality of your VR studio.

By following these steps, beginners can utilize Unreal Engine to create a virtual reality design and prototyping studio. This project not only introduces users to VR development but also highlights the potential of virtual spaces for collaborative and creative work in various disciplines.

To sum up this chapter, building smart working in digital metaverse cities, each prototype explores how digital twin and metaverse technologies can revolutionize the concept of smart working, offering new possibilities for collaboration, training, and productivity in virtual environments. By leveraging the strengths of various development tools, these prototypes could pave the way for innovative working methods that transcend traditional office boundaries.

CHAPTER 15

Digital Twin Metaverse Prototypes: *Smart Entertainment and Cities*

As we step into this chapter, the excitement builds as we explore a collection of eight pioneering prototypes that define the essence of entertainment and urban life in the digital twin metaverse. This chapter is not just about conceptual ideas; it's about bringing those ideas to life through detailed prototyping examples that demonstrate the breadth and depth of possibilities in smart entertainment and city planning.

From the immersive experiences of a virtual art gallery and a digital twin museum to the adrenaline rush of a metaverse theme park and the serene escape of a virtual public park, each prototype showcases the innovative use of digital twin and metaverse technologies to enhance our leisure and urban experiences. And in this vibrant lineup of prototypes, we proudly introduce a groundbreaking concept—the metaverse music festival. This prototype stands as a testament to the power of digital twin metaverse technologies in transforming how we experience music and community, bringing together artists and audiences from across the globe in a dynamic, interactive virtual space.

CHAPTER 15   DIGITAL TWIN METAVERSE PROTOTYPES: SMART ENTERTAINMENT AND CITIES

Through the meticulous use of tools discussed in Chapters 11 and 12, such as Unreal Engine for detailed 3D visualization and spatial audio, coupled with the interactive capabilities of AI-driven platforms, we guide you through the creation of each prototype. These hands-on examples not only inspire but also equip you with the knowledge to craft your own digital twin metaverse experiences.

Join us as we embark on a journey through smart living, working, and now exhilarating entertainment within the boundless realms of digital twin metaverse cities. This chapter is about envisioning a future where every facet of city life is enhanced by digital innovation—a future that is not just imagined but built, one prototype at a time.

1. Virtual Concert and Event Arena

Harnessing the power of Unreal Engine for its high-fidelity graphics and immersive environments, we will create a prototype of a virtual concert and event arena. Figure 15-1 presents a conceptual design of virtual concert and event arena—the blueprint we aspire to replicate in our prototype. This space could host live performances, virtual meetups, and large-scale events, featuring interactive elements such as live polls, virtual merchandise stores, and social spaces for attendees to interact.

Creating a virtual concert and event arena using Unreal Engine involves several steps, tailored to beginners eager to dive into the world of digital twin metaverse development. Unreal Engine (U5) is chosen for its advanced graphics capabilities and immersive environments, making it ideal for developing a visually stunning virtual concert arena. Here's a step-by-step guide to start this project:

CHAPTER 15　DIGITAL TWIN METAVERSE PROTOTYPES: SMART ENTERTAINMENT AND CITIES

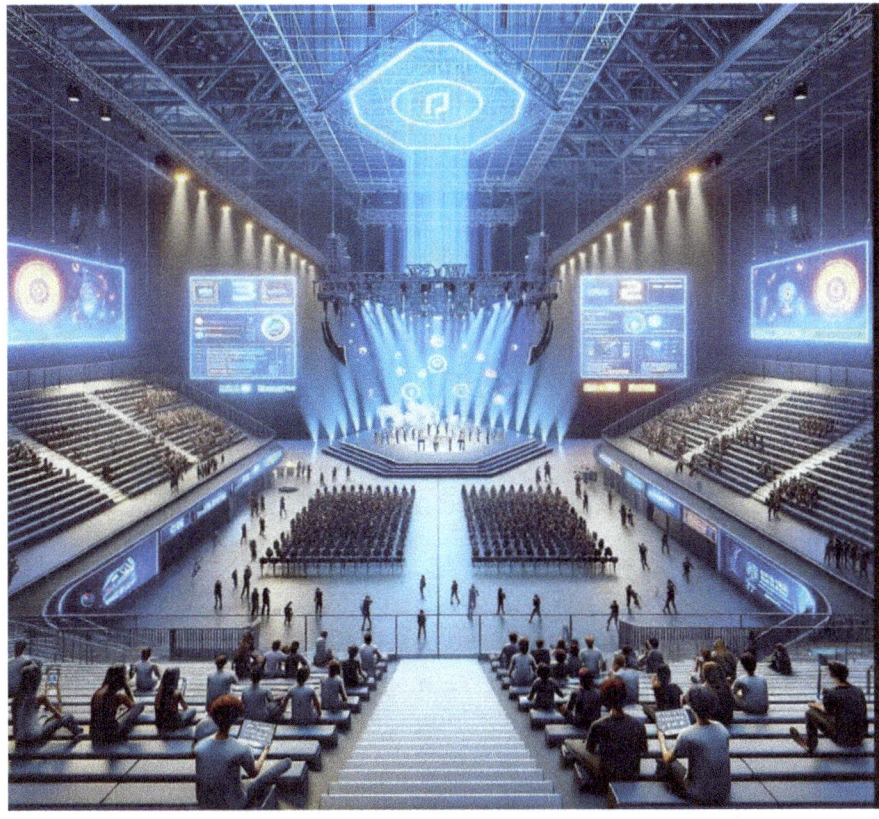

Figure 15-1. *Conceptual design of virtual concert and event arena (author's development with Dall-E)*

Step 1: Getting Started with Unreal Engine

- Download Unreal Engine: Visit the (https://www.unrealengine.com/en-US/)
  and download the Epic Games Launcher. Install it on your computer, create an Epic Games account if you don't already have one, and navigate to the Unreal Engine to install the latest version of Unreal Engine.

CHAPTER 15   DIGITAL TWIN METAVERSE PROTOTYPES: SMART ENTERTAINMENT AND CITIES

- Create a New Project: Open the Epic Games Launcher, go to the Unreal Engine tab, and click "Launch" under the latest version. Select "Games" in the New Project Categories and choose the "Blank" template. Make sure "With Starter Content" is selected to include basic assets in your project. Name your project "VirtualConcertArena" and select a suitable location on your computer to save it.

CHAPTER 15 DIGITAL TWIN METAVERSE PROTOTYPES: SMART ENTERTAINMENT AND CITIES

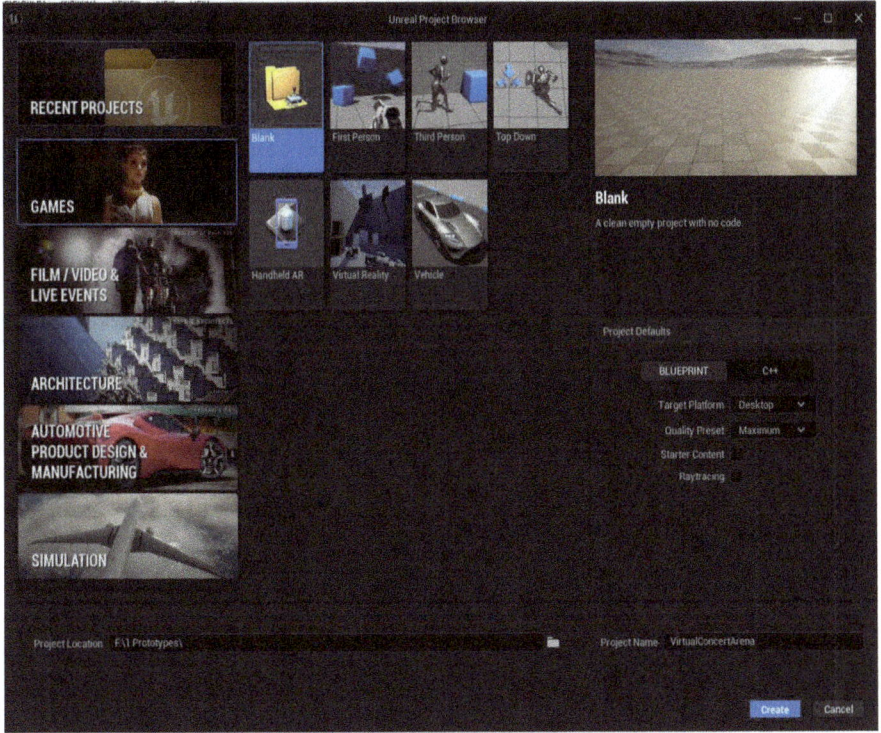

Step 2: Familiarizing Yourself with the UE Interface

- Explore the Interface: Spend some time getting familiar with the main areas of the Unreal Engine interface, including the viewport (where you'll see your project in 3D), Content Browser (where your assets are stored), World Outliner (a list of all objects in your scene), and Details Panel (shows properties of the selected object).

CHAPTER 15   DIGITAL TWIN METAVERSE PROTOTYPES: SMART ENTERTAINMENT AND CITIES

- Basic Navigation: Learn to navigate the viewport using your mouse and keyboard. Holding the right mouse button and moving your mouse allows you to look around, while WASD keys let you move through the scene. Scrolling the mouse wheel zooms in and out.

Step 3: Building the Arena

- Layout: Start by creating the basic layout of your concert arena using the "Geometry" tools found in the "Modes" panel. Use simple shapes (cubes, spheres) to block out the stage, audience areas, and other major components of your venue.

- Applying Textures: Enhance the visual appeal of your basic structures by applying textures. Open the "Content Browser," navigate to the "Starter Content" ➤ "Materials," and drag and drop materials onto your geometry objects to apply them.

CHAPTER 15   DIGITAL TWIN METAVERSE PROTOTYPES: SMART ENTERTAINMENT AND CITIES

Step 4: Adding Interactivity

- Blueprints: Unreal Engine's visual scripting system, Blueprints, allows you to add interactivity without writing code. Start simple by creating a light that turns on and off when a player approaches. Go to "Content Browser" ➤ "Add New" ➤ "Blueprint Class," select "Actor" as the parent class, and name it "InteractiveLight."

CHAPTER 15   DIGITAL TWIN METAVERSE PROTOTYPES: SMART ENTERTAINMENT AND CITIES

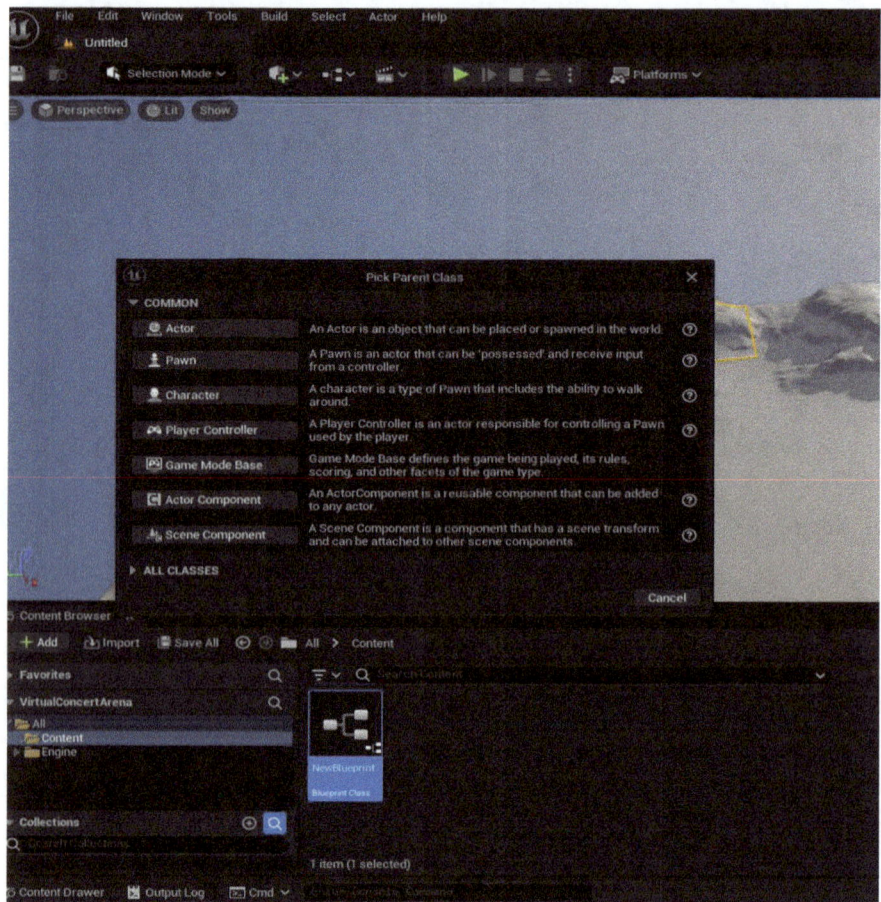

Now it's your turn   *As you venture further into the realm of digital twin metaverse city development, I encourage you to continue the remaining steps and enhance your prototype by adding rich, realistic scenery, fine-tuning materials, and weaving in greater interactivity. Your engagement and dedication to this work are invaluable— embrace this chance to innovate and hone your expertise in crafting the digital landscapes of tomorrow...*

- Editing Blueprints: Double-click your new Blueprint to open the editor. Use the "Event Graph" to create logic that turns a light component on or off based on player proximity. Unreal Engine provides plenty of tutorials on getting started with Blueprints.

Step 5: Populating the Scene

- Assets: Populate your concert arena with assets from the "Starter Content" or Unreal Engine Marketplace. Add seats, stages, screens, and lights to make your arena come to life. Use the drag-and-drop method from the "Content Browser."

- Custom Assets: For more personalized content, consider creating or downloading additional assets. Software like Blender can be used to create custom models that you can import into Unreal Engine.

Step 6: Testing and Iterating

- Playtest: Click the "Play" button in the toolbar to enter Play Mode and explore your virtual arena. Experience the space from the attendee's perspective, interact with the elements you've scripted, and make note of any changes you'd like to make.

- Iterate: Development is an iterative process. Based on your tests, return to the editor to tweak the layout, adjust Blueprints, or add new features to enhance the experience.

Step 7: Sharing Your Prototype

- Packaging: Once satisfied with your virtual concert arena, package your project for others to explore. Go to "File" ➤ "Package Project" and select the platform you want to package for (e.g., Windows, Mac). Follow the prompts to complete the packaging process.

- Distribution: Share your packaged project with others by hosting it on a file-sharing service or creating a dedicated website for your virtual concert arena.

This guide provides a foundational starting point for beginners to embark on creating a virtual concert and event arena in Unreal Engine. As you become more comfortable with the tools and processes, you'll be able to add more complexity and detail to your projects. Remember, learning Unreal Engine is a journey—make use of online tutorials, community forums, and Unreal Engine's extensive documentation to expand your skills.

2. Interactive Public Art Installations

Using Unity and Meta Spark, we will develop interactive public art installations that blend AR with physical spaces in the metaverse city. Figure 15-2 presents a conceptual design of interactive public art installations—the blueprint we aspire to replicate in our prototype. These installations could offer augmented reality (AR) experiences accessible via mobile devices, encouraging public engagement and blending digital art with the urban landscape.

CHAPTER 15   DIGITAL TWIN METAVERSE PROTOTYPES: SMART ENTERTAINMENT AND CITIES

Figure 15-2. *Conceptual design of interactive public art installations (author's development with Dall-E)*

To develop "interactive public art installations" that blend AR with physical spaces in the metaverse city using Unity and Meta Spark, follow these step-by-step instructions. This guide is designed for beginners with no prior experience with these tools.

Step 1: Unity Setup and Basic Scene Creation

- Download Unity Hub: Visit the (`https://unity.com/downloa4`) and install Unity Hub.

- Install Unity Editor: Through Unity Hub, install the latest version of the Unity Editor suitable for 3D projects.

CHAPTER 15   DIGITAL TWIN METAVERSE PROTOTYPES: SMART ENTERTAINMENT AND CITIES

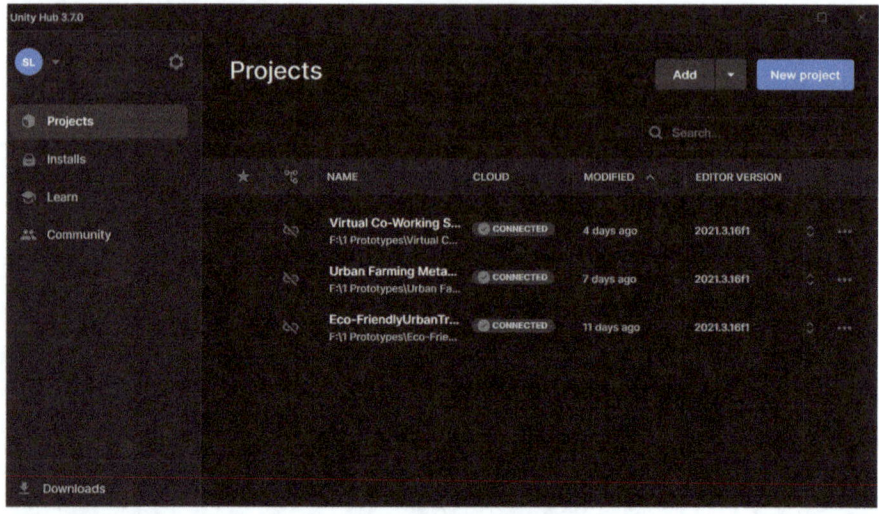

- Create a New Project: Open Unity Hub, go to the "Projects" tab, click "New," choose the "3D" template, and name your project "PublicArtInstallation."

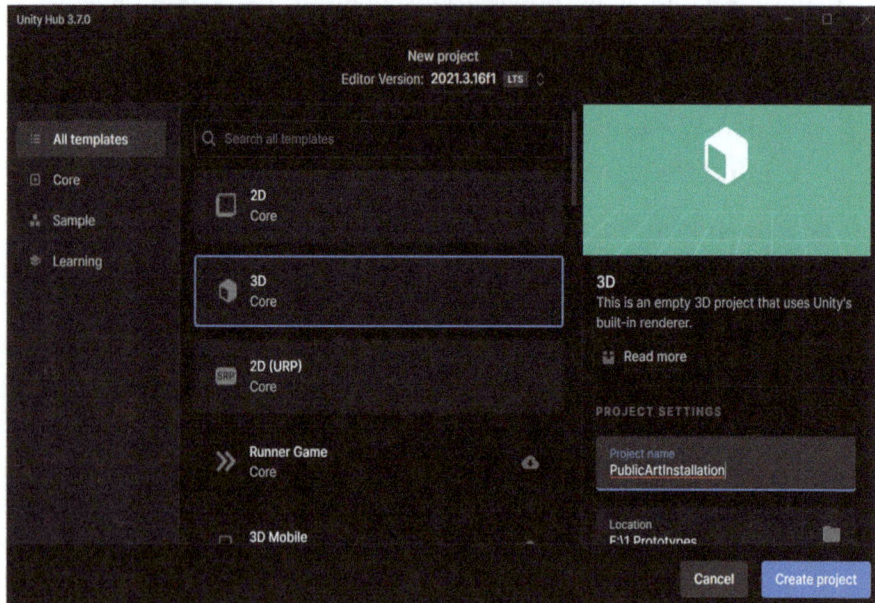

CHAPTER 15   DIGITAL TWIN METAVERSE PROTOTYPES: SMART ENTERTAINMENT AND CITIES

Step 2: Building the 3D Installation

- Scene Setup: Open your new project. You'll see a default scene with a camera and a directional light. This is your canvas.

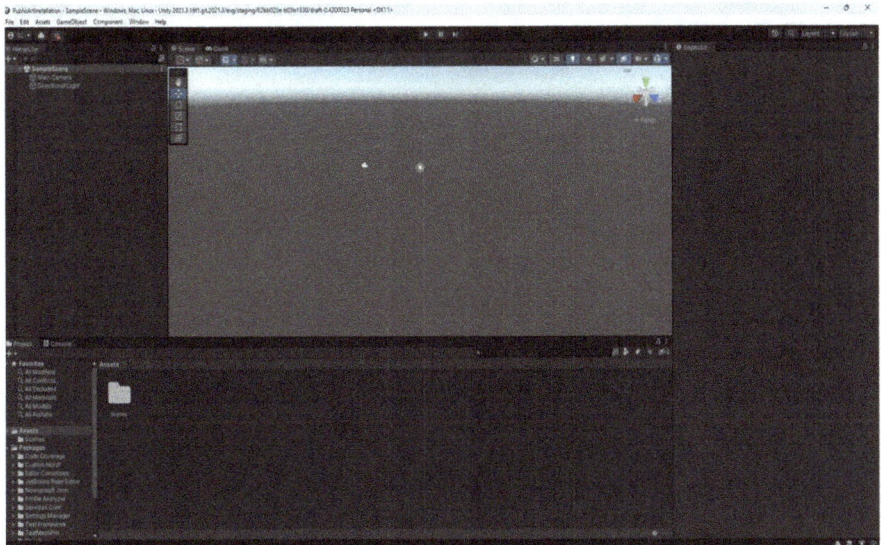

- Import Assets: For art assets, you can create your own in a 3D modeling tool like Blender or use free assets from the Unity Asset Store. To access the store, click "Window" ➤ "Asset Store" and search for assets like sculptures, abstract art models, or any other art forms you envision in your installation.

363

CHAPTER 15   DIGITAL TWIN METAVERSE PROTOTYPES: SMART ENTERTAINMENT AND CITIES

- Place Assets in Your Scene: Drag and drop assets from the "Assets" folder to the scene. Arrange them to create your art installation. Use the transform tools in the toolbar to move, rotate, and scale your objects.

- Add Interactivity: To make parts of your installation interactive, you'll need to attach scripts. For a simple interaction (e.g., changing color on click), right-click the "Assets" folder, create a new C script, name it "ColorChange," double-click to open it in Visual Studio or your preferred IDE, and enter a basic script to change the object's color when clicked. Unity's (https://docs.unity3d.com/ScriptReference/) is a great resource for learning how to write scripts for various interactions.

CHAPTER 15   DIGITAL TWIN METAVERSE PROTOTYPES: SMART ENTERTAINMENT AND CITIES

Step 3: Using Meta Spark for AR Experience

- Download Meta Spark Studio: Visit the (https://sparkar.facebook.com/ar-studio/download/) and install Meta Spark Studio on your computer.

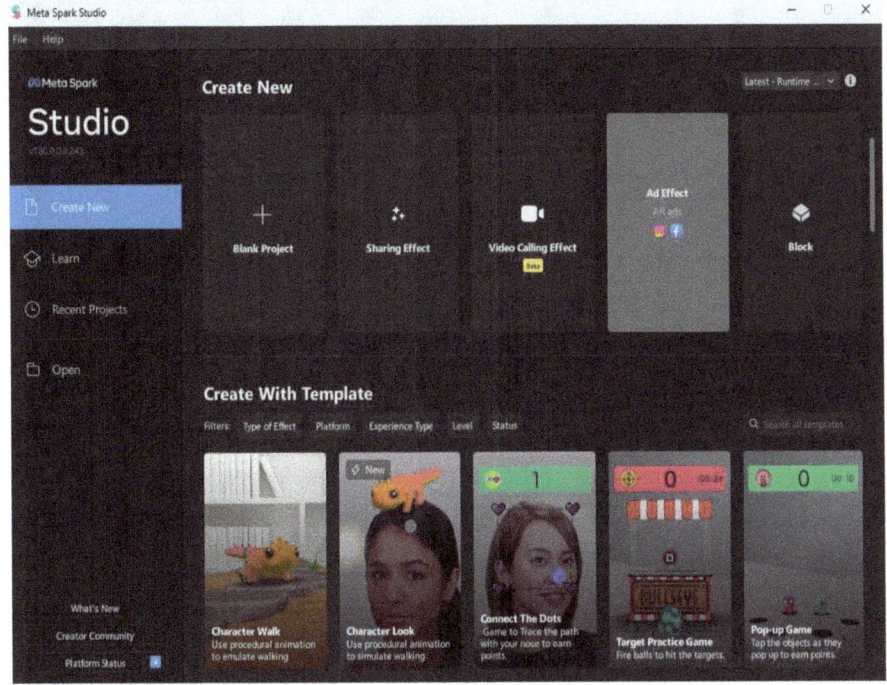

- Explore Tutorials: Since you're a beginner, take some time to explore the official (https://sparkar.facebook.com/ar-studio/learn/tutorials/) to get familiar with the interface and basic functionalities.

CHAPTER 15   DIGITAL TWIN METAVERSE PROTOTYPES: SMART ENTERTAINMENT AND CITIES

Step 4: Creating AR Overlay for the Installation

- Start a New Project: Open Meta Spark Studio and start a new project aimed at creating an AR experience.

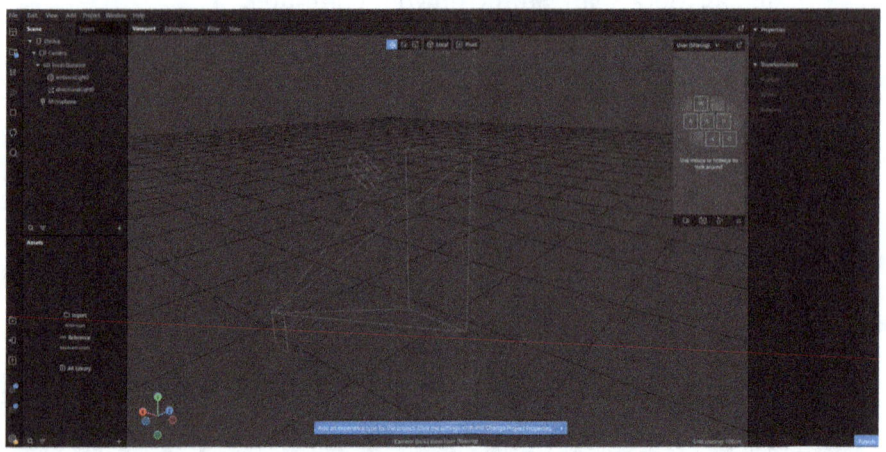

Now it's your turn   *As you venture further into the realm of digital twin metaverse city development, I encourage you to continue the remaining steps and enhance your prototype by adding rich, realistic scenery, fine-tuning materials, and weaving in greater interactivity. Your engagement and dedication to this work are invaluable—embrace this chance to innovate and hone your expertise in crafting the digital landscapes of tomorrow...*

- Import 3D Art: Import the 3D models of your public art installation. These can be simplified versions of the Unity assets for optimal performance in AR.

- Add Interactivity and AR Features: Use Meta Spark's patches and scripting capabilities to add interactivity to your AR experience. This could include animations, informational pop-ups, or interactive elements that users can engage with using their mobile devices.

- Test Your AR Experience: Use the Meta Spark Player app to test your AR experience on a mobile device. Make adjustments as necessary to ensure the experience is engaging and functions well in a real-world environment.

Step 5: Publishing Your AR Experience

- Prepare for Publishing: Follow Meta Spark's guidelines for publishing AR experiences, ensuring your project meets all requirements.

- Submit Your Project: Submit your AR experience for review directly within Meta Spark Studio. Once approved, it will be accessible to users on Instagram and Facebook, allowing them to interact with your public art installation in augmented reality.

By following these steps, you'll create an interactive public art installation that leverages the power of Unity for 3D model creation and Meta Spark for augmented reality experiences, enriching the urban landscape of your digital twin metaverse city.

3. Metaverse Theme Park

We will leverage Roblox Studio's capabilities to create a prototype of a metaverse theme park and complete with virtual rides, games, and attractions. Figure 15-3 presents a conceptual design of a metaverse theme

CHAPTER 15   DIGITAL TWIN METAVERSE PROTOTYPES: SMART ENTERTAINMENT AND CITIES

park—the blueprint we aspire to replicate in our prototype. This theme park could offer personalized experiences based on user preferences, featuring AI-guided tours and interactive, story-driven adventures.

Creating a prototype of a metaverse theme park using Roblox Studio involves several steps, tailored to beginners. Here's a step-by-step guide to get started:

Figure 15-3. *Conceptual design of a metaverse theme park (author's development with Dall-E)*

CHAPTER 15   DIGITAL TWIN METAVERSE PROTOTYPES: SMART ENTERTAINMENT AND CITIES

Step 1: Downloading and Installing Roblox Studio

- Go to the (https://www.roblox.com/creat5) and click the "Start Creating" button to download the installer. Follow the prompts to install Roblox Studio on your computer.

Step 2: Familiarizing Yourself with the Interface

- Upon opening Roblox Studio, take some time to familiarize yourself with the interface. Key areas include the viewport (where your game world is displayed), the explorer window (where you see the hierarchy of your game elements), and the properties window (where you can edit the attributes of selected objects).

Step 3: Starting a New Project

- Choose a template that suits a theme park layout, such as the "Obby" (obstacle course) template, which provides a basic structure that you can modify. This will give you a starting point with terrain and some basic elements.

CHAPTER 15   DIGITAL TWIN METAVERSE PROTOTYPES: SMART ENTERTAINMENT AND CITIES

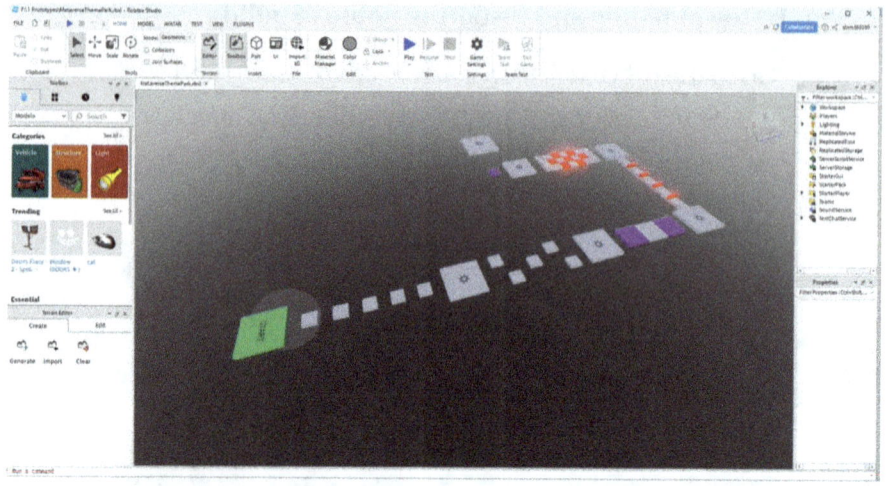

Step 4: Designing the Layout of your Theme Park

- Use the Terrain Tools in Roblox Studio to sculpt your theme park's landscape. Consider creating different areas for various attractions, like a roller coaster section, a water park area, and a fantasy land.

- You can add paths and decorations using the Toolbox, which contains a vast library of models and assets created by the Roblox community.

CHAPTER 15   DIGITAL TWIN METAVERSE PROTOTYPES: SMART ENTERTAINMENT AND CITIES

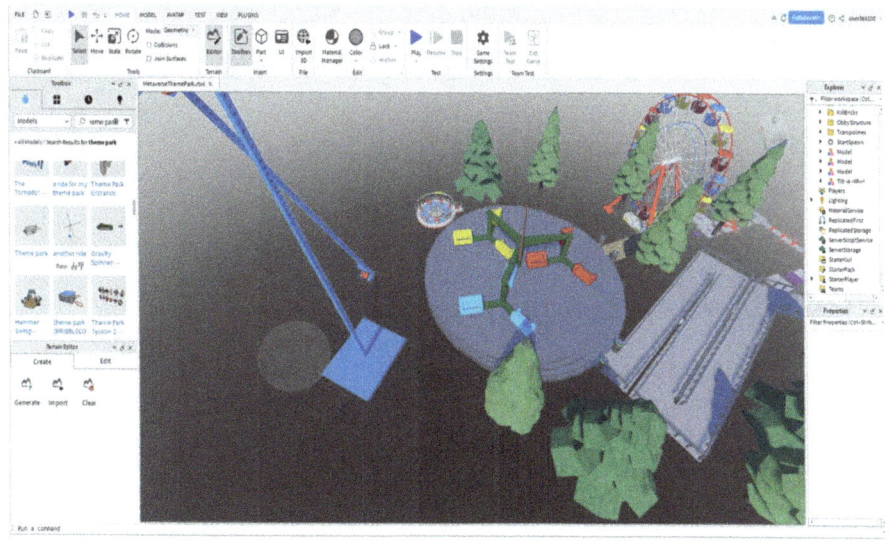

Now it's your turn   *As you venture further into the realm of digital twin metaverse city development, I encourage you to continue the remaining steps and enhance your prototype by adding rich, realistic scenery, fine-tuning materials, and weaving in greater interactivity. Your engagement and dedication to this work are invaluable—embrace this chance to innovate and hone your expertise in crafting the digital landscapes of tomorrow...*

Step 5: Creating Rides and Attractions

- To build a ride, you can start with basic shapes and assemble them into complex structures. For a roller coaster, for example, use cylinders and blocks to create the track and supports.

- Use the "Anchor" property to secure parts of your rides to the terrain, ensuring they don't fall apart when the game runs.

- For moving parts, like a Ferris wheel or carousel, you'll need to learn some basic scripting in Lua (Roblox's programming language) to make them rotate or move.

Step 6: Scripting Interactivity

- Roblox Studio uses Lua for scripting game logic. Start with simple scripts to make rides operational. For instance, you can script a roller coaster to move along the track when a player sits in a cart.

- There are plenty of tutorials and documentation on Roblox's Developer Hub that cover scripting basics. A simple script to start a ride could check for a player entering a vehicle and then move the vehicle along a predefined path.

Step 7: Personalizing Experiences

- Implement game mechanics that allow for personalization. This could include a script that remembers a player's favorite rides or customizes characters with theme park merchandise.

- Use Roblox's data store services to save player preferences and progress, ensuring a personalized experience every time they visit your theme park.

Step 8: Testing and Iteration

- Regularly test your theme park by playing the game in Roblox Studio. Look for bugs and areas of improvement. Use the feedback to make adjustments.

CHAPTER 15   DIGITAL TWIN METAVERSE PROTOTYPES: SMART ENTERTAINMENT AND CITIES

- Consider inviting friends or other Roblox users to test your park and provide feedback.

Step 9: Publishing Your Theme Park

- Before publishing, ensure your theme park is optimized for performance. This includes reducing the complexity of models and scripts where possible and ensuring the game runs smoothly on different devices.

- When you're ready, publish your theme park to Roblox. Go to the "File" menu in Roblox Studio and select "Publish to Roblox As…." Follow the prompts to complete the publishing process.

- Share your theme park with the community through Roblox's social features, forums, and social media. Engage with players and consider their feedback for future updates.

Creating a metaverse theme park in Roblox Studio is a journey of creativity and learning. Start simple and gradually incorporate more complex features as you become more comfortable with the tools and scripting. Remember, game development is an iterative process, so keep refining your theme park based on player feedback and new ideas you learn along the way.

4. Digital Twin Museums and Galleries

Leveraging Unity's versatile development platform and extensive asset store, we're set to craft a prototype of digital twin museums and galleries. This virtual setting aims to redefine cultural exploration, offering globally accessible, immersive art and history experiences. Figure 15-4 will illustrate a conceptual design of a digital twin museum—the vision

CHAPTER 15   DIGITAL TWIN METAVERSE PROTOTYPES: SMART ENTERTAINMENT AND CITIES

we seek to bring to fruition in our prototype. With Unity, this digital museum will not only showcase precise digital replicas of renowned artworks and historical artifacts but will also integrate interactive educational experiences and augmented reality (AR) features to deepen visitor engagement. From AI-guided virtual tours revealing the stories behind each artifact to interactive exhibits that breathe life into history, this prototype will open a new dimension of cultural and educational enrichment within the digital twin metaverse city.

Figure 15-4. *Conceptual design of a digital twin museum (author's development with Dall-E)*

CHAPTER 15   DIGITAL TWIN METAVERSE PROTOTYPES: SMART ENTERTAINMENT AND CITIES

Building a digital twin museum in Unity involves a series of steps from conceptualization to final deployment. Here's a detailed guide to help develop this prototype:

Step 1: Initial Setup

- Download Unity Hub from the official Unity website and install Unity Editor (preferably the latest version for access to new features).

- Create a New Project in Unity Hub, selecting a 3D template for the museum.

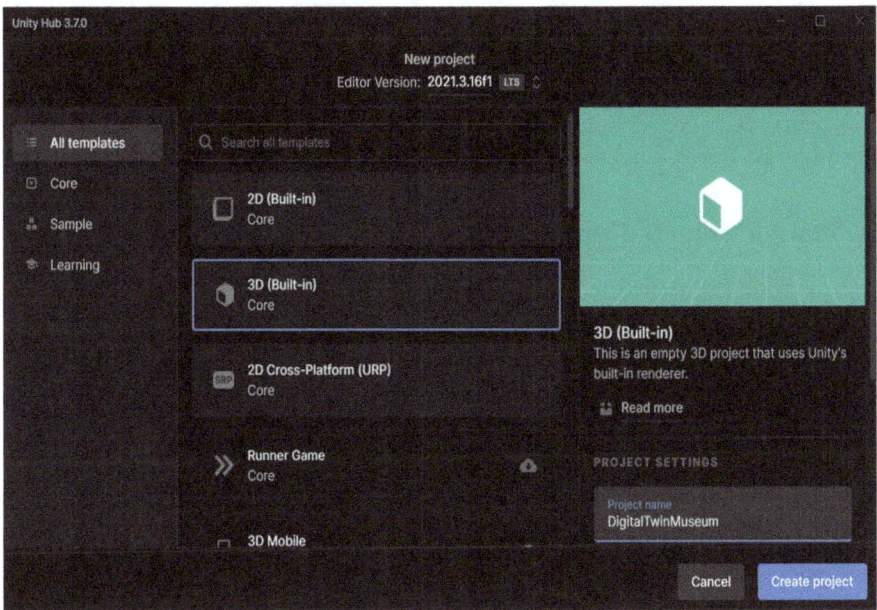

CHAPTER 15   DIGITAL TWIN METAVERSE PROTOTYPES: SMART ENTERTAINMENT AND CITIES

- Get familiar with the Unity 3D working environment:

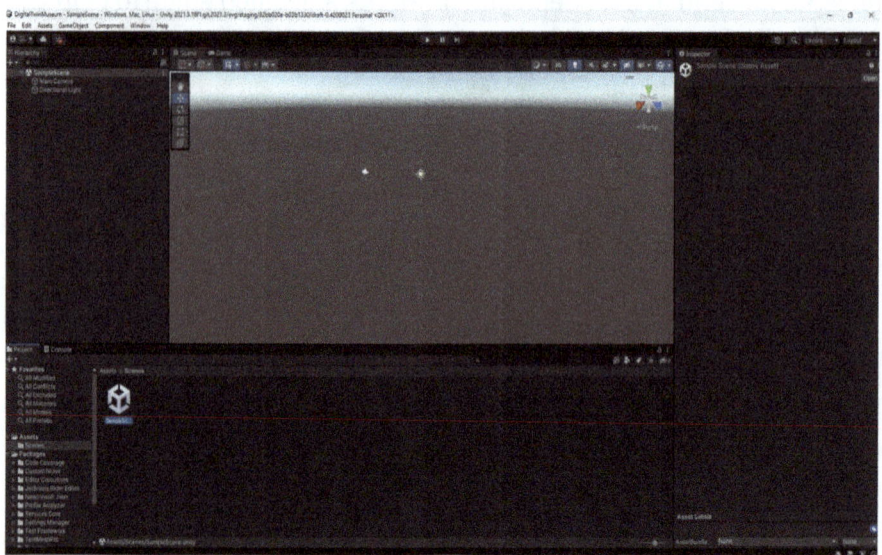

Step 2: Design the Museum Layout

- Sketch the Museum Layout: Before diving into Unity, draft a rough sketch of your museum's layout, including exhibition halls, corridors, and any specific areas for interactive exhibits.

CHAPTER 15   DIGITAL TWIN METAVERSE PROTOTYPES: SMART ENTERTAINMENT AND CITIES

Now it's your turn   *As you venture further into the realm of digital twin metaverse city development, I encourage you to continue the remaining steps and enhance your prototype by adding rich, realistic scenery, fine-tuning materials, and weaving in greater interactivity. Your engagement and dedication to this work are invaluable—embrace this chance to innovate and hone your expertise in crafting the digital landscapes of tomorrow…*

- Model the Structure: Use Unity's ProBuilder tool for basic modeling or import detailed 3D models from software like Blender or SketchUp. Create walls, floors, ceilings, and necessary structural elements.

Step 3: Populate the Museum

- Acquire or Create Artifacts: Source 3D models of artifacts and artworks. Websites like Sketchfab or TurboSquid offer a variety of models, or you can create custom models.

- Import Models: Import these models into your Unity project and place them throughout your museum's galleries.

Step 4: Implement Interactivity

- Create Informational Pop-ups: Utilize Unity's UI system to create pop-ups that appear when visitors interact with an exhibit, providing historical context or artist information.

- Add Audio Guides: Record or source audio descriptions for key exhibits and implement an audio playback system when a visitor approaches or selects an artifact.

Step 5: Integrate AR and VR

- Set Up VR Support: Follow Unity's guidelines to set up your project for VR, ensuring it's compatible with your target VR hardware.

- Implement AR Features: For AR, use Unity's AR Foundation to create augmentations such as holographic displays of artifacts or interactive historical scenes that overlay onto the physical environment.

Step 6: Lighting and Effects

- Adjust Lighting: Use Unity's lighting system to highlight exhibits effectively and create the desired atmosphere within different sections of the museum.

- Add Environmental Effects: Implement subtle effects like particle dust in the air or dynamic shadows to enhance realism.

Step 7: Navigation System

- Design a Navigation Interface: Create a user-friendly interface that allows visitors to navigate through the museum, either through a point-and-click system for desktop or motion controllers for VR.

- Implement Pathfinding: Use Unity's NavMesh system to allow AI-guided tours to navigate through the museum, leading visitors between exhibits.

Step 8: Optimization and Testing

- Optimize Performance: Ensure your museum runs smoothly across devices by optimizing models, textures, and effects. Unity's Profiler tool can help identify performance bottlenecks.

- Test Extensively: Conduct thorough testing on your target platforms, gathering feedback to refine user experience and interactivity.

Step 9: Deployment

- Build Your Project: Once satisfied, build your project for the chosen platforms (WebGL, stand-alone, VR/AR devices).

- Publish: Share your digital twin museum online or through app stores, providing access to users worldwide.

CHAPTER 15 DIGITAL TWIN METAVERSE PROTOTYPES: SMART ENTERTAINMENT AND CITIES

This detailed, step-by-step approach offers a foundation for creating a digital twin museum in Unity, blending educational content with interactive technology to deliver an engaging and informative experience. Remember, the key to a successful prototype lies in iteration and feedback—continuously refine your museum based on user interaction and feedback to enhance its educational value and engagement.

5. Smart Sports Complex

With CryEngine's realistic environmental rendering and physics simulation, we will develop a prototype of a smart sports complex that hosts virtual sports events and interactive training sessions. Figure 15-5 presents a conceptual design of a smart sports complex—the blueprint we aspire to replicate in our prototype. This complex could simulate real-world physics for various sports, offer virtual training programs with AI coaches, and host esports competitions in a digitally replicated stadium.

CHAPTER 15   DIGITAL TWIN METAVERSE PROTOTYPES: SMART ENTERTAINMENT AND CITIES

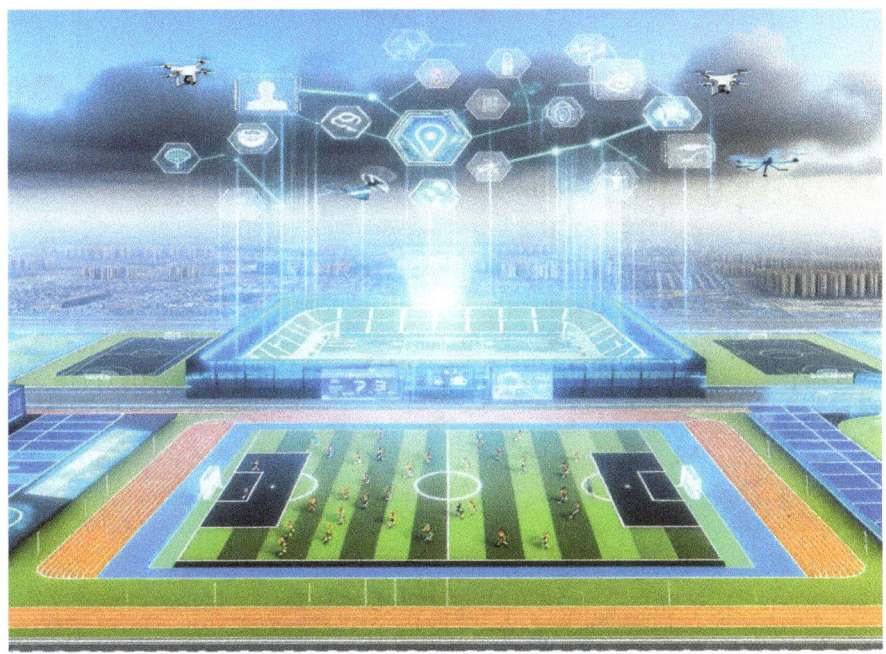

Figure 15-5. Conceptual design of smart sports complex (author's development with Dall-E)

Creating a smart sports complex prototype in a digital twin metaverse city using CryEngine involves several steps, designed to guide beginners through the process from start to finish. CryEngine is chosen for its advanced rendering capabilities and physics simulation, ideal for creating realistic sports environments. Here's how to get started:

Step 1: Familiarize Yourself with CryEngine

- Download CryEngine: First, visit the (https://www.cryengine.com/) and download the CryEngine launcher. Install the engine on your computer.

CHAPTER 15   DIGITAL TWIN METAVERSE PROTOTYPES: SMART ENTERTAINMENT AND CITIES

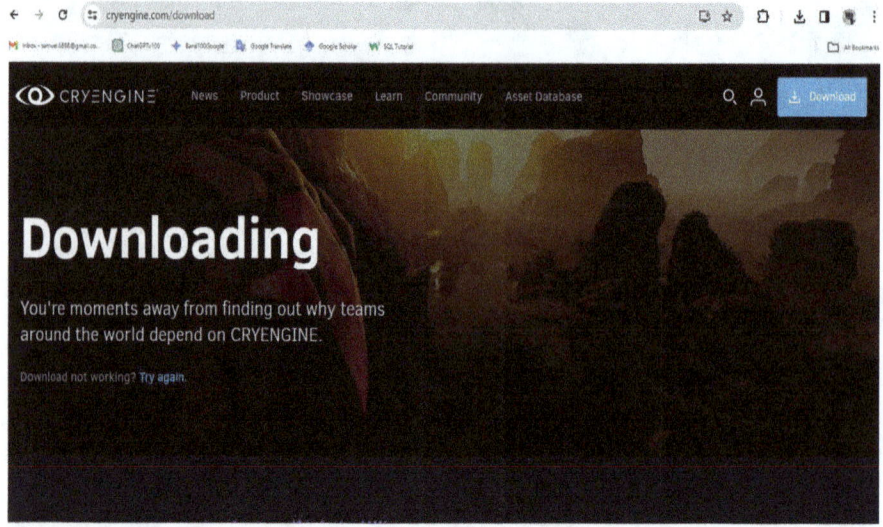

- Explore Tutorials: CryEngine provides a range of tutorials for beginners. Start with the basics to understand the interface, key tools, and functionalities. CryEngine's documentation and YouTube channel are great resources.

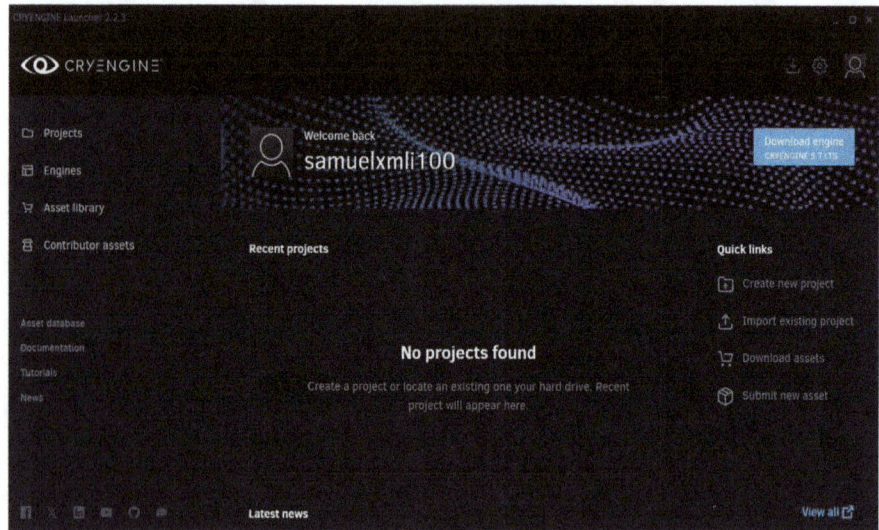

Step 2: Conceptualize Your Sports Complex

- Define the Scope: Decide on the sports to include in your complex. Consider a mix of indoor and outdoor sports for variety.

- Sketch the Layout: Draft a basic layout of your complex, including fields, courts, stadiums, and other facilities like locker rooms or training areas.

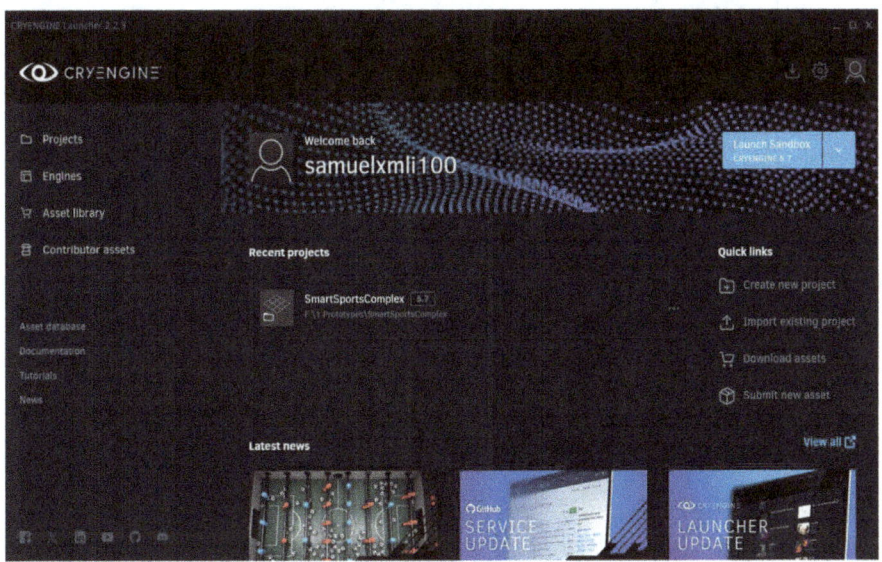

Step 3: Create the Environment

- Start a New Project: In CryEngine, create a new project tailored for your sports complex. Choose a template that best fits an outdoor environment if available.

CHAPTER 15   DIGITAL TWIN METAVERSE PROTOTYPES: SMART ENTERTAINMENT AND CITIES

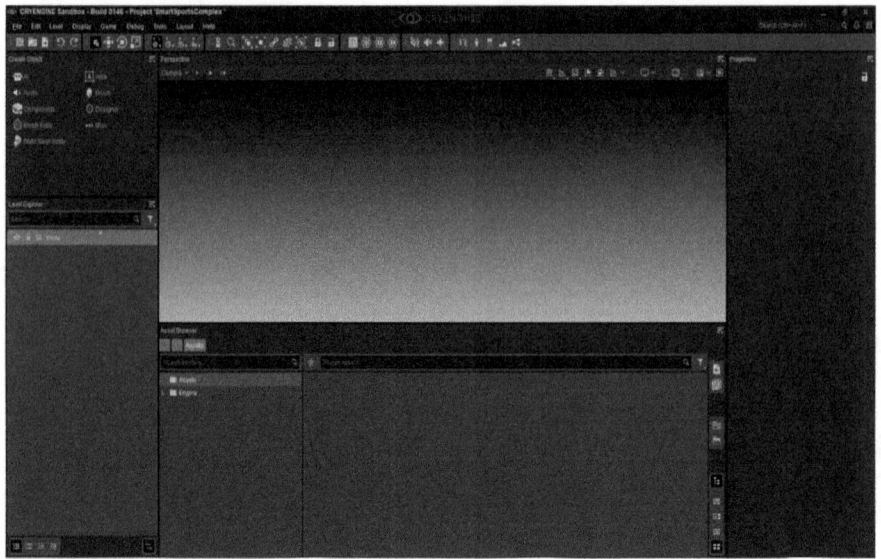

Now it's your turn   *As you venture further into the realm of digital twin metaverse city development, I encourage you to continue the remaining steps and enhance your prototype by adding rich, realistic scenery, fine-tuning materials, and weaving in greater interactivity. Your engagement and dedication to this work are invaluable—embrace this chance to innovate and hone your expertise in crafting the digital landscapes of tomorrow...*

- Design the Terrain: Use the Terrain Editor to sculpt the landscape of your sports complex. Include areas for different sports and adjust elevations for realism.

- Add Textures: Apply textures to your terrain for grass, tracks, pools, etc. CryEngine's material editor allows for detailed customization to achieve realistic looks.

Step 4: Add Sports Facilities and Assets

- Import Assets: Utilize CryEngine's Marketplace or create your own models for sports facilities like soccer fields, basketball courts, and running tracks. Import these models into your project.

- Place Assets: Arrange your sports facilities according to your layout. Adjust scaling, rotation, and positioning for a natural setup.

Step 5: Implement Physics and Interactivity

- Set Up Physics: Apply physical properties to objects that require interaction, like balls or training equipment. CryEngine's physics system will help simulate realistic movements and interactions.

- Create Interactive Elements: For training modules or interactive games, use Flow Graph (CryEngine's visual scripting system) to add logic and interactivity, such as scoring systems or AI opponents.

Step 6: Integrate AI Coaches and Training Programs

- Develop AI Characters: Use CryEngine's AI tools to create coach characters who can guide users through training programs. Script simple behaviors like demonstrating exercises or giving feedback.

- Script Training Sessions: Design training sessions with clear objectives and challenges. Use Flow Graph to sequence activities and track player progress.

Step 7: Testing and Optimization

- Test Your Prototype: Regularly test your sports complex by playing through the training sessions and using the facilities. Look for bugs or areas of improvement.

- Optimize Performance: Ensure your complex runs smoothly across devices. Utilize CryEngine's profiling tools to identify and fix performance bottlenecks.

Step 8: Share Your Prototype

- Prepare for Release: Once satisfied with your prototype, make any final adjustments based on feedback.

- Publish: Use CryEngine's deployment options to share your smart sports complex. Consider uploading it to a platform where others can experience and provide feedback on your creation.

Remember, developing a complex prototype like a smart sports complex is an iterative process. Don't hesitate to go back and refine elements based on testing and feedback. Engage with the CryEngine community for support and inspiration as you bring your digital twin metaverse city to life.

6. City-Wide Game and Scavenger Hunt

Combining the spatial computing capabilities of SpatialOS with the narrative generation potential of ChatGPT, we will create a city-wide game or scavenger hunt that players can participate in across the digital twin metaverse city. Figure 15-6 presents a conceptual design of a city-wide game and scavenger hunt—the blueprint we aspire to replicate in our prototype. This game could incorporate historical landmarks, puzzles, and challenges that encourage exploration and learning about the city's culture and history.

Creating a city-wide game or scavenger hunt in a digital twin metaverse city using SpatialOS for spatial computing and ChatGPT for narrative generation involves several steps. This guide is designed for beginners, detailing each phase from conceptualization to deployment.

Figure 15-6. Conceptual design of city-wide game and scavenger hunt (author's development with Dall-E)

Step 1: Conceptualizing the Game

- Define Objectives: Decide what players will achieve. Is it to learn about the city's history, discover hidden places, or solve puzzles related to landmarks?

- Storyboard: Sketch out a rough storyline or flow of the scavenger hunt. Incorporate historical facts, myths, or interesting stories about the city that ChatGPT can help generate.

Step 2: Setting Up Development Environments

- Install SpatialOS: Go to the (https://improbable.io/) website, sign up, and download the SpatialOS SDK. Follow the installation guide to set up the SDK on your system.

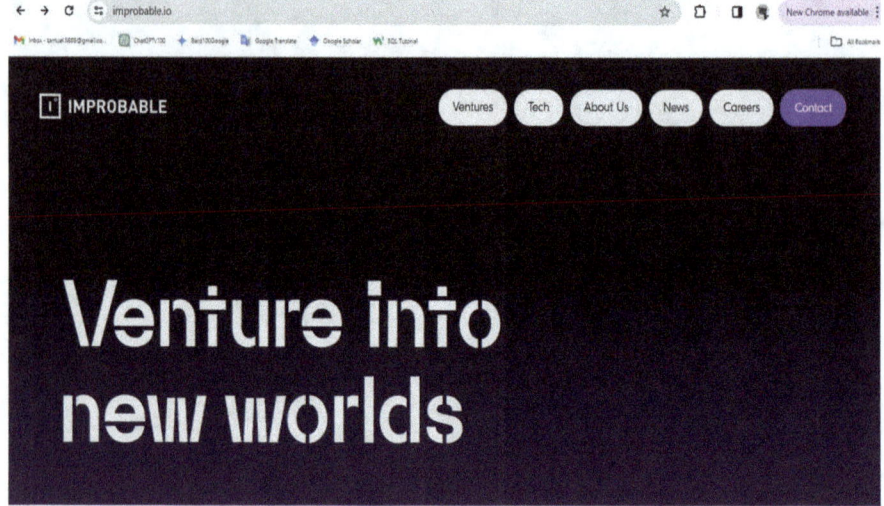

- Install Unity or Unreal Engine: Choose your preferred game development engine. For Unity, visit the (https://unity.com/downloa4), and for Unreal Engine, visit the (https://www.unrealengine.com/en-US/download). Install the engine following the provided instructions.

CHAPTER 15   DIGITAL TWIN METAVERSE PROTOTYPES: SMART ENTERTAINMENT AND CITIES

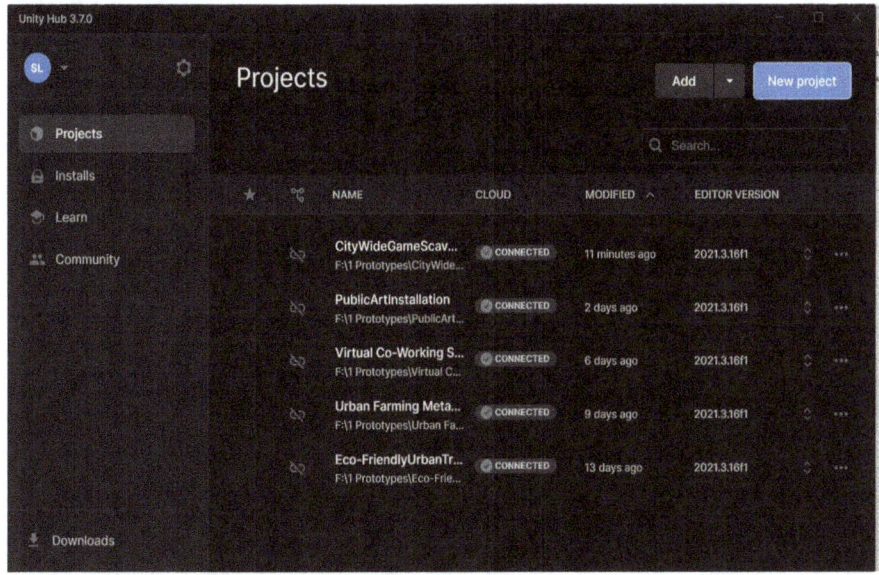

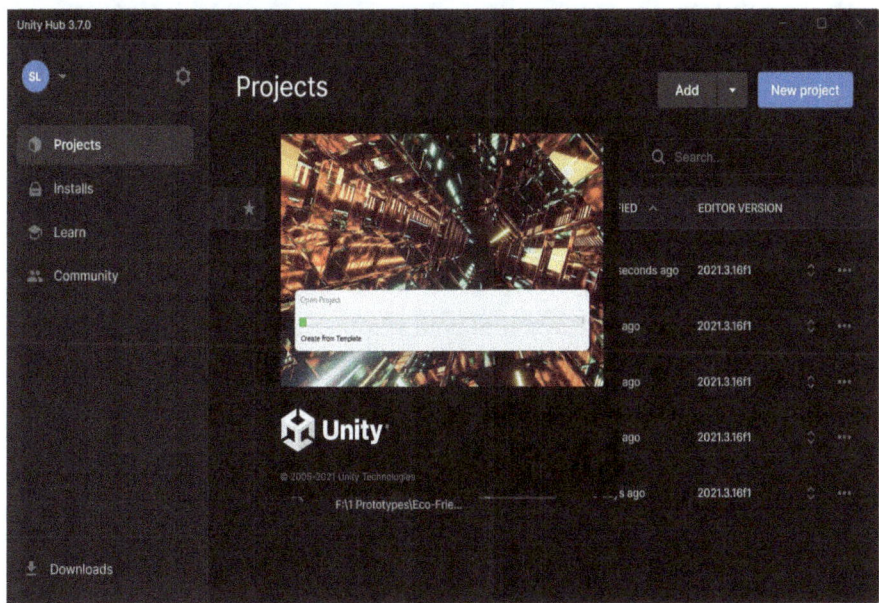

CHAPTER 15   DIGITAL TWIN METAVERSE PROTOTYPES: SMART ENTERTAINMENT AND CITIES

- Configure SpatialOS with Unity/Unreal Engine: Follow the SpatialOS documentation to integrate SpatialOS with your chosen engine. This typically involves installing SpatialOS plugins or GDK (Game Development Kit) for Unity or Unreal.

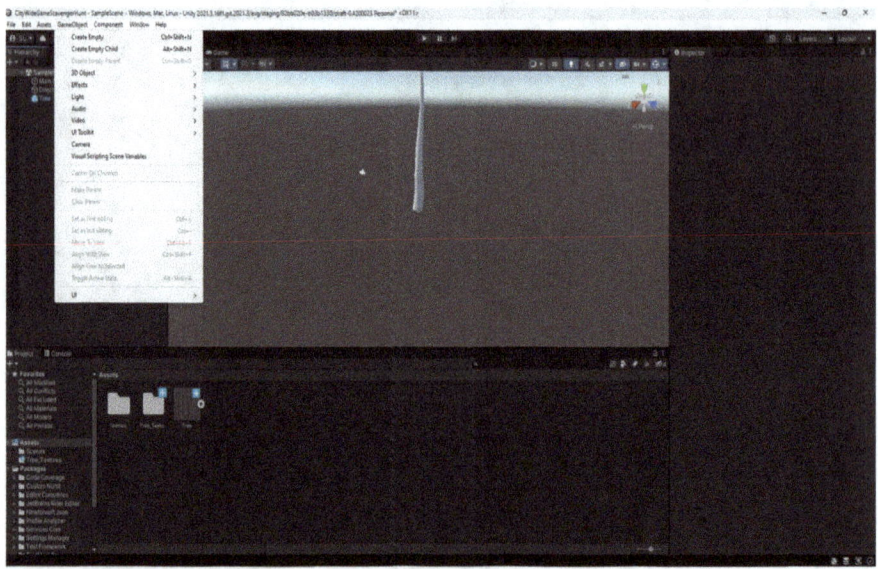

Step 3: Building the Digital Twin City

- Create the City Layout: Use Unity or Unreal Engine to model the basic layout of your digital twin city. Import city maps, buildings, and landmarks as 3D models. Many cities have 3D data available for public use, or you can create simple representations.

CHAPTER 15   DIGITAL TWIN METAVERSE PROTOTYPES: SMART ENTERTAINMENT AND CITIES

Now it's your turn   *As you venture further into the realm of digital twin metaverse city development, I encourage you to continue the remaining steps and enhance your prototype by adding rich, realistic scenery, fine-tuning materials, and weaving in greater interactivity. Your engagement and dedication to this work are invaluable—embrace this chance to innovate and hone your expertise in crafting the digital landscapes of tomorrow...*

- Import to SpatialOS: Once your basic city layout is ready in Unity or Unreal Engine, import it into SpatialOS. This allows your city to leverage SpatialOS's cloud-based computation for scalability and real-time updates.

Step 4: Integrating ChatGPT for Narrative Generation

- Generate Content: Use ChatGPT to create interesting stories, clues, and puzzles related to the city's landmarks. You can prompt ChatGPT with specific historical events or cultural aspects of the city to generate engaging content.

- Implement Content in Game: Incorporate the narratives and puzzles generated by ChatGPT into your game. Use Unity or Unreal Engine's scripting capabilities to create NPCs (non-player characters), dialogues, and puzzle mechanics based on the content.

Step 5: Adding Game Mechanics

- Set Objectives and Rewards: Define clear objectives for each stage of the scavenger hunt. Use Unity or Unreal Engine to program rewards for completing puzzles or discovering new locations.

- Implement Player Tracking: Use SpatialOS's spatial computing capabilities to track players' movements across the city, manage interactions with game elements, and update the game state in real time.

Step 6: Testing and Deployment

- Local Testing: Use the local deployment feature of SpatialOS to test the game on your machine. Check for bugs, narrative flow, and player engagement.

- Cloud Deployment: Once satisfied with local tests, deploy your game to the cloud using SpatialOS. This allows players from different locations to participate in the scavenger hunt.

Step 7: Launch and Iterate

- Launch: Open your game to players. Use social media and gaming forums to invite players to your digital twin city's scavenger hunt.

- Collect Feedback: Gather player feedback on gameplay, narrative elements, and technical performance.

CHAPTER 15   DIGITAL TWIN METAVERSE PROTOTYPES: SMART ENTERTAINMENT AND CITIES

- Iterate: Use the feedback to improve the game. Update narratives with ChatGPT, refine puzzles, and optimize performance using SpatialOS and your development engine.

Creating a city-wide game or scavenger hunt in a digital twin metaverse requires a blend of creative storytelling, technical skills in game development, and leveraging advanced tools like SpatialOS and ChatGPT. This guide provides a foundational approach, encouraging beginners to explore, learn, and create engaging metaverse experiences.

7. Metaverse Music Festival Experience

Diving into the future of live music with the metaverse music festival experience, we will develop a prototype that brings the electrifying atmosphere of music festivals into the digital twin metaverse cities. Figure 15-7 presents a conceptual design of a metaverse music festival experience—the blueprint we aspire to replicate in our prototype. This innovative concept allows users to experience live concerts and festivals in a virtual environment that replicates real-world festival venues with stunning accuracy and immersive detail.

CHAPTER 15   DIGITAL TWIN METAVERSE PROTOTYPES: SMART ENTERTAINMENT AND CITIES

Figure 15-7. *Conceptual design of metaverse music festival experience (author's development with Dall-E)*

Step 1: Downloading Unreal Engine

- Visit the Unreal Engine Website: Go to https://www.unrealengine.com/ and sign up or log in if you already have an account.

- Install Unreal Engine: Run the downloaded installer and follow the on-screen instructions. Make sure to include the necessary components for game development, such as the UE4 editor and basic project templates.

CHAPTER 15   DIGITAL TWIN METAVERSE PROTOTYPES: SMART ENTERTAINMENT AND CITIES

Step 2: Setting Up Your Project

- Open the Epic Games Launcher: After installation, open the launcher and go to the "Unreal Engine" tab.

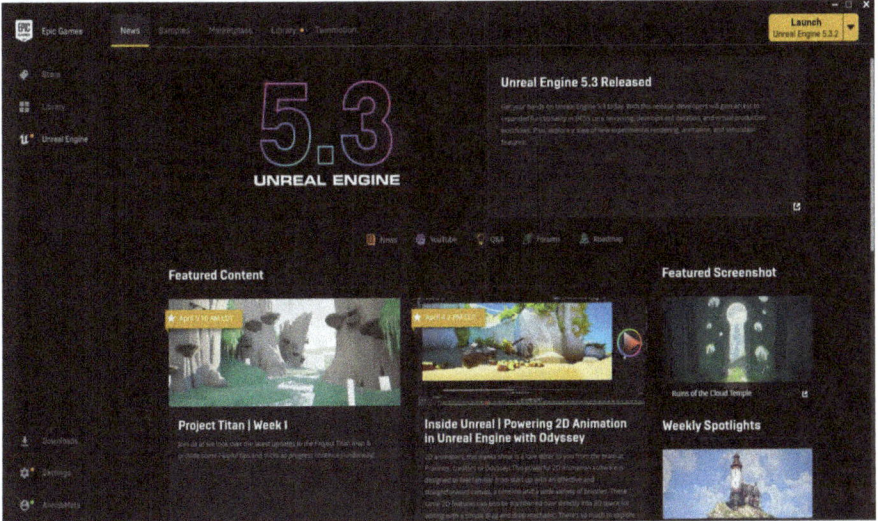

- Create a New Project: Click "Launch" under the version of UE5 you installed, and then choose "New Project" from the main screen.

- Choose a Template: For a music festival, select the "Third-Person" template to give attendees a character to navigate the festival grounds. Ensure "Blueprint" is selected as the project's programming language for easier visual scripting.

- Project Settings: Name your project "MetaMusicFestival" and specify the desired location on your computer. Make sure to set the quality level to "High" and include starter content.

395

CHAPTER 15 DIGITAL TWIN METAVERSE PROTOTYPES: SMART ENTERTAINMENT AND CITIES

- Create Project: Click "Create Project" to initialize your new metaverse environment.

Step 3: Designing the Environment

- Explore Starter Content: Investigate the starter content provided by Unreal Engine to familiarize yourself with available assets like trees, buildings, and props.

- Creating the Terrain: In the "Modes" panel, select "Landscape" to start shaping your festival grounds. Use the sculpt tools to create hills, valleys, and flat areas for stages and audience spaces.

CHAPTER 15   DIGITAL TWIN METAVERSE PROTOTYPES: SMART ENTERTAINMENT AND CITIES

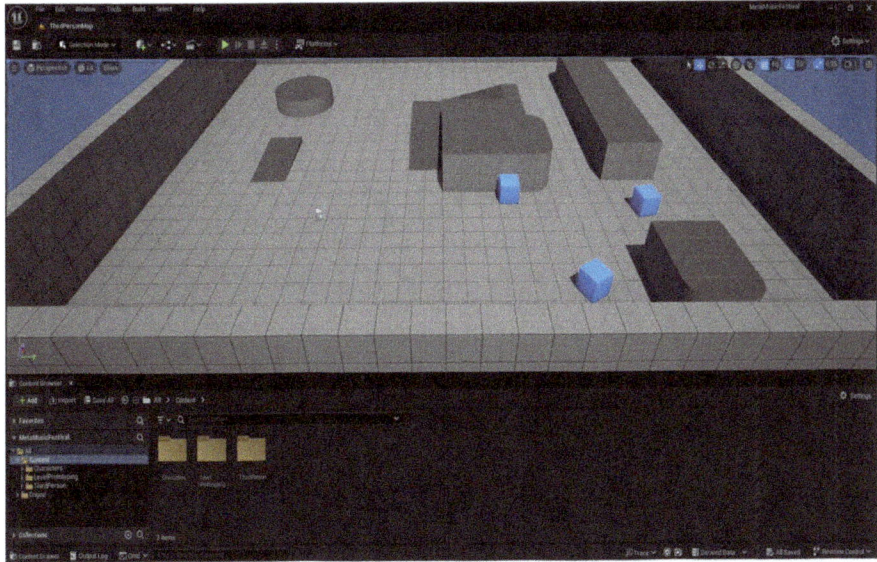

- Adding Assets: Drag and drop assets from the starter content or import custom assets to build your festival scene. This includes stages, screens, lighting rigs, and crowd barriers.

CHAPTER 15   DIGITAL TWIN METAVERSE PROTOTYPES: SMART ENTERTAINMENT AND CITIES

- Implement Lighting: Use the "Light" options to add a directional light for the sun and spotlight for stage lighting. Adjust the intensity and color to mimic the time of day or night for your festival.

Now it's your turn   *As you venture further into the realm of digital twin metaverse city development, I encourage you to continue the remaining steps and enhance your prototype by adding rich, realistic scenery, fine-tuning materials, and weaving in greater interactivity. Your engagement and dedication to this work are invaluable—embrace this chance to innovate and hone your expertise in crafting the digital landscapes of tomorrow…*

Step 4: Adding Interactivity

- Place a Character Spawn Point: In the "Modes" panel, navigate to "Basic" and drag a "Player Start" actor into your scene. This designates where players will start upon entering your metaverse.

- Creating Interactive Elements: Use Blueprints to add interactivity, like starting a music track when a character approaches a stage or triggering lights when night falls.

- Add Music and Sound Effects: Import music tracks and sound effects, placing audio sources around your stages and interactive elements to create an immersive atmosphere.

Step 5: Testing and Iteration

- Playtest Your Festival: Click the "Play" button in the Unreal Editor to enter your festival as the player character. Explore the environment, interact with elements, and note any areas for improvement.

- Iterate Based on Feedback: Make adjustments based on your experiences. This might include altering the landscape, adding more interactive elements, or improving the lighting and sound design.

Step 6: Packaging Your Prototype

- Package Your Project: Once satisfied with your prototype, go to "File" ➤ "Package Project" ➤ "Windows" (or your preferred platform) to create an executable version of your metaverse music festival.

- Distribute or Share: Share your packaged project with others to explore your digital twin metaverse city's entertainment prototype.

Remember, developing in Unreal Engine is a process of learning and experimentation. Don't hesitate to utilize Unreal Engine's extensive documentation and community forums for additional guidance and tips.

Creating a metaverse music festival prototype with Unreal Engine is a transformative experience that combines the thrill of design with the power of interactivity. Starting with downloading Unreal Engine, you dive into designing the festival's terrain, selecting and placing vibrant assets, and injecting life into the scene with dynamic lighting and sound. Implementing interactivity via Blueprints makes the environment not just visually captivating but engaging. Through playtesting, you refine the prototype, ensuring it delivers a compelling experience. The journey concludes with packaging the project, making your digital twin metaverse festival ready to share and explore. This prototyping adventure is a blend of creativity, technology, and iterative design, showcasing the potential of digital twin cities in the metaverse.

8. A Metaverse City Prototype Using Unreal Engine (UE)

In this closing prototype of the book, we're taking a leap from theoretical exploration to practical creation. Inspired by a dazzling sample metaverse city courtesy of Unreal Engine 5's official documentation, we embark on a journey of crafting our own full-scale metaverse city. This will be a testament to the array of skills we've honed throughout the book—a showcase of proficiency in digital twin metaverse city-building gleaned from our hands-on experience with various smart city prototypes. Step by step, we'll stitch together the fabric of a comprehensive metaverse city,

CHAPTER 15   DIGITAL TWIN METAVERSE PROTOTYPES: SMART ENTERTAINMENT AND CITIES

stitching virtual threads into a tapestry of interactive urban spaces. Join me in harnessing Unreal Engine 5 to elevate our metaverse vision from concept to reality.

The metaverse sample city shown in Figure 15-8 is created using UE5 by SideFx's Houdini, provided by Epic Games as an official UE tutorial document.[1] And it demonstrates to generate data to create a working simulated metaverse city world by populating assets, driving AI simulation, audio, and visual simulations.

Figure 15-8. *Building a metaverse sample city and freeway prototype using UE5 (source: UE official tutorial[2])*

---

[1] *City Sample Quick Start for Generating a City and Freeway in Unreal Engine 5 | Unreal Engine 5.0 Documentation*

[2] https://academy.unrealengine.com/totara/dashboard/index.php

CHAPTER 15   DIGITAL TWIN METAVERSE PROTOTYPES: SMART ENTERTAINMENT AND CITIES

More specially, here are eight steps to build such a metaverse sample city according to the UE official tutorial document:

[1] Project Setup and Configuration: Users need to open the Metaverse City Sample Project and create folder locations to import the data generated in Houdini for the target city. As a result, a new folder named for the target city and two folders within the named geometry.

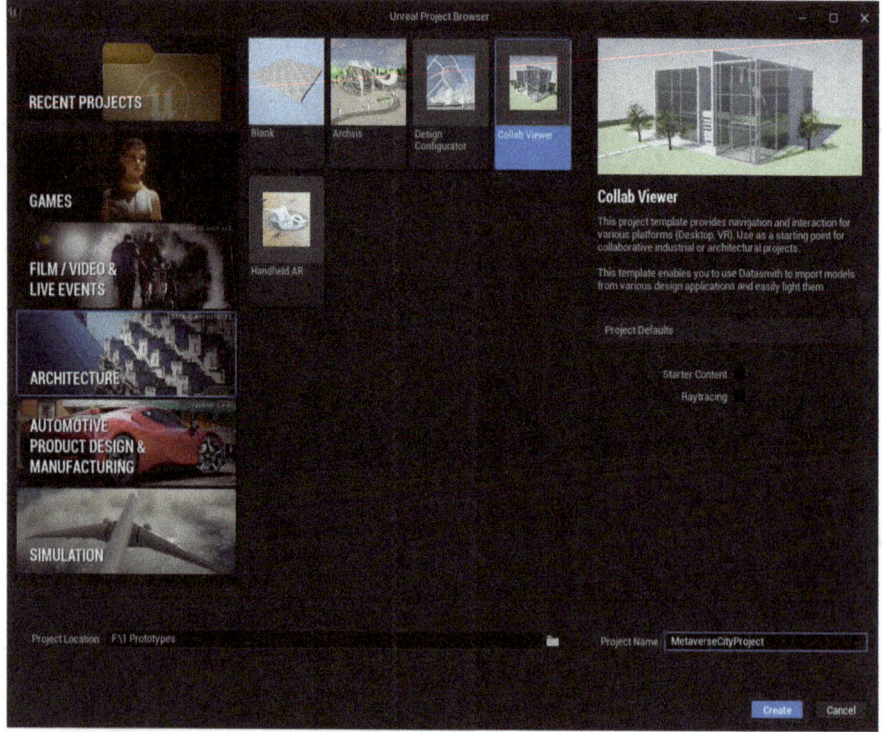

[2] Importing the City Data into Unreal Engine: In this step, the geometry and point cloud data files are imported and saved as assets in the folders created in step 1. As a result, these assets are used in the following steps to start generating the target city.

CHAPTER 15   DIGITAL TWIN METAVERSE PROTOTYPES: SMART ENTERTAINMENT AND CITIES

[3] Preparing an Open World Level: In this step, users create a new level from a templated city Open World Level. This template level provides a starting point for creating the target city like the one from City Sample, with its own lighting and skybox set up and blueprint spawners used to populate data.

[4] Running the Rule Processor Generation: All the data needed to start generating the target city has been imported into the engine, then have a map to load and save it. In this step, users use the Rules Processor for the city and freeway point cloud data you imported into the engine. The Rules Processor maps the generated point cloud data from Houdini Engine to rules that tell Unreal Engine how to use that data to populate the world. Once the Rules Processor has completed processing the data, the city can be loaded into the Level Viewport using the World Partition Editor. Once loaded, users can fly out and inspect your city shown in Figure 15-9.

403

CHAPTER 15   DIGITAL TWIN METAVERSE PROTOTYPES: SMART ENTERTAINMENT AND CITIES

[5] Setting Up Point Cloud Data for the Zone Graph for Traffic: While users have a city to work with, there are two Blueprint Spawners (BS) included with the level that set up the city. With these BS, users can duplicate some data assets used with the small city for the target city, and these data assets rely on point cloud data which is imported.

[6] Running the Zone Graph Generation for Traffic: In this step, users use an editor utility widget made specifically for performing tasks of generating a Zone Graph for lanes of traffic using the point cloud data you assigned to data assets and Blueprint Spawners before. Once the Zone Graph editor utility widget has run, which populates the data from both the parking spaces and traffic lights to the data assets, users can now visualize the navigation that is generated from that data inside the Level Viewport shown in Figure 15-9.

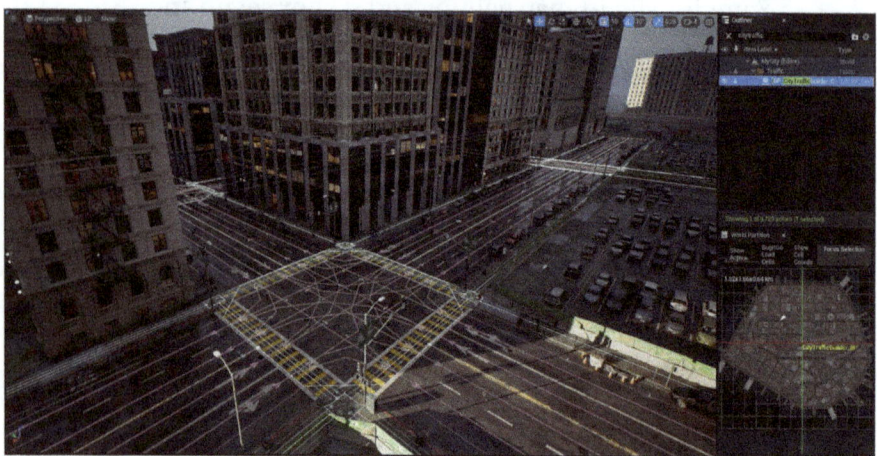

Figure 15-9. *A metaverse city at street level: streetlights, traffic, and parking spaces (source: UE official tutorial[3])*

---

[3] https://academy.unrealengine.com/totara/dashboard/index.php

[7] Generating World Partition Holds for Your City: An important part of building a metaverse city is that it likely has parts that need to be seen from far distances. The World Partition system handles far distances through Hierarchical Level of Detail (HLODs) that can combine many objects into single, large actors that can be streamed in and out dynamically. For an example of the target city, the next step is to generate your own HLODs that can be streamed in and out dynamically using World Partition. The size of the city can contribute to how long it takes for HLODs to be generated for your level. Users can use the in-editor tools to do this through the Build menu or by closing the project and using a Windows Command Prompt to do so, with the latter method taking less time.

[8] End Results: In this final step, users place a Player Start in the target city level where the users want to spawn in while launching the game. Finally, a metaverse smart city has been successfully built using the source files provided for Houdini Engine to build a procedural city, importing and setting up in UE5. And the users can explore and play through their own metaverse city shown in Figure 15-10.

CHAPTER 15   DIGITAL TWIN METAVERSE PROTOTYPES: SMART ENTERTAINMENT AND CITIES

Figure 15-10. *Playing around the prototyping metaverse city created by Unreal Engine 5 (source: UE official tutorial[4])*

Having immersed yourself in the official Unreal Engine Sample City tutorial, you're now poised to embark on the exciting venture of constructing your own metaverse city prototype with Unreal Engine 5. Here's a step-by-step guide to ignite your journey into metaverse city creation:

Step 1: Familiarize with UE5 Interfaces with Sample City Temple

- Open the City Sample project in UE5. Figure 15-11 shows your startup screen of creating a metaverse city prototype using a *UE sample city temple.* And it also shows the content organizational structure and recommended development platform requirements.

---

[4] https://academy.unrealengine.com/totara/dashboard/index.php

CHAPTER 15   DIGITAL TWIN METAVERSE PROTOTYPES: SMART ENTERTAINMENT AND CITIES

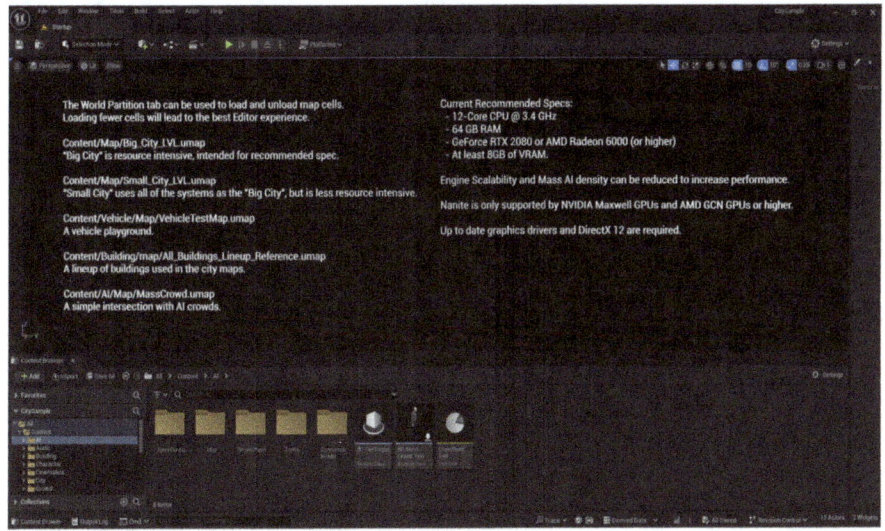

Figure 15-11. *Creating a metaverse city prototype using a UE sample city template (startup screen)*

- Spend some time exploring the interface if you're not already familiar with it. UE5 might have a learning curve if you're new to the engine.

Step 2: Review the City Sample

- Before you start creating, review the City Sample (see Figure 15-12 as a city example).

- Look at the provided content, including the AI, Audio, Building, Character, Cinematics, City, and Crowd folders, to understand how the sample city is structured.

CHAPTER 15   DIGITAL TWIN METAVERSE PROTOTYPES: SMART ENTERTAINMENT AND CITIES

Figure 15-12. Sample city within a UE sample city template

Now it's your turn   *As you venture further into the realm of digital twin metaverse city development, I encourage you to continue the remaining steps and enhance your prototype by adding rich, realistic scenery, fine-tuning materials, and weaving in greater interactivity. Your engagement and dedication to this work are invaluable—embrace this chance to innovate and hone your expertise in crafting the digital landscapes of tomorrow...*

Step 3: Modify the Environment

Begin modifying the existing city environment to make it your own. You can adjust the layout, add new buildings, or change the landscape to start giving your city a unique look and feel.

Step 4: Create New Assets

If you're aiming to design a city with a particular theme or style, you may need to create new assets or import them from other sources. UE5's Quixel Bridge integration allows for easy importing of high-quality assets.

Step 5: Scripting Logic

If you want to add interactive elements or simulate specific behaviors in your city, you'll need to use Blueprints or C++ coding in UE5 to script the logic. For instance, you may want to add traffic lights that change color or have cars that follow paths.

Step 6: Test and Iterate

Regularly test your prototype to check the interaction of elements within your city. Use UE5's Play mode to walk through your city and ensure everything functions as expected.

Step 7: Performance Optimization

As your city grows, keep an eye on performance. Use UE5's profiling tools to find and fix performance bottlenecks. A metaverse city can be resource-intensive, so optimization is key.

Step 8: Documentation

Follow the guide provided by Unreal Engine at the link you've mentioned. This will have specific steps tailored to the City Sample template you're working with.

Step 9: Learning Resources

Utilize learning resources available from Epic Games and the UE5 community. Tutorials, forums, and official documentation will be incredibly valuable as you build your prototype.

Step 10: Collaboration and Feedback

If possible, get feedback from others who have experience in UE5 or who are also interested in metaverse city development. Collaborating with peers can provide fresh perspectives and valuable insights.

CHAPTER 15   DIGITAL TWIN METAVERSE PROTOTYPES: SMART ENTERTAINMENT AND CITIES

Remember that creating a prototype can be an iterative process, so be prepared to cycle through designing, testing, and refining multiple times. If you encounter any issues or specific questions while working with the City Sample or UE5, feel free to ask for more detailed assistance. Good luck with your own metaverse city project!

As we draw the curtains on this chapter, we have witnessed the transformative power of digital twin metaverse prototypes, not just as theoretical constructs but as palpable realities within our grasp. From the thrumming heart of virtual concert arenas to the introspective silence of digital twin museums and galleries, we've ventured through smart sports complexes and city-wide games that fuse play with urban space. These eight prototypes stand as beacons of innovation, each a testament to the possibilities that lie at the intersection of imagination, technology, and civic life.

Now, we stand at the threshold of Part 6, encapsulated in Chapters 16–18. Here, the baton is passed to you, the reader, the visionary, the city builder, to move from conception to action. We will tackle the real-world challenges of managing and sustaining the momentum of smart city projects, the subtleties of change management during transitions, and the indispensable leadership skills required to steer these complex endeavors toward success.

The journey forward is both an invitation and a challenge: to not only dream of the digital twin metaverse cities but to actualize them. In these final chapters, we will arm you with the strategies, the methodologies, and the courage to lead the charge in shaping the future of our urban landscapes. Let's embrace this new era of urban innovation, where every step forward is a stride toward redefining the very essence of city living. Prepare to be inspired, to learn, and, most importantly, to do. The canvas of the future awaits your touch.

PART VI

What Is Next: Just Do It

Embarking on the thrilling conclusion of our journey through the digital twin metaverse cities, Part 6 beckons us to reflect on the intricate challenges and managerial acumen required for these urban marvels. The previous chapters have provided us with a virtual toolbox and vivid showcases of cutting-edge prototypes, painting a portrait of what the future holds for smart cities that are not just digitally enabled but truly digitally transformed.

As we turn the page to Chapter 16, we'll unravel the art of managing triumphant smart city projects amid the shadows of potential risks like budgetary constraints and user adoption hurdles. In Chapter 17, we'll venture into the dynamic world of change management, a pivotal force in steering the metamorphosis of cities in the age of rapid digitalization. The final chapter, Chapter 18, elevates our discourse to leadership—here lies the crucible where vision is forged into reality, demanding new leadership competencies attuned to the rhythm of this digital epoch.

This part isn't merely a collection of theoretical musings but a call to arms—a proclamation that now is the time to transmute knowledge into action. It's a manifesto for innovators, urban developers, policymakers, and every passionate individual ready to embrace the baton of transformation and sprint toward a smarter, more interconnected urban existence. So, brace yourselves to leap into practice, to navigate the digital waves, and to become the architects of tomorrow's digital twin metaverse cities in this exhilarating era of artificial intelligence.

# CHAPTER 16

Managing Successful Smart City Projects

This chapter unravels the essence of project management as the linchpin for the successful construction of digital twin metaverse cities. It defines project management as a systematic methodology crucial for the precise organization, planning, and control of projects, ensuring they are delivered on time and within budget while satisfying stakeholder requirements. Introducing the Program Evaluation and Review Technique (PERT) as a pivotal planning tool, the chapter highlights its role in task sequencing, resource allocation, and critical path identification. Furthermore, it explores Agile Project Management with a focus on Scrum, underscoring its suitability for managing large-scale, complex projects like digital twin cities through iterative, flexible, and team-centric approaches. Merging the methodical insights of PERT with the dynamism of Agile and Scrum, the chapter advocates for a strategic balance in navigating project schedules and resources, aiming to steer ambitious smart city projects toward fruition.

The construction of a digital twin metaverse city is a meticulous process, orchestrated through a series of successful projects that leverage the cutting-edge architecture detailed in Chapter 5, the comprehensive digital twinning process outlined in Chapter 6, and the pioneering ICTs and showcases from Chapters 7–10. Despite the innovative approach, these smart city projects harbor substantial risks, including budget overruns, delays, suboptimal return on investment, and challenges in user adaptability. Echoing the findings of Mansfield et al. [137], the dichotomy between a project's technical success (80% probability) and its commercial success (20% probability) starkly highlights the precarious nature of such undertakings, with an overall project success rate plummeting to a mere 16%. This alarming statistic underscores the imperative for robust project management as a key success factor in navigating the complexities inherent in developing successful digital twin metaverse cities. It is through the lens of effective project management that we can address and mitigate these risks, ensuring that the visionary blueprint of a digital twin metaverse city, as conceptualized through the innovative architectures, processes, and technologies discussed in earlier chapters, transitions from a theoretical model to a tangible, thriving urban ecosystem.

A project is an interconnected set of tasks with specific start and end points, aimed at achieving a particular outcome with allocated resources [129]. Project management (PM) adopts a systematic and phased method to define, organize, plan, monitor, and control these tasks [133]. The essence of project management lies in ensuring that projects are delivered on time, within budget, and in alignment with the stakeholders' agreed-upon specifications. This definition not only highlights the procedural aspect of project management but also underscores its strategic role in facilitating successful project outcomes. This approach is integral to the construction of digital twin metaverse cities, as outlined in earlier chapters, where meticulous planning, resource allocation, and stakeholder collaboration are critical. By refining project management practices, projects related to digital twinning and the deployment of innovative technologies discussed in previous sections can be more effectively realized, ensuring these ambitious initiatives meet their intended goals and deliver tangible benefits.

Project planning is crucial for achieving project success. It involves setting clear goals, segmenting the project into manageable stages, identifying tasks, defining deliverables, sequencing activities, allocating resources, estimating task durations, and balancing the budget and schedule. The Program Evaluation and Review Technique (PERT) plays a vital role in this process by establishing the sequence of activities, facilitating resource allocation, and identifying the project's critical path [134]. As illustrated in Figure 16-1, a PERT diagram simplifies project management from start to finish, highlighting both sequential and parallel tasks. The diagram's critical path—marked in red from the start through tasks B and E to the finish—represents the sequence of activities that determines the project's shortest completion time. Delays in any task along this path directly impact the project's overall completion timeline. Therefore, managing tasks on the critical path efficiently is paramount for keeping the project within time and budget constraints, leading to successful outcomes. This strategic emphasis on project planning and critical path management aligns with the principles discussed in previous chapters, emphasizing the meticulous approach required for the successful realization of digital twin metaverse cities.

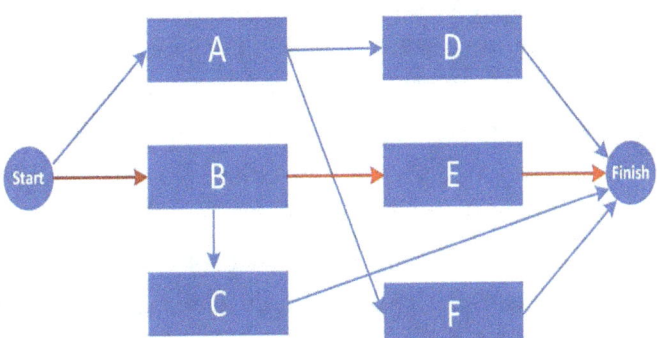

Figure 16-1. PERT diagram for project management (author's development)

Agile Project Management (APM) with Scrum has gained prominence in managing the software development life cycle and is increasingly adopted for large-scale projects like the construction of digital twin metaverse cities, owing to its iterative, team-oriented, and flexible methodology [135]. This approach is particularly beneficial for complex projects requiring adaptation to rapidly changing requirements, reconciliation of divergent stakeholder interests, and enhancement of communication and collaboration, thereby ensuring maximal productivity. Unlike the traditional Waterfall model, which is linear and sequential, APM with Scrum offers a dynamic framework that fosters continuous improvement and responsiveness to change [138], making it ideally suited for the innovative and multifaceted nature of digital twin metaverse city projects. This adaptability aligns with the foundational principles detailed in earlier chapters, emphasizing the need for agile methodologies in navigating the complexities of modern urban development.

The Agile Project Management (APM) Scrum framework, illustrated in Figure 16-2, is designed to address complex, adaptive challenges efficiently, fostering a high-value delivery of products or services [136]. It is grounded on principles of transparency, inspection, and adaptability, facilitated by an engaging APM Scrum process. Projects are segmented into manageable components: the "Product Backlog," the "Sprint Backlog," and daily engagements in the "Daily Scrum." This process involves a cohesive team effort from various roles—Scrum Master, Product Manager, Business Analyst, Developer, and Tester—collaborating from the initial scrum meeting to the day's end solution delivery. This methodology not only accelerates project deliverables but also promotes an agile culture of collaboration and teamwork. Unlike traditional, rigid organizational structures, Scrum's flexibility and adaptability encourage a more fluid and responsive project management approach.

CHAPTER 16   MANAGING SUCCESSFUL SMART CITY PROJECTS

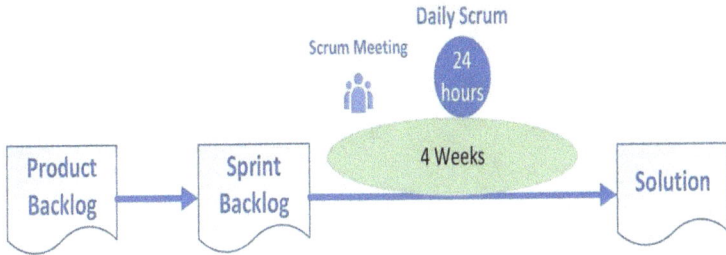

Figure 16-2. *Agile Project Management (APM) with Scrum process (author's development)*

In conclusion, leveraging both the Program Evaluation and Review Technique (PERT) and Agile Project Management (APM) models presents a formidable strategy for the successful development of large-scale digital twin metaverse cities. These methodologies provide a robust framework for navigating the complexities of such ambitious projects, ensuring a balanced allocation of resources and adherence to project timelines. By applying a scientific approach to project management, these techniques not only enhance the likelihood of success but also offer a pathway to overcoming the inherent challenges of building sophisticated smart city ecosystems. The integration of PERT's structured planning with APM's flexibility allows for an adaptive and responsive project management process, crucial for the dynamic and evolving nature of digital twin environments. This harmonious combination promises to steer these complex initiatives toward their envisioned outcomes, marking a significant advancement in the creation of the digital twin metaverse cities that are both innovative and sustainable.

CHAPTER 17

Navigating Change: Smart City Transformation and Cutover Strategies

In this chapter, we explore the pivotal role of citizen support and adaptability to new smart applications as critical factors for the success of digital twin metaverse cities. This chapter delves into the intricacies of change management (CM) strategies, which are indispensable for cities and businesses aiming to harness innovative ICTs to maintain a competitive edge. It posits that the essence of successful digital transformation lies in effectively managing and steering change, coupled with ensuring a seamless transition for citizens. Highlighting Lewin's Change Management Model and the Nudge Theory, the chapter underscores their relevance in the digital twin metaverse city context. Lewin's model unfolds through three phases, Unfreezing, Changing, and Refreezing, designed to facilitate a smoother transition. Conversely, the Nudge Theory, rooted in behavioral science, emphasizes the power of subtle prompts in influencing decisions and behaviors. These models aim to mitigate citizen apprehension and streamline the adaptation process during the creation of digital twin metaverse cities, ultimately enhancing investment returns, forging a competitive advantage, and empowering citizens to navigate and thrive in the emerging smart urban landscapes.

While Information and Communication Technologies (ICTs) are foundational in constructing a digital twin metaverse city, the engagement and adaptation of citizens to smart applications emerge as a crucial success factor for the ultimate functionality and livability of smart cities. This intersection emphasizes the critical role of change management (CM) in enabling cities and businesses to stay competitive by embracing innovative ICTs for operational effectiveness, adhering to the imperative "digitize or die." Effective change management entails strategies that support seamless adaptation by individuals, including structured processes for requesting changes and systems to monitor and respond to such requests, thereby maximizing the city's return on investment (ROI) through digital transformation. Enhanced efficiency and productivity from these transformations contribute to improved life quality in digital twin metaverse cities. Hussain et al. [124] articulate that change management's purpose is to continually adapt an organization's direction, structure, and capabilities to meet the evolving needs of both external and internal customers, acknowledging the necessity for organizations to quickly respond to global changes. Understanding the drivers behind organizational and individual change, as well as what motivates these shifts, is essential. By employing behavioral change theories and models, like Lewin's Change Management Model and the Nudge Theory, we can gain insights into the factors influencing human behavior and facilitate the successful digital transformation of digital twin metaverse cities.

Kurt Lewin's Change Model shown in Figure 17-1 provides a comprehensive framework for understanding and facilitating change, capturing the essence of how individuals and organizations navigate transitions. This model delineates a three-stage process: Unfreeze, Change, and Refreeze. Initially, it advocates for creating an awareness of the need for change, thereby preparing the mind for a shift ("Unfreeze").

Following this, it moves to the "Change" phase, where the actual transition occurs, encouraging adoption of new behaviors or processes. Finally, the "Refreeze" stage solidifies these changes, integrating them into everyday practice. This systematic approach is crucial for managing the transformation in digital twin metaverse cities, ensuring that changes are not only implemented but also embraced and sustained over time. By applying Lewin's model, stakeholders can facilitate a smoother transition toward innovative urban living, aligning with the principles discussed throughout this book.

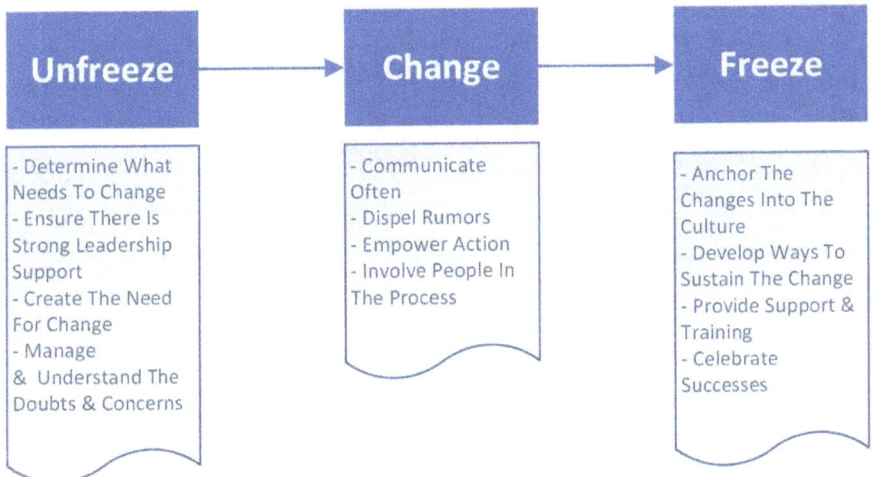

Figure 17-1. Lewin's Change Model—Unfreeze, Change, and Refreeze (source: author's development based on [126])

The initial stage of Kurt Lewin's Change Model, "Unfreeze," involves preparing individuals for change by motivating them to recognize the necessity of altering their current behaviors or practices. This phase is crucial for overcoming inertia and reluctance, requiring clear communication to educate and persuade individuals about the benefits of change [125]. As people progress to the "Change" phase, they start adapting their behaviors, a process that can present challenges,

CHAPTER 17 NAVIGATING CHANGE: SMART CITY TRANSFORMATION AND CUTOVER STRATEGIES

including discomfort and resistance, due to the apprehension of new methods and the perceived loss of familiar habits. Effective planning and communication are essential to facilitate this transition and gain widespread buy-in. The final "Refreeze" stage solidifies these new behaviors or practices as the standard, reinforcing positive changes through rewards and acknowledgment, and supported by policies that promote these new norms. This structured approach ensures that changes are not only implemented but become integrated and sustainable within the organization or community, ultimately leading to improved outcomes and efficiencies.

The Nudge Theory represents a modern and dynamic approach within behavioral science, focusing on how subtle prompts can influence individuals' perceptions, judgments, and actions in the real world [127]. This theory posits that small interventions, or nudges, can significantly impact decision-making processes. As illustrated in Figure 17-2, to effectively implement change through nudging, it's essential to clearly articulate the changes, view these changes from the citizens' perspectives, present evidence supporting the best choices, frame changes as options, solicit and heed feedback, minimize barriers to change, and sustain momentum by celebrating short-term achievements. This nuanced approach facilitates smoother transitions by gently guiding individuals toward desired behaviors or decisions, making it a valuable tool in the realm of digital twin metaverse cities' development.

CHAPTER 17   NAVIGATING CHANGE: SMART CITY TRANSFORMATION AND CUTOVER STRATEGIES

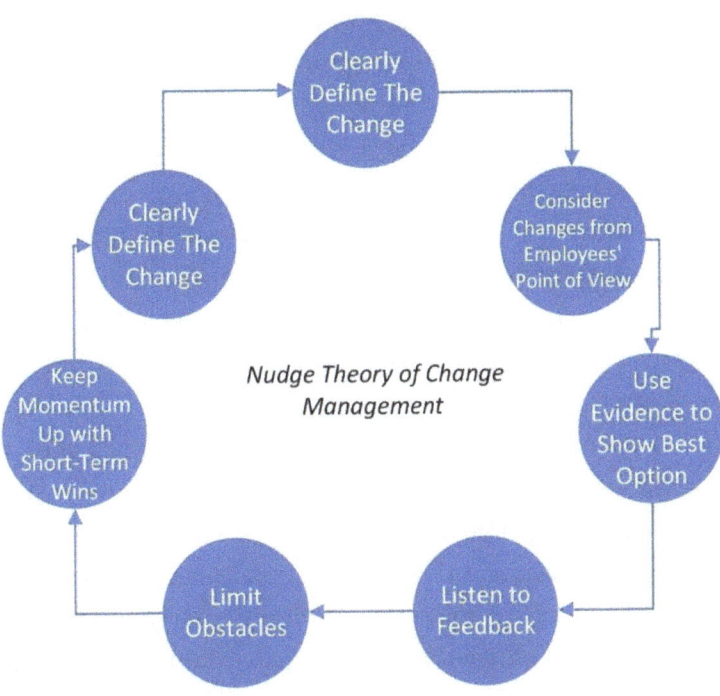

Figure 17-2. Nudge Theory of Change Management (source: author's development based on [128])

Within the Nudge Theory, three pivotal nudges—perception, motivation, and ability and simplicity—play crucial roles in guiding successful organizational change. The theory emphasizes altering the organizational behavior perception, recognizing that individuals interpret changes differently, and, thus, understanding their perspectives is key to identifying and overcoming barriers to change. Motivational nudges serve to actively engage citizens, making the change personally relevant and compelling. For complex changes, emphasizing the ease of adoption and enhancing individual capability through simplification can significantly improve the assimilation of new behaviors. These strategic nudges collectively enhance the adaptability and acceptance of change within the community.

CHAPTER 17 NAVIGATING CHANGE: SMART CITY TRANSFORMATION AND CUTOVER STRATEGIES

In summary, the exploration of Lewin's Change Management Model and the Nudge Theory within this chapter illuminates the path for cities transitioning to digital twin metaverse ecosystems. By leveraging these strategic frameworks, urban developers can effectively mitigate resistance, guiding communities through change with clarity and care. These methodologies do more than just smooth the transition; they bolster the digital transformation journey, leading to tangible benefits such as enhanced return on investment (ROI), a distinct competitive edge, and the empowerment of communities to navigate and thrive in new digital habitats.

The incorporation of these models underscores a critical message: embracing change with agility, flexibility, and a commitment to ongoing innovation is not optional but a necessity for those looking to lead in the rapidly evolving digital era. As cities and businesses adopt cutting-edge Information and Communication Technologies (ICTs), these change management strategies become indispensable tools in fostering acceptance, minimizing disruption, and paving the way for a future where digital and physical realms merge seamlessly, offering unprecedented opportunities for growth, efficiency, and enhanced quality of life.

CHAPTER 18

Leadership for the Future: New Skills for Smart City Development and Management

In this chapter, we will venture into the realm of leadership, uncovering the pivotal skills necessary for steering urban digital transformations in the era of artificial intelligence. Central to constructing a digital twin metaverse city, these leadership skills become the linchpin for managing the intricacies and challenges unique to smart city development. We spotlight four indispensable leadership attributes: humility, adaptability, engagement, and vision.

Humility enables leaders to welcome novel ideas and appreciate contributions across all echelons. Adaptability empowers them to pivot and capitalize on emerging opportunities, as well as to mitigate potential threats. Engagement is about fostering a connection to the team's goals and sustaining motivation, while vision focuses on delineating precise

CHAPTER 18 LEADERSHIP FOR THE FUTURE: NEW SKILLS FOR SMART CITY DEVELOPMENT AND MANAGEMENT

and ambitious objectives. This discussion is enriched by the interactional framework of leadership and the incorporation of the OCEAN model, which highlights the trait of openness as a catalyst for creativity. Furthermore, the narrative integrates Maslow's hierarchy of needs as a foundational element for effective leadership in this dynamic landscape.

Ultimately, leaders who embody humility, adaptability, engagement, and vision are exceptionally equipped to guide the complex journey of urban digital transformation, paving the way for the successful realization of the digital twin metaverse cities in the AI era. As highlighted in Chapter 7, the current AI revolution, featuring breakthroughs like ChatGPT and Gemini LLM, is not only permeating daily life but also playing a crucial role in shaping the smart cities of tomorrow. These AI advancements are crucial to creating a digital twin metaverse city, a concept where the integration of "smartness" into urban infrastructures is no longer a luxury but a necessity.

Leadership in the dynamically evolving terrain of digital transformation necessitates a profound navigation of a world where AI, exemplified by ChatGPT, enriches human interactions within digital domains, and advanced tools like Gemini LLM spearhead the creative endeavors crucial for metaverse development. For those at the helm—be it project managers, team leaders, functional managers, or city officials—the role extends beyond mere technological proficiency. It encompasses steering cultural and strategic shifts, vital for harnessing AI's full potential in urban digitalization.

Such leaders are entrusted with leveraging AI to untangle complex challenges, cultivate novel urban services, and meld the virtual with the physical seamlessly, thus enhancing the lived experience within digital twin metaverse cities. Mastery over these technological advancements isn't just beneficial; it's essential. It facilitates informed urban planning, boosts operational efficiencies, and cultivates a more immersive, engaging environment for citizens, thereby enriching the very essence of smart city living.

CHAPTER 18   LEADERSHIP FOR THE FUTURE: NEW SKILLS FOR SMART CITY DEVELOPMENT AND MANAGEMENT

In general, leadership consists of both hard and soft parts of leadership skills. The hard part refers to the factual and cognitive aspects of leadership, whereas the soft part includes the personality traits and attitude behavior to achieve an objective. These hard and soft elements have been a part of leadership for thousands of years. And the concept of leadership has been upgraded from time to time. Therefore, with the advent of AI, it is imperative that new leadership is required to drive AI revolution during building smart metaverse cities. According to the leadership research by CP, Wade, and Jordan published in *Harvard Business Review*,[1] four new leadership skills—*humility, adaptability, engagement*, and *vision*—will play a vital role in effective leadership during the AI era, which can also apply to building digital twin metaverse cities.

1. Humility in AI-Driven Smart City Leadership

Humility is indispensable in the fast-paced realm of AI and smart city evolution. As AI tools like ChatGPT and Gemini LLM become integral to societal functions, leadership transcends its traditional confines, embracing a humble approach to knowledge and innovation from every corner of the organization. This humility fosters an environment where novel ideas, such as utilizing ChatGPT for enhancing metaverse city services, are not just acknowledged but celebrated. It's about leaders being ready to learn from AI's insights, even when they challenge conventional wisdom. In the construction of digital twin metaverse cities, humility means shifting from authoritative directives to fostering a culture of collaboration and continuous learning.

---

[1] *As AI Makes More Decisions, the Nature of Leadership Will Change (hbr.org)*

2. Adaptability in Smart City Leadership

Adaptability is crucial for leaders in the era of AI and digital twin metaverse cities. It's the ability to swiftly navigate and adapt to technological advancements and unexpected challenges, championing innovation and change. Leaders exemplify adaptability by integrating AI technologies to enhance city operations and citizen experiences, constantly seeking innovative solutions across diverse sectors. This agility enables leaders to transform potential disruptions into strategic advantages, ensuring the successful development of smart, sustainable urban landscapes.

3. Engagement for Smart City Cohesion

Engagement is fundamental as cities evolve into digital metaverse ecosystems. Effective leaders ensure a deep connection with both the implementation team and the broader community, bridging the gap between advanced AI technologies and their practical, beneficial use for all residents. Engagement means maintaining a collective focus on enhancing city living and fostering a culture of innovation, ensuring every team member is aligned with the vision of transforming urban centers into intelligent, connected spaces.

4. Visionary Leadership in the AI Era

A clear, compelling vision is the cornerstone of effective leadership, especially as we step into the future of AI-driven smart cities. Leaders must articulate a forward-looking vision that encompasses the integration of AI into urban infrastructures, envisioning a seamlessly connected metaverse city. This vision serves as a unifying force, inspiring and guiding all stakeholders toward a shared goal of creating more efficient, sustainable, and user-friendly urban environments. Visionary leaders inspire their teams to embrace AI advancements, driving the transformation of cities into dynamic digital twin metaverse cities that anticipate and meet future needs.

According to the interactional framework for leadership shown in Figure 18-1, the construct of leadership emerges from the dynamic interplay between the leader, the followers, and the situational context [130]. This framework is pivotal as we navigate the AI era, where technology is not just an enabler but a transformer of cities into smart, interconnected metaverses. The role of the *leader* evolves to interact with an ever-changing landscape, where their personality and behavior must be adaptable to the challenges and opportunities presented by AI technologies. *Followers*, too, are not static entities but active participants whose values, beliefs, norms, and attitudes toward AI and change are crucial. They need leaders who can guide them through the transition, ensuring that their contributions are valued and their concerns addressed.

The *situational* context is equally significant; leaders must have the foresight to understand and anticipate the conditions that will shape the future of smart cities. They must navigate through the complexities of integrating systems like AI-driven traffic management or responsive public services, which require not only technical knowledge but the ability to foresee societal impacts and ensure the technology is implemented in ways that enhance the city's livability.

For instance, the successful implementation of an AI technology such as ChatGPT in city governance would require leaders to demonstrate these interactional skills. They would need to interact effectively with their teams to understand and leverage the technology, communicate with the populace to foster acceptance and usage, and analyze the situational dynamics to ensure the technology meets the city's unique challenges and opportunities.

Therefore, the interactional framework becomes a lens through which we can view leadership in the AI era: it's about engaging with a diverse group of stakeholders, understanding the implications of AI technologies, and effectively leading the charge in building the digital twin metaverse cities that are not only smart but also sustainable and inclusive.

Figure 18-1. Interactional framework of leadership (source: author's development based on[130])

The OCEAN leadership model, also known as the Five-Factor Model [131], is pivotal in understanding the multifaceted nature of leadership qualities, particularly highlighting the significance of humility in the realm of innovative leadership. This model delineates human personality across five dimensions—openness, conscientiousness, extraversion, agreeableness, and neuroticism—each contributing unique attributes essential for leadership in the rapidly evolving digital twin metaverse city landscape.

- **Openness** is critical, especially for leaders navigating the complexities of AI-era innovations within smart cities. It embodies a leader's adaptability and creativity, crucial for embracing novel technologies like ChatGPT for citizen engagement or leveraging Gemini LLM for urban planning simulations. Leaders exemplifying high openness are not just receptive to new ideas; they actively seek them, fostering an environment where imaginative solutions can thrive.

- **Conscientiousness** ensures that leaders are organized, dependable, and diligent, qualities that enable the meticulous planning and execution needed for integrating advanced technologies into urban infrastructures.

- **Extraversion** facilitates dynamic interaction with teams and stakeholders, enabling leaders to advocate for visionary projects effectively, such as AI-driven public safety initiatives or sustainable urban designs enabled by digital twins.

- **Agreeableness** enhances a leader's capacity to collaborate and empathize with diverse groups, ensuring that the development of smart cities is inclusive and benefits all citizens.

- **Neuroticism**, though typically associated with sensitivity to stress, in a balanced measure can make leaders more attuned to the challenges and pressures of pioneering smart cities, driving them to seek innovative solutions proactively.

Particularly, the dimension of openness aligns with the concept of humility in leadership, where a genuine trust in the contributions of others, regardless of their hierarchy or experience, is paramount. This approach not only builds credibility but also galvanizes a culture of mutual respect and collective intelligence. For example, a leader who embraces ideas from a young intern with fresh insights on incorporating VR for virtual city tours demonstrates humility and openness, essential for fostering innovation and building credibility.

In constructing digital twin metaverse cities, leaders who embody these OCEAN traits, particularly openness and humility, are better equipped to steer their teams through the uncharted territories of smart urban development. By valuing contributions from all levels, these leaders not only enhance their credibility but also empower their teams, paving the way for revolutionary changes that shape the cities of the future. *Adaptability* is another trait possessed by successful leaders nowadays. In this, one should be innovative and creative. Creative intelligence is one, and it deals with the ability to produce new and useful tasks. A leader must be engaged in the team's objectives and goals during a specific situation.

In aligning with the company's objectives, a leader's role extends beyond mere coordination; it entails fostering a unified team spirit and actively motivating and inspiring team members. Drawing upon Maslow's hierarchy of needs [132]—a framework comprising physiological, safety, belongingness and love, esteem, and self-actualization needs—a leader can tailor their motivational strategies to address the diverse aspirations and concerns of their team. This nuanced approach recognizes that employees' needs vary, ranging from basic job security to more complex desires for achievement and personal growth.

For instance, in the context of developing digital twin metaverse cities, a leader might address physiological and safety needs by ensuring job stability and a safe working environment amid the rapid technological advancements. To fulfill the need for belongingness and love, the leader could cultivate a collaborative team culture that values each member's contributions, making everyone feel integral to the project's success.

CHAPTER 18 LEADERSHIP FOR THE FUTURE: NEW SKILLS FOR SMART CITY DEVELOPMENT AND MANAGEMENT

Addressing esteem needs, a leader could recognize individual and team achievements in developing innovative AI applications for urban planning, thereby boosting morale and fostering a sense of pride in their work. For employees seeking self-actualization, leaders could provide opportunities for professional growth, such as leading a new project using cutting-edge technologies like ChatGPT or Gemini LLM, enabling team members to explore their full potential.

Furthermore, it is crucial that every employee and team member has a clear understanding of the firm's goals or vision. This clarity ensures that all efforts are cohesive and directed toward a common objective, such as building a sustainable and efficient digital twin metaverse city that enhances urban living. By integrating Maslow's theory into their leadership approach, leaders can create an environment where motivation thrives, and every team member is engaged and committed to the collective vision.

This chapter crystallizes the imperative leadership qualities needed to navigate the construction and management of the digital twin metaverse cities in the AI era. Leadership in this transformative landscape requires a composite of humility, adaptability, engagement, and vision. These qualities are not just beneficial but essential for leaders, including project managers, team leaders, event organizers, and city officials, as they steer through the challenges and opportunities presented by urban digital transformation.

- **Humility** encourages leaders to remain open to new ideas, fostering an environment where innovation can arise from any quarter, irrespective of hierarchy. This quality ensures that the diverse and potentially groundbreaking perspectives, especially those influenced by emerging AI technologies, are acknowledged and integrated into the development process.

- **Adaptability** emphasizes the necessity for leaders to pivot in response to the dynamic nature of technological innovation and urban development. The rapid evolution of AI technologies demands a leadership style that is not only responsive but also anticipative of future shifts, ensuring that smart city infrastructures remain resilient and forward-thinking.

- **Engagement** underscores the importance of leaders being deeply connected with their team's goals and objectives. This connection is crucial for maintaining team cohesion and motivation, especially in the complex and often unpredictable journey of building digital twin metaverse cities, where team members must navigate new technological landscapes together.

- **Vision** highlights the need for clear, specific, and attainable goals. Leaders must articulate a compelling and understandable vision for the organization, ensuring that all members are aligned and motivated toward achieving the collective aim of transforming urban environments through digital innovation.

These leadership skills are corroborated by various leadership theories, illustrating that successful navigation through the urban digital transformation process is contingent upon embodying these four critical leadership attributes. As we transition into the remaining of this book, the focus will shift toward more specific aspects of digital twin metaverse city development, building on the foundational leadership principles outlined in this chapter.

Conclusion and Calling for Immediate Actions

As we approach the culmination of this insightful journey with *Building Digital Twin Metaverse Cities: Revolutionizing Cities with Emerging Technologies*, it is imperative to reflect on the extensive knowledge and insights distilled from Chapters 1-18. This narrative has meticulously charted the transformative blueprint for digital twin metaverse cities, offering a beacon of hope amid the escalating challenges of global urbanization.

We embarked on this exploration with an examination of the rapid pace of urban migration and its resultant challenges—overcrowded housing, relentless traffic, overstretched healthcare, and dwindling resources. The call for innovative solutions led us to envision a new paradigm of urban development, intricately woven with the threads of emerging technologies.

Our exploration unveiled an architectural masterpiece—the blueprint of digital twin metaverse cities. This blueprint serves as a catalyst for a digital renaissance, intertwining the physical city with its virtual counterpart through a dynamic, living representation that evolves continually. Central to this vision are the novel theoretical foundations laid out in Chapters 5 and 6, where we introduced an architectural design and digital twinning process that seamlessly integrates the physical and digital realms of urban development. These chapters not only propose a new blueprint for city planning but also ignite a digital renaissance, emphasizing the dynamic evolution of cities in sync with their digital twins. Moreover, this novel theoretical foundation proposed a seamless integration of physical and digital realms, heralding a new era of city planning and digital renaissance.

Our journey through the core and enabling technologies unraveled the critical role of 5G, IoT, AI, robotics, AR/VR, fog computing, and blockchain in sculpting an interconnected urban ecosystem poised to redefine our living, working, and interaction paradigms. Among the 28 innovative digital twin and metaverse development tools explored were AWS IoT TwinMaker, Microsoft Azure Digital Twins, Nvidia's Omniverse, Roblox, Blender, ChatGPT, Gemini, Unity, and Unreal Engine, each heralding unique capabilities to foster a cradle of innovation.

The practical applications and engineering prototypes demonstrated the transition from theoretical frameworks to real-world implementations, showcasing dynamic traffic management, intelligent energy systems, robotic assistance, and more. Highlighted prototypes, including sustainable smart homes, virtual healthcare clinics, smart education centers, and a metaverse city prototype, among others, illustrate the transformative potential and practical applicability of our digital twin metaverse vision.

As we delved into the human aspect of this technological revolution, the pivotal role of project managers, team leaders, and city officials was emphasized. Leadership qualities such as humility, adaptability, vision, and engagement emerged as the navigational beacons through the intricacies of urban digital transformation.

This narrative culminates in a compelling call to action, urging governments, city planners, business leaders, and ICT innovators to heed the pressing need for urban digitalization. The emergence of smart city revolution is upon us, demanding a unified effort to leverage ICTs for creating more sustainable, efficient, and citizen-responsive urban landscapes.

CONCLUSION AND CALLING FOR IMMEDIATE ACTIONS

We close this book with a clarion call to action, urging each reader to harness the insights, theories, and practical guidance provided to build the digital twin metaverse cities of tomorrow. These cities, envisioned as monuments to human ingenuity and collaborative spirit, promise a legacy of innovation and sustainability for future generations. Let's embark on this transformative journey, turning the potential of the digital twin metaverse cities into a tangible reality.

APPENDIX A

Building Digital Twin–Based Modern Management Information Systems (MMIS)

This appendix provides an added value or bonus for our readers as it will introduce an innovative modern management information systems (MIS) architecture based on the digital twin metaverse concept, similar to the approach discussed in this book for building digital twin smart cities. The discussion kicks off by shedding light on the deficiencies of existing MIS architectures, such as isolated data islands, inadequate decision support, internal-centric focus, high maintenance costs, and limited support for novel business strategies. Key requirements for a contemporary MIS are then outlined, emphasizing a robust external focus, swift data-driven decision-making, automation, and flexibility. The proposed digital twin metaverse-based MIS architecture seamlessly integrates physical and digital aspects across six layers: physical assets, management functions,

APPENDIX A   BUILDING DIGITAL TWIN–BASED MODERN MANAGEMENT INFORMATION SYSTEMS (MMIS)

data collection, data platform, intelligent services utilizing the Data Analytics Flywheel (DAFW) for the digital twinning process, and firm governance. The DAFW serves as the core of the MIS architecture, driving complete automation and the generation of intelligent services. The appendix concludes with practical examples showcasing the application of this MIS architecture in diverse enterprises, including Tesla Gigafactory, Amazon Go, supply chain management, robotaxi services, and airports. Overall, the proposed architecture aims to effectively tackle current MIS challenges and align with the dynamic needs of digital enterprises.

Management Information System (MIS)

Management information systems (MIS) are integral to the operational and strategic framework of contemporary organizations [122][123]. These systems serve as a technological backbone, providing critical data processing and business intelligence required for agile decision-making, thereby enhancing organizational efficiency and effectiveness.

A well-structured MIS encompasses an array of components, including hardware, networking infrastructure, software applications, databases, and the expertise of IT professionals. At its foundation lies the IT architecture, which is constructed upon guiding principles and frameworks that direct the acquisition, development, and integration of IT resources to align with and fulfill the enterprise's strategic objectives.[1]

Transactional MIS and strategic MIS represent the two foundational categories of these systems. The former focuses on the processing of routine data for essential operations such as order processing, inventory management, and accounting. The latter, on the other hand, leverages business intelligence tools for higher-order decision-making processes such as reporting, predictive analysis, and strategic planning.

---

[1] https://www.gartner.com/en/information-technology/glossary/architecturee

APPENDIX A   BUILDING DIGITAL TWIN–BASED MODERN MANAGEMENT INFORMATION SYSTEMS (MMIS)

The current MIS architecture depicted in Figure A-1 illustrates how an MIS infrastructure must not only facilitate day-to-day operations but also empower the management and strategic tiers of an organization. By breaking down an enterprise MIS into subsystems such as supply chain management (SCM), customer relationship management (CRM), enterprise resource planning (ERP), and business intelligence (BI), we see how an integrated approach can provide a holistic view of organizational operations and enable informed decision-making at every level.

As organizations evolve toward the digital twin metaverse city model discussed throughout this book, the traditional MIS architecture needs to adapt. Emerging technologies such as AI, IoT, and big data analytics call for an MIS that is not just a repository of information but an active, intelligent participant in decision-making processes. The digital twin concept redefines MIS, transforming it from a static system to a dynamic, interactive framework capable of simulating and analyzing real-world scenarios in real time, thus significantly advancing the capability to forecast, strategize, and execute with precision.

For example, a digital twin–based MIS in an automotive manufacturing enterprise, like the Tesla Gigafactory, could use real-time data and AI to optimize the entire production life cycle, anticipate maintenance needs, and tailor vehicles to consumer preferences even before they hit the showroom floor. Similarly, Amazon Go's retail environment could utilize such an MIS to manage logistics, track inventory, and enhance the customer shopping experience through a seamless blend of physical and virtual interactions.

In a nutshell, MIS is not just supporting infrastructure but the central nervous system of an organization. The proposed digital twin metaverse-based MIS architecture aims to supersede traditional systems, offering unparalleled insights and controls to steer enterprises toward their future, prepared to meet the demands of the ever-changing market and technological landscape.

APPENDIX A BUILDING DIGITAL TWIN–BASED MODERN MANAGEMENT INFORMATION SYSTEMS (MMIS)

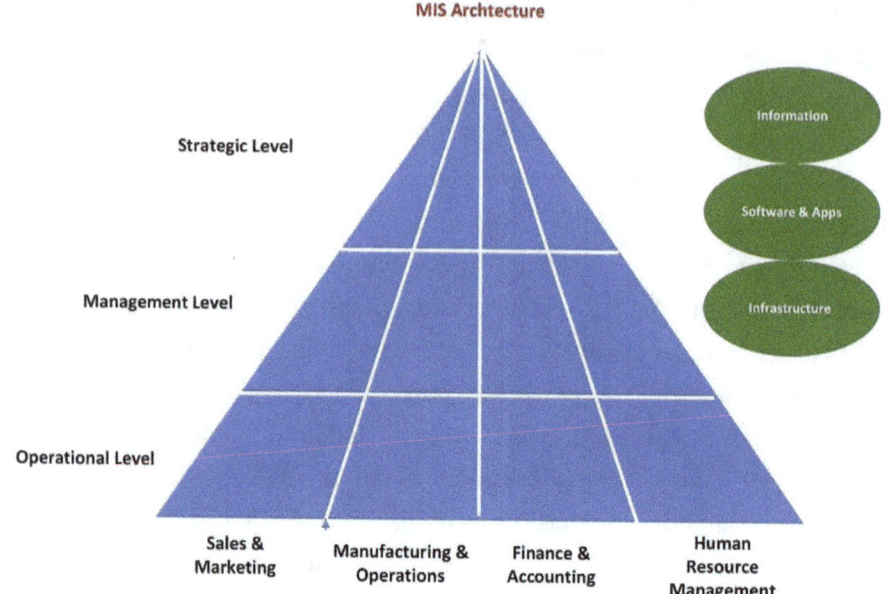

Figure A-1. Current MIS architecture (source: author's development based on [122])

The Challenges of Contemporary MIS Architecture

The MIS architecture of yesteryear, typified in Figure A-1, is increasingly at odds with the dynamism of today's digital economy. The blueprint of isolated data islands, as expounded in the previous section, represents a fragmented era. These islands—enclaves of isolated data, born from disparate systems implemented by independent teams over decades—are the vestiges of the Industry 3.0 paradigm. SAP, Microsoft, and Salesforce.com have each, in their own way, contributed to these segmented landscapes, leading to an integrated communication conundrum and data dissonance.

APPENDIX A   BUILDING DIGITAL TWIN–BASED MODERN MANAGEMENT INFORMATION SYSTEMS (MMIS)

The ripple effect of these siloed structures is a weakened backbone for decision support. As data gets duplicated and compartmentalized, the potential for holistic data analytics, necessary for strategic decision-making, is undermined. This architecture lacks the agility and acuity needed for the kind of swift, data-driven decision-making that is hallmark to thriving in the digital age.

Our focus has historically been inward, looking at internal management processes—from inventory and logistics to finance and HR—with little regard for the broader ecosystem. This contrasts starkly with the Internet-based, platform-centric models explored in Chapter 4, such as those leveraged by Amazon, Uber, and Airbnb, which thrive on external collaboration within a two-sided market.

The maintenance burden of these legacy systems is colossal. Entrenched in proprietary IT infrastructure and shackled to an array of vendor-specific applications, companies find themselves in a Sisyphean struggle against obsolescence and escalating costs. The focus on keeping the lights on means innovative development and strategic initiatives take a back seat.

Take the examples of Tesla Gigafactory[2] and Amazon Go[3]—discussed in the appendixes—where an outdated MIS architecture would falter in supporting the real-time, data-intensive operations that these futuristic enterprises rely on. From supply chain dynamics to customer interactions, the need for a cohesive, intelligent system architecture is evident. The traditional MIS model is not built to underpin such modern, digitally driven business strategies as platform business models, knowledge economies, and automated business processes—all essential to survival and success in a data-dominant world.

---

[2] https://www.tesla.com/gigafactory
[3] https://www.forbes.com/sites/andriacheng/2019/01/13/why-amazon-go-may-soon-change-the-way-we-want-to-shop/?sh=1d2a17de6709

APPENDIX A   BUILDING DIGITAL TWIN–BASED MODERN MANAGEMENT INFORMATION SYSTEMS (MMIS)

Key Requirements of Modern MIS (MMIS)

To surmount the challenges outlined in preceding chapters, a modern MIS architecture must meet pivotal requirements, tailored for the burgeoning era of digital enterprises:

- Strong External Focus: The digital transformation ushering in the Industry 4.0 era necessitates digital enterprises to form robust networks. As detailed in Chapter 4, these networks span suppliers, customers, and third-party partners, forming a two-sided market to capitalize on network effects for exponential growth. Modern MIS must thus facilitate this extroverted ecosystem, underpinning the expansive reach of a digital platform economy.

- Rapid Data-Driven Decision-Making: In the age of "dataism," decision-making has become an immediate, data-centric process. Real-time business intelligence is crucial; for instance, a firm must rapidly assess metrics like sales and customer satisfaction to make pivotal decisions—be it scaling production or altering service offerings. As Chapters 4–6 reveal, modern MIS must therefore embody the agility and capability for data-driven decision-making, transforming data into actionable insights for strategic and operational agility.

- Automation and Intelligent Services: Digitalization has pivoted businesses toward full automation, as highlighted by examples like Tesla's Gigafactory and Amazon Go—enterprises that epitomize efficiency and exemplify the shift toward reduced human intervention. Coupled with the move toward

APPENDIX A BUILDING DIGITAL TWIN–BASED MODERN MANAGEMENT INFORMATION SYSTEMS (MMIS)

servitization [121]—a transition to service-oriented revenue models—this trajectory underscores a strategic push for modern MIS to support automation and intelligent, service-led innovation, shown in Figure A-2.

- Flexibility and Innovation: Today's fast-paced, technology-driven market demands enterprises to be nimble and inventive. With each chapter of this book, from the foundational understanding of emerging technologies to the practicalities of their application, it's evident that modern MIS must be both flexible and innovative, undergirding the rapid evolution of business operations and customer services that define contemporary society.

These requirements lay the groundwork for the next phase—a modern MIS architecture predicated on the digital twin metaverse concept, poised to tackle the extant MIS inadequacies and align with the emergent dynamics of digital businesses. The convergence of these principles will pave the way for enterprises to not only survive but thrive in the unfolding landscape of the digital age.

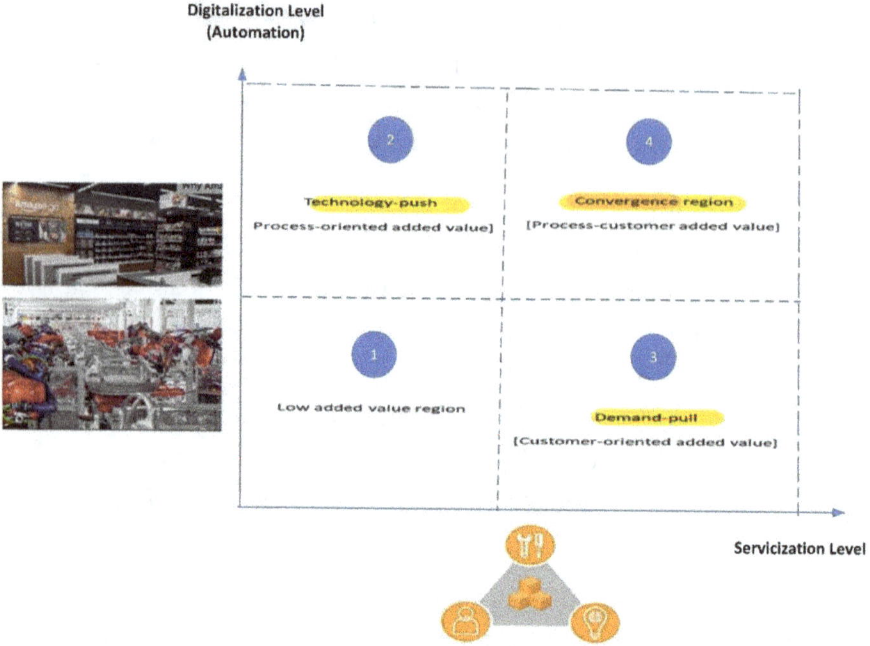

APPENDIX A BUILDING DIGITAL TWIN–BASED MODERN MANAGEMENT INFORMATION SYSTEMS (MMIS)

Figure A-2. *Industry 4.0—automation (digitalization) and servicization (source: author's development based on [121])*

A Digital Twin Metaverse–Based Modern MIS Architecture

In the evolving landscape of digital enterprises, the incorporation of a digital twin metaverse–based modern MIS architecture represents a pivotal shift toward unprecedented operational efficiency and strategic agility. As depicted in Figure A-3, this architecture draws inspiration from the cutting-edge design of the digital twin metaverse cities (Figure 5-1, Chapter 5) and leverages the data-driven decision-making process exemplified in smart city management (Figure 6-5, Chapter 6). At the core of this innovative model lies the Data Analytics Flywheel (DAFW), functioning as the vital heart that propels two strategic imperatives:

APPENDIX A   BUILDING DIGITAL TWIN–BASED MODERN MANAGEMENT INFORMATION SYSTEMS (MMIS)

complete automation and the generation of intelligent services, thereby revolutionizing the operational dynamics of modern digital powerhouses like Tesla's Gigafactory and Amazon Go retail environment.

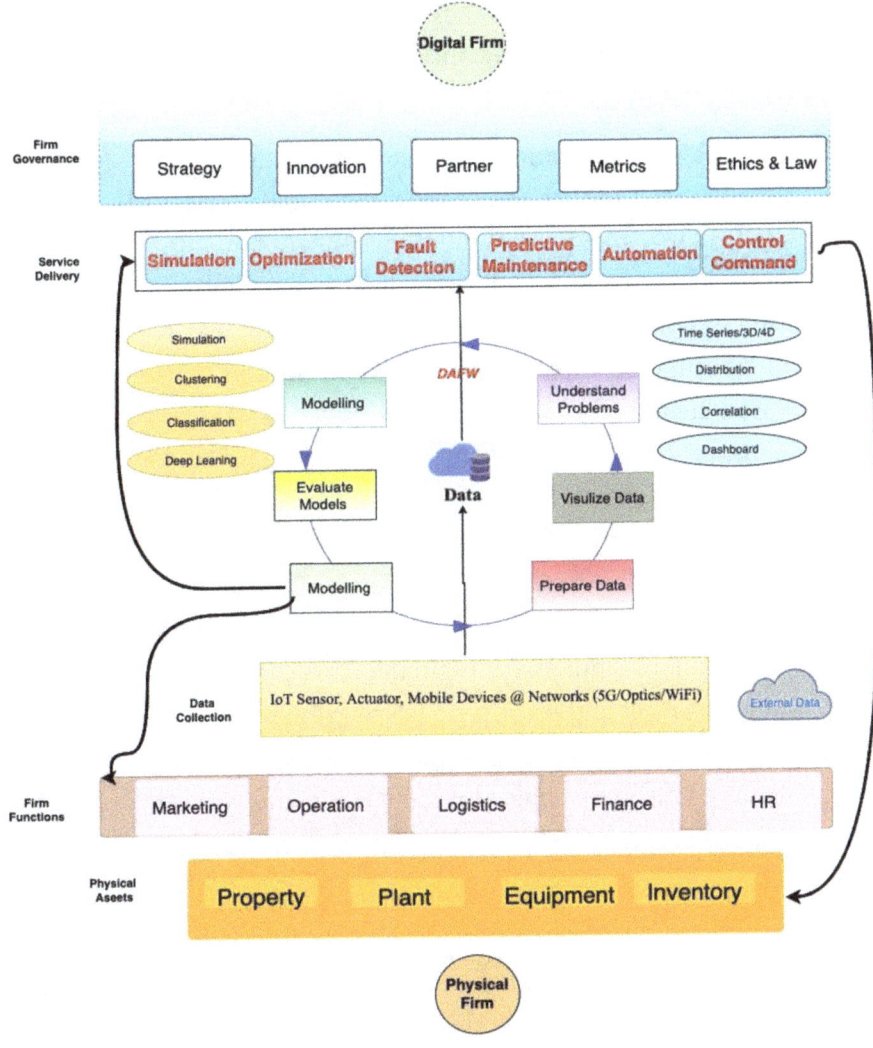

Figure A-3. *A digital twin metaverse–based modern MIS architecture (source: author's development)*

APPENDIX A   BUILDING DIGITAL TWIN–BASED MODERN MANAGEMENT INFORMATION SYSTEMS (MMIS)

More specifically, a modern firm must be a digital twin metaverse-based digital enterprise because of the ongoing digital transformation process, resulting in a physical firm at the bottom and a digital firm on the top as mirrored digital twin metaverse shown in Figure A-3.

- **Digital Twin Metaverse and Physical-Digital Firm Integration**

    The essence of a modern firm, as illuminated through our model, transcends traditional boundaries to embody a dual existence: a tangible physical firm grounded in real-world assets and an ethereal digital firm within the metaverse, each mirroring the other in a seamless continuum. This duality acknowledges the physical assets—property, plant, equipment, and inventory (PPE)—as foundational elements according to the generally accepted accounting principles (GAAP),[4] yet emphasizes a strategic pivot toward a digital platform economy to enhance flexibility and foster innovation. Emblematic of this shift are platforms such as Uber and Airbnb, which minimize physical assets in favor of leveraging partner resources, and tech giants like Google and Meta Platforms, which operate with virtually no physical assets.

---

[4] https://www.accounting.com/resources/gaap/#:~:text=Generally%20accepted%20accounting%20principles%2C%20or,approved%20accounting%20methods%20and%20practices

APPENDIX A   BUILDING DIGITAL TWIN–BASED MODERN MANAGEMENT INFORMATION SYSTEMS (MMIS)

- **Transforming Management Functions into Intelligent Services**

    At the second layer of our architecture, traditional management functions—marketing, operations, logistics, finance, and human resources—are reimagined as intelligent services through the application of data-driven decision-making (DDDM), empowered by DAFW. This transformation is crucial for managing both tangible and intangible assets efficiently, aiming to maximize profitability through innovation and strategic asset management.

- **Data Collection As a Strategic Layer**

    The third layer prioritizes real-time data collection through an extensive network of IoT sensors, actuators, mobile devices, and telecommunication infrastructures, including Wi-Fi, Bluetooth, and 5G. This layer is pivotal in monitoring, analyzing, and optimizing physical assets to ensure optimal return on assets (ROA). It embraces a holistic data strategy that encompasses both internal and external data sources, tailored to the firm's privacy policies and strategic goals.

- **The Heartbeat: Data Analytics Flywheel (DAFW)**

    DAFW stands at the heart of this architecture, analogous to the human heart, incessantly pumping vitality into the digital firm's operations. It encompasses data visualization, machine learning, and a spectrum of analytics applications—ranging from new product design and online platform development to digital marketing and IoT automation. This relentless process cycles through understanding business problems, data preparation, visualization, modeling, evaluation, and deployment of optimal models, thus triggering business intelligence services essential for operational excellence and innovation.

- **Illustrative Example: Tesla Gigafactory**

  A practical embodiment of this architecture is seen in Tesla's Gigafactory, where real-time IoT data collection from physical assets is integrated into the DAFW. This enables a virtual representation of the Gigafactory, accessible through AR/VR headsets, facilitating simulation, optimization, and automation of the manufacturing processes. Such a digital twin metaverse–based MIS architecture not only enhances operational efficiency but also supplants traditional ERP systems, streamlining processes across various management functions.

- **Governance and Strategic Direction**

  At the zenith of our architecture lies the Firm Governance layer, empowering top management to focus on strategic directions, business model innovation, and operational metrics improvement, free from the constraints of daily operations. This layer underscores the architecture's capacity to foster full automation and generate intelligent services, thereby enhancing operational performance and facilitating rapid, data-driven decision-making.

APPENDIX A   BUILDING DIGITAL TWIN–BASED MODERN MANAGEMENT INFORMATION SYSTEMS (MMIS)

In summary, the proposed digital twin metaverse-based MIS architecture is a testament to the synergistic fusion of digital and physical realms, driving full automation, intelligent service generation, and operational excellence. This architecture not only meets but exceeds modern MIS requirements, offering unparalleled flexibility, innovation, and strategic depth, setting a new standard for digital enterprise operations in the 21st century.

More Interesting Examples of Digital Twin Metaverse–Based MIS (MMIS)

To captivate the readers and provide them with a comprehensive understanding of the versatile applications of the proposed digital twin metaverse-based MIS architecture, we delve into a range of fascinating examples. These instances showcase how modern digital enterprises across various sectors can leverage this advanced framework to achieve significant efficiency gains, enhance customer experiences, and pioneer new service models.

1. Amazon Retailing MIS: Pioneering Automation and Personalization

In the realm of retail innovation, a store embracing the digital twin metaverse-based MIS, as illustrated in Figure A-3, can transcend traditional operational limitations to achieve a paradigm of full automation, exemplified by the Amazon Go experience. Upon entering, customers, with preregistered accounts, are seamlessly identified via sophisticated store cameras utilizing advanced face recognition technologies embedded within the Data Analytics Flywheel (DAFW). This process not only ensures security but also marks the beginning of a highly personalized shopping journey.

APPENDIX A BUILDING DIGITAL TWIN–BASED MODERN MANAGEMENT INFORMATION SYSTEMS (MMIS)

The DAFW leverages the customer's historical shopping data to navigate them toward their preferred items, offering a personalized shopping experience that is both efficient and engaging. This personalization extends further as the DAFW employs intelligent recommendation algorithms, such as Naïve Bayes and decision trees, alongside AI-driven insights to suggest complementary items based on the contents of the customer's current shopping cart. These recommendations are not random but are carefully curated to enhance the shopping experience, making it not just personalized but also intuitively responsive to the customer's immediate and evolving preferences.

The pinnacle of this automated retail experience is the checkout process or, rather, the absence of it in the conventional sense. Customers conclude their shopping by simply walking out with their selected items, eliminating the need for physical checkouts. Transactions are processed automatically, with shopping lists and invoices sent directly to the customer's email. This seamless integration extends to the store's accounting systems, where transactions are recorded with no need for manual entry, thereby reducing administrative overhead and potential for human error.

This hypothetical yet entirely feasible example illustrates how retail stores, powered by digital twin metaverse–based MIS, can achieve a level of operational automation and service innovation that was previously unimaginable. Store owners, liberated from day-to-day operational concerns, can remotely oversee store performance—from the office, home, or even the beach—through digital simulations of the physical store. This remote oversight capability allows for strategic focus on expansion, inventory enhancement, and overall shopping experience optimization, all informed by real-time customer data analytics.

While Amazon Go represents a pioneering example, the application of digital twin metaverse–based MIS in retail can extend into various innovative domains:

APPENDIX A   BUILDING DIGITAL TWIN–BASED MODERN MANAGEMENT INFORMATION SYSTEMS (MMIS)

- Virtual Fitting Rooms: Apparel stores could use AR and VR technologies to create virtual fitting rooms, where customers can try on clothes virtually, combining the convenience of online shopping with the confidence of in-store purchases.

- Smart Inventory Management: Using IoT sensors, retailers can achieve real-time inventory tracking and automated replenishment, ensuring optimal stock levels and reducing waste from overstocking or stockouts.

- Enhanced Customer Loyalty Programs: By integrating data analytics with digital twin technology, retailers can design highly personalized loyalty programs, offering rewards and promotions that truly resonate with individual customer preferences and behaviors.

The envisioned Amazon Retailing MIS, grounded in the digital twin metaverse–based MIS architecture, exemplifies the transformative potential of digital innovation in retail. By harnessing the power of automation, personalization, and real-time data analytics, retailers can not only enhance operational efficiency and customer satisfaction but also open new avenues for growth and innovation. This journey toward a fully automated, intelligent service-oriented retail environment underscores the broader themes of digital transformation and the pivotal role of MIS in shaping the future of modern digital enterprises.

APPENDIX A   BUILDING DIGITAL TWIN–BASED MODERN MANAGEMENT INFORMATION SYSTEMS (MMIS)

2. SCM MIS: Revolutionizing Supply Chain with Digital Twins

The proposed digital twin metaverse–based MIS architecture heralds a new era in supply chain management, offering businesses the ability to replicate their real-world assets, processes, and human interactions within a digital environment. This transformative approach facilitates the production of higher-quality products and services, optimizes logistics, lowers costs, and cultivates superior customer experiences. For instance, envision a global T-shirt business leveraging the capabilities of a leading digital twin platform like Microsoft Azure IoT to create a comprehensive digital representation of its supply chain.

Taking Contoso Apparel as an illustrative example, this business can harness the Azure Digital Twins platform[5] to construct a digital mirror of its entire supply chain. Utilizing tools like Digital Twins Explorer, Contoso Apparel[6] can dynamically visualize and analyze each segment of its operations—from the factory floor and inventory management to shipping logistics and retail distribution. This granular insight enables real-time identification and analysis of any quality issues that may arise, be it in the manufacturing process, during transit, or at the point of sale.

The Data Analytics Flywheel (DAFW) plays a pivotal role in this ecosystem, employing models to assess manufacturing quality, monitor shipping conditions (e.g., container moisture levels), and ensure optimal handling at retail outlets. Intelligent services, powered by analytics results from the DAFW, can initiate proactive measures such as pausing assembly lines for maintenance, halting upcoming shipments, or reallocating

---

[5] https://azure.microsoft.com/en-us/services/digital-twins/
[6] https://youtu.be/ScmK-bKJ4MI

APPENDIX A   BUILDING DIGITAL TWIN–BASED MODERN MANAGEMENT INFORMATION SYSTEMS (MMIS)

production to alternate facilities. These actions are not merely reactive but strategically designed to minimize business disruption, safeguard continuity, and enhance overall supply chain resilience.

While the Contoso Apparel example highlights the capabilities of digital twin technology in the apparel industry, the application of digital twin metaverse-based MIS architecture extends far beyond, offering transformative potential across a myriad of sectors:

- Pharmaceuticals: In the highly regulated pharmaceutical industry, digital twins can simulate manufacturing processes to ensure compliance with quality standards, optimize production, and manage the distribution of sensitive products under controlled conditions.

- Agriculture: Digital twins of agricultural ecosystems can optimize resource usage (water, fertilizers, etc.), predict crop yields, and enhance sustainable farming practices by monitoring and simulating environmental and soil conditions.

- Automotive: For automotive manufacturers, digital twins enable the simulation of production lines, supply chain logistics, and even the performance of vehicles in various conditions, leading to improved manufacturing efficiency and product quality.

- Energy Sector: In energy production and distribution, digital twins can optimize grid operations, forecast energy demand, and enhance the maintenance and operation of renewable energy sources, thereby ensuring reliability and efficiency.

APPENDIX A   BUILDING DIGITAL TWIN–BASED MODERN MANAGEMENT INFORMATION SYSTEMS (MMIS)

The integration of digital twin metaverse-based MIS architecture into supply chain management represents a leap toward operational excellence and strategic agility. By enabling a holistic and dynamic representation of supply chains, businesses can achieve unprecedented levels of transparency, efficiency, and resilience. This approach not only improves product quality and logistics but also drives innovation, ensuring businesses are well equipped to meet the demands of the modern digital economy.

3. Robotaxi Services: Navigating the Future of Urban Mobility

AI-driven autonomous driving technology, represented by pioneering firms like GM's Cruise and Google's Waymo, marks a paradigm shift in urban transportation, offering a glimpse into a future where commuting is not just about getting from point A to point B, but an experience tailored to individual preferences and needs.[7] The commercialization of robotaxi services in urban centers like San Francisco,[8] facilitated by regulatory approvals, signifies the dawn of a new era in public transportation, one that promises enhanced efficiency, safety, and environmental sustainability.

- **Integrating Digital Twin Metaverse–Based MIS Architecture**

    The application of our proposed digital twin metaverse–based MIS architecture, as depicted in Figure A-3, offers robotaxi firms a robust framework

---

[7] https://www.therobotreport.com/cruise-opens-driverless-robotaxi-service-sf-public/
[8] https://techcrunch.com/2022/02/28/waymo-to-begin-charging-for-robotaxi-rides-in-san-francisco/

APPENDIX A BUILDING DIGITAL TWIN–BASED MODERN MANAGEMENT INFORMATION SYSTEMS (MMIS)

to innovate and deliver intelligent services. The architecture's heart, the Data Analytics Flywheel (DAFW), plays a critical role in harnessing commuter data to not only optimize operational logistics but also to refine customer engagement strategies. Machine learning models, such as logistic regression and support vector machines, combined with AI, analyze data from various sources, including competitor insights and customer feedback, to identify trends and preferences in real time.

- **Personalization at the Core of Robotaxi Services**

    The true potential of robotaxi services lies in their ability to offer highly personalized experiences. By analyzing rider preferences—ranging from vehicle class selection to desired interior ambiances—robotaxi firms can assign vehicles that best match individual customer profiles, ensuring each journey is not just a ride, but a tailored experience. This focus on customization extends beyond the physical attributes of the ride to include dynamic route optimization, real-time adjustments to travel schedules, and even personalized entertainment options during the commute.

- **Beyond Transportation: Envisioning a New Lifestyle**

    The widespread adoption of robotaxi services could significantly alter the urban lifestyle, reducing the reliance on personal vehicle ownership. With vehicles being idle 95% of the time, the shift toward robotaxi services not only promises a more efficient use of resources but also contributes to a reduction in urban congestion and environmental impact. This transition supports a broader vision of smart, sustainable cities, where digital twin technologies enable a seamless, interconnected urban ecosystem.

- **Expanding the Horizon with Innovative Examples**
  - Dynamic Urban Planning: Digital twins can simulate traffic patterns and demand scenarios, helping cities optimize road use and public transportation networks in harmony with robotaxi services.
  - Integrated Mobility Solutions: Robotaxis can become part of a larger, multimodal transportation system, connecting with public transit, bike-sharing, and pedestrian pathways for comprehensive urban mobility.
  - Enhanced Safety Features: Leveraging real-time data, robotaxis can incorporate advanced safety protocols, adjusting to weather conditions, traffic anomalies, and emergency situations, ensuring passenger safety at all times.

Robotaxi services, empowered by digital twin metaverse–based MIS architecture, stand at the forefront of transforming urban mobility. By focusing on personalization, efficiency, and integration with broader urban ecosystems, robotaxi firms can not only enhance customer satisfaction but also contribute to the development of smart, sustainable cities. This innovative approach to transportation underscores the profound impact of digital transformation on modern enterprises, paving the way for a future where technology and human-centric design converge to create enriching, life-enhancing experiences.

APPENDIX A   BUILDING DIGITAL TWIN–BASED MODERN MANAGEMENT INFORMATION SYSTEMS (MMIS)

4. Airport MIS: Elevating Airport Operations and Security with Digital Twins

Implementing the digital twin metaverse-based MIS architecture, as outlined in Figure A-3, provides a transformative pathway for airports to achieve unprecedented levels of operational efficiency, safety, and passenger satisfaction. Through the utilization of advanced Unreal Engine (U5) tools, airports can construct a comprehensive digital twin, enabling managers to monitor every aspect of the airport environment and aircraft operations with unparalleled precision.[9]

- **Seamless Monitoring and Enhanced Security**

    The digital replication of airport facilities through a metaverse-based MIS architecture offers continuous, real-time visibility into all airport operations. Managers can access this digital environment via various devices, including TVs, computers, mobile phones, or AR/VR headsets, ensuring they can oversee and respond to operational nuances 24/7. This capability is crucial for enhancing airport safety and security, allowing for the immediate identification and resolution of potential issues or threats within the airport premises or related to aircraft.

- **Optimization of Flight Scheduling and Operational Logistics**

    At the heart of this digital transformation is the Data Analytics Flywheel (DAFW), equipped with sophisticated simulation and optimization models.

---

[9] https://youtu.be/sKnsd-ssOgcring

APPENDIX A BUILDING DIGITAL TWIN–BASED MODERN MANAGEMENT INFORMATION SYSTEMS (MMIS)

These tools enable dynamic adjustments to flight schedules and operational routing, optimizing resource allocation, minimizing delays, and improving overall airport efficiency. By leveraging real-time data, airports can streamline operations, reduce congestion, and ensure a smoother passenger experience.

- **Advancements in Aircraft Maintenance and Safety**

   Further enriching the potential of this architecture, DAFW employs predictive maintenance and fault detection models to enhance aircraft performance and reliability. These models analyze vast amounts of data from aircraft sensors to predict and prevent potential maintenance issues before they impact flight operations. This proactive approach to maintenance not only improves aircraft safety but also significantly enhances traveler satisfaction by ensuring flights are safe, reliable, and on schedule.

- **Beyond Operational Efficiency: Enriching Passenger Experience**

   The digital twin metaverse–based MIS architecture paves the way for a range of intelligent services that extend beyond operational excellence, focusing on elevating the passenger experience:

   - Personalized Journey Planning: Passengers can use apps connected to the airport's digital twin to receive personalized journey plans, including real-time updates on flight status, security wait times, and gate changes.

- Virtual Navigation Assistance: AR/VR technologies integrated with the digital twin can offer passengers virtual navigation assistance, providing a stress-free way to find gates, lounges, and amenities within the airport.

- Smart Baggage Handling: Advanced tracking and management systems, informed by the digital twin, ensure that baggage handling is more efficient and less prone to errors, providing passengers with peace of mind.

By embracing a digital twin metaverse-based MIS architecture, airports can not only achieve full automation and enhanced operational efficiency but also offer rich, intelligent services that significantly improve safety, security, and the passenger experience. This innovative approach to airport management marks a significant leap toward the future of air travel, where digital and physical realms converge to create safer, more efficient, and passenger-centric airports.

Summary

In this exploration of the digital twin metaverse cities and the pioneering digital twin metaverse-based MIS architecture, we journeyed through a revolutionary proposal designed for the modern digital enterprise. This architecture integrates the physical and digital realms across six layers—physical assets, management functions, data collection, data platforms, intelligent services powered by the Data Analytics Flywheel (DAFW), and firm governance. Central to this architecture, the DAFW is instrumental in achieving full automation and generating rich, intelligent services that cater to the evolving needs of customers, enabling top management to focus on strategic initiatives such as business model innovation and navigating the complexities of the digital age.

APPENDIX A BUILDING DIGITAL TWIN–BASED MODERN MANAGEMENT INFORMATION SYSTEMS (MMIS)

The transformative potential of this architecture was vividly demonstrated through examples like Tesla's Gigafactory, Amazon Go, SCM, robotaxi services, and airports. These enterprises epitomize the seamless integration of automation and intelligent service generation, establishing a blueprint for digital transformation within the modern economy. The narrative underscores the critical role of innovative architectural frameworks in bridging the digital and physical worlds, thereby facilitating operational excellence, sustainability, and a competitive advantage in the rapidly evolving digital landscape.

As this book concludes with the discussion on state-of-the-art tools and prototypes, it aims to empower readers to lead their digital twin initiatives, catalyzing the next phase of urban and enterprise digital transformation. This concluding call to action emphasizes the urgency of innovative solutions for harnessing emerging ICT technologies, highlighting the book's vision for a smarter, more interconnected world. The digital twin metaverse–based MMIS architecture provides a comprehensive roadmap for future enterprises to thrive amid digital advancements, ensuring resilience and growth in an era marked by unprecedented technological evolution.

Bibliography

[1] World Population Review (2021). Vancouver Population 2021. https://worldpopulationreview.com/world-cities/vancouver-population

[2] Mohanty, S. P., Choppali, U., & Kougianos, E. (2016), "Everything you wanted to know about smart cities: the Internet of things is the backbone," IEEE Consumer Electronics Magazine, 5 (3), 60–70. doi: 10.1109/MCE.2016.2556879.

[3] Barlow M & Levy-Bencheton C. (2018), "Smart cities, smart future: showcasing tomorrow," John Wiley & Sons.

[4] Gassmann O Böhm Jonas & Palmié M (2019), "Smart Cities: Introducing Digital Innovation to Cities," Emerald Publishing Limited.

[5] Marr B (2020), Tech Trends in Practice: The 25 Technologies That Are Driving The 4th Industrial Revolution (1st ed.). United Kingdom: John Wiley and Sons Ltd.

[6] Brown S (2020), The Innovation Ultimatum: How six strategic technologies will reshape every business in the 2020s, Wiley; 1 ed.

BIBLIOGRAPHY

[7] Lal R & Houghtalin A (2018) "Smart City Strategy: Amsterdam, Barcelona, and Atlanta," Harvard Business School Publishing. https://store.hbr.org/product/smart-city-strategy-amsterdam-barcelona-and-atlanta/518092?sku=518092-PDF-ENG

[8] Benedikt O (2016) "The valuable citizens of smart cities: The case of Songdo city," Graduate Journal of Social Science, 12 (2), 17–36.

[9] Baltzan P & Phillips A, (2018), Business Driven Information Systems, McGraw-Hill Education; 6th edition, ISBN: 0073376892, 978-1259111082.

[10] Li XM, De M, Hipel KW (1994) "A DSS architecture for multiple participant decision making," In Systems, Man, and Cybernetics: Humans, Information and Technology, 1994, IEEE International Conference 2 (5) 1208–1214.

[11] Stephenson, N. (1992). Snowcrash, London: ROC.

[12] Mystakidis, S. (2022). Metaverse. *Encyclopedia*, *2*(1), 486–497.

[13] Wang, Y., Su, Z., Zhang, N., Xing, R., Liu, D., Luan, T. H., & Shen, X. (2022). A survey on metaverse: Fundamentals, security, and privacy. *IEEE Communications Surveys & Tutorials*.

[14] Grieves M and Vickers J (2016), "Digital Twin: Mitigating Unpredictable, Undesirable Emergent Behavior in Complex Systems," in: Transdiscipl. Perspect. Complex Syst, 85–113, doi:10.1007/978.

[15] Glaessgen E and Stargel D (2012), "The digital twin paradigm for future NASA and U.S. Air Force vehicles," in Proc. 53rd AIAA/ASME/ASCE/AHS/ASC Struct. Struct. Dyn. Mater. Conf., 2012.

[16] Apte P and Spanos C (2021), "The Digital Twin Opportunity," MIT Sloan Management Review, 63 (1), 15–17.

[17] Tao F, Zhang H, Liu A, and Nee AY (2019), "Digital Twin in Industry: State-of-the-art," IEEE Transactions on Industrial Informatics, 15 (4), 2405.

[18] Peters B (2017) "IBI Group's top 10 smart city strategy success factors." Toronto, Canada: IBI Group.

[19] Dameri RP (2015) "Searching for Smart City definition: a comprehensive proposal." International Journal of Computers & Technology, 11 (5).

[20] Mahizhnan A (1999) "Smart cities. The Singapore case," Cities, 16 (1), 13–18.

[21] Giffinger R, Fertner C, Kramar H, Kalasek R, PichlerMilanoviü N & Meijers E. (2007), "Smart Cities: Ranking of European Medium-Sized Cities," Vienna, Austria: Centre of Regional Science (SRF), Vienna University of Technology.

[22] Purnomo F and Prabowo H (2016) "Smart city indicators: A systematic literature review." Journal of Telecommunication, Electronic and Computer Engineering (JTEC), 8 (3), 161–164.

BIBLIOGRAPHY

[23] Lu Q, Xie X, Heaton J, Parlikad AK & Schooling J. (2020) "From BIM towards digital twin: Strategy and future development for smart asset management," Studies in Computational Intelligence, 853, 392–404.

[24] Wirth R and Hipp J, "CRISP-DM: Towards a standard process model for data mining," In Proceedings of the 4th International Conference on the Practical Applications of Knowledge Discovery and Data Mining, 2000, 29–39.

[25] Todorovic D (2011) "What is the origin of the Gestalt principles?", Humana Mente Journal of Philosophical Studies, 17, 1–20.

[26] Provost F and Fawcett T, Data Science for Business, by, New York University, O'Reilly, 2013, ISBN 1449361323, 9781449361327.

[27] Domingos P, 2015, The Master Algorithm: How the quest for the ultimate learning machine will remake our word, ISBN-10:0465094279, Basic Books.

[28] Dahlman E, Mildh G, Parkvall S, Peisa J, Sachs J, Seln Y, and Skld J (2014) "5G wireless access: Requirements and realization," IEEE Communications Magazine, 52 (12), 42–47.

[29] Lescop D, Pujol F, and Henten A. (2016) "Mobile Dynamics: The Path to 5G: Introduction," DigiWorld Economic Journal, 102, 9–12.

[30] Hammoudeh MA (2020) "Policy Model for Sharing Network Slices in 5G Core Network," Journal of Information Technology Management, 12 (2), 79–89.

[31] Gupta A and Jha RK (2015) "A survey of 5G network: Architecture and emerging technologies," IEEE Access, 3, 1206–1232.

[32] Xia X, Yuan X, Liang Y, and Zhang (2020). "Research on 5G network slicing enabling the smart grid," Dianzi Jishu Yingyong, 46 (1), 17–21.

[33] Miao Y, Jiang Y, Peng L, Hossain MS, and Muhammad G (2018) "Telesurgery Robot Based on 5G Tactile Internet." Mobile Networks & Applications 23 (6), 1645-54. doi:10.1007/s11036-018-1110-3.

[34] Guevara L & Cheein AF (2020) "The Role of 5G Technologies: Challenges in Smart Cities and Intelligent Transportation Systems," Sustainability 12 (16), 6469.

[35] Gkonis P., Trakadas PT, and Kaklamani, DI (2020) "A Comprehensive Study on Simulation Techniques for 5G Networks: State of the Art Results, Analysis, and Future Challenges," Electronics, 9 (3), 46.

[36] Zanella A, Bui N, Castellani A, Vangelista L, and Zorzi M (2014) "Internet of Things for smart cities," IEEE Internet Things Journal, 1 (1), 22–32.

[37] Restuccia D, D'Oro S, and Melodia T (2018), "Securing the Internet of Things in the age of machine learning and software-defined networking," IEEE Internet Things J., 5 (6), 4829–4842.

BIBLIOGRAPHY

[38] Farooq U, Hasan NU, Baig I, and Shehzad N (2019) "Efficient adaptive framework for securing the Internet of things devices," EURASIP J Wireline Communication Network,1, 210.

[39] Demchenko Y, Membrey P, Grosso P, Laat C (2013), "Addressing Big Data Issues in Scientific Data Infrastructure," First International Symposium on Big Data and Data Analytics in Collaboration (BDDAC 2013), San Diego, California, USA.

[40] Nguyen G, Dlugolinsky S, Bobák M, Tran V, López, Malík P, HluchL (2019), "Machine Learning and Deep Learning Frameworks and Libraries for Large-Scale Data Mining: A Survey." Artificial Intelligence, 52, 77–124.

[41] Houssami N, Kirkpatrick-Jones G, Noguchi N, Lee CI (2019) "Artificial Intelligence (AI) for the early detection of breast cancer: a scoping review to assess AI's potential in breast screening practice." Expert Review Medical Devices 16, 351–362.

[42] Kratzke N (2018) "A brief history of cloud application architectures," Applied Sciences, 8 (8).

[43] Miyachi C (2018) "What is "Cloud"? It is time to update the NIST definition?", IEEE Annals of the History of Computing, 5 (3), 6–11.

[44] Rashid A and Chaturvedi A (2019) "Cloud computing characteristics and services a brief review," International Journal Computer Science Engineering, 7 (2), 421–426.

[45] Mell P and Grance T (2011) "The NIST definition of cloud computing," National Institute of Standards and Technology, Special Publication, 53 (6), 50.

[46] El-Haddadeh R (2019) "Digital innovation dynamics influence on organizational adoption: the case of cloud computing services," Information Systems Frontier, DOI. 10.1007/ s10796-019-09912-2.

[47] Mahmud R, Kotagiri R, and Buyya R (2018) "Fog computing: A taxonomy, survey and future directions," In Internet of Everything. Singapore: Springer, 2018, pp. 103–130.

[48] Nakamoto S (2008) "Bitcoin: A peer-to-peer electronic cash system," Bitcoin, 2008.

[49] Crosby B, Nachiappan MC, Pattanayak N, Verma P, & Kalyanaraman V (2016) "Blockchain Technology: Beyond Bitcoin," Applied Innovation 2, 6–9.

[50] Turi, A. N. (2020) "Technologies for Modern Digital Entrepreneurship," Apress Springer, 2020, `https://doi.org/10.1007/978-1-4842-6005-0`

[51] Saberi S, Kouhizadeh M, Sarkis J (2018) "Blockchain technology: A panacea or pariah for resources conservation and recycling?", Resour. Conserv. Recycl. 130, 80–81.

[52] Rochet J and Tirole (2003) "Platform competition in two-sided markets," Journal of the European Economic Association, 1 (4), 990–1029.

[53] Metcalfe B (2013). "Metcalfe's law after 40 years of Ethernet," IEEE Computer, 46, 26–31.

BIBLIOGRAPHY

[54] Varian, HR, Microeconomic Analysis, New York, NY: Norton, 1984.

[55] Li S (2021), "Short or Long Review? Text Analytics and Machine Learning Approaches to Online Reputation," International Journal of Business and Management Research (IJBMR), 9 (1), 28–40, e-ISSN: 2347-4696.

[56] Li XMS (2021), "Online Platform Market Reputation Systems," Scholars' Press, Book SBN-10: 6138954548, ISBN-13: 978-6138954545.

[57] Raj M & Seamans R. (2019) "Primer on artificial intelligence and robotics," Journal *of Organization Design,* 8 (1). https://doi.org/10.1186/s41469-019-0050-0

[58] Angelo JA (2003) "Robotics: a reference guide to the new technology." IEEE Communications Magazine. 41(12), 60–67. Dec. 2003 ISSN: 0163-6804. INSPEC Accession Number: 7950580.

[59] Birk A (2011) "What is robotics? An interdisciplinary field is getting even more diverse." IEEE Robotics and Automation Magazine, December 8, 2011.

[60] Niemeyer G, Preusche C, and Hirzinger g, "Telerobotics," in Springer Handbook of Robotics. New York, NY, USA: Springer-Verlag, 2008, ch. 31.

[61] Liu Y & Xu Y (2019), "Summary of cloud robot research." In Proceedings of the 2019 25th International Conference on Automation and Computing (ICAC), Lancaster, UK, September 5–7, 2019; IEEE: New York, NY, USA, 2019; pp. 1–5.

[62] Marr B (2019) "The Important Difference Between Virtual Reality, Augmented Reality and Mixed Reality." Forbes Magazine, 19, July 2019.

[63] Farshid M, Paschen J, Eriksson T & Kietzmann J (2018) "Go boldly!: Explore augmented reality (AR), virtual reality (VR), and mixed reality (MR) for business," *Business Horizons, 61* (5), 657–663.

[64] Steinicke F (2016) "Being Really Virtual: Immersive Natives and the Future of Virtual Reality," Springer, Switzerland.

[65] Dipietro L, Sabatini AM, and Dario P (2008), "A survey of glove-based systems and their applications," IEEE Trans. Syst., Man Cybern.-Part C, 38 (4) 461–482.

[66] Silvestri B (2020) "The Future of Fashion: How the Quest for Digitization and the Use of Artificial Intelligence and Extended Reality Will Reshape the Fashion Industry After Covid-19," ZoneModa Journal, 10 (2), 61–73.

[67] Gopinathan J and Noh (2018), "Recent trends in bioinks for 3D printing. Biomater, 22, 11. https://doi.org/10.1186/s40824-018-0122-1

[68] Shahrubudin N, Lee TC & Ramlan, R (2019) "An overview on 3D printing technology: technological, materials, and applications," Procedia Manufacturing, 35, 1286–1296.

[69] Attaran M (2017) "The rise of 3-D printing: The advantages of additive manufacturing over traditional manufacturing." Business Horizons, 60(5), 677-688.

[70] Pereira GR, Gasi F & Lourenço SR (2019) "Review, Analysis, and Classification of 3D Printing Literature: Types of Research and Technology Benefits," International Journal of Advanced Engineering Research and Science, 6 (6), 167-187.

[71] Shahrubudin N, Leea TC, Ramlan R (2019) "An overview on 3D printing technology: Technological, materials, and applications," Procedia Manufacturing,35, 1286-1296.

[72] Fang EH & Kumar S (2018) "The Trends and Challenges of 3D Printing." Encyclopedia of Information Science and Technology, Fourth Edition, 4382-4389.

[73] Redwood B, Schffer F & Garret B (2017) "The 3D printing handbook: technologies, design and applications," 3D Hubs.

[74] Frauenfelder M (2014) "Make: Ultimate Guide to 3D Printing," Maker Media, Inc.

[75] Matthews MJ, Guss G, Khairallah SA, Rubenchik AM, Depond PJ & King WE (2016) "Denudation of metal powder layers in laser powder bed fusion processes." Acta Materialia, 114, 33-42.

[76] Yang H, Lim JC, Liu Y, Qi X, Yap YL, Dikshit V, Yeong WY & Wei J (2017) "Performance evaluation of projet multi-material jetting 3D printer," Virtual and Physical Prototyping, 12 (1), 95-103.

[77] Kumar KP & Pumera M (2021) "3D-Printing to Mitigate Covid-19-19 Pandemic," Advanced Functional Materials, 31(22), 2100450.

[78] Palevicius V, Uspalyte-Vitkuniene R, Damidavicius J, Karpavicius T (2020), "Concepts of development of alternative travel in autonomous cars," Sustainability 12, 8841.

[79] Thierer AD & Hagemann R (2014) "Removing Roadblocks to Intelligent Vehicles and Driverless Cars," Wake Forest Journal of Law and Policy, 5, 339.

[80] Levinson J, Askeland J, Becker J, Dolson J, Held D, Kammel S, Kolter J, Langer D, Pink O, Pratt V, Sokolsky M, Stanek G, Stavens D, Teichman A, Werling M, and Thrun S (2011) "Towards fully autonomous driving: Systems and Algorithms," in Proc. IEEE IV, Jun. 2011, pp. 163–168.

[81] Zeiler MD & Fergus R (2014), "Visualizing and understanding convolutional neural networks," In ECCV, 2014.

[82] Caesar H, Bankiti V, Lang AH, Sora VE, Liong Q, Xu A, Krishnan Y. Pan G, Baldan, and O. Beijbom (2019) "nuScenes: A multimodal dataset for autonomous driving," in Proc. IEEE Conf. Comput. Vis. Pattern Recognit., 2020, 11621–11631.

[83] Beiker S (2021) "Legal Aspects of Autonomous Driving," 52 Santa CLARA L. REV. 1145, available: https://heinonline.org/HOL/Page?collection=journals&handle=hein.journals/saclr52&id=1200&men_tab=srchresults

[84] Maurer M, Gerdes JC, Lenz B & Winner H (2016) "Autonomous driving: technical, legal and social aspects." Berlin, Heidelberg: Springer Open.

[85] Tang Y, Dananjayan S, Hou C, Guo Q, Luo S, He Y (2020) "A survey on the 5G network and its impact on agriculture: challenges and opportunities," Comput. Electron. Agric. 180105895. 10.1016/j.compag.2020.105895.

[86] Prathibha SR, Hongal A, Jyothi MP (2017) "IoT based monitoring system in smart agriculture" (2017) International Conference on Recent Advances in Electronics and Communication Technology, 81-84.

[87] Pozniak H (2019) "Are wildfires getting worse." Engineering & Technology 14 (1), 68-72.

[88] Gondchawar N & Kawitkar RS (2016) "IoT based smart agriculture." *International Journal of advanced research in Computer and Communication Engineering*, 5 (6), 838-842.

[89] Ding G, Wu Q, Zhang L, Lin Y, Tsiftsis TA & Yao YD (2018) "An amateur drone surveillance system based on the cognitive Internet of Things." *IEEE Communications Magazine*, 56 (1), 29-35.

[90] Craigen D, Diakun-Thibault N, & Purse R (2014) "Defining cybersecurity." *Technology Innovation Management Review*, 4 (10).

[91] Jang-Jaccard J & Nepal S (2014). "A survey of emerging threats in cybersecurity." Journal of Computer and System Sciences, 80 (5), 973-993.

[92] Laudon KC & Traver CG (2021) "E-commerce - Business, Technology, and Society," Boston, MA: Pearson (16th ed).

[93] Peltier TR (2016) "Information Security Policies, Procedures, and Standards: guidelines for effective information security management," CRC Press.

[94] Grigorescu S, Trasnea B, Cocias T, & Macesanu G (2020) "A survey of deep learning techniques for autonomous driving," *Journal of Field Robotics*, 37(3), 362–386.

[95] Agarwal A (2011) "The security risks associated with cloud computing." *International Journal of Computer Applications in Engineering Sciences*, 1, 257–259.

[96] Boeckl K, Fagan M, Fisher W, Lefkovitz N, Megas KN, & Scarfone K (2019) "Considerations for managing Internet of Things (IoT) cybersecurity and privacy risks." Gaithersburg: US Department of Commerce, National Institute of Standards and Technology.

[97] Shafiq M, Tian Z, Sun Y, Du X & Guizani M (2020) "Selection of effective machine learning algorithm and Bot-IoT attacks traffic identification for internet of things in smart city." *Future Generation Computer Systems*, 107, 433–442.

[98] Mahmood A, Zhang WE & Sheng QZ (2019) "Software-defined heterogeneous vehicular networking: The architectural design and open challenges." Future Internet, 11 (3), 70.

[99] Liu CC, McArthur S & Lee SJ (2016) "Smart grid handbook," 3 volume set (Vol. 1). John Wiley & Sons.

[100] Jiang L, Liu DY & Yang B (2004) "Smart home research." In *Proceedings of 2004 international conference on machine learning and cybernetics*, 2, 659–663. IEEE.

[101] Ejaz W, Naeem M, Shahid A, Anpalagan A, & Jo M (2017) "Efficient energy management for the internet of things in smart cities." *IEEE Communications magazine*, 55 (1), 84–91.

[102] Quigley JM, Raphael S & Smolensky E (2001) "Homeless in America, homeless in California." *Review of Economics and Statistics*, 83 (1), 37–51.

[103] Yoshiura N, Fujii Y & Ohta N (2013), "Smart street light system looking like usual street lights based on sensor networks." In *13th International Symposium on Communications and Information Technologies (ISCIT)*, 633–637. IEEE.

[104] El-Faouri, FS, Sharaiha M, Bargouth D & Faza A (2016) "A smart street lighting system using solar energy." In *2016 IEEE PES Innovative Smart Grid Technologies Conference Europe (ISGT-Europe)* 1–6. IEEE.

[105] Schmaltz E, Melvin EC, Diana Z, Gunady EF, Rittschof D, Somarelli JA,& Dunphy-Daly MM (2020). "Plastic pollution solutions: emerging technologies to prevent and collect marine plastic pollution." *Environment international*, 144, 106067.

[106] Kim H, Mokdad L & Ben-Othman J (2018) "Designing UAV surveillance frameworks for smart city and extensive ocean with differential perspectives." *IEEE Communications Magazine, 56*(4), 98–104.

[107] Akib A, Tasnim F, Biswas D, Hashem MB, Rahman K, Bhattacharjee A & Fattah SA (2019) "Unmanned floating waste collecting robot." In *TENCON 2019-2019 IEEE Region 10 Conference (TENCON)* (pp. 2645–2650). IEEE.

[108] Baker SB, Xiang W & Atkinson I (2017) "Internet of things for smart healthcare: Technologies, challenges, and opportunities." *IEEE Access, 5,* 26521–26544.

[109] Lum MJ & Friedman D, Sankaranarayanan G, King H, Fodero K, Leuschke R,& Sinanan, MN (2009), "The RAVEN: Design and validation of a telesurgery system." *The International Journal of Robotics Research, 28* (9), 1183–1197.

[110] Charlon Y, Bourennane W, Bettahar F & Campo E (2013) "Activity monitoring system for elderly in a context of smart home." *IRBM, 34* (1), 60–63.

[111] Bellarhmouch Y, Jeghal A, Tairi H, & Benjelloun N (2022) "A proposed architectural learner model for a personalized learning environment." *Education and Information Technologies,* 1–21.

[112] Tikhomirov V, Dneprovskaya N & Yankovskaya E (2015), "Three dimensions of smart education." In *Smart Education and Smart e-Learning,* 47–56, Springer, Cham.

BIBLIOGRAPHY

[113] Li C, Guo J, Zhang G, Wang Y, Sun Y & Bie R (2019) "A blockchain system for E-learning assessment and certification." In *2019 IEEE International Conference on Smart Internet of Things (SmartIoT)*, 212–219. IEEE.

[114] Polacco A & Backes K (2018) "The amazon go concept: Implications, applications, and sustainability." Journal of Business and Management, 24(1), 79-92.

[115] Wankhede K, Wukkadada B & Nadar V (2018) "Just walk-out technology and its challenges: A case of Amazon Go," In *2018 International Conference on Inventive Research in Computing Applications (ICIRCA)* (pp. 254–257). IEEE.

[116] Hong I, Park S, Lee B, Lee J, Jeong D & Park S (2014) "IoT-based smart garbage system for efficient food waste management." *The Scientific World Journal, 2014.*

[117] Keerthana B, Raghavendran SM, Kalyani S., Suja P & Kalaiselvi VKG (2017) "Internet of bins: Trash management in India." In *2017 2nd international conference on computing and communications technologies (ICCCT)* (pp. 248–251). IEEE.

[118] Boukerche A & Coutinho RW (2018) "Smart disaster detection and response system for smart cities." In 2018 IEEE Symposium on Computers and Communications (ISC3) (pp. 01102–01107). IEEE.

[119] Adl S, Iron D & Kolokolnikov, T (2011) "A threshold area ratio of organic to conventional agriculture causes recurrent pathogen outbreaks in organic agriculture." *Science of the Total Environment, 409*(11), 2192-2197.

[120] Grogan A (2012) "Smart farming." *Engineering & Technology, 7* (6), 38-40.

[121] Frank AG, Mendes GH, Ayala NF & Ghezzi, A (2019). "Servitization and Industry 4.0 convergence in the digital transformation of product firms: A business model innovation perspective." Technological Forecasting and Social Change, 141, 341-351.

[122] Laudon K & Laudon JP, "Essentials of Management Information Systems," 2nd ed., Prentice Hall, 1997.

[123] Reynolds G (2015). Information technology for managers. Cengage Learning.

[124] Hussain, S. T., Lei, S., Akram, T., Haider, M. J., Hussain, S. H., & Ali, M. (2018). Kurt Lewin's change model: A critical review of the role of leadership and employee involvement in organizational change. *Journal of Innovation & Knowledge, 3*(3), 123-127. https://doi.org/10.1016/j.jik.2016.07.002

[125] MSG. (2018). *Kurt Lewin's change management model: The planned approach to organizational change.* Management Study Guide - Courses for Students, Professionals & Faculty Members. https://www.managementstudyguide.com/kurt-lewins-change-management-model.htm

BIBLIOGRAPHY

[126] 9m Consulting (September 18, 2019). *Lewin's change model | 9m consulting Lewin's change model.* https://9mconsulting.com/newsletter/lewins-change-model/

[127] Umar (2020). *What is nudge theory?* CMI. https://changemanagementinsight.com/nudge-theory-in-change-management/

[128] 9m Consulting (September 21, 2019). *Nudge theory changes the model.*

[129] Richard, W (2003), *Operations management,* http://196.188.170.250:8080/jspui/bitstream/123456789/2612/1/POM NOTES.pdf.

[130] Hughes, R. L., Ginnett, R. C., & Curphy, G. J. (2021). The international framework for analyzing Leadership. In *Leadership: enhancing the lessons of experience,* McGraw Hill Education.

[131] McCrae, R. R., & Costa, P. T. (1987). Validation of the five-factor model of personality across instruments and observers. *Journal of personality and social psychology, 52*(1), 81.

[132] Maslow, A. H. (1943). A theory of human motivation. *Psychological review, 50*(4), 370.

[133] Allen, M et al. (2014) "A framework for project success," *Journal of Information Technology and Economic Development, 5* (2), 1-17.

[134] Simmons LF (2002) "Project management-critical path method (CPM) and PERT simulated with Process Model." In *Proceedings of the Winter Simulation Conference* (Vol. 2, pp. 1786-1788). IEEE.

[135] Hidalgo, E. S. (2019) "Adapting the scrum framework for agile project management in science: case study of a distributed research initiative," *Heliyon*, 5 (3), e01447.

[136] Schwaber & Sutherland (2013), "The scrum guide. The definitive guide to scrum: the rules of the game." `http://www.scrumguides.org/docs/scrumguide/v1/scrum-guide-us.pdf`

[137] Mansfield E (1972). *Research and innovation in the modern corporation*. Springer.

[138] Bassil Y (2012). "A simulation model for the waterfall software development life cycle." *arXiv preprint arXiv:1205.6904*.

Index

A

Adaptability, 85, 141, 236, 414, 416, 419, 423, 425–428, 431, 433, 434, 438
Adaptability in smart city leadership, 428
A Digital twin metaverse-based modern MIS architecture, 448–455
Aeroponics, 167
Agile project management (APM) with Scrum process, 415–417
A home monitoring systems for smart senior caring, 139, 140
AI-powered virtual assistants, 171, 313, 339–344
Airport MIS
  Elevating airport operations and security with digital twins, 461–463
Amazon AWS IoT, 32
Amazon AWS IoT TwinMaker, 174–176, 208, 438
Amazon Go, 148–152, 442, 443, 445, 446, 453, 454, 464

Amazon Go Store, 149, 150, 152
Amazon Retailing MIS pioneering automation and personalization, 453–455
Amazon Sumerian, 221, 222, 224, 260
A Metaverse city prototype using Unreal Engine (UE), 400–410
Amsterdam, 9, 12, 22
Anatomy of a smart streetlight system, 124
An exponential growth of IoT devices from 2015 to 2025, 58
An organizational cybersecurity capacity, 104
Ansys, 31, 171, 194
Ansys Twin Builder, 194–196, 208
Aquaponics, 167
AR and VR continuum, 88, 89
Artificial intelligence (AI), 9, 11, 17, 43, 53, 83, 112, 132, 178, 211, 263, 313, 352, 426
Artificial neural networks (ANN), 43
Atlanta, 12, 22

INDEX

Augmented reality (AR), 82, 83, 88–92, 107, 143, 144, 147, 153, 160, 161, 171, 213, 215, 221–224, 229, 244, 257–260, 274, 275, 277, 280, 281, 287, 288, 290, 294, 295, 313, 321–326, 360, 361, 365–367, 374, 378, 455
Augmented reality training modules, 171, 313, 321–326
Augmented/virtual reality (AR/VR), 9–11, 13, 18, 45, 52, 90, 92, 257, 260, 438, 452, 461
Autodesk Maya, 233–236, 260
Autodesk Tandem, 205–209
Automation and intelligent services, 442, 446, 447, 449, 452, 453, 463, 464
Autonomous driving (AD), 54, 67, 69, 82, 83, 96–100, 112, 198, 219, 458
AWS IoT, 32, 171
AWS IoT TwinMaker, 174–176, 208, 438
Azure Digital Twin, 32, 171, 177–179, 208, 438, 456

B

Barcelona, 12, 22
Bibliography, 465–489
Big data analytics, 51, 62–65, 82, 112, 123, 150, 154, 163, 168, 443

Blender, 32, 171, 230–233, 260, 267, 304–306, 309, 312, 359, 363, 377, 438
Blockchain, 9, 18, 31, 51, 73–76, 82, 119, 134, 138, 144, 146, 160, 161, 168, 197, 254, 256, 257, 260, 327, 328, 330, 332, 438
Bosch IoT Suite, 171, 197–199
Building digital twin based modern management information systems (MMIS), 441–464
Building information model (BIM), 25

C

Calling for immediate actions, 437–439
Change management (CM), 410, 411, 419, 420, 423, 424
ChatGPT for metaverse, 245–247
ChatGPT large language AI model, 171
City function layer, 29
City management and governance, 31
City-wide game and scavenger hunt, 386–393, 410
Classification, 42, 44, 46, 49, 66
Cloud computing, 9, 10, 51, 53, 70–73, 82, 85, 101, 154, 165, 177, 203, 252
Clustering, 42, 44, 46, 49
Conceptual framework of smart education, 142, 143

INDEX

Convolutional neural networks (CNN), 43, 97–99
Covid-19, 8, 9, 134
Covid-19 pandemic, 77, 81, 86, 95, 100, 130, 133, 135, 137, 141, 144, 148
CRISP-DM process, 36–38, 44, 46
CryEngine, 227–229, 260, 380–386
Current MIS architecture, 443, 444
Cutting-edge development tools, 211–261
Cybersecurity, 46, 52, 53, 65, 76, 82, 83, 102–107

D

Dassault Systèmes 3D EXPERIENCE, 188–191, 208
Data analytics, 20, 35, 38, 40–42, 50, 51, 59, 62–67, 101, 107, 112, 119, 123, 140, 148, 150, 151, 154, 163, 168, 200, 204, 443, 445, 448, 454, 455
Data Analytics Flywheel (DAFW), 35, 46–51, 115, 116, 169, 442, 448, 451–454, 456, 459, 461–463
Data analytics process and techniques, 40, 42–45
Data collection layer, 29, 76, 106, 169
Data-driven digital twinning process (DDTP), 15, 27, 28, 32, 35, 43, 45–47, 49, 50

Data platform, 15, 27, 31, 47, 73, 164, 442, 463
Data visualization, 31, 38–39, 44, 49, 65, 451
Decentraland SDK, 171, 254–257, 260, 327–329, 331
Decision automation, 40, 42
Deep learning (DL), 42–44, 46, 49, 50, 65, 66, 112, 149, 151, 160
Descriptive analytics, 41
Diagnostic analytics, 41
Different types of 3D printers, 93
Digital city, 12, 27, 28, 30–32, 47, 70, 72, 211, 212, 260
Digital platform main components, 81
Digital platforms, 9, 51, 76–82, 280, 446, 450
Digital twin, 10, 11, 17, 27, 35, 53, 83, 111, 129, 173, 218, 263, 314, 351, 413, 419, 425
Digital twin development tools, 173–209
Digital twin metaverse cities
 Core, 111–128
 services, 129–170
Digital twin metaverse city prototypes, 10
Digital twin museums and galleries, 373–380, 410
Digital twinning process-based decision making for smart metaverse cities, 45
Digital twins in five dimensions, 21

485

INDEX

Digital twins in three dimensions, 21
Digital twin smart cities, 15, 128, 170, 441
Dragnet, 101, 102
Drone and UAV, 100-103
Drone applications, 100, 101

E

Eco-friendly urban transportation hub, 281-289
Emerging technologies, 1, 17, 18, 25, 51-52, 82, 87, 107, 109, 111, 112, 132, 168, 214, 222, 428, 443, 447
Engagement, 24, 31, 49, 81, 116, 146, 155, 161, 165, 246, 260, 270, 273, 281, 289, 295, 303, 304, 310, 319, 325, 331, 337, 338, 343, 347, 358, 360, 366, 371, 374, 377, 380, 384, 391, 392, 398, 408, 416, 420, 425-427, 429, 431, 435, 438, 459
Engagement for smart city cohesion, 429

F

5G, 9-11, 17, 22, 23, 29, 51, 53, 55-58, 61, 62, 64, 65, 82, 87, 98, 103, 112, 123, 125, 132-134, 140, 152, 156, 158, 164, 438, 451

5G mobile networks, 53-57, 61
5G networking, 9, 58, 87
Flexibility and innovation, 447

G

GE Digital Predix, 171, 191-193, 208
Gemini for Metaverse, 248-250
GE Predix, 32, 67, 68
Gestalt principles of visual perception, 38
Google Gemini's Large Language Model (LLM)

H

Hierarchical ocean surveillance drone/UAV system, 127
Humility, 60, 425-428, 431-434, 438
Humility in AI-driven smart city leadership, 428
Hydroponics, 167
Hydroponics vertical farming, 167

I, J

IBM Maximo Asset Monitor, 171, 185-188, 208
Index, 163
Industry 4.0, 57, 446, 448
automation (digitalization) and servicization, 448

Interactional framework of leadership, 426, 431
Interactive public art installations, 171, 360–367
Internet of Things (IoT), 9, 11, 17, 28, 45, 54, 97, 112, 132, 174, 264, 438
IoT based smart healthcare systems, 132

K

Key performance indicators (KPIs)
　product details, 40
　profit, 38–40
　sales, 40
Key requirements of modern MIS (MMIS), 446–447
Kurt Lewin's Change Model, 420, 421

L

Leadership for the future, 425–435
Lewin's Change Model
　Change, 420, 421
　Refreeze, 420–422
　Unfreeze, 420, 421

M

Major challenges for smart city projects, 13
Management information systems (MIS), 12, 63, 71, 441–464
Managing successful smart city projects, 413–417
Megacities, 5, 22
Meta Platform for Facebook Metaverse, 20, 257
Meta Spark, 32, 171, 212, 257–261, 273–275, 277, 280, 290, 294–296, 321–326, 360, 361, 365–367
Metaverse, 10, 11, 17, 27, 35, 53, 83, 111, 129, 173, 211, 263, 314, 351, 413, 419, 425
Metaverse as digital twins and digital native continuum, 19
Metaverse music festival experience, 393–400
Metaverse theme parks, 171, 351, 367–373
Microsoft Azure Digital Twins, 32, 177–179, 208, 438
MIS architecture, 441–453, 456–458, 460–464

N

NASA, 20, 89, 167
Navigating change
　smart city transformation and cutover strategies, 419–424
Nudge Theory of Change Management, 423
Nvidia Omniverse, 171, 212, 218–221, 260, 438

INDEX

O

OCEAN leadership model, 431
OCEAN model, 426
Oracle Digital Twin, 202–205, 208
Our solution overview, 9

P, Q

PERT diagram for project management, 415
Physical city, 15, 27–31, 46, 47, 59, 65, 70, 169, 437
Physical city layer, 28, 169
PowerBI, 38
Predictive analytics, 41, 149, 151, 187, 188, 193, 201, 203
Prescriptive analytics, 40, 41, 151
Problem statement, 1, 7–10
Professional development and networking hub, 333–339
Program evaluation and review technique (PERT), 413, 415, 417
Project management, 24, 413–417
Prototypes
 entertainment and city, 351–410
 smart living, 24, 263–312, 352
 smart working, 313–349
PTC ThingWorx, 171, 182–185, 208
Public safety and emergency response simulation, 296–304
Python, 38, 64, 235, 342

R

R, 38, 64
Rapid data-driven decision-making, 446, 452
Rapid global urbanization, 3–10
RAVEN system, 134
Research gap, 11–13
Roblox, 32, 224–226, 292, 294–296, 335, 338, 373, 438
Roblox Studio, 171, 211, 224–226, 260, 290–296, 333–335, 338, 339, 367–370, 372, 373
Robotaxi services
 navigating the future of urban mobility, 458–460
Robotic automation, 52, 83–87
Robotics, 9–11, 17, 18, 22, 23, 45, 46, 52, 67, 70, 82–87, 107, 121, 126, 127, 132, 135, 136, 154, 160, 161, 168, 438

S

SAP Digital Twin, 200–202, 208
SCM MIS
 revolutionizing supply chain with digital twins, 456–458
Service delivery platform, 15, 28, 31, 49, 106, 127, 140
Siemens MindSphere, 180–182, 208
SketchUp, 236–239, 260, 377

INDEX

Smart cities, 9–13, 17, 22–25, 27–33, 35, 44–50, 57–62, 70, 82, 87, 95, 103, 107, 111, 115, 122, 123, 127, 128, 130, 140, 154, 159, 160, 169–171, 174, 175, 177, 178, 181, 183, 186, 189, 192, 195, 198, 199, 201, 204, 206, 208, 213, 216, 219, 221, 222, 225, 228, 231, 234, 237, 240, 243, 246, 248, 252, 255, 258, 400, 405, 410, 411, 413–417, 419–436, 438, 441, 448
Smart city indicator, 15, 17, 23–25, 27, 29, 31, 47
Smart city showcases, 109, 111–170
Smart disaster prediction, discovery, 164
Smart disaster response, 162–166, 169
'Smart economy,' 24
Smart education, 141–147, 171
Smart education centers, 290–296, 438
Smart energy, 116
Smart environment, 24, 125–128
Smart garbage management systems for food waste, 157
'Smart government,' 24
Smart green energy, 113–116
Smart healthcare, 130–137
Smart homes, 57, 116–119, 128, 171, 264–273, 438
Smart home systems within digital twin metaverse cities, 118
Smart housing, 24, 120
Smart living, 10, 24, 263–312, 352
Smart office management system, 313, 327–333
Smart people, 24
Smart recycling, 155, 159–161
Smart retailing, 147–155
Smart senior caring, 137–140
Smart sports complex, 380–386, 410
Smart sports complexes, and culminate in a comprehensive metaverse city prototype, 10
Smart streetlight, 123–125, 128
Smart transportation, 111–113, 128
Smart vertical farming, 166–170
Snow Crash, 18
South Korea, 8, 10
SpatialOS, 171, 251–254, 260, 296, 297, 299–304, 386–388, 390–393
Strong external focus, 446
Supervised learning (SPL), 42, 43, 46
Sustainable smart homes, 171, 264–273, 438
Sustainable smart homes and virtual healthcare clinics to smart education centers, 171, 438

489

INDEX

T

Tableau, 38–40, 58, 64, 86
Tesla, 67, 96, 105, 112, 442, 443, 445, 446, 449, 452, 464
Tesla gigafactory, 442, 445, 446, 449, 452, 464
The Heartbeat: Data Analytics Flywheel (DAFW), 451–452
The network effects in digital platform, 79
3D, 17, 18, 46, 48, 64, 94, 143, 144, 175, 194, 206, 212, 215–224, 230–244, 264, 265, 267, 294, 306, 309, 316, 323, 324, 344, 345, 348, 352, 355, 361–363, 366, 367, 375–378, 390
3D printed house by Icon, 122
3D printing (3DP), 9, 52, 82, 83, 92–95, 107, 120–122, 133
The six smart city indicators, 23, 24, 29
Tilt Brush, 242–244, 260
Traditional data "silo" management information system (MIS), 12
Traditional linear business, 78
Two-sided digital platform, 78

U

Uber, 12, 76, 77, 79, 445, 450
Unique selling points, 11–13

Unity, 32, 171, 212–215, 226, 229, 250, 251, 260, 263–265, 267–269, 273, 281–283, 285, 287–289, 304, 305, 308, 309, 311, 312, 314–317, 320, 321, 360–363, 366, 367, 374–376, 378, 380, 388, 390–392, 438
Unity and Unreal 3D Engine, coupled with the AI-driven insights provided by OpenAI ChatGPT, 352
Unreal Engine (UE), 32, 171, 211, 215–218, 250, 251, 260, 263, 264, 270, 272, 273, 296–301, 303, 304, 314, 344–346, 348, 349, 352–355, 357, 359, 360, 388, 390–396, 400–410, 438, 461
Unsupervised learning (USPL), 42, 46
Urban Farming and Green Spaces, 304–312

V

Vehicular network, 112
Virtual concert and event arena, 352–360
Virtual co-working spaces, 316
Virtual healthcare clinic, 171, 273, 274, 280, 281, 438
Virtual reality (VR), 9, 19, 42, 83, 88–92, 107, 143, 144, 147, 213, 221, 235, 241–244, 254, 257, 290, 344–349

Virtual reality design and prototyping Studio, 344–349
Virtual Singapore (VP), 35, 47–48
Vision, 20, 33, 47, 50, 51, 90, 115, 128, 134, 140, 150, 160, 166, 169, 170, 189, 219, 251, 373, 401, 411, 425–429, 434, 435, 437, 438, 460, 464
Visionary leadership in the AI era, 429–435
VR headset structure, 91

W, X, Y

Waymo, 87, 97, 112, 458
What Is Next–Just Do It, 411
Wind and solar energy intermittent problems, 114

Z

ZBrush, 171, 239–242, 260

GPSR Compliance

The European Union's (EU) General Product Safety Regulation (GPSR) is a set of rules that requires consumer products to be safe and our obligations to ensure this.

If you have any concerns about our products, you can contact us on

ProductSafety@springernature.com

In case Publisher is established outside the EU, the EU authorized representative is:

Springer Nature Customer Service Center GmbH
Europaplatz 3
69115 Heidelberg, Germany

www.ingramcontent.com/pod-product-compliance
Lightning Source LLC
LaVergne TN
LVHW010332260326
834688LV00036B/676